Property Rights from Below

Recent years have seen a globalization of property rights as the Western conception of property over land has extended across the world. As formerly community-owned land and natural resources are privatized and titling schemes proliferate, *Property Rights from Below* questions the trend toward treating land as a commodity and explores alternatives to the Western model.

As we enter an era of resource scarcity and as competition for land and associated natural resources increases, purchasing power cannot become the sole criterion for land allocation; and the law of supply and demand in increasingly financialized markets cannot become the sole metric through which the value of land is determined. Using a range of examples from around the world, *Property Rights from Below* demonstrates that alternatives to this model often emerge from social innovations supported by local communities and that there is an urgent need for a broader political imagination when it comes to land governance.

This innovative cross-disciplinary perspective on the pressing problems surrounding global property rights will be of interest to academics, students and professionals with an interest in property law, development economics and land governance.

Olivier De Schutter is Professor at the University of Louvain (UCL), Belgium, and at SciencesPo (Paris). He is also a member of the United Nations Committee on Economic, Social and Cultural Rights. He was the United Nations Special Rapporteur on the right to food between 2008 and 2014 and has been a visiting professor at Columbia University and at Berkeley University, USA.

Balakrishnan Rajagopal is a professor at the Massachusetts Institute of Technology, USA, where he is the head of the International Development Group at the Department of Urban Studies and Planning and the founding director of the Program on Human Rights and Justice and the Displacement Research and Action Network. He is an active member and one of the founders of the Third World Approaches to International Law (TWAIL) network of scholars.

Routledge Complex Real Property Rights Series
Series editor: Professor Spike Boydell
University of Technology Sydney, Australia

Real Property Rights are central to the global economy and provide a legal framework for how society (be it developed or customary) relates to land and buildings. We need to better understand property rights to ensure sustainable societies, careful use of limited resources and sound ecological stewardship of our land and water. Contemporary property rights theory is dynamic and needs to engage thinkers who are prepared to think outside their disciplinary limitations.

The Routledge Complex Real Property Rights Series strives to take a transdisciplinary approach to understanding property rights and specifically encourages heterodox thinking. Through rich international case studies our goal is to build models to connect theory to observed reality, allowing us to inform potential policy outcomes. This series is both an ideal forum and reference for students and scholars of property rights and land issues.

Property, Place and Piracy
Edited by James Arvanitakis & Martin Fredriksson

Wicked Valuations
People and Landed Property
Michael McDermott

Compulsory Property Acquisition for Urban Densification
Edited by Glen Searle

Pseudo-Public Spaces in Chinese Shopping Malls
Rise, Publicness and Consequences
Yiming Wang

Property Rights from Below
Commodification of Land and the Counter-Movement
Edited by Olivier De Schutter and Balakrishnan Rajagopal

For more information about this series, please visit: www.routledge.com/Routledge Complex-Real-Property Rights-Series/book-series/CRPRS

Property Rights from Below

Commodification of Land and the
Counter-Movement

**Edited by Olivier De Schutter
and Balakrishnan Rajagopal**

LONDON AND NEW YORK

First published 2020 by Routledge

2 Park Square, Milton Park, Abingdon, Oxon OX14 4RN
605 Third Avenue, New York, NY 10017

Routledge is an imprint of the Taylor & Francis Group, an informa business

First issued in paperback 2022

Publisher's Note

The publisher has gone to great lengths to ensure the quality of this
reprint but points out that some imperfections in the original copies
may be apparent.

British Library Cataloguing-in-Publication Data
A catalogue record for this book is available from the British Library

Library of Congress Cataloging-in-Publication Data
A catalog record for this book has been requested

ISBN: 978-1-138-65724-3 (hbk)
ISBN: 978-1-03-233742-5 (pbk)
DOI: 10.1201/9781315621463

Typeset in Times New Roman
by Apex CoVantage, LLC

Contents

Contributors

An Ansoms is Professor in Development Studies at the Université Catholique de Louvain (Belgium). She leads the Centre for Development Studies. She holds a PhD in economics and is involved in research on natural resource dynamics, poverty and inequality in the Great Lakes Region. She pays particular attention to the challenges of rural development and land conflicts in land-scarce (post-) conflict environments. She coordinates an interdisciplinary action-research project titled "Land Rush" (www.land-rush.org). In Congo, her team's research focuses on natural resource conflicts. In Rwanda, she coordinates a research project on the role of civil society and local administration in agrarian and land policies in Rwanda. The team had extensive expertise on research ethics in conflict-prone environments.

Antonio Azuela, Vice President of FIU (Iberoamerican Federation of Urbanists), is a member of the Social Research Institute at UNAM (Mexico's National University). Since the late 1970s he has conducted research on urban and environmental law from a socio-legal perspective. From 1994 to 2000 he acted as General Attorney for the Environment (*Procurador Federal de Protección al Ambiente*) in the Mexican government. He is a cofounder of IRGLUS (International Research Group on Law and Urban Space) within the International Sociological Association. His recent research focuses on environmental conflicts and on the urbanization of the rural world.

Giuseppe Davide Cioffo (European Network for Central Africa – EurAc, Belgium) is a program and policy officer. He is interested in the social and environmental dynamics linked to Green Revolution models as well as in small family farming and agrarian change in developing countries. He is preparing to defend his thesis on the processes of agrarian modernization in Rwanda at the Université Catholique de Louvain.

Klara Claessens is a postdoctoral researcher for the Department of Earth and Environmental Sciences, Division of Geography and Tourism (KU Leuven) and the Institute of Development Policy (University of Antwerp). She works on the political ecology of natural resources and natural resource governance in the Great Lakes Region. She coordinates an international master program in sustainable development at KU Leuven (www.susdev.eu).

Priscilla Claeys received her PhD in political and social sciences from the University of Louvain (UCLouvain) in 2013 and is now a senior research fellow in Food Sovereignty, Human Rights and Resilience at the Centre for Agroecology, Water and Resilience (CAWR), Coventry University (UK). She worked as Advisor to the UN Special Rapporteur on the right to food from 2008 to 2014. She previously worked for a number of human rights organizations and development NGOs. In 2015, she published a book with Routledge entitled *Human Rights and the Food Sovereignty Movement: Reclaiming Control*, in which she looks at the creation of new human rights by transnational agrarian movements.

Hanoch Dagan is the Stewart and Judy Colton Professor of Legal Theory and Innovation, the director of the Edmond J. Safra Center for Ethics at Tel Aviv University and a former dean of its Faculty of Law. Among his many publications are over 80 articles in major law reviews and journals as well as seven books, including *Property: Values and Institutions* (Oxford University Press, 2011), *Reconstructing American Legal Realism & Rethinking Private Law Theory* (Oxford University Press, 2013) and *The Choice Theory of Contracts* with Michael A. Heller (Cambridge University Press, 2017). He is currently working on a new book – *A Liberal Theory of Property* (Cambridge University Press, forthcoming 2020). Professor Dagan has been a visiting professor at Yale, Columbia, University of Michigan, Cornell, UCLA and University of Toronto law schools. He delivered keynote speeches and endowed lectures at Singapore, Alabama, Toronto, Queensland, Cape Town and Oxford. Dagan is a member of the American Law Institute and of the International Academy of Comparative Law.

Tsilly Dagan is a professor of law at Bar-Ilan University, Israel. Her book *International Tax Policy: Between Competition and Cooperation* (Cambridge University Press, 2018) has won the Frans Vanistendal IBFD award for the best publication in international law in 2017. Professor Dagan is also the author of numerous articles including "Rights for Sale" with Talia Fisher, 96 *Minnesota Law Review* 90 (2011); "The Currency of Taxation", 84 *Fordham Law Review* 2537, (2016) and "The Tax Treaties Myth", 32 *NYU Journal of International Law and Politics* 939 (2000).

Luís Felipe Perdigão de Castro is a lawyer (OAB-DF), master in agribusiness (Propaga/UnB) and PhD candidate at the Department of Latin American Studies (ELA) at the University of Brasilia (UnB). He is Professor and Head of the Law Department at Faciplac and Professor and Head of the Department of Public Law at Unidesc. His main research themes are land struggles, agrarian law, agrarian social movements, territorial rights, agribusiness and agrarian conflicts in Latin America.

Sheila R. Foster is a joint professor of law and public policy at Georgetown University. Professor Foster writes in the areas of property, environmental law and justice, urban land use law and policy and state and local government. Her most recent work explores questions of property, urban law and governance through the lens of the "commons", exemplified by her article *The City as a Commons* in the Yale Law and Policy Review (2016) and a forthcoming MIT Press Book, *The Co-City* (both with Christian Iaione). As Codirector of the International Laboratory for the Governance of the Commons (LabGov), Professor Foster is currently engaged with a groundbreaking applied research project, the "Co-Cities Project". The Co-Cities project is collecting data on public policies and local projects from over 100 cities around the world that are spurring collaborative economies as drivers of local economic development, inclusive urban regeneration and social innovation in urban services provision. LabGov is applying the Co-City methodology in cities around the world, including New York City, Amsterdam, Sao Paolo and Rome, among others.

Sonia Katyal is Chancellor's Professor of Law and Codirector of the Berkeley Center for Law and Technology at the University of California, Berkeley. Professor Katyal is the coauthor of *Property Outlaws* with Eduardo M. Peñalver (Yale University Press, 2010), which studies the intersection between civil disobedience and innovation in property and intellectual property frameworks. In March of 2016, Katyal was selected by US Commerce Secretary Penny Pritzker to be part of the inaugural US Commerce Department's Digital Economy Board of Advisors. Katyal also serves as Affiliate Scholar at Stanford Law's Center for Internet and Society and is a founding advisor to the Women in Technology Law organization. She also serves on the Executive Committee for the Berkeley Center for New Media (BCNM) and on the Advisory Board for Media Studies at UC Berkeley.

Philip McMichael is Professor of Development Sociology at Cornell. His research is informed by a world-historical perspective and focuses on food regimes and food sovereignty. He authored *Food Regimes and Agrarian Questions* (Fernwood, 2013), *Development and Social Change: A Global Perspective* (Sage, 2016, 6th edition) and the award-winning *Settlers and the Agrarian Question* (Cambridge, 1984). In addition, he edited *Contesting Development: Critical Struggles for Social Change* (Routledge, 2010) and *Biofuels, Land and Agrarian Change* with Jun Borras and Ian Scoones (Routledge, 2011). He is a member of the Civil Society Mechanism in the UN Committee on World Food Security (CFS), has worked with UNRISD, the FAO and IPES and has collaborated with La Vía Campesina and the IPC for Food Sovereignty.

Emery Mushagalusa Mudinga has a long experience in peace building, conflict resolution, community service and research on armed groups' dynamics in the DRC. Mushagalusa is a lecturer and holds a PhD in political sciences from the Université Catholique de Louvain; his research focused on land grabs dynamics and peasants' resistance in Africa. Mushagalusa is politically committed to advocating about youth access to jobs and decision-making positions in the different institutions.

Aymar Nyenyezi Bisoka is currently a lecturer and postdoctoral researcher. Nyenyezi Bisoka received his PhD at the Université Catholique de Louvain (UCLouvain), Belgium, with a background in legal and political studies. His postdoctoral researches focus on issues of power and resistance in relation with access to natural resources in the Great Lakes Region. Nyenyezi Bisoka is involved in teaching and coordinating research-action projects in Belgium (UCLouvain), Burundi (University of Burundi), DRC (Catholic University of Bukavu and the Higher Institute of Rural Development) and Rwanda.

Saskia Sassen is the Robert S. Lynd Professor of Sociology and Member, The Committee on Global Thought, Columbia University (www.saskiasassen.com). Her latest books are the fifth, fully updated edition of *Cities in a World Economy* (Sage, 2018) and *Expulsions: Brutality and Complexity in the Global Economy* (Harvard University Press 2014, now out in 18 languages.) She is the recipient of diverse awards – including multiple doctor *honoris causa* and the Principe de Asturias 2013 Prize in the Social Sciences – and has been made a foreign member of the Royal Academy of the Sciences of Netherland.

Sérgio Sauer is a professor at the University of Brasilia (UnB) in the postgraduate program for Environment and Rural Development (Mader) of the Planaltina campus (FUP) and in the Centre for Sustainable Development (CDS/UnB). He holds a research scholarship from the Brazilian Conselho Nacional de Desenvolvimento Científico e Tecnológico (CNPq). He is a fellow of the Terra de Direitos and was a national rapporteur for food and land rights of the Plataforma DhESCA-Brazil from 2010 to 2014. His main research themes are land struggles, agrarian social movements, land, territory, agribusiness and its social and environmental impacts in the Cerrado and Amazon regions.

J. Phillip Thompson has served as Deputy Mayor for Strategic Policy Initiatives in the city of New York since 2018. Prior to this appointment, he was Associate Professor of Political Science and Urban Planning at MIT's Department of Urban Studies and Planning, where he taught on housing and economic development, urban politics, post-disaster planning, social movements, and race and ethnicity in American politics. He authored *Double Trouble: Black Mayors, Black Communities and the Struggle for Deep Democracy*, published in 2006 by Oxford University Press. Before joining MIT, he worked as Deputy General Manager of the New York Housing Authority and as Director of the Mayor's Office of Housing Coordination.

Acknowledgements

This volume emerged from a conference organized at MIT in February 2014 on "Rethinking Property", organized by the MIT Displacement Research and Action Network under the direction of Prof. Balakrishnan Rajagopal and in collaboration with Prof. Olivier De Schutter. Most papers in this volume grew out of presentations at that conference. The support of MIT-MISTI and the MIT Department of Urban Studies and Planning are gratefully acknowledged for the support of this conference. The assistance provided by Alpen Sheth, then a doctoral student at MIT, is also gratefully acknowledged for the organization of the conference. We also wish to acknowledge the support provided by the editor at Routledge, Ed Needle, Patrick Heatherington and other staff. Prof. Rajagopal would also like to acknowledge the many brilliant graduate students at MIT who have brought deeper understanding of property and land-use law over the years, as participants in his course "Legal Aspects of Property and Land Use".

Foreword

Real property rights are central to the economy and provide a legal framework for how society (be it developed or customary) relates to land and buildings. Property rights are both institutional arrangements and social relations. We need to better understand property rights to ensure sustainable societies, careful use of limited resources and sound ecological stewardship of our land and water.

Land conflict is all around us – from corporate and political corruption over land dealings in the developed world, to land grabs in developing countries, to compromised indigenous property rights, to resource exploitation. At a time where global food security, water security and shelter are paramount, an understanding of property rights is key to sustainability.

Contemporary property rights theory is dynamic and this series strives to engage thinkers who are prepared to step beyond their disciplinary limitations. 'Property rights' is a broad term that is fundamentally about social relations. Real property rights, obligations and restrictions can be found in and change across the full range of human societies, both in time and space. Property rights research has emerged from a broad range of disciplines including (but not limited to) archaeology, anthropology, business studies, economics, ethics, geography, history, law, philosophy, planning, psychology, and sociology. What makes this series special is that it facilitates a transdisciplinary approach to understanding property rights and, specifically, promotes heterodox thinking.

In *Property Rights from Below: Commodification of Land and the Counter-Movement*, Olivier De Schutter and Balakrishnan Rajagopal draw together a diverse group of authors and perspectives in a volume that quintessentially encapsulates the heterodox aspiration of the series. They offer a critique of the dominant models and conceptions of contemporary property while offering alternative transdisciplinary understandings to the prevailing neoliberal agenda grounded in social movements.

A central theme in the volume challenges contemporary and institutional notions of property. We are taken on an exploration that came to a head in 2008 with the global food crisis and global financial crisis. In the aftermath, an exacerbation of land grabs coupled with an escalation of land titling and privatisation ensued in developing nations; meanwhile, developed nations witnessed a spectacular rise in evictions as mortgage debt exceeded property resale values, and recession resulted in unpaid property taxes. De Schutter and Rajagopal expose the duality of contemporary property rights in that they both protect land users with security of tenure *and* increase their vulnerability by encouraging dispossession.

This volume is carefully structured in three parts. The first sees contributing authors explore the global push for land commodification in an era of competition between urban growth, resource exploitation and 'carbon imperialism'. In the second part, authors explore social mobilisation around land and resources, with the ensuing counter-movement over food sovereignty and peasants rights from 'below', which includes social justice, self-determination and civil disobedience that push the boundaries of accepted neoliberal notions of the institution of property. The third part juxtaposes rebuilding the commons as an alternative way forward to the prevailing neoliberal orthodoxy of commodification and possessive individualism.

Excited? You should be. De Schutter and Rajagopal have assembled compelling contributions that invite the reader to rethink – nay – reimagine the notion of property, grounded on the inventiveness of a groundswell of social movements in the face of growing resistance towards commodification. Such a 'counter-movement from below' postulates the importance and power of community based understanding of people, place and property and in particular the use, conservation and management of their land and resources.

Synthesising the transdisciplinary and geopolitically diverse range of case studies articulated within the three parts of the volume, De Schutter and Rajagopal provide a compelling manifesto for us to reimagine our relationship with property in the 2020s and beyond. They also provide a road-map for governments, think-tanks, intergovernmental organisations and NGOs to acknowledge common-property regimes, limit constitutional autonomy on local communities, and rethink private property law (notably titling, security, acquisition and eminent domain).

As De Schutter and Rajagopal highlight, this counter-movement is neither new nor radical thinking. Many of these ideas are endorsed in the 'Voluntary Guidelines on the Responsible Governance of Tenure of Land, Fisheries and Forests in the Context of National Food Security' adopted in 2012 by the Committee on World Food Security. Yet the views are heterodox as, like the Voluntary Guidelines, they are counter to the prevailing neoliberal orthodoxy of commodification, climate imperialism and resource exploitation.

It is time for us to individually and collectively rethink and reimagine 'property rights from below' . . . and push our elected representatives, politicians and governments to do the same.

Enjoy.

Spike Boydell, General Editor
Sydney, Australia
November 2019

1 Property rights from below

An introduction to the debate

Olivier De Schutter and Balakrishnan Rajagopal

At the juncture of the multiple global crises that we are witnessing – food, water, ecological and political – is the increasing contestation over property. Especially intense concerning property in land and land-use arrangements secured by law, these crises have resulted in increased displacement, dispossession, evictions and concentrations of inequality in access to resources. These crises, and the struggles they have generated, provide the main motivations for the questions that arise in this volume.

There are two distinct contributions that we aim to make. First, we aim to critique the dominant models and conceptions of property and their distributional consequences and explore alternative understandings of property such as the commons. Second, we intend to highlight the juris-generative role of social movements and their contestations for the transformation of the law and politics of property, at several scales, from international to the very local. In doing both, we reveal our intention to echo many of the concerns and approaches adopted in earlier works in law and social sciences as being "from below" in contradistinction to traditional approaches in the social sciences or law, which focus on actors and approaches "from above". A central element of such approaches to law from below is the role of social movements and dissident understandings and ideas and to reinterpret them as being more central to the understanding of law and social sciences. In international law, Rajagopal launched the effort through *International Law from Below* (2003). This volume attempts to be the first to try this approach in the realm of private law. It takes an approach that combines international law – especially human rights law and property law in dialogue with insights from experts in other disciplines such as sociology, history and political science – with a focus on law and social movements. In this effort, it shares much in common with many concerns that led to critical and progressive approaches to property in law, from Third World Approaches to International Law (TWAIL) (Ngugi 2004), Critical Legal Studies (Kennedy and Michelman 1980), Feminism (Lim and Bottomley 2007), Critical Race Theory (Harris 1993) and Progressive Property Theory (Peñalver and Katyal 2010).

A central question in our volume, and in many of the critical strands of the literature on property, is what to make of the institution of property itself. This question is not new and has been with us at least since the nineteenth century.

What to do with property? Is the institution corrupt beyond redemption, due to its role in upholding the class structure of capitalism, or can it be reformed to become a tool of progressive politics? It is this debate that led to the famous polemics between Karl Marx and Pierre-Joseph Proudhon in the 1840s. Marx was initially an admirer of Proudhon, at the time the most famous of the French socialists. Proudhon published his tract *What is property?* in 1840. The book caused a scandal, in part because of the provocative statement with which it opened: "property", Proudhon claimed, "is theft". Marx admired the boldness of the formula. He was only 26 at the time; to read a pamphlet as radical written by a man almost ten years older than him could only have made a strong impression on the young German intellectual. Indeed, it is in order to pay homage that he sought to meet Proudhon when he spent the month of July 1844 alone in Paris, as his wife Jenny had returned to Trier to visit the family.

We don't know how the meeting went. Yet, after Proudhon published *Système des contradictions économiques ou philosophie de la misère* in 1846, Marx retorted in June 1847 with his *Misère de la philosophie* (*Poverty of Philosophy*) (Marx 1952 [1847]), in which he attacked Proudhon for remaining wedded to bourgeois values and for seeking to save a capitalist system by reformist proposals, when Marx of course expected capitalism to collapse under the weight of its own contradictions. Engels too would later attack Proudhon for his legal fetishism and petty bourgeoisie attitudes in his discussion of the housing question in Europe (1872).

Part of the debate concerned the question whether property, as an institution, could be reformed or whether it should be simply abolished in a communist society. Proudhon was seen as a dangerous anarchist by most of his readers and certainly by the intellectual establishment at the time. The Academy of Besançon, to which he had dedicated his pamphlet *What is property?*, was so disconcerted that it felt compelled to disavow the work publicly, denying any responsibility for the content, and a vote was organized to strip Proudhon of the grant they had been providing him. (Since the two-thirds majority was not reached, Proudhon could keep the money, but he had to take the blame.) To Marx and Engels however, Proudhon was trying to save capitalism, remaining blind to the forces of history that would inevitably lead to its ruin. Proudhon's critique of property, indeed, did not go at the heart of the institution. What he was denouncing was its abuse by the owners who used the monopoly rights conferred upon them by the right to property to coerce others into making unreasonable concessions (as happens when the owner of capital forces workers to labour against wages that barely allow them to survive). Marx believed that the faith of Proudhon in the possibility of changing that state of affairs was naïve; henceforth, it is he who, together with his new intellectual partner Friedrich Engels, would keep the radical flame alive.

In a way, the debate could be seen as terribly outdated – not simply because the specter of communism is not haunting us today as it was a century and a half ago, but also because the absolute character of property as an institution has long since been challenged. The various limitations Proudhon had envisaged to "domesticate" it and to ensure it would not be abused have become banal; what was then seen as revolutionary would appear to us today as largely harmless. Yet, at the same time, the more fundamental question forming the background of the debate – Should progressives call for a more equal distribution of property or denounce the institution of private property itself? – is more alive than ever. Indeed, it has reemerged with particular political urgency in the current struggles of social movements; the question of the role of property and how it should be protected was spectacularly revived in 2008, when the financial crisis followed the global food price crisis in close succession. It is this revival and the contestations that accompanied it that form the background of this volume and provide its main source of inspiration.

1. The crises of 2008 and the revival of the debate on property rights

The first reason we have witnessed a renewed interest in the question of the role of property is because land has become a target for financial speculation, with its exchange value increasingly detached from its use value. The origins of this development have been discussed elsewhere (De Schutter 2011). The high volatility of agricultural markets since the mid-2000s, culminating in the global food price crisis of the spring of 2008, is explained by the growing pressures on land and by fears concerning the scarcity of resources relative to a rise in demand – for food of course, but also for fuel and fiber. This increased volatility of markets sent a clear message both to the buyers of agricultural commodities (the agrifood companies in particular) and to governments. Agricultural markets henceforth would be less and less reliable, and therefore strategies of vertical integration, by taking direct control of the most productive agricultural land, should be accelerated. The result was what nongovernmental organizations soon denounced as "land grabbing": in many parts of the world, and particularly in relatively weakly governed countries with corrupt governmental elites, the best land was bought, or leased through long-term arrangements (typically for 33 or 99 years), depriving the local land users from access to natural resources. The most affected were small farmers whose land had not been titled. The government considered these farms to be its own property, which could be sold to private investors or foreign states, to groups depending on communal lands (artisanal fishers needing access to fishing grounds and pastoralists using open grazing grounds) and to indigenous groups, who depended on the products of the forests (Haralambous et al. 2009; Cotula et al. 2009; Deininger et al. 2010; Kugelman and Levenstein 2009; Center for Human Rights and Global Justice 2010; De Schutter 2011).

Just months after the rise in the prices of agricultural commodities rocked the markets, a financial and economic crisis sent waves across the world – arguably the most important such crisis to hit the global economy since the Great Recession of 1929. Again, the triggering factors are well-known, and again they have much to do with how property rights have evolved. During the two decades that preceded the crisis, households in many industrial countries were encouraged to take loans from banks in order to finance the acquisition of flats or houses. As the price of houses seemed to rise endlessly, investing in real estate seemed a wise and safe strategy both for homeowners and for the lenders. Banks were eager to provide loans, not so much because of the interest rates that applied (the rates were in fact low in the beginning, one reason why clients were encouraged to borrow), but especially because of the commissions both bank employees and salespersons perceived on the transactions. Those loans were then "securitized", repackaged as financial products that banks sold to other financial institutions. This continued, more or less unnoticed until it was discovered that, following a rise in interest rates and the explosion of the housing bubble, the borrowers might default. The financial assets held by the creditors had become "toxic". However, since these assets had by then spread across the financial system, the realization led to a sudden loss of confidence and to an almost complete freeze on interbank lending. That was the start of the crisis. Since most institutions that had been lending to people who wanted to acquire a house were themselves heavily indebted, their inability to borrow money meant they might go bankrupt – as did Lehman Brothers on September 15, 2008. A spectacular rise in the number of evictions resulted, as millions of households found that, while the value of their houses had dramatically fallen, they had accumulated considerable debts that they were unable to repay.

In both these developments, the role of property as an institution plays a decidedly ambiguous role. On one hand, it is tempting to see the role of progressives as having to defend property against the land grabs threatening the livelihoods of small farmers in the Global South (as well as in some parts of the Northern hemisphere) and against the wave of housing evictions that followed the financial crisis of 2008–2009. On the other hand, perhaps counterintuitively, it is property itself – or more precisely, the commodification of resources and of assets essential to a life in dignity – that allowed the crisis to have such massive impacts.

The reactions that followed the global food price crisis of 2008 provide a vivid illustration of this ambiguity. Land grabs did not start in 2008. The crisis significantly accelerated a process of dispossession, however, which a growing number of nongovernmental organizations and social movements then started to denounce as threatening the land users' access to the resources on which they depended for their livelihoods – for farming or fishing, for access to wild fruits, for water or for fuelwood. The immediate and obvious response to this threat was to speed up processes of land titling, which had been so popular in the preceding decade, for instance in the context of the privatization of the economies of Central and Eastern Europe. Clarifying property rights by such schemes was meant to provide security of tenure: to allow slum dwellers to be recognized as owners of their homes in the informal settlements where they were staying, or to allow small farmers to be protected from eviction from the land that they cultivated. Indeed, in the classic defense of titling programs provided by Hernando de Soto in his most important book, *The Mystery of Capital* (de Soto 2000), the security of tenure favoured through titling should encourage individual landowners to make the necessary investments in the land, thus improving their living conditions and, in rural areas, enhancing the productivity of the cultivated plot of land. The occupants, it was supposed, would not invest in their land unless they were certain to be protected from the risk of losing it. In addition, as emphasized by de Soto, titling of their property should have allowed the owners to mortgage their land and thus to obtain access to the credit necessary to make such investments. In the famous metaphor used by de Soto, this process transforms "dead (physical) assets" – "where assets can not be readily turned into capital, can not be traded outside narrow local circles where people know and trust each other, can not be used as collateral for a loan, and can not be used as a share against an investment" – into "live" capital that can be mobilized for investment (de Soto 2000: 6).

Yet, there is a profound ambiguity in the neoliberal promotion of property rights. Security of tenure is but one side of the coin; the other is the establishment of a market for land rights, allowing a more fluid transfer of property rights – a lowering of transaction costs, increasing the liquidity of these markets – to ensure productive assets go to the most efficient user. The intellectual roots of the argument are in the work of Ronald H. Coase, the 1991 Laureate of the Nobel Prize in Economics and the real intellectual godfather of law and economics. Coase famously argued that if transaction costs are low enough (and ideally, reduced to zero), the freedom of transactions will result in solutions that are most economically efficient (Coase 1960). The basic reasoning is simple enough: the buyer of property will pay the price he considers reasonable, taking into consideration the streams of income that are expected to flow from making a productive use of the assets acquired; therefore, if such assets are transferred to the highest bidder, as a well-functioning market for property rights should allow, they should ultimately be captured by the economic actors who can use them most productively, thus contributing to general economic growth.

This of course is not about preserving the rights of the land user by strengthening ownership rights. It is the exact opposite: it is about commoditizing land to make sure its productive function is maximized by being used by buyers with the deepest pockets and, thus, whose ability to invest in production is highest. This has sometimes been described as "fertilizing soil with money". But in good neoliberal newspeak, this is now repackaged as "security of tenure": a 1987 study by two authors of the World Bank proposes that "the ability of an occupant to undertake land transactions that would best suit his interests" should be considered part of "security of tenure" (Feder and Noronha 1987: 159).

But commodification of land rights can result in exclusion, just as direct expropriation does. This may happen through four mechanisms. First, the process of titling itself may be captured by the elites. When the United Nations-sponsored Commission for the Legal Empowerment of the Poor (CLEP) delivered its final report in 2008, it noted that "[i]n many countries, speculators preempt prospective titling programmes by buying up land from squatters at prices slightly higher than prevailing informal ones. Squatters benefit in the short term, but miss out on the main benefits of the titling programme, which accrue to the people with deeper pockets" (CLEP 2008: 80, citing J.-Ph. Platteau 2000: 68; on the risks of elite capture, see also K. Firmin-Sellers and P. Sellers 1999). The Commission on the Legal Empowerment of the Poor also remarked that titling schemes may be manipulated or tainted by corruption; and, it added, the formalization of property may be too costly or complex for the poorest segment of the population to benefit. These statements are remarkable. Not so much because of their substance, of course: it is hardly new that elites are better positioned to reap the benefits of public programmes shaped with progressive intentions, a phenomenon economists sometimes refer to as the "Matthew effect". But it is noteworthy that this is said by a commission established at the initiative of a range of governments from different regions, working together with the United Nations Development Programme (UNDP) and the United Nations Economic Commission for Europe, and placed under the co-chairmanship of Hernando de Soto and Madeleine Albright. Indeed, the CLEP was conceived as an independent body largely in order to provide support to the bold claims made by de Soto about insufficiently developed property rights being the main cause of the lack of development. Rather than supporting these claims, however, the CLEP provided ammunition to its critics. That it took many observers by surprise only gives more weight to its calls to treat titling with caution.

Elite capture of titling processes is not the only problem. Once property has been formalized and land demarcated, taxes may be imposed, and more easily collected, by the public authorities. This may present an opportunity to better finance public services. But it may also have exclusionary effects: it may occur that the poorest are not be able to pay those taxes and are forced to sell off the land as a result. More generally, the rural poor may be tempted to sell off land in order to overcome temporary economic hardship such as a bad harvest or a fall in the farmgate prices received for their crops. A 2003 report on land rights authored by a World Bank official, for instance, clearly recognizes that land markets could encourage such "distress sales", thus potentially increasing insecurity of tenure rather than reducing it (Deininger 2003: 96–98; see also B. Cousins et al. 2005: 3).

Even more troubling, whether to pay those taxes or whether to make the necessary investments in their houses or on their cultivated lands, the poor (who by definition have no liquid capital of their own) may be tempted to mortgage their land in order to have access to credit. But even if this works – even if, that is, lenders are willing to provide loans – the risk is that the debts will accumulate and the land will finally be seized by the lender. The commodification of land, in such a case, will have made the loss of land possible, rather than having protected the land user from its risk. This is the sad story of many rural households in the Global South, but it is also the drama of many families in rich countries who were lured into borrowing during the housing bubble of the early 2000s and who were then threatened by evictions once the interest rates went up and the value of their houses fell.

This risk, it is worth noting, should not be seen as *failure* of the system or as a problem that should be remedied in order for the system to proceed more smoothly. Instead, it is *inherent in the very process of commodification of property rights* that gives property its value. It has been written that, in de Soto's view, the problem with informal forms of tenure is not so much too little security of tenure, but instead *too much*: the problem with "dead capital" is that it cannot be lost, because it cannot be sold or mortgaged (T. Mitchell 2006: 7). Indeed, de Soto is explicit about this, noting that one of the benefits of formal property systems is that they make people "accountable", encouraging people "in advanced countries" to "respect titles, honor contracts, and obey the law", because of "the possibility of forfeiture" (de Soto 2000: 55–56). In other terms, the counterpart of the improved security of tenure that formalization of property is meant to allow is the *insecurity* resulting from the possibility of losing property – whether because the household finds itself unable to reimburse the lender after having mortgaged the land, because the levels of taxes makes them unaffordable and forces the family to leave, or (where rural farming households are concerned) because the household finds it impossible to expand its property following the speculation fuelled by the titling process, and thus cannot achieve the economies of scale required to be competitive on markets.

Thus, property rights have a dual function: they protect land users *and* they increase their vulnerability; they provide security of tenure *and* they encourage dispossession. This duality, a characteristic of commodification itself, is not relevant only to small-scale farmers or other land users in developing countries, whose legal systems are still considered immature; it is also important to understand the impacts of the recent financial and economic crises on low-income and middle-class households in rich countries.

The city of Detroit, Michigan, provides a perfect example. Like many other localities in the United States, in which households were encouraged to borrow during the boom – mortgaging their houses, whose value was meant to continue to increase – a large number of families lost their homes after the bubble burst. For that population, the shock was especially damaging, since it came together with General Motors filing for bankruptcy in June 2009 (forcing the federal government to intervene to rescue the company, which sold a number of its assets) and after years during which the population of the city decreased. Detroit, which boasted about 1 million residents in 2000, has lost one-third of its population since then. In 2012 and 2013 however, a new threat emerged. It was reported at the time that "nearly half of the owners of Detroit's 305,000 properties failed to pay their tax bills [during the year 2012], exacerbating a punishing cycle of declining revenues and diminished services for a city in a financial crisis" (MacDonald and Wilkinson 2013). Since the municipality of Detroit faced significant cash constraints and did not wish to send a wrong signal to local taxpayers, it started imposing severe penalties on the residents who did not pay their taxes on time (at some point, late payers faced up to 18 percent interest rates, although the rates have been reduced since), without creating any exception for the poorest families, and initially, without revising the estimated value of the homes for the calculation of the real estate tax since the peak reached in the early 2000s. The result was a massive rise in tax foreclosures – in effect expulsions – ordered by the tax authorities of Wayne County (which the city of Detroit is part of) following the auctioning off of the houses of delinquent taxpayers in order to allow the city to recover what it was owed. The phenomenon reached alarming levels in the mid-2010s, with a large number of houses being sold by auction and often bought off (at an extremely low price) by speculators, accelerating the dispossession of the working class in a city that the financial and economic crisis had already hit so hard.

The process met with resistance from local communities, of course. Non-profit organizations such as the United Community Housing Coalition, working in collaboration with the anti-poverty advocates Michigan Legal Services, sought to stem this trend, and in fact succeeded in avoiding a large number of tax foreclosures. The city authorities themselves, aware that tax foreclosures would only accelerate population flight and potentially lower the tax base further, have changed course more recently. Detroit's owner-occupied foreclosures fell from a peak of 6,408 in 2015 to 708 at risk in 2018, and tax foreclosures of all city-occupied homes (including renter-occupied) went down 84 percent since 2015, with 1,517 homes at risk in 2018, compared to 9,111 three years earlier (Stafford 2018).

The example of Detroit provides a vivid illustration of a more general problem: the commodification of property leads to the allocation of use rights being based on purchasing power, rather than need. Once they are subject to market mechanisms, the goods or resources go to the highest bidder, not to those who most deserve support, or (to borrow language from utilitarian ethics) to those whose utility would be most increased by having access to the goods or resources concerned. Economic efficiency in the allocation of goods or resources has all to do with those with the deepest pockets further monopolizing wealth, and it is only for the ease of language that we describe markets, conveniently, as responding to consumers' "needs". The same bias affects our understanding of prices. Economists typically describe prices as reflecting the relative scarcity of goods. This, in turn, leads them to draw this optimistic conclusion: if there is too little of a thing in comparison to what society demands, the price shall go up so that more of that thing shall be produced, and a return to a "natural" price, rewarding the producer's efforts at an appropriate rate, shall be inevitable in the long run. In fact however, prices are an indicator not of scarcity, but of demand, as expressed by those with purchasing power. It is this purchasing power, rather than the needs of those who own little and cannot afford to pay, that guides production choices: the richer you are, the more votes you have in influencing the allocation of resources. As noted by Scitovsky, this means that the marketplace is analogous to a plutocracy: it is "the rule of the rich", he wrote, "where each consumer's influence on what gets produced depends on how much he spends" (Scitovsky 1992: 8). For the poor, scarcity may be very real, and yet the market will not respond; market actors will not step up production if there is no solvent demand to respond to. In fact, this applies doubly to land and to housing needs because one cannot grow more land to satisfy needs and because it requires time and planning to increase significantly the supply of housing.

Confronted with land grabs affecting the weakest and most disempowered land users, as well as with speculation on housing making unaffordable to the middle-class in rich countries even the very houses that they inhabit, a contemporary Proudhon might have argued for a rapid expansion of titling schemes to protect land users from evictions and for social programmes to allow each household to acquire a house. A contemporary Marx might have stepped in, however, to warn against this version of "petty bourgeois socialism" – the expression appears in the *Manifesto of the Communist Party* in a transparent allusion to Proudhon (Marx and Engels 1848: 430). Instead, he might have warned against the risks inherent in grounding social relations in property, as if redistribution of property rights rather than the institution of property itself were the chief problem.

Marx's solution to the problem of property, however, was unimaginative. He did denounce, of course, the process of "enclosures", which between the sixteenth and the nineteenth centuries drove off many small peasants from the land they used to cultivate. Marx saw this "robbery of the common lands" and its "transformation into modern private property" as one of the major processes of primitive accumulation that "conquered the field for capitalistic agriculture, [making] the soil part and parcel of capital, and [creating] for the town industries the necessary supply of 'free' and outlawed proletariat" (Marx 1952 [1847]: 364). Yet, perhaps because he feared to be denounced as a utopian or as inimical to progress, and because he directed his message not to agrarian but to industrialized societies, he advocated not for new and democratic forms of governing property (this he preferred to leave to his contemporaries Robert Owen or Charles Fourier), but for the collectivization of factors of production, which he argued should be in the hands of the workers.

Despite its important limitations however, Marx's critique still anticipates the revival of the "commons" as a new form of property relations located beyond private property (subject to market mechanisms) and state property (in the hands of a state bureaucracy). This reinvention of the institution of property cannot be left to social critics. What we are seeing, emerging from the struggles of peasant communities and indigenous peoples against land grabs, and from the fight of urban groups against gentrification of whole neighbourhoods, relegating the poor to the outskirts, is that it is the social movements, today, that are defining the new contours of property. This book is largely about this attempt to redefine property from below. We provide below a brief overview of its contents.

2. From commodification of land to the emerging alternatives

The book is divided in three parts of comparable length. A first series of contributions, forming Part I of the book, is about competition for resources, dispossession and exclusion. Part II is about social movements' contributions to challenging dominant conceptions of property and natural resource allocation. Part III, finally, discusses how the legal framework can be "enabling": how the shift away from privatization and commodification and toward the revival of the commons can be supported. A brief overview follows.

A. *The global commodification of land and competition for resources*

In Chapter 2, Saskia Sassen revisits her earlier work (Sassen 2008, 2014) to provide a "long view" of current land grabs. She demonstrates how the current wave of land acquisitions and leases, particularly in the Sub-Saharan African region, has its source in the forced transformation of the economies of the countries concerned during the 1980s and 1990s. After having been encouraged in the 1970s to borrow from Western banks in order to finance industrialization policies and the building of infrastructures (these banks were flush with liquidities thanks to the rising price of oil, leading to a massive amount of "petrodollars" being made available), these countries were confronted with the sudden rise of interest rates imposed by the Federal Reserve in 1979 in order to combat inflation in the United States. They suddenly discovered that their debt had become impossible to repay, and the International Monetary Fund only agreed to provide them temporary support if they submitted to drastic conditions, euphemistically referred to as "structural adjustment". To repay their debt, these countries not only had to slash down the public sector; they also had to focus their economic development on exports in order to obtain access to hard currencies. What resulted is what Sassen calls an extractive economy, benefiting Western companies and impeding local development. "Predatory formations" emerged, which she sees as a constellation of legal reforms (facilitating the arrival of foreign investors and free trade) of an export-led economy (discouraging diversification and leading these countries to focus on the exploitation of raw materials) and of corrupt governmental elites that act as intermediaries between the interests of Western multinational corporations and local communities.

While Chapter 3 by Philip McMichael also discusses the phenomenon of land grabbing and proposes to take the "long view" (seeing the current wave of land grabs as a symptom of something deeper at work), his emphasis is on how capitalism has managed to co-opt environmental challenges into its programme, presenting market-based solutions as the solution to the major environmental threats of resource depletion and climate change. This approach resonates, of course, with the themes developed in this introduction. After all, it is Garrett Hardin, an *ecological* economist (the first of his kind, according to one of the founders of the discipline, Herman Daly) whose work led many to conclude that the privatization of resources that had been governed hitherto as commons was the only way to avoid their depletion in the face of growing demand and the threat of scarcity. Many market-based "solutions" to climate change, moreover, are more or less directly derived from Coase's theorem, referred to in Section 1 of this introductory chapter, which sees market exchanges as a means to identify the most economically efficient allocation of resources, an allocation of resources that shall prevail, provided that transactions are allowed to go unimpeded quite apart from how the law assigns rights and duties. (The most well-known of such "solutions" is the emissions trading scheme included in the 1997 Kyoto Protocol on Climate Change as a way to allow industrialized countries to compensate their inability to reduce emissions by buying unused "assigned amount units" from countries who are not using fully their assigned emission quotas.[1]) In other terms, while the commodification of nature is now presented as a means to preserve scarce resources and to reconcile economic efficiency with the need to remain within planetary boundaries, it leads to a new form of "carbon imperialism" (an expression McMichael borrows from Servaas Storm 2009) – an imperialism that, as ever, serves the interests of the economic actors, the large corporations, who are best positioned to seize the opportunity.

Chapter 4, by An Ansoms and her coauthors, has a very different focus. Taking as its departure point two rounds of land reform in the Democratic Republic of Congo, it shows how the coexistence of different systems of tenure (customary and based on civil law, respectively), far from constituting a source of legal insecurity and a potential cause of conflict, allowed local actors involved in conflicts over land to design hybrid solutions best-suited to their needs. The key ingredient in addressing conflict, it would seem, resides less in the existence of a legal regime devoid of ambiguity and providing clear-cut solutions than in affordable and accessible mechanisms of conflict resolution that allow for institutional innovation.

Both the approach adopted, richly documented by empirical findings, and the conclusions reached are highly original. Whereas conventional wisdom would insist that we need clearly defined property rights, thus lowering transaction costs to allow a market for land rights to emerge, these authors suggest that local actors should be allowed to "transgress" existing rules, in order to find (or, better expressed perhaps, to *invent*) forms of ownership and use of resources that can accommodate the various competing interests. This, perhaps, is one illustration of the "constitutional-level" prerogatives discussed in our concluding chapter, where we note the importance of allowing local communities not only to implement operational-level rules and to decide on collective-choice rules, but also to decide how these latter rules would be shaped. In other words, the chapter by An Ansoms and her coauthors provides an illustration of the usefulness of granting constitutional autonomy to local actors in order to allow ownership of the institutional solutions they design in the shadow of legal prescriptions. Legal insecurity, according to that logic, is not necessarily a liability: it can in fact provide an opportunity for institutional innovation.

B. Social mobilization and the counter-movement

Part II of the book brings together four contributions on how social movements mobilize around land and resources and how they have in fact exercised this institutional imagination, drawing inspiration from the approach to law and social movements that one of us has taken (Rajagopal 2003a, 2003b, 2005). Chapter 5, by J. Phillip Thompson, offers a historical overview of how workers' unions gradually shifted from purely corporatist claims, focusing on the defense of their members, to broader struggles not only about social justice but also about racial integration. The chapter not only provides an instructive illustration of how social movements evolve, redefining their claims in the course of the struggles they lead; it also describes how the various ways in which the fight for social justice and the fight for racial equality can either compete with one another, or complement each other. J. Phillip Thompson suggests that if "property from below" is to succeed, it is by social movements becoming mature enough to enter into such broad coalitions, moving beyond parochial struggles in the defense of narrowly defined group interests.

Can civil disobedience and, more generally, breaking the law form part of a strategy to change the structure of property? In Chapter 6, Sonia Katyal and Eduardo Peñalver provide a fascinating account of occupation and improvement of underused (but privately owned) urban land as a strategy of resistance. They take as a departure point the collapse of the housing market in 2008 and the large amount of foreclosures that resulted in the following years. The reaction, in many neighbourhoods, was to illegally occupy property. The tactic was not entirely new: already in the late 1970s, groups such as the Association of Community Organizations for Reform Now (ACORN), relied on squatting as a form of protest. Yet, the authors draw our attention to what is specific to "acquisitive outlaws", in contrast to the "expressive outlaws", who break the law in order to send a symbolically powerful message. The civil rights-era forms of civil disobedience did not pretend to change the law by violating it. They did protest against laws deemed unfair or discriminatory, of course. But civil disobedience was about expressing discontent, not about taking change in their own hands: it is this that "acquisitive outlaws" attempted, in some cases successfully (see also, on this phenomenon, Alexander 2015 and Quarta and Ferrando 2015, as well as the chapter by Sheila R. Foster in this volume). Katyal and Peñalver conclude that these outlaws provide an important service to legal reform: "far from being lawless, devoid of order or regulatory impulse", they open "sophisticated avenues for legal reform", by drawing attention to the scandal of underused urban property, and in many cases, by "reshaping the political landscape of urban neighborhoods".

Chapter 7, by Sergio Sauer and Luís Felipe Perdigão de Castro, provides a detailed discussion of land conflicts in Brazil and brings together a number of the themes running through the three preceding chapters. The Brazilian Landless Rural Workers' Movement (MST), after all, relies on a strategy of "occupations" in part to denounce the fact that huge tracts of land owned by large landowners remain unproductive: this, the MST claims, fails to fulfill the "social function" of property as envisaged in Articles 184 to 186 of the 1988 Constitution, which in that regard – though it is far from unique[2] – is more explicit than most constitutional documents. The MST would thus qualify as "acquisitive outlaws" in Katyal and Peñalver's terminology. They are not only protesters: they seek to establish new settlements (the so-called "agrarian reform settlements"), which they seek to have recognized and made permanent. Moreover, broad alliances are formed in the question of agrarian reform and a more equitable distribution of land, between landless families, indigenous peoples, Quilombolas and traditional communities. Finally, these actors demand access to land and territorial rights in a variety of forms that move far beyond a claim to have access to private property: the dimension of institutional innovation, put forward in the contribution by An Ansoms and her coauthors, is central to the experience of Brazilian social movements. What emerges from this discussion is what one might call the *constitutive* dimension of land struggles: both the social identities of the different communities taking part in these struggles and their role in the public space evolve as new relationships to lands and territories are invented, often through hybrid institutions that borrow from various paradigms, ranging from that of indigenous peoples' relationships to their territories to the classic form of private property.

The last chapter of this part, by Priscilla Claeys, describes the role played by the transnational agrarian movement established in 1993, La Via Campesina (LVC), to challenge the increased speculation of farmland and the phenomenon of land grabs that developed especially between 2007 and 2012. In part, this chapter complements the analyses by Saskia Sassen and Philip McMichael in recalling the factors that have led to the increased commodification of land. Its specific focus however is on the reliance by the peasants' organizations grouped within LVC of a human rights framework, invoking specifically a "right to land and territory" – a right that is emerging gradually in international law at the intersection of the right to food, to housing, and to cultural identity and that is developed per analogy with the right of indigenous peoples to their land and territories (see De Schutter 2010a, 2010b, 2011a). The contribution of Priscilla Claeys is based on large number of interviews of leaders and activists within the food sovereignty movement in order to assess the choice to frame their claims in human rights terms.

The inquiry is particularly instructive for two reasons. First, for social movements, to adopt such a framing is not without a cost. The language of human rights and the mechanisms through which human rights are monitored and enforced remain specialized: the language is that of human rights experts, and it is experts who populate the mechanisms. Even the most robust legal and policy frameworks designed to support the right to food may lack any self-instituting dimension. For all these reasons, human rights (although they ensure an indispensable protective function) may also be seen in other respects as disempowering – as robbing rights-holders of their ability to define the objectives of their struggles for justice and to define the pathways toward realizing them (Kennedy 2002, 2005, 2012; Hopgood 2013; Engle 2011). Secondly, the "right to land and territory" (as well as the "right to food sovereignty") has been imported by the transnational peasant movement into bodies such as the United Nations Human Rights Council and the Committee on World Food Security. If the Via Campesina is to be co-opted into such processes, with their particular codes of behavior, sets of actors and relationships built on reciprocity, does it mean that it may lose its ability to invent new solutions? Will it have to compromise? Will "leaders" emerge within the organization, monopolizing the role of spokespersons, at the risk of making it more difficult for the members of the movement to be heard? According to a recent count, the Via Campesina now brings together 182 local and national organizations across the world, scattered over more than 80 countries across Asia, Africa, Europe and the Americas, and represents an estimated 200 million farmers. Is it realistic to believe that the Via Campesina shall escape the dangers of bureaucratization, if it is to be an effective participant in a UN process such as the CFS – one that requires expertise, the building of networks among the community of diplomats, an ability to articulate clearly and forcefully one's demands and, perhaps most challenging of all, an ability to strike compromises?

Priscilla Claeys shows how two "master frames" – the "food sovereignty" and the "peasants' rights" frames, respectively – are used in combination in order to argue for a "right to land and territory", and thus contribute to a new understanding of property, "from below". She concludes in a rather optimistic mode: only by providing space for social movements to thus "co-construct" the meaning of human rights, and to contribute to their evolution, can human rights proclaimed in international instruments retain their vitality; "the value of human rights" to the activists, she notes, "lies not in their supposed universality but in their very contestability: only through global public dialogue can we make sure that human rights are relevant, and can be considered universal". In other terms, it is only when human rights are challenged from below that their proclamation from above can be seen as legitimate and effective. Ultimately, human rights shall remain empty promises – the legal embodiment of ethical values, perhaps, but with a weak ability to make a difference in people's everyday lives – unless their meaning is permanently reinvented by the very groups that they seek to protect and backed by popular mobilization. It is perhaps true that governments respond to shame and that they care about their standing as members of the international community (Chayes and Chayes 1995); but they care also, perhaps even more, about public opinion mobilizing. Pressure "from below" is therefore vital for human rights to remain meaningful and to provide an effective bulwark against the impacts of globalization and commodification.

C. Shaping alternatives: from commodification to rebuilding the commons

Part III, finally, brings together four chapters that address more explicitly the phenomenon that was referred to above as the revival of the commons. How can the law support the establishment and the maintenance of the "commons", where economic incentives to contribute are absent, and where the temptation of opportunistic behavior remains always present? Which kind of government is required if the objective is to support citizens-led initiatives that take the form of projects inspired by the philosophy of the commons?

In Chapter 9, Hanoch Dagan and Tsilly Dagan explore the fundamental question of how a "liberal" commons regime can be maintained against the temptation of "exit" and of opportunistic behavior by potential free riders. The departure point of the authors is that, whereas a number of economic and social benefits can be derived from a commons (including economies of scale and the spreading of risk across all members), the establishment and maintenance of a commons may be in tension with the liberal commitment to individual autonomy where "exit" of members is restricted in order to avoid the temptation of free riding on others' efforts. In social liberal commons in particular, where the primary objective of the collective is not to make a profit on the market, it may be tempting for participants to enter when they may benefit and to leave when they are asked to contribute: such behavior, as it results in over-use or in under-investment, would soon lead the project to collapse. Dagan and Dagan therefore ask how the various parties' interests can be realigned in order to support the commoners' collective activities. They discuss how this objective could be attained by regulating the governance of such commons more precisely: by internalizing externalities around individual use and investment decisions; by democratizing a set of fundamental management decisions, thus shifting authority from individual to group control, and making the expression of "voice" within the collective a more attractive option than to "exit" and finally, by "de-escalating tensions around entry and exit", for instance by allowing for certain restrictions to the right to exit in order to prioritize the negotiation of solutions based on interpersonal trust. Finally, using the tax regime applied in Israel to the *kibbutzim* as an example, they show how taxation may, both by its economic impacts and by its expressive of "symbolic" functions, favor reciprocity and trust within the commons: for instance, whereas the *kibbutz* business activities are taxed, the services provided by members to other members within the community escape taxation, which avoids such services being "commodified" and perceived as such by the community members. In the words of the authors, such an example shows how "the law can support the governance of the commons and the commoners' collective activities and help preserve their non-commodified features by both setting the internal rules of the game and providing external incentives, notably through the way these activities are taxed".

In Chapter 10, Sheila R. Foster explores the link between the project of a "right to the city" – the vision first outlined by Henri Lefebvre in 1968 and promoted now by the urban geographers such as David Harvey – and the emergence of "urban commons" – the phenomenon of urban residents reclaiming space and resources to develop non-market-based projects. She highlights how the language and discourse of the commons can constitute an important means to realize or instantiate the right to the city. Though operating from within a property rights framework, the "commons" approach is grounded on the idea that property should perform a social function. It can also be deeply democratizing. The Bologna regulation (allowing, in effect, social actors of the city to propose certain projects based on the philosophy of the commons and seek support to implement them) and the notion of Bologna as a "co-city" that it seeks to embody provides a striking illustration of the connection between both: by encouraging the emergence of commons in Bologna, this regime also favors the move toward a decentralized and experimentalist form of governance in which the city does not "lead", but "enables", stimulating the emergence of social innovations.

Chapter 11, by Antonio Azuela, discusses what property looks like once we remove one of its components – the privilege to sell. He addresses specifically the impacts of inalienability of land, using the example of the Mexican institutions of the *ejidos* and of the *comunidades*. On one hand, he notes that the prohibition imposed on *ejidatarios* to transfer land may (like the restrictions to exit discussed in the chapter by Dagan and Dagan) strengthen community life and facilitate agreement within the *ejido* as to how their natural resources should be used; it may also encourage a sustainable use of the resources, such as forests, protecting such resources from the impacts of commodification. On the other hand however, particularly with the progress of urbanization, the institution of the *ejido* may lead to social exclusion. The case of the *avecindados* illustrates this: in contrast to the *ejidatarios*, the *avecindados*, although they reside within the community and contribute to its welfare by their work, are not formally part of the original *ejido*, and therefore they cannot take part in the deliberations about major decisions concerning the collective. The inalienability of the *ejido* land, moreover, may deprive from access to land the landless poor, with important consequences on their livelihoods and their right to housing. In sum, Antonio Azuela calls for a shift from a discussion conducted at a high level of generality between a neoliberal camp that believes in the superiority of market-based solutions (particularly from the point of view of economic efficiency) and communitarians who tend to romanticize institutions that are premised on the existence of strong community life, to one that is empirically informed by social realities.

Altogether, the contributions assembled in this volume are an invitation to reimagine property and to connect a discussion on the institution of property (the bundle of prerogatives that constitutes it) with a discussion on the future of democratic governance and how communities can design the rules by which they are governed, without those rules being imposed on them from the outside or from the above. The inventiveness of social movements is striking: operating at times at the border of illegality, they are experimenting with new ways of organizing social relations in the use of resources. Whether state bureaucracies shall be able to match this inventiveness by strengthening their ability to learn from local experimentation remains to be seen: it is this challenge they must now face.

Notes

1 Such emissions trading schemes were introduced in Article 17 of the Kyoto Protocol to the United Nations Framework Convention on Climate Change (Kyoto, December 11, 1997, entered into force on February 16, 2005 (UN doc. FCCC/CP/L.7/Add.1, 10 December 1997; 37 ILM 22 (1998)). The Kyoto Protocol complemented the United Nations Framework Convention on Climate Change, which was opened for signature on May 9, 1992, and entered into force on March 21, 1994 (1771 UNTS 107; 31 ILM 851 (1992)).
2 See Foster and Bonilla (2011), and the contribution of Sheila R. Foster as chapter 10 in this volume.

Works cited

Alexander, L. T. (2015) Occupying the Constitutional Right to Housing. *Nebraska Law Review*, 94, 245–301.
Center for Human Rights and Global Justice. (2010) *Foreign Land Deals and Human Rights: Case Studies on Agricultural and Biofuel Investment*. New York, New York University School of Law.
Chayes, A. and Chayes, A. H. (1995) *The New Sovereignty: Compliance with International Regulatory Agreements*. Cambridge, Harvard University Press.
CLEP (High-Level Commission on the Legal Empowerment of the Poor). (2008) *Final Report*. New York, United Nations.

Coase, R. H. (1960) The Problem of Social Cost. *Journal of Law and Economics*, 3, 1–44.

Cotula, L., Vermeulen, S., Leonard, R. and Keeley, J. (2009) *Land Grab or Development Opportunity? Agricultural Investment and International Land Deals in Africa*. London and Rome, IIED-FAO-IFAD.

Cousins, B., Cousins, T., Hornby, D., Kingwill, R., Royston, L. and Smit, W. (2005) *Will Formalizing Property Rights Reduce Poverty in South Africa's 'Second Economy'? Questioning the Mythologies of Hernando de Soto*. Programme for Land and Agrarian Studies Policy Brief Debating Land Reform, Natural Resources and Poverty, No. 18, October, Cape Town, PLAAS.

Deininger, K. (2003) *Land Policies for Growth and Poverty Reduction: A World Bank Policy Research Report*. Report No. 26384, Washington, DC and Oxford, World Bank and Oxford University Press.

Deininger, K. and Byerlee, D. (2010) *Rising Global Interest in Farmland: Can It Yield Sustainable and Equitable Benefits?* Washington, DC, World Bank.

De Schutter, O. (2010a) Access to Land and the Right to Food. Interim Report of the Special Rapporteur on the Right to Food to the 65th Session of the General Assembly, UN Doc. A/65/281.

De Schutter, O. (2010b) The Emerging Human Right to Land. *International Community Law Review*, 12, 303–334.

De Schutter, O. (2011) The Green Rush: The Race for Farmland and the Rights of Land Users. *Harvard International Law Journal*, 52 (2), 503–559.

de Soto, H. (2000) *The Mystery of Capital: Why Capitalism Triumphs in the West and Fails Everywhere Else*. New York, Basic Books.

Engels, F. (1872) *The Housing Question*. 3rd ed. Moscow: Progress Publishers, 1970.

Engle, Karen. 2011. On Fragile Architecture: The UN Declaration on the Rights of Indigenous Peoples in the Context of Human Rights, *European Journal of International Law*, 22 (1): 141–163.

Feder, G. and Noronha, R. (1987) Land Rights Systems and Agricultural Development in Sub-Saharan Africa. *World Bank Research Observer*, 2 (2), 143–169, DOI: 10.1093/wbro/2.2.143.

Firmin-Sellers, K. and Sellers, P. (1999) Expected Failures and Unexcepted Successes of Land Titling in Africa. *World Development*, 27 (7), 1115–1128, DOI: 10.1016/S0305-750X(99)00058-3.

Foster, S. and Bonilla, D. (2011) Symposium: The Social Function of Property: A Comparative Perspective. *Fordham Law Review*, 80, 1003–1015.

Haralambous, S., Liversage, H. and Romano, M. (2009) *The Growing Demand for Land: Risks and Opportunities for Smallholder Farmers*. International Fund for Agricultural Development Discussion Paper for Round Table 2, Thirty-Second Session of IFAD's Governing Council, Rome, IFAD.

Harris, C. I. (1993) Whiteness as Property. *Harvard Law Review*, 106 (8) (June), 1707.

Hopgood, S. (2013) *The Endtimes of Human Rights*. Ithaca, NY, Cornell University Press.

Kennedy, D. (2002) The International Human Rights Movement: Part of the Problem? *Harvard Human Rights Journal*, 15, 101.

Kennedy, D. (2005) *The Dark Sides of Virtue: Reassessing International Humanitarianism*. Princeton, Princeton University Press.

Kennedy, D. (2012) The International Human Rights Regime: Still Part of the Problem? In: Dickinson, R., Katselli, E., Murray, C. and Pedersen, O. W. (eds.), *Examining Critical Perspectives on Human Rights*. Cambridge, UK, Cambridge University Press, 19–34.

Kennedy, D. and Michelman, F. (1980) Are Property and Contract Efficient? *Hofstra Law Review*, 8 (3): 711–770.

Kugelman, M. and Levenstein, S. L. (eds.). (2009) *Land Grab? The Race for the World's Farmland*. Washington, DC, Woodrow Wilson International Center for Scholars.

Lim, H. and Bottomley, A. (eds.). (2007) *Feminist Perspectives on Land Law*. London: Routledge and Cavendish.

MacDonald, C. and Wilkinson, M. (2013) Half of Detroit Property Owners Don't Pay Taxes. *Detroit News*, February 21 (republished on June 14, 2018).

Marx, K. (1952 [1847]) Capital, F. Engels (ed.), S. Moore and E. Aveling (trans.). In: Hutchins, R. M. (ed.), *Great Books of the Western World*. Chicago, University of Chicago Press, vol. 50.

Marx, K. and Engels, F. (1952 [1848]) Manifesto of the Communist Party, S. Moore (trans.). In: Hutchins, R. M. (ed.), *Great Books of the Western World*. Chicago: University of Chicago Press, vol. 50.

Mitchell, T. (2006) *The Properties of Markets: Informal Housing and Capitalism's Mystery*. Working Paper No. 2, Cultural, Political Economy Working Paper Series, Lancaster, Institute for Advanced Studies in Social and Management Sciences, Lancaster University.

Ngugi, J. M. (2004) Re-Examining the Role of Private Property in Market Democracies: Problematic Ideological Issues Raised by Land Registration. *Michigan Journal of International Law*, 25, 467.

Peñalver, E. M. and Katyal, S. K. (2010) *Property Outlaws: How Squatters, Pirates and Protestors Improve the Law of Ownership*. New Haven, CT, Yale University Press.

Platteau, J.-P. (2000) Does Africa Need Land Reform? In: Toulmin, C. and Quan, J. (eds.), *Evolving Land Rights, Policy and Tenure in Africa*. London, DFID-IIED-NRI, 51–74.

Quarta, A. and Ferrando, T. (2015) Italian Property Outlaws: From the Theory of the Commons to the Praxis of Occupation. *Global Jurist*, 15 (3), 261–290.

Rajagopal, B. (2003a) *International Law from Below: Development, Social Movements and Third World Resistance*. Cambridge, Cambridge University Press.

Rajagopal, B. (2003b) International Law and Social Movements: Challenges of Theorizing Resistance. *Columbia Journal of Transnational Law*, 41, 397.

Rajagopal, B. (2005) The Role of Law in Counter-Hegemonic Globalization and Global Legal Pluralism: Lessons from the Narmada Valley Struggle in India. *Leiden Journal of International Law*, 18 (3), 1.

Sassen, S. (2008) *Territory, Authority, Rights: From Medieval to Global Assemblages*. 2nd rev. ed. Princeton, NJ, Princeton University Press.

Sassen, S. (2014) *Expulsions: Brutality and Complexity in the Global Economy*. Cambridge, MA, Belknap Press of Harvard University Press.

Scitovsky, T. (1992) *The Joyless Economy: The Psychology of Human Satisfaction.* New York and Oxford, Oxford University Press.

Stafford, K. (2018) *Detroit Home Tax Foreclosures: Why They's Dropped Dramatically.* Detroit, MI: Detroit Free Press, July 18.

Storm, S. (2009) Capitalism and Climate Change: Can the Invisible Hand Adjust the Natural Thermostat? *Development and Change*, 40 (6), 1011–1038.

Part I

The global commodification of land and competition for resources

2 When primitive accumulation inhabits advanced systems

Saskia Sassen

There is an older history that lies behind the current conditions we see in so many Global South economies. It begins in the 1980s with the so-called "restructuring programs" of the IMF and World Bank. These programs weakened and impoverished many of the struggling national governments, especially in Sub-Saharan Africa – today also a key site for land grabs.

Too often overlooked is the fact that by the 1960s and 1970s, many of these countries were beginning to develop mass manufacturing and a middle class employed in government bureaucracies. A good part of this was destroyed by the new phase of capitalism that took off in the 1980s and transformed much of Africa and Latin America into sources for primary goods. It is well-known that unlike manufacturing, economies dependent on mining, plantations and imports of all consumer goods do not enable the growth of prosperous working and middle classes. Nor do they enable government elites to prioritize the larger common good of a country.

By the 1980s and early 1990s, a growing number of these countries were losing ground. One key factor was the rise of neoliberalism. It pushed these countries to open up their economies to large global consumer firms and destroyed their local commerce and manufacturing. The final hit came when national debt exploded in the 1980s in much of sub-Saharan Africa; this debt explosion was in good part due to the recycling of so-called post-1973 OPEC dollars by the large transnational banks of that period.

This destruction of emerging industrial economies and the rapidly growing government debt set the stage for weak negotiating capabilities on the part of Global South governments. One consequence was the land and water grabs that took off in the 2000s, which recent research has studied in detail (Anseeuw et al. 2012; Cotula 2011; Land Matrix, 2016a, 2016b; Byerlee et al. 2011; UNCTAD 2009; Borras et al. 2011; De Schutter 2011).

A key element of my argument is that this older history that took off in the 1980s led to the start of a downward cycle – for governments, the economy and the people in many of the countries that today are subject to large land and water grabs. In my research I find that this weakening of newly independent states, especially in Sub-Saharan Africa, was one key factor that enabled the current large-scale acquisitions of land by foreign governments and foreign firms.

The first section develops these issues, leading into a subsequent section that focuses on a specific, powerful vector with enormous consequences for these countries: that government debt enabled the implementation of extractive logics by foreign enterprises. These logics redirected development away from local entities and needs.

1. The many faces of advanced capitalism

One outcome of this longer history, and the central focus in this paper, is the presence of new forms of primitive accumulation *inside* more advanced capitalism itself, a thesis I develop at length elsewhere (Sassen 2014). In other words, this is a kind of primitive accumulation that is not a deviation or what is still incomplete in advanced capitalism. It is integral to that advanced capitalism. Thus land grabs, water grabs, burning down floras to plant palm, expelling small holder growers to develop mines and build office parks and more can all be seen as akin to primitive accumulation even though they use some of the most complex legal, financial and insurance instruments to achieve this. Further, in standard measures of economic growth they register as a growth in GDP, compared to the small-holder economies they replaced; thus they obscure the facts of growing poverty and displacement, not to mention often severe degradation of land and water bodies.

The turn to neoliberalism also escalated borrowing, partly as a function of the ongoing recycling of vast OPEC oil income, much of which was being handled by the large transnational banks. This became a key factor pushing loans onto Global South governments and enterprises that had not asked for them. For instance, Mogadishu (Somalia) was a middle-class city with a large educated workforce and a prosperous working class. The seeds of indebtedness were laid.

When national debt exploded in the 1980s in much of sub-Saharan Africa, partly due to the recycling of so-called post-1973 OPEC dollars, the possibility of economic and social progress was thwarted. Key reasons were the imposition of regimes that prioritized debt repayment and the opening of markets to powerful foreign firms. This weakened the state, thereby impoverishing the middle classes, and it destroyed the indigenous manufacturing and commercial sectors, which could not compete with large mass-market foreign firms.

A key element of my argument is that this older history that took off in the 1980s led to the start of a downward cycle – for governments, the economy and the people in many of the countries that today are subject to large land and water grabs. This weakening of newly independent states, especially in Sub-Saharan Africa, was one key factor enabling the current large-scale acquisitions of land by foreign governments and foreign firms. One outcome in the current phase of this downward cycle is the presence of new forms of primitive accumulation inside more advanced capitalism itself. As I discuss in greater detail elsewhere (Sassen 2008), the recent wave of land grabs can be approached with a theory of change that has as one core dynamic the fact that condition x or capability y can shift organizing logics and thereby actually change valence even if it may look the same. Thus, for instance, the massive expulsion of people due to the current phase of land grabs is not necessarily simply more of the same – more poor, more displaced, more downward mobility. It may be part of a new organizing logic that alters the valence and systemic character of poverty and downward mobility. Thus land grabs, water grabs, burning down floras to plant palm, expelling small holder growers to develop mines and build office parks and more can all be seen as akin to primitive accumulation even though they use some of the most complex legal, financial and insurance instruments to achieve this. Further, in standard measures of economic growth, they register as a growth in GDP, compared to the small- holder economies they replaced; thus they obscure the fact of growing poverty and displacement, not to mention often severe degradation of land and water bodies.

2. Extractive logics camouflaged as gifts

The key logic at work that matters for my analysis is the systemic conditioning that took place and has shaped the evolution of much of the Global South in the past several decades. Debt servicing became one key instrument for this conditioning: it weakened the governments of debtor countries by forcing them to pay grow- ing shares of national revenue for interest on their debts rather than engaging in economic development. Further, it made these governments susceptible to signing unfavorable deals with global firms, especially in extractive industries. This was catastrophic, as it did not further mass manufacturing by national firms nor did it draw foreign investment to this sector. This is extremely damaging to the long- term development of a country. We know from multiple research studies that mass manufacturing is a sector that can generate a modest but effective middle class and a prosperous working class, both key elements for developing an economy.

Even before the economic crises of the mid-1990s that hit a vast number of countries as they implemented neoliberal policies, the debt of poor countries in the South had rapidly grown from US $507 billion in 1980 to US $1.4 trillion in 1992. Debt service payments alone had increased to $1.6 trillion, more than the actual debt. From 1982 to 1998, indebted countries paid four times their original debts, and at the same time, their debt stocks went up by four times. Africa's debt-to-Gross National Product ratios were especially high in the late 1990s: 123 percent, compared with 42 percent in Latin America and 28 percent in Asia.[1]

These countries had to use a significant share of their total revenues to service these debts. For instance, Africa's payments reached $5 billion in 1998, which means that for every $1 in aid, African countries paid $1.40 in debt service in 1998. Debt-to-Gross National Product (GNP) ratios were especially high in Africa, where they stood at 123 percent in the late 1990s, compared with 42 percent in Latin America and 28 percent in Asia. By 2003, debt service as a share of exports only (not overall government revenue) ranged from extremely high levels for Zam- bia (29.6 percent) and Mauritania (27.7 percent) to significantly lower levels com- pared with the 1990s for Uganda (down from 19.8 percent in 1995 to 7.1 percent in 2003) and Mozambique (down from 34.5 percent in 1995 to 6.9 percent in 2003).

By 2006, the poorest 49 countries (i.e. "low income countries" with less than $935 per capita annual income) had debts of $375 billion. If to these 49 poor countries we add the "developing countries", we have a total of 144 countries with a debt of over $2.9 trillion and $573 billion paid to service debts in 2006 (Jubilee

Debt Campaign 2013). Since then there has been an effort by the international system to reduce these debts.

Thus inside capitalism itself we can characterize the relation of advanced to traditional capitalism as one marked by predatory dynamics rather than merely evolution, development or progress.[2] At its most extreme this can mean immiseration and exclusion of growing numbers of people who cease being of value as workers and consumers. But it also means that traditional petty bourgeoisies and traditional national bourgeoisies cease being of value. I see the latter as part of the current systemic deepening of capitalist relations.

3. Conclusion

One brutal way of putting it is to say that the natural resources of much of Africa and good parts of Latin America and Asia have long counted more for investors than the people on those lands counted as consumers and as workers. This is not an accident or something that went wrong. This is part of the systemic deepening of advanced capitalist relations of production. We have left behind the varieties of Keynesianism that thrived on the accelerated expansion of prosperous working and middle classes – even if with high inputs of racisms of all sorts.

What marks the difference of developing countries overwhelmed by powerful foreign actors with the Keynesianism of the developed world was the valuing, even if partial, of people *as workers and consumers*. This was critical for the deepening of capitalism in the West. The emphasis was on the *making* of capitalist relations of production, whether those of early or of advanced capitalism.

Today it is resource-extraction that is ascendant. We see the making of a systemic transformation. Older forms of "advanced" capitalist economies are being destroyed or incorporated into the operational space of a new type of extractive capitalism.

Notes

1 There were also some reasonably good outcomes – though just among a very few countries. Thus by 2003, debt service as a share of exports (not overall government revenue) ranged from extremely high levels for Zambia (29.6 percent) and Mauritania (27.7 percent) to significantly lowered levels (compared to the 1990s) for Uganda (down from 19.8 percent in 1995 to 7.1 percent in 2003) and Mozambique (down from 34.5 percent in 1995 to 6.9 percent in 2003).
2 It is not clear to what extent Marx's analysis of primitive accumulation (to explain the relationship between capitalism and pre-capitalist economies) might illuminate this relationship between traditional capitalism and the new types of advanced capitalism (see Sassen 2014).

Works cited

Anseeuw, Ward, Lily Alden Wily, Lorenzo Cotula, and Michael Taylor. 2012. *Land Rights and the Rush for Land: Findings of the Global Commercial Pressures on Land Research Project*. Rome: International Land Coalition.

Cotula, Lorenzo. 2011. *The Outlook on Farmland Acquisitions.* Rome: International Land Coalition.

Borras, Saturnino M., Jr., Jennifer C. Franco, Cristobal Kay, and Max Spoor. 2011. *Land Grabbing in Latin America and the Caribbean Viewed from Broader International Perspectives.* New York: United Nations.

Byerlee, Derek, Klaus Deininger, Jonathan Lindsay, Andrew Norton, Harris Selod, and Mercedes Stickler. 2011. *Rising Global Interest in Farmland: Can It Yield Sustainable and Equitable Benefits?* Washington, DC: World Bank.

De Schutter, Olivier. 2011. "How Not to Think of Land Grabbing: Three Critiques of Large-Scale Investments in Farmland." *Journal of Peasant Studies* 38(2):249–279.

Jubilee Debt Campaign. 2013. "How Big Is the Debt of Poor Countries?" Retrieved January 10, 2016 (http://jubileedebt.org.uk/faqs-2/how-big-is-the-debt-of-poor-countries).

Land Matrix. 2016a. "Dynamics Overview." Land Matrix. Retrieved January 13, 2016 (continuously updated) (www.landmatrix.org/en/get-the-idea/dynamics-overview/).

Land Matrix. 2016b. "Land Matrix: The Online Public Database on Land Deals." Land Matrix. Retrieved January 13, 2016 (www.landmatrix.org/en/).

Sassen, Saskia. 2008. *Territory, Authority, Rights: From Medieval to Global Assemblages.* 2nd rev. ed. Princeton, NJ: Princeton University Press.

Sassen, Saskia. 2014. *Expulsions: Brutality and Complexity in the Global Economy.* Cambridge, MA: Belknap Press of Harvard University Press.

UNCTAD. 2009. World investment report 2009. Transnational corporations, agricultural production and development. UNCTAD.

3   Land grab governance and the crisis of market rule

Philip McMichael

While land grabbing is integral to the modern history of capitalism, its drivers (and their justifications) have changed over time. Generally, historical cycles of capital accumulation have depended on new ecological frontiers to replace under-reproduced nature (relative exhaustion of natural resources), defer absolute exhaustion and renew accumulation (Moore 2000). Representation of cycles of frontier expansion depends on prevailing forms and temporal exigencies of rule (e.g. colonial/imperial, national security or market).

Explicit recognition of the exhaustion of resources and associated ecosystem services materialized in the last quarter of the twentieth century following the 1970s oil crisis and the rise of the environmental movement. The *Scientific American* observed: "self-conscious, intelligent management of the earth is one of the great challenges facing humanity as it approaches the 21st century" (Clark 1989, 47). This sentiment expressed a new form of environmental appropriation: substituting the concept of "sustainable development" launched by the Brundtland Commission (WCED 1987) for the earlier call for "limits to growth" (Meadows et al. 1972), for example. The 1992 Earth Summit institutionalized this appropriation, redefining the atmosphere and biodiversity as a "global commons" to be managed for waste sinks and food security. At the time, Wolfgang Sachs defined *global ecology* as the "rational planning of the planet for Northern security" (1993, 20). The intervening years have seen the development of institutional and market-driven management of the global commons: the World Bank's Global Environmental Facility, the Kyoto Protocol's Clean Development Mechanism, the Reducing Emissions from Deforestation and Forest Degradation (REDD) programme, the carbon-trading scheme designed under the United Nations Framework Convention on Climate Change and the consolidation of a mandated biofuel industry.

When the food-price and financial crises of the mid-late 2000s occurred, they stimulated a triple movement: (1) a new engagement with agriculture and food security as necessary to millennial development and security, (2) an extension of financialization into agriculture as a relatively safe refuge, with commodities incorporated into index funds and land redefined as a financial asset and (3) an official renewal of the trope of planetary rational planning in land and green grabbing. These shifts, enabled or sanctioned by public authorities, express a neoliberal reflex in recycling market problems as solutions. This reflex enlists the state system in the service of commodifying landscapes to "feed the world" and "save the planet" via market/profit incentives.[1]

In a more fundamental sense, this is a capitalization reflex. It involves a global power grab[2] in the name of market solutions. Here, capital operates as a mode of power, where the market "with its universalizing price architecture and encompassing discounting, is not a diffusion of power but the very precondition of power" (Nitzan and Bichler 2009, 306).[3] Through the device of the capital market, investors seek to capitalize future income streams, and "since income streams are generated by social entities, processes, organizations and institutions, we end up with capitalization discounting not [only] the so-called 'sphere of economics', but potentially every aspect of society" (Bichler and Nitzan 2009). In this way, state and corporate power come to control the conditions of social reproduction (DiMuzio 2012, 371). Such a *preemptive* strategy expresses the reproductive instincts of states and investors in subordinating land and ecosystems to the price form, as a governance mechanism, to render them accessible to market metrics, and to preclude alternative solutions.

This chapter historicizes the land/green grab through the lens of neoliberal governance mechanisms.[4] These elaborate principles and partnerships to commandeer land, labor and ecosystems as new commodities serve to usurp and concentrate resource control in the name of rational planning for human survival, promoting private power through public authority.[5] As Polanyi (1957) reminds us, markets are instituted, and markets in land and ecosystem services are no exception. What is distinctive *at this time* is the deployment of markets as mechanisms of control over (largely) common property resources to reorganize the world in a quest for security, displacing risk on to vulnerable populations and ultimately threatening the very survival of the earth.

1. The discourse and technology of globalism

In the last quarter of the twentieth century, environmental feedbacks (pollution of atmosphere, waterways and oceans; chemicalization; global warming) signaled an imminent absolute exhaustion of nature, triggering the UN Conference on Environment and Development (UNCED) known as the Earth Summit in 1992. Here, in addition to reducing greenhouse gas emissions (GHGs) and reducing ocean pollution and ozone-layer depletion, forests in the Global South in particular were to be managed as carbon sinks and for biodiversity preservation: bioregions of intrinsic (ecological) value to a Northern-led accumulation drive, now redefined as "sustainable development". As Sachs noted: "Far from 'protecting the earth', environmental diplomacy which works within a developmentalist frame cannot but concentrate its efforts on rationing what is left of nature" (1993, 13). At the same time, by classifying the atmosphere and biodiversity as a global commons, the Bank's Global Environmental Facility (GEF) "was able to override the local claims of those who rely on local commons and effectively assert that everyone has a right of access to them, that local people have no more claim to them than a corporation based on the other side of the globe" (Hildyard 1993, 34; cf Gupta 1998, 292). Sachs continued:

> To put the outcome of UNCED in a nutshell: the governments at Rio came around to recognizing the decline of the environment, but insisted on relaunching development. . . . There were conventions on biodiversity, climate and forests, but no conventions on agri-business, automobiles or free trade. This indicates that UNCED attempted to secure the natural resources and waste sinks for economic growth in favour of the global middle class, rather than to embark upon a path towards industrial self-limitation and local regeneration.
>
> (1993, 3)

Anticipating my argument below, Gupta claims that such "global environmentalism is part of a qualitative transformation of the world economy whose ramifications go far beyond mere *intensification* of existing trends" – foreshadowing "the creation of a set of institutions and practices that make up, in Foucauldian terms, a new technology of government" (1998, 293). This was justified at the Earth Summit opening session by the UNCED Secretary General in the following way: "we are all in this together" with agreements needing to "serve the common interests of the entire human family" (Ibid, 302).

Over a decade later, the specter of absolute exhaustion received renewed attention. In 2005, the UN's *Millennium Ecosystem Assessment*[6] claimed that the past half-century of economic development "has resulted in a substantial and largely irreversible loss in the diversity of life on Earth" (2005, 1). In 2007, the UN Environment Programme stated that "the planet's water, land, air, plants, animals and fish stocks were all in 'inexorable decline'." The following year, the Stratigraphy Commission of the Geological Society of London, the world's oldest association of Earth scientists, warned:

> The combination of extinctions, global species migrations and the widespread replacement of natural vegetation with agricultural monocultures is producing a distinctive contemporary biostratigraphic signal. These effects are permanent, as future evolution will take place from surviving (and frequently anthropogenically relocated) stocks.
>
> (quoted in Davis 2010, 31)

In context of the food and financial crises, public authorities reconvened to mark a new stage in "rational planning" of the planet.

2. Crisis management and agriculture

With the renewal of rational planning in recognition of a new threshold in planetary history, the global ecology trope acknowledges the centrality of agriculture to addressing energy, climate change and ecosystem deterioration. The UN/World Bank initiated International Assessment of Agricultural Science and Technology for Development (IAASTD) entitled its Executive Summary of the Synthesis Report "Agriculture at a Crossroads" (2008). And while the UN's *Millennium Ecosystem Assessment* noted that "agricultural expansion will continue to be one of the major drivers of biodiversity loss well into the twenty-first century" (2005, 22), the World Bank's *World Development Report* declared, "it is time to place agriculture afresh at the center of the development agenda" (2007, 1). The food crisis precipitated responses juggling these priorities of sustainability and development, conditioned by neoliberal policy.

Much of the official discourse at the Rome Food Summit (2008) surrounding the food crisis viewed it as an opportunity to reverse a long period of declining investment in agriculture and to secure world food supplies (FAO 2008), and for smallholders to take advantage of high food prices by accelerating their incorporation into national and global markets. FAO Director General Jacques Diouf wrote in a May 2008 press release that "high food prices represent an excellent opportunity for increased investments in agriculture by both the public and private sectors to stimulate production and productivity", adding that "governments, supported by their international partners, must now undertake the necessary public investment and provide a favourable environment for private investments" (quoted in Urquhart 2008).

African farmers, representing a substantial remnant of the world's peasantry, became the new object of development overnight, with the promise of public-private partnership investment to improve productivity via agro-industrialization. This attempt to recycle modern solutions to modern problems[7] is reminiscent of Moore's claim that capital's world-ecological regimes are simultaneously ecologically crisis-*attenuating* and crisis-*generating* (2011). In other words, official intervention activated this dynamic in targeting peasantries to "feed the world", but now as corporate value chain "outgrowers".[8]

At the same time, the IAASTD Report declared "business as usual is not an option", given the combination of climate, energy, water and food crises, and it went on to question industrial agriculture and transgenic foods as the solution to the social and ecological crises associated with global agribusiness, on the grounds that markets fail to adequately value environmental and social harm (2008, 20). The Report also questioned the salience of a market-driven approach to the agri-food question and its productivist (macro-nutrient) focus versus an integrative view of food, resource and nutritional security (Ibid, 17–18) – underlining agriculture's multifunctional contribution to complex socio-ecological reproduction issues.[9] Finally, IAASTD noted: "international trade in agricultural commodities and food, as currently organized, sets consumers in different countries into competition for the same land and water resources. For example, the global average agricultural land availability is 0.25 ha per person, yet food consumption in many countries, particularly developed countries, makes a much larger claim on this resource."[10]

This issue of "ghost acres" is, arguably, at the center of the global ecology episteme, since much of the subsequent development of this new initiative in "rational planning" to resolve food deficits projected for the future targets access to land across the Global South[11] for food and fuel crops. Land access takes two particular forms: (1) land grabs that retitle and reclassify land as "vacant" or "unused" or "unproductive", leading to the displacement and/or marginalization of small producers from their ancestral lands, including common lands, and (2) incorporating farmers into "value-chains" risking dispossession, given that important actors such as the Gates Foundation –the chief financier of the Alliance for a Green Revolution in Africa (AGRA) – suggests that commercial development of African agriculture "will require some degree of land mobility and a lower percentage of total employment involved in direct agricultural production" (quoted in Mittal 2009). Either way, the agro-industrial paradigm is favored as the solution to putative food shortages and transition to green fuels. While the second form of land access is not typically included in the land grab debate, the mobilization of outgrowers is a form of land grab, as it depends on capturing land through farm labor once farmers have been incorporated into contract relations associated with "value-chain" agriculture, whether such land remains nominally in the hands of the contract farmer or is alienated through the inevitable debt relations attending this form of agriculture (McMichael 2013b).

Investing in southern lands is partly a function of productivity decline on northern lands. Industrial agriculture has experienced a declining biophysical productivity, with soil depletion and efficiency of nitrogen use falling from 60 to 20 percent from the 1950s to the 1990s (Van der Ploeg 2010, 100). The costs of "biophysical override" have risen with prices of inputs amplified by rising energy costs and agribusiness conglomeration (Weis 2007). Consequently agribusiness migrates offshore to take advantage of cost-reducing investments in land, water and labor in developing countries and the prospect of untapped markets for agro-inputs provided by newly recruited outgrowers. "Ghost acres," therefore, are not simply about an expanding frontier of production,[12] but also a crisis-attenuating strategy on the part of agribusiness. The scale of the ghost acre phenomenon is distinctive to this juncture and brings about a series of public-private partnerships.

The recent, corporate food regime (1980s–) has intensified a long-term appropriation of lands in the Global South for commodities sold on world markets via the devices of structural adjustment and the disciplines imposed under the World Trade Organization (WTO) agreements, requiring states to recalibrate agricultural production for export with the aid of foreign investment. Current interventions deepen the ghost acre phenomenon, via land grabbing, still requiring host-state sponsorship of land acquisition by local and foreign investors, but within a decidedly more globalist framework. The Bank's use of satellite imagery is an approach that "assumes that land and resources can be quantified by objective, distant images, and that the myriad uses, customs, and benefits informing the interests of land users can be captured, guaranteed and marketized through written, formally-demarcated rights" (Narula 2013, 169–170). Expropriating land users has a long history, systematized during the colonial era. Currently, a new cycle of resource grabbing involves land conversion for flex crops (Borras et al. 2012) and the new bioeconomy, compounding the crisis of market rule.[13]

3. Crisis of market rule

Market rule is more than simply the protection of economic interests or private property rights, rather "it acts to canonize these rights, to make them inalienable and unassailable" from notions of public good (McMichael and Peine 2005). This is termed the *constitutionalization* of market regulation – where "constitutionalism is viewed as the means of placing law, or the rule of law, above politics" (Howse and Nicolaidis 2003, 75).[14] As with any hegemonic order, it is never absolute or complete, currently challenged by initiatives to rethink property rights within the framework of food/land sovereignty (Monsalve Suárez 2013; McKeon 2015). The current moment involves intensification of a "double movement" (Polanyi 1957), as the dominant order is challenged by reliance on human and peasants' rights within the UN system, by the counter-proposals emanating from social movements and civil society – including the Civil Society Mechanism (CSM) within the Committee on World Food Security (CFS) – and by a multiplicity of land and environmental struggles in different places, against the background of the legitimacy crisis of the rule of the market.[15]

The crisis of market rule is multifaceted, including food, financial and ecological crises, a trade regime crisis as states and sovereign wealth funds acquire land, overriding WTO rules with "agro-security mercantilism" (McMichael 2013a) and a general crisis of governmentality. The latter refers to the mortgaging of public capacities to structural-adjustment programs of austerity, making land and green investments more attractive to host states in the Global South. While these processes manifest crisis, including attempts at crisis attenuation, they *compound* crisis in deepening the globalist project and its commodification of land and ecosystem services. In so doing, the material crisis becomes an ontological[16] crisis (of exclusion): reducing lands, forests and waterways to a uniform price metric regardless of their meaning and use-value to communities of small producers, forest dwellers and fishers. Not only are material cultures discursively homogenized, but also their inhabitants are trivialized as residual, unproductive or as environmental risks, and summarily evicted, relocated with often disingenuous claims for "improvement"[17] or removed from their natural practices.[18]

The imposition of the *global commons* definition is a class act. It attempts a virtual one-time alienation of landscapes to those with financial power, naturalizing the market as the arbiter of efficient allocation of resources, and as a global crisis-management mechanism. The extension of land grabbing to green grabbing (commodification of ecosystems), internalizes "externalized" (uncounted) environmental costs of industrial development – incentivizing protection of nature or selling nature to save it (McAfee 1999) by redefining it as "natural capital". With respect to the REDD program, which enables the exchange of permits (carbon credits) to pollute by linking forest protection financing with global carbon markets, the UNEP stated:

> Essentially REDD+ is an investment focusing on retaining or enhancing natural capital, and provides an opportunity to enable countries to move towards

realizing green development. Where conditions are favourable, REDD+ potentially represents an important, possibly even the pre-eminent, strand in a natural capital centric investment strategy . . . . (which) . . . . explicitly *acknowledges that we are reaching limits in our use of the natural environment* and that the true environmental and social costs of our current economic development and growth models must be taken into account in devising any future development solutions.

(Sukhdev et al. 2011, 2, emphasis added)

In this way the natural world is alienated *en masse* as the virtual commodity[19] *par excellence* for a global ecology project privileging investor rights. Thus, in colonizing the environment and environmental practices as a virtual market, Monbiot remarks that the EU's Emissions Trade Scheme "has seized something which should belong to all of us – the right, within the system, to produce a certain amount of carbon dioxide – and given it to the corporations" (2006, 46). Smith notes that "any choice over what kinds of environments and landscapes are to be produced, and for what purposes, increasingly passes from any semblance of broad social discussion into narrow class control orchestrated through the market" (2007, 26).

The intensified commodification of nature and natural resources via land/green grabs represents an ecological *crisis-attenuating* strategy. For example, with the enclosure of land for biofuels, the EU Energy Commissioner claimed they are "the only known substitute for fossil fuels in transport today. They contribute to our security of energy supply, reduce greenhouse gas emissions and create jobs in rural areas" (quoted in Gilbertson et al. 2007, 7). Evidence to date suggests that biofuels are likely to increase emissions and barely make a dent in energy needs.[20] Crisis attenuation is for the system of capital accumulation: lending it a green legitimacy at the same time as a new green frontier for capital is created. The consequence, ontologically, is a redefinition of nature and its relation to humanity and social reproduction via a market calculus. Not only does this allow corporations and investors to control and exercise pollution rights, it also threatens the rights to habitat and associated livelihoods of land/water users and forest dwellers. While capital can offset its impact on the earth, profitably and at a distance, rural populations lose the right to common-pool resources with carbon credit and REDD schemes that compromise their lifeworlds via what Storm calls "carbon imperialism" (2009). Through the device of a scarcity calculus, demand for environmental services increases their market value "in ways that out-compete other forms and practices of value for the landscapes providing them" (Idem). In other words, "the commodification of nature forestalls democratic choice" (Monbiot 2012). That is, through subjection to the price form, the use value of landscapes or ecosystems is determined, not by the needs of land users, but by the thirst for accumulation of those who manage and manipulate markets. Thus, land is grabbed for its use value in producing fungible crops (or offsetting incommensurable carbon emissions elsewhere). Where corn, soy and palm oil double and triple as food, feed or fuel crops responding to price signals, their value derives from considerations of profit rather than a social or ecological calculus.

Such fetishism of agricultural and "natural" commodities is *ultimately a property relation* concealing the power and control vested in the exercise of market rule(s). The conversion of farming and forestry to commodity (rather than life-world) production is an exercise of propertied power, whereby agribusiness or carbon investments reconfigure the use value of land and/or labor. The latter case involves a double movement of dispossession and *remaking* of land users.

Conversion to carbon forestry illustrates this double conversion via market rule. Thus Lacandon maize farmers, facing unfair competition from the dumping of (NAFTA-style) subsidized corn in the Mexican markets, are compelled to embrace carbon forestry as a survival strategy (Osborne 2011). There is a double enclosure at work: first, through the price form *campesinos* find their corn unable to compete with cheapened imported corn, forcing them to seek alternative sources of income; and second, they resort to carbon forestry as the principal source of alternative income as determined by the new value of timber/forestry production subsidized by carbon credits. Ultimately, the extension of "land control" via market rule displacing *milpa* labor and elaborating forestry systems to offset carbon emissions represents the exercise of property relations as "new enclosures" (Peluso and Lund 2011).

4. Commodification and the reformulation of public authority

The Lacandon case provides a lens on an important shift in authority relations associated with the commodity fetishism underlying land/green grabbing. The transformation of peasant farming (from maize culture to carbon forestry) simultaneously signals a shift in the meaning of "state-controlled territories" from a spatial to a relational understanding.[21] How territory is governed and exploited is not simply the domain of sovereign states, rather it depends on the mode of states' participation/complicity in international regimes (trade and carbon) that transform conditions for land users.[22] The internalization of a market calculus reformulates livelihood possibilities by subjecting citizens to economic enclosure. The embedding of market relations within state practices and authority structures abstracts sovereignty via processes of deterritorialization – by enclosure of land and ecosystem processes in a global regime of standardized commodification (whether real or virtual).

The compromise of sovereignty has two aspects. Indebted states, and local elites, mortgage public authority to private ends to capture foreign exchange or investments, and territory is redefined as a source of present and future income – thereby alienating control of habitat to investors or conservation organizations with no relation to national territory other than a financial calculus. A case in point is MacDonald's account of conservation organizations – whose members "become ontologically complicit with the knowledge categories of the institutional field . . . that structures and provides the material resources and legitimacy needed to support the organization's existence" (2013, 241). The commodification of nature is the operative principle, rendering "conservation an instrument for the accumulation of capital and a vehicle through which capital interests could gain access to sites of 'nature as capital'" (2013, 234). His ethnography of the International Union for Conservation of Nature (IUCN) observes that, from a distance (without field experience), the IUCN accumulates selective knowledge of conservation sites across the world – the goal being "to rationalize and then modify situated knowledge or practice within ideological boundaries of understanding subscribed to by transnational organizations" (MacDonald 2013, 235). While this process may be resisted and/or modified,[23] it represents an ontological projection of global planning of landscapes via commodification, reducing meanings, practices and processes of human/nature interaction to a universal price form.

Such projection of global value relations[24] reformulates property relations[25] in two senses: (1) the meaning of property in land shifts from national/cultural territory to the status of a scarce (global) resource targeted for capitalization and (2) disposition over land and ecological resources is "centralized" as *proprietary control* vested in public authority.[26] Thus politically instituted market mechanisms (notably the use of eminent domain by central governments to commandeer land) override the rights of land users to their habitats and their re-deployment.[27] Such mechanisms are designed to ensure the reproduction of the global market, in both present *and future* senses. It is important here to stress that "public authority" is embodied not only in governments but also intergovernmental organizations and multilateral institutions, where the latter represent interstate hierarchies, projecting forms of governance as control.[28] In this sense, Gupta views global environmental accords (emanating from the Earth Summit) as "part of a larger process that is weakening the intimate links between 'nation' and 'state'" (1998, 314), where transnational governance overrides the social contract.

5. Reformulating property relations

Following Earth Summit (1992) concern with the future of biodiversity and carbon sinks, *current* concern now includes the future of energy and of food. Resolving these material constraints involves redefining them as opportunities for capitalization, as arenas of "sustainable development'" States enlist in the capitalization process with subsidies and payments, backstopping capital accumulation and renewing legitimacy by incentivizing production of food and green fuel. In this sense, new solutions to valorize nature represent methods of social control through which dominant visions of what count as viable futures are reproduced (DaCosta and McMichael 2007).

Valorization of future resources is accomplished by an elaboration of governing principles in the name of the market, affording control to corporate interests. This is, in effect, a reformulation of property as a *future claim* embodied in the enlistment of public authority in expanding the commodity frontier in land, labor, water and carbon to meet the needs of the future. In this way the crisis of market rule is expressed in the perversion of the Brundtland Commission's understanding of sustainable development – thus, current responses to ecological crisis produce a "development that meets the needs of the present [*by* in place of *without]* compromising the ability of future generations to meet their own needs". Here, the conversion of land and ecosystems into financial assets confers a new dimension on the property relation. This is a phenomenon of the *conjuncture*, in which property relations no longer simply exclude by enclosure. Through the refocusing of public authority on a project of "planetary rational planning", market rule exerts a proprietary ontological claim over "available"[29] landed, or virtual,[30] resources – in the name of global security.

Thus, rather than question the trajectory of market rule that has impoverished public authority, degraded ecosystems and mortgaged the future to highly unequal consumption relations, the crisis initiates a new chapter in naturalizing the market as the way forward. This implicates states directly, as political elites seek legitimacy and creditworthiness by internalizing the rationality of global currency[31] and capital markets. Market rule operates via a "global financial architecture"[32] complemented by WTO trade rules and regional/bilateral trade agreements. Under these institutional circumstances, states incorporate multilateral protocols and recalibrate public policies toward private goals with significant sovereignty effects, justified by claims for increased productivity, debt-reduction, export enhancement and rural development.

The enlistment of states in addressing the crisis expresses the "paradox of sovereignty". Here, the construction and internalization of market rule within the operation of the state system underscores that sovereignty is "both more absolute in its 'purely political' prerogatives than other historical forms of rule, and yet highly ambiguous as a measure of actual power" (Rosenberg 2001, 131). A striking example is the Ethiopian government's recent sponsorship of "deterritorialization" via long-term land rental agreements to foreign investors to modernize production of an unspecified range of exportable crops. Opposition politicians view these agreements to be less about the land and its produce and more about government brokering of international influence via secret deals, so that "the party in power is an intermediary without which no one can get a piece of the action" (Liberti 2013, 24). Whether the state alienates land and resources via the complicity of local chiefs or community leaders (Vermeulen and Cotula 2010), often with unmet promises, or, as in Ethiopia where the party in power controls subnational authorities, the sovereignty paradox extends to the local region, as village land is redefined for national (that is, commercial) purposes.[33] Thus, in Tanzania land designated as the property of the local village has been redefined by the government as "general" land to lease to biofuel companies (Ibid, 174–5), and in Mozambique, where community boundaries are imprecise, land law manipulations "have generally weakened communities' ability to protect their land from a government that favors an influx of foreign investors" (Friends of the Earth 2010, 13),[34] including bank-supported jatropha crops. The "paradox of sovereignty" is not simply about the formal alienation of land and dislodging land users, but a substantive threat to food sovereignty with the expansion of agrofuels and other agro-export crops.

Just as governments, in competition with other host states (Peters 2013, 546), have come to broker land deals, so brokerage becomes an operating principle of conservation organizations (as in the above IUCN case). FAO Müller's account of the FAO's "technical interventions" in southern states reveals its ambiguous legacy, driven ultimately by financial dependence (2013). For the case in point, providing technical advice to the Nicaraguan state on a food sovereignty law by which its parliament intended to "establish an effective instrument that would attenuate the effects of international trade agreements and the world market", the FAO attempted to steer a "technical" course between contending interests regarding the form of agricultural development (Müller 2013, 207). It resulted in what Müller calls a "gloss of harmony": juxtaposing language acknowledging the right to food sovereignty but "without prejudice to the exercise of the right to free enterprise and trade" (Ibid, 210). This, then, enabled the FAO to broker the 2008 EU Food Facility Programme, which distributed green revolution seeds and agro-inputs "according to a global methodology determined by the donor" (Ibid, 211). To finance this package, three million euros were dedicated to Nicaragua, to increase farmer productivity and improve farmer entrepreneurial capacities – and the "discourse of urgency was complemented here by a rhetoric of empowering smallholder farmers to feed themselves and produce for the market" (Idem).[35] Müller concludes:

> The FAO has become, over the last twenty years, more and more dependent on donor countries as funding to the institution itself has been constantly reduced. Losing part of its institutional autonomy, it has thus started to act as a "broker" between food-exporting donor countries and food-insecure receiver countries. The funding of specific projects and programmes by donor countries has thus become vital to the authority and survival of the FAO itself.
>
> (2013, 211)

In short, just as the public authority of states is increasingly governed by financial calculus, so it is with development and conservation organizations, whose initiatives are increasingly driven by and for private power. In this way the crisis of public authority expresses the crisis of market rule in both cause and effect.

6. Land grab governance

Fallout from the 2008 food crisis confirmed the Bank's new emphasis on mobilizing small-scale farming (2007), and stimulated jockeying for influence among the various international and intergovernmental agencies and the G-20. While the crisis rejuvenated the FAO's Committee for World Food Security (CFS) as the multilateral organization most appropriate to addressing the food and hunger question, with a significant reform in 2009 admitting civil society input, the G-20[36] has maneuvered to take "an increasingly prominent role in the global governance of food security" and to declare itself "the *de facto* coordinator of international development finance" (Murphy and Wise 2013, 23, 25). Such initiatives raise the question of governance as the:

> FAO, and CFS are established under international law with formal governance systems and clear mandates, with inclusive, if sometimes messy, procedures that bring different agencies and stakeholders to the table. The G-20 has none of this. It is an invitation-only group of some of the world's most powerful economies. . . . Much of the G-20's work takes place hidden from public view. The G-20's assertion of leadership in development finance, including a response to the food security crisis, undermines accountability in the international system, and weakens the efforts of the organizations and inter-agency processes that should be solving the problems. . . . Meanwhile, donor support for agriculture and food security, which comes mostly from G-20 countries, is largely channeled not through GAFSP with its broad mandate for coordination, but through bilateral ODA heavily influenced by private sector interests.
>
> (Ibid, 25)

The Global Agriculture and Food Security Programme (GAFSP), a multi-donor trust fund to support country-led programs, emerged from the G-8 Summit in L'Aquila, Italy (2009). Given its focus on support for small-scale and women farmers engaged in subsistence agriculture, it has been largely overshadowed by bilateral forms of Overseas Development Assistance (ODA), which have concentrated investments in land grabs, conservation agriculture and GMOs (Ibid, 15, 17). The trajectory of public funding via ODA and World Bank programs favors farmers with marketable surpluses (Ibid, 16, 18) in partnership with the private sector. This general goal is expressed by the Citizens Network for Foreign Affairs (CNFA), an organization funded by USAID and DFID (with seed and chemical supplier trustees): "leveraging the power of private enterprise – from large multinational corporations to local input supply stores – is the best route to sustainable, market-based development solutions" (quoted in War on Want 2012, 7).[37]

The consolidation of public-private partnerships is very much a product of the crisis conjuncture and the market-centered response. The 2008 Food Summit in Rome and the G-8 Summit in L'Aquila established the broad terms of reference: "among the challenges to which the G8 has increasingly turned is *global economic development: as an expression of shared humanity* and in recognition of the growing interconnectedness of the world economy and in the contribution of low- and middle-income countries to global economic well-being" (G8 2012a, 1, italics added). Global food security is the goal, with the European Commission taking the lead, creating the EU Food Facility, geared toward "pro-poor research and the strengthening of the global governance of the food system" (Murphy and Wise 2012, 16). As stated previously, the FAO's role in implementing the Food Facility Programme is ambiguous, given its dependence on private funding and its sponsorship of green revolution packages. Similarly, states exhibit the paradox of sovereignty in administering land acquisitions.

Access to farmland was the centerpiece of the G-8's New Alliance for Food Security and Nutrition (NAFSN) – a partnership between the G-8, the African Union, the New Partnership for Africa's Development (NEPAD), several African governments,[38] and over 100 private corporations, initiated in 2012. NAFSN appears to have been a counter-move to the reform of the CFS, with the goal of "accelerating the flow of private capital" to African agriculture by reformulating governing mechanisms to commandeer African land, water and labor and to further monopolize seeds and markets. Such governing mechanisms, termed *Cooperation Framework Agreements (CFAs)*, involve commitments by host states to facilitate access to key agricultural lands, using data bases, resettlement policies and measures that authorize communities "to engage in partnerships through leases or sub-leases" (Paul and Steinbrecher 2013, 5).[39] In addition, following a pattern of non-consultation with producer and civil society organizations and confidential letters of intent signed between corporations and governments (Oxfam 2013, 6), New Alliance partners must confirm their intentions to "take account of" the CFS responsible agricultural investment principles (rai) and the Voluntary Guidelines on the Responsible Governance of Tenure of Land, Fisheries and Forests (Paul and Steinbrecher 2013, 6).

Access to key farmland targets a series of African Agricultural Growth Corridors as sites selected for agro-industrialization projects (with infrastructural facilities) organized by private corporations. Access involves either displacement through land grabs[40] or value-chain incorporation of peasants as outgrowers.[41] Either form of access depends on government sanction, including land leasing. Thus the NASFN's CFA for Tanzania reads:

> Tanzania is a showcase for publicprivate partnership in agricultural growth, exemplified by the development of its Southern Agricultural Growth Corridor (SAGCOT). This strategic investment blueprint is a model for inclusive and strategic collaboration among government, donors and the private sector . . . The Government of Tanzania intends to focus its efforts, in particular, on increasing stability and transparency in trade policy; improving incentives for the private sector; developing and implementing a transparent land tenure policy; developing and implementing domestic seed policies that encourage increased private sector involvement in this area.
>
> (G8 2012a, 1, 2)

For the private sector's part,

> Monsanto will support the Tanzanian government's plans to improve nutrition and livelihoods of farmers in the Southern Agricultural Growth Corridor of Tanzania with key investments and partnerships that strengthen the maize and vegetable value chains. Plans include increased access to finance through a partnership with Opportunity International, introduction of 3–5 new maize hybrids suitable for Tanzania and available royalty-free to seed companies; strengthening of agrodealer networks to provide more choices to farmers; a

partnership on soil health with the Earth Institute; and creation of opportunities that provide farmers with improved access to markets.

(Ibid, 12)

In addition, the agreement between the G-8 and Ghana includes a summary of the long-term visioning of Norwegian fertilizer company, Yara International:

Yara has committed to a broader sub-Saharan Africa strategy, applying an integrated multi-country approach. At a pan-African level, Yara is currently undertaking a significant business development activity to identify the most competitive location to develop a world-class fertilizer production facility . . . Of critical importance in choosing a location is the overall local and regional agricultural development potential, where a *world-scale manufacturing facility can act as a catalyst to growth in the agricultural sector and underpin the viability of sustainable food production.* Yara would aim to combine an investment in such a production facility with a range of integrated agricultural growth and development approaches, such as the development of regional fertilizer hubs and holistic value chain initiatives.

(G8 2012b, 15, italics added)

Whether land is obtained (grabbed) through leases or accessed through out-grower relations, NAFSN-affiliated companies[42] represent "the whole supply chain, from seeds, chemical inputs, production, processing, transport and trade to supermarkets" (Paul and Steinbrecher 2013, 2). Overall goals are

to identify suitable land for investors; to help the private sector to control and increase the use of agricultural inputs (fertilizers) and 'improved' (hybrid or GM) seeds and halt the distribution of free and 'unimproved' seeds (farmer varieties, often well adapted to local conditions and needs); and to mobilize public largesse to assist investors.

(Ibid, 4)

With respect to consultative arrangements, Oxfam's assessment is telling:

Unlike CAADP,[43] the New Alliance has not developed guidance outlining the roles and responsibilities of stakeholders, including POs and CSOs. Nor are there specific benchmarks for their participation in the development of CFAs or implementation of New Alliance activities. Consequently, actors in each country – chiefly donors and government officials – are free to decide whether and how to engage stakeholders.

(Oxfam 2013, 5)

In other words, such public-private partnerships tend to exclude substantive input of communities, smallholders and their organizations, and certainly eschew principles of food sovereignty and agro-ecology as pathways to food security. While such initiatives promise development opportunities for smallholders, arguably they are more likely "to put Africa's land, water and seeds [and labor] under the control of international traders and investors" (Ibid, 13).[44]

The appearance of NAFSN as an alternative form of global food security governance to that of the CFS (with its Tenure Guidelines that recommend strengthening of recognition of customary property tenure and women's land rights), signals a substantial counter-movement by investor, retailer and agribusiness interests in the state system to appropriate the future for industrial agriculture.[45] Projections of rising global demand for food combined with recognition of potential markets for agro-inputs among small farmer communities match land grabbing with outgrowing (value chains) in a bid to capitalize on "available" farmland. Thus the Alliance for a Green Revolution in Africa (AGRA) intones:

> In all instances, governments need to make sure the land is used productively. In general, it is important for governments to promote investment in agriculture and to develop input and output markets. In doing so, farmers will be encouraged to invest, land values will increase, and land holdings will be induced to adjust – thereby becoming more efficient.
>
> (2013, 37)

7. Conclusion

In these ways, the commodification of land and ecosystems proceeds apace, by direct grabbing or indirect control through value-chains and emission offsets. Either way, the meaning of the natural world is reduced to price-governed fractions of complex natural interactions, and farming systems are degraded by projects of capitalization of soil and waterways, enclosing the future. The complicity of public authorities in alienating common property resources, and/or subsidizing private agribusiness in the name of global food security, reveals the deepening of commodity relations as market power conditions policy-making and management of the future. This is an era in which the state/finance nexus fetishizes social reproduction as a market function, deepening the use of the market to consolidate capital's power via overlapping sovereignties. Landed property is not only increasingly privately commandeered, but also its capture for offshore production, speculation or carbon sinks (as offsets) forecloses possibilities for managing landscapes for the common good rather than for private gain. This is a double foreclosure: on democratic access and control, and on land-use practices that work with, rather than against, nature. In this sense, the property regime under construction, through commodification, is not just a bid for profit, but for long-term control, in the (problematic) name of "shared humanity".

Notes

1 Susan Payne, CEO of Emergent Asset Management (a UK investment fund), declared, "Farmland in sub-Saharan Africa is giving 25 percent returns a year and new technology

can treble crop yields in short time frames . . . Agricultural development is not only sustainable it is our future. If we do not pay great care and attention now to increase food production by over 50 percent before 2050, we will face serious food shortages globally" (quoted in Vidal 2010).

2 *See* Kerssen (2013), who characterizes Honduran land grabbing as a political power grab (the 2009 coup) against a substantial land sovereignty movement challenging "internal" land grabbing for oil palm plantations.

3 "For the capitalist, the real thing is the nominal capitalization of future earnings. This capitalization is not 'connected' to reality; it is the reality. And what matters in that reality is not production and consumption, but power. This nominal reality of power is the capitalist *nomos*, and that should be our starting point" (Nitzan and Bichler 2009, 182).

4 Cerny conceptualizes such mechanisms as "embedded neoliberalism" (2008). See also McMichael and Peine (2005).

5 A neoliberal paradox.

6 Melissa Leach suggests the Millennium Ecosystem Assessment popularized the concept of "ecosystem services" (Foster 2012), stimulating the application of the price form to natural processes.

7 Santos (2002) argues there are few modern solutions to modern problems – the modern problem here being discounting (the value of) small farming cultures, and the assumption that corporate agriculture and markets, which have already marginalized such cultures, are the only solution to food insecurity (McMichael 2013c).

8 As such, contract farmers are subject to extractivist relations (Van der Ploeg 2009, 77–78).

9 Conventional agro-industrial emphasis is on agricultural output, rather than function, focusing on developing capacity for seeds and fertilizer inputs. The alternative conception of raising productivity is as "food output per acre rather than yield per plant" where farming is diverse, needing investment in "ecologically sound and socially just technologies" (Murphy 2008).

10 IAASTD. 2008. "Food Security in a Volatile World," Issues in Brief. Available at: www.agassessment.org/docs/10505_FoodSecurity.pdf

11 Of course land grabbing extends to the US, the EU (including "Eastern" Europe) Australia and so on, but for the purposes of this paper I focus on the Global South.

12 But they certainly remain so – as former UK Secretary of State for International Development Andrew Mitchell observed in July 2011: "If this is a moment of opportunity in many places across Africa, it is also a moment of huge opportunity for business . . . this Coalition Government is working to make it easier for companies to do business in Africa . . . Africa is the next, maybe even the last, big market" (War on Want 2012, 3).

13 By "market rule" I mean the institutional elaboration of neoliberal policy whereby states serve markets and the price form governs the development calculus.

14 Currently, there are a number of challenges by states and human rights organizations to suits filed at the World Bank-based International Center for the Settlement of Investment Disputes, regarding investor-rights provisions, increasingly being enforced through bilateral and multilateral treaties (notably, the North American Free Trade Agreement (NAFTA) and now the Trans-Pacific Partnership (TTP) and Transatlantic Trade and Investment Partnership (TTIP)) – arguably an indication of corporate mobilization to deploy legal force to gain access to foreign markets via border-hopping investment (Broad and Cavanagh 2014; Hansen-Kuhn and Suppan 2013).

15 Resistance takes a variety of forms: including government restrictions on foreign acquisitions of land in Argentina and Brazil (Perrone 2013; Borras et al. 2012), land governance reforms in Burkina Faso, Kenya, Tanzania and Liberia (Wuethrich 2013), and use of the Voluntary Tenure Guidelines to inform land struggles in India, Mali, Uganda, Argentina and Italy (McKeon 2015, 4), documentation of land grabbing forms and extent in Europe to encourage application of the Guidelines in the EU (TNI 2013),

land occupation by social movements in Argentina (Brent 2013), and indigenous struggles to defend territory in Guatemala (Alonso-Fradejas 2013) and Honduras (Kerssen
2013).

16 I use *ontology* to refer to "an implicit organization of the world and its inhabitants"
(Trouilliot 1995, 73).

17 See, e.g. Daniel (2010), Cotula (2011), Grajales (2011).

18 MacDonald reports on a "cash for wild-life swap" in Northern Pakistan by the International Union for Conservation of Nature (IUCN), which "offered to generate cash
for the village by selling a limited number of hunting permits to foreign hunters in
exchange for an agreement from village leaders that villagers would discontinue hunting ibex for subsistence purposes" (with no evidence that the latter threatened ibex
numbers) (2013, 231).

19 "Virtualism . . . operates at both the conceptual and practical levels, for it is a practical
effort to make the world conform to the structures of the conceptual" (Carrier 1998, 2).
This conception complements Nitzan and Bichler's notion that the market episteme
and its price form is the precondition and expression of power.

20 See Crutzen (2007) and Fargione et al. (2008). On current projections and alternative
energy targets, the International Energy Agency calculates that along with other renew-
ables, industrial biofuels are expected to supply no more than 9 percent of the world's
global energy consumption (GRAIN 2007, 6).

21 Consider Peluso's observation that territorialization is "an expression of relationships
that emerge, operate, and converge across and within localities, national spaces and
global networks" (2005, 13).

22 Creating, for example, dependent "environmental subjects" (Peluso and Lund 2011,
669).

23 Thus: "the emergence of REDD+ has been strongly influenced by the assertion of
political and cultural values tied to land by indigenous peoples' mobilizations at local,
national and transnational levels. The mobilizations have highlighted the value of land
as a place of belonging, as sacred territories and/or for the exercise of political self-
determination . . . mobilizations have driven this ongoing process of revalorization by
targeting global-level governance and international law (e.g. the UN Declaration on
the Rights of Indigenous Peoples and the principle of Free, Prior and Informed Consent) and the strategies of inter-national conservation organizations, yet also influenced
national and subnational legislation and local-level practices, such as revenue-sharing
around protected areas" (Sikor 2013, 2).

24 For elaboration of "global value relations", see McMichael (1999), and Araghi (2003).

25 Indeed: "the aggregation of economic rights is not so defining of [corporate] globalization as the attempt to *institutionalize* property rights on a global scale. Sheer size
or scale may distinguish the twenty-first-century corporation, but the privileging of
corporate rights over citizens' rights via institutional transformations is more profound.
Nowhere is this more dramatic than in the participation of states in the elaboration of
global market rule" (McMichael 2005, 599).

26 Brooks details a parallel process of the CGIAR centralizing bio-fortification research –
away from a food systems frame toward a more reductionist vision, setting "targets for
generic, scalable, 'gold standard' technologies", in the Challenge Program, which "was
designed with the needs of future 'strategic partnerships' with the transnational private
sector in mind" – allowing its "role of broker to be transformed into that of gatekeeper"
(2011, 72–74).

27 In the Lacandon case cited, the reconfiguration of livelihoods on the land is not necessarily of the producers' making – however much it may be presented as income
enhancement or productive improvement.

28 Thus "the South also recognizes that discourses of environmental degradation pose a
distinctive new kind of threat to national sovereignty because of their stress on northern
control of remedial measures" (Gupta 1998, 315).

29 De Schutter underlines the manipulability of the concept of "available land", that is, land with less than 25 people per square kilometre (Liberti 2013, 91).

30 As in "ecosystem services", which may in fact be unclaimed by ecosystem inhabitants, given that they co-produce such "services" without naming them, separately.

31 Liberti reports that the Ethiopian government wants dollars to modernize "and in order to obtain foreign currency it is prepared to undersell its own resources" such as land (Liberti 2013, 16).

32 Financial deregulation has enabled the shift in international financial governance "from states to 'private' institutions such as the Bank of International Settlements" (Nesvetailova and Palan 2010, 7–8). In this context, the World Bank, the International Monetary Fund (IMF) and the Bank of International Settlements (BIS) pair with the Organization for Economic Cooperation and Development (OECD), the G-8 and the G-20 in coordinating central banks and treasury departments "to constitute an evolving global financial architecture for an international version of the state-finance nexus" (Harvey 2011, 51).

33 Liz Alden Wily emphasizes that African lands with customary tenure are easily targeted for state appropriation because of "legal manipulations, which deny that local indigenous (customary) tenures deliver property rights, thereby legalizing the theft of the lands of the poor or subject peoples" (Alden Wily 2012, 751).

34 Mozambique reputedly depends on ODA to fund half its national budget, rendering it particularly vulnerable to donor pressure, such that domestic customary rights abuses are shared with other investing governments (Künnemann and Monsalve Suárez 2013, 132).

35 Reference to the "discourse of urgency" captures an important dimension of "rational planning of the planet" – and resonates in Liberti's observation that: "The great land grab feeds primarily on differences in knowledge and means; it is gauged and articulated in the distance that separates rural populations who have lived undisturbed for years in their fields, and certain characters who appear out of nowhere promising them development . . ." (2013, 194).

36 The rationale for G-20 strong-arm tactics under President Sarkozy's leadership is that G-20 countries "account for 65 percent of all agricultural land, 77 percent of global production of cereals, and 80 percent of world trade in agricultural products" (Murphy and Wise 2013, 23).

37 In a related initiative, presumably managing the taking into account of the Voluntary Tenure Guidelines, the "USAID has been leading the effort to develop a comprehensive database of all land governance programs funded by members of the Global Donor Working Group on Land. So far we have collected information on approximately 600 programs in over 92 countries with a total value of about 2 billion dollars. The database contains information on the location, duration, funding and scope of each program. As well as information on what specific aspects of the Voluntary Guidelines are being supported by each program" (Myers 2014).

38 To date, the G-8 has signed Cooperation Framework Agreements (CFAs) since the New Alliance formed in May 2012 with Benin, Burkina Faso, Côte d'Ivoire, Ethiopia, Ghana, Malawi, Mozambique, Nigeria and Tanzania (Oxfam 2013, 3). However, NAFSN is currently stalled under review, given the paucity of results and the recent withdrawal of France on the grounds that it preferred to avoid land grabbing and support established small-farming systems via agroecological intensification (*Le Monde*, February 12, 2018). Meanwhile the African Development Bank appears to be emulating this initiative with a new African Investment Forum (2018), designed to attract pension funds and other institutional finance to reduce the risk of private investment in large-scale agriculture.

39 Murphy and Wise comment: "the requirement that African governments 'improve investment opportunities' sounds hauntingly like the conditionalities of old (and current, much-criticized, bilateral investment agreements) and nothing like the country-led,

accountable and transparent aid policies that donors have pledged themselves to follow in the last several years" (2012).

40 For example, in the Nacala Corridor in Mozambique, Brazilian and Japanese investors are leasing, at minimal cost, land declared abandoned, but used by millions of small farmers – prompting La Via Campesina to call for a moratorium on all large-scale agricultural investments and recognition of common lands for use by local peasants (Paul and Steinbrecher 2013, 9).

41 Tanzania's Southern Agricultural Growth Corridor (SAGCOT) of 7.5 million ha includes 2 million ha farmed by smallholders (Paul and Steinbrecher 2013, 9).

42 E.g. Monsanto, Cargill, Dupont, Syngenta, Nestlé, Unilever, Itochu, Yara International, etc.

43 The Comprehensive Africa Agricultural Development Program (CAADP), formed as an inter-state project to promote country-led programs, has substantial experience in consulting with civil society organizations in national agricultural planning. It has also caught the financial attention of the G-8's New Alliance as a legitimacy grab.

44 Mozambique, for example, is required to write legislation promoting "partnerships" and to eliminate distribution of free and unimproved seeds, while "any constraints on the behaviour of corporate investors in Africa (such as the CFS guidelines on land tenure) remain voluntary, while the constraints on host nations become compulsory" (Monbiot 2013). Oxfam reports a consistent pattern of land and water acquisition putting farmers at risk (and discounting CFS Tenure Guidelines), as well as promoting seed and input policies privileging the private sector and its intellectual property rights (2013, 7).

45 Thus new "food security" interventions tend to promote "more investment rather than better policies as the solution to the food crisis" (McKeon 2013, 108) – threatening to deepen food insecurity in regional and class terms.

Works cited

Action Aid. 2009. *Assessing the Alliance for a Green Revolution in Africa*. ActionAid International.

AGRA. 2008. 'AGRA and the Millennium Challenge Corporation launch a historic collaboration to provide Africa's farmers with technologies, infrastructure and financing.' *Alliance for a Green Revolution in Africa*, June 11. Available at: www.agra-alliance.org/content/news/detail/682/

AGRA. 2013. Annual Report. *Alliance for a Green Revolution in Africa*.

Alden Wily, L. 2012. 'Looking back to see forward: The legal niceties of land theft in land rushes.' *The Journal of Peasant Studies*, 39(3): 751–775.

Alonso-Fradejas, Alberto. 2013. Land and sovereignty in the Americas. *Food First/TNI Issue Brief No 1*.

Araghi, Farshad. 2003. 'Food regimes and the production of value: Some methodological issues.' *The Journal of Peasant Studies*, 30(2): 41–70.

Bichler, Shimshon, and Jonathan Nitzan. 2009. 'Capital as power: Toward a new cosmology of capitalism.' Presentation at Seventh International Rethinking Marxism Conference, U Mass, Amherst, November. Available at: www.bnarchives.net

Borras, S., J. Franco, S. Gómez, C. Kay, and M. Spoor. 2012. 'Land grabbing in Latin America and the Caribbean.' *The Journal of Peasant Studies*, 39(3–4): 845–872.

Brent, Zoe. 2013. *Land Conflicts in Argentina: From Resistance to Systemic Transformation*. (Land & Sovereignty in the Americas Series, No. 4). Oakland, CA: Food First/Institute for Food and Development Policy and Transnational Institute.

Broad, Robin, and John Cavanagh. 2014. 'A strategic fight against corporate rule.' *The Nation*, February 3: 21–25.

Brooks, Sally. 2011. 'Is international agricultural research a global public good? The case of rice biofortication.' *The Journal of Peasant Studies*, 38(1): 67–80.

Carrier, James. 1998. 'Introduction.' In *Virtualism and Its Discontents*, ed. James Carrier and Daniel Miller. New York: Oxford University Press.

Cerny, Philip. 2008. 'Embedding neoliberalism: The evolution of a hegemonic paradigm.' *The Journal of International Trade and Diplomacy*, 2(1): 1–46.

Clark, William C. 1989. 'Managing planet earth.' *Scientific American*, 261: 46–54.

Cotula, Lorenzo. 2011. *Land Deals: What's in the Contracts?* London: IIED.

Crutzen, Paul. 2007. *Chemistry World*, September 21.

DaCosta, Dia, and Philip McMichael. 2007. 'The poverty of the global order.' *Globalizations*, 4(4): 588–602.

Daniel, Shepard. 2010. *(Mis)Investment in Agriculture: The Role of the International Finance Corporation in Global Land Grabs*. Oakland, CA: The Oakland Institute.

Davis, Mike. 2010. 'Who will build the ark?' *New Left Review*, 61: 10–25.

Deininger, K., and D. Byerlee. 2011. 'The rise of large farms in land abundant countries: Do they have a future?' *Policy Research Working Paper 5588*. Washington, DC: World Bank Development Research Group Agriculture & Rural Development Team.

DiMuzio, Tim. 2012. 'Capitalizing a future unsustainable: Finance, energy and the fate of market civilization.' *Review of International Political Economy*, 19(3): 363–388.

Diouf, Jacques, and J.-M. Severino. 2008. 'Africa must grow to rely on its own farms.' *Guardian Weekly*, May 2.

FAO. 2008. 'Boosting food production in Africa's "breadbasket areas".' *FAO Newsroom*, June 4. Available at: www.fao.org/newsroom/en/news/2008/1000855/index.html

Fargione, J., J. Hill, D. Tilman, S. Polasky, and P. Hawthorne. 2008. 'Land clearing and the biofuel carbon debt.' *Science*, February 7.

Foster, Joanna M. 2012. 'Q&A: The underside of "green" transactions.' *The New York Times*, June 20. Available at: http://green.blogs.nytimes.com/2012/06/20/q-and-a-the-dark-side-to-green-transactions/?_r=0

Friends of the Earth. 2010. *The Jatropha Trap? The Realities of Farming Jatropha in Mozambique*. Issue 118.

G8. 2012a. The "New Alliance for Food Security and Nutrition" in Tanzania. G8 Cooperation Framework.

———. 2012b. The "New Alliance for Food Security and Nutrition" in Ghana. G8 Cooperation Framework.

Gilbertson, T., et al. 2007. *Paving the Way for Agrofuels: EU Policy, Sustainability Criteria and Climate Calculations*. Amsterdam: Transnational Institute.

GRAIN. 2007. 'A new green revolution for Africa?' *Briefing*. Available at: www.grain.org/briefings/

Grajales, Jacobo. 2011. 'The rifle and the title: Paramilitary violence, land grab and land control in Colombia.' *The Journal of Peasant Studies*, 38(4): 771–792.

Gupta, Akhil. 1998. *Postcolonial Developments: Agriculture in the Making of Modern India*. Durham: Duke University Press.

Hansen-Kuhn, Karen, and Steve Suppan. 2013. *Promises and Perils of the TTIP: Negotiating a Transatlantic Agricultural Market*. Minneapolis: Institute for Agriculture and Trade Policy and Berlin: Heinrich Böll Foundation.

Harvey, David. 2011. *The Enigma of Capital*. Oxford & New York: Oxford University Press.

Hildyard, Nicholas. 1993. 'Foxes in charge of the chickens.' In *Global Ecology*, ed. Wolfgang Sachs. London: Zed Books.

Howse, R., and K. Nicolaidis. 2003. 'Enhancing WTO legitimacy: Constitutionalization or global subsidiarity?' *Governance: An International Journal of Policy, Administration, and Institutions*, 16(1): 73–94.

International Assessment of Agricultural Knowledge, Science and Technology for Development (IAASTD). 2008. *Executive Summary of the Synthesis Report*. Available at: www.agassessment.org/docs/SR_Exec_Sum_280508_English.pdf

Kerssen, Tanya. 2013. *Grabbing Power: The New Struggles for Land, Food and Democracy in Northern Honduras*. Oakland: Food First Books.

Künnemann, Rolf, and Sofia Monsalve Súarez. 2013. 'International human rights and the governance of land: Enforcing standards or enabling scrutiny?' *Globalizations*, 10(1): 123–140.

Liberti, Stefano. 2013. *Land Grabbing: Journeys in the New Colonialism*. London: Verso.

MacDonald, Kenneth Iain. 2013. 'Nature for money: The configuration of transnational institutional space for environment governance.' In *The Gloss of Harmony: The Politics of Policy-Making in Multilateral Organizations*, ed. B. Müller, 227–254. London: Pluto Press.

McAfee, Kathleen. 1999. 'Selling nature to save it? Biodiversity and the rise of green developmentalism.' *Environment and Planning D: Society and Space*, 17(2): 133–154.

McKeon, Nora. 2013. '"One does not sell the land upon which the people walk": Land grabbing, transnational rural social movements, and global governance.' *Globalizations*, 10(1): 105–122.

———. 2015. *Food Security Governance: Empowering Communities, Regulating Corporations*. London: Routledge.

McMichael, Philip. 1999. 'The global crisis of wage-labour.' *Studies in Political Economy*, 58: 11–40.

———. 2005. 'Globalization.' In *The Handbook of Political Sociology: States, Civil Societies and Globalization*, ed. Thomas Janoski, Robert Alford, Alexander Hicks and Mildred Schwartz. Cambridge: Cambridge University Press.

———. 2009. 'Banking on agriculture: A review of the *World Development Report* (2008).' *Journal of Agrarian Change*, 9(2): 235–246.

———. 2013a. 'Land grabbing as security mercantilism in international relations.' *Globalizations*, 10(1): 47–64.

———. 2013b. 'Value-chain agriculture and debt relations: Contradictory outcomes.' *Third World Quarterly*, 34(4): 671–690.

———. 2013c. *Food Regimes and Agrarian Questions*. Halifax: Fernwood Press.

McMichael, Philip, and Emelie Peine. 2005. 'Globalization and Governance.' In *Agricultural Governance: Globalization and the New Politics of Regulation*, ed. Vaughan Higgins and Geoffrey Lawrence. Abingdon, UK: Routledge.

Meadows, D.H., Meadows, D.L., Randers, J. and Behrens III, W.W. 1972. *The Limits to Growth. A Report for the Club of Rome*. New York: Universe Books.

Millennium Ecosystem Assessment. 2005. *Ecosystems and Human Well-Being*. Washington, DC: Island Press.

Mittal, Anuradha. 2009. 'Introduction.' In *Voices from Africa: African Farmers and Environmentalists Speak Out against a New Green Revolution in Africa*, ed. Anuradha Mittal and Melissa Moore. The Oakland Institute.

Monbiot, George. 2006. *Heat: How to Stop the Planet Burning*. London: Allen Lane.

———. 2012. 'Putting a price on the rivers and rain diminishes us all.' *The Guardian*, August 6.

———. 2013. 'Africa, let us help - just like in 1884.' *Grain*, June 11. Available at: https://www.grain.org/e/4742 (last consulted 20 Oct. 2019).

Monsalve Suárez, Sofia. 2013. 'The Human Rights framework in contemporary agrarian struggles.' *The Journal of Peasant Studies*, 40(1): 239–290.

Moore, Jason. 2000. 'Environmental crises and the metabolic rift in world-historical perspective.' *Organization & Environment*, 13(2): 123–157.

———. 2011. 'Ecology, capital & the nature of our times: Accumulation & crisis in the capitalist world-ecology.' *Journal of World-System Research*, 17(1): 107–146.

Müller, Birgit. 2013. 'The loss of harmony: FAO guidance for food security in Nicaragua.' In *The Gloss of Harmony: The Politics of Policy-Making in Multilateral Organizations*, ed. B. Müller, 202–226. London: Pluto Press.

Murphy, Sophia. 2008. 'Will free trade solve the food crisis?' *Food Ethics Council*, 3(2). Available at: www.foodethicscouncil.org.

Murphy, Sophia, and Tim Wise. 2012. 'G-8 punts on food security . . . to the private sector.' *Institute for Agriculture and Trade Policy*, May 22. Available at: www.iatp.org/blog/201205/g-8-punts-on-food-security

———. 2013. 'Resolving the food crisis: The need for decisive action.' *Aljazeera*, January 30.

Myers, Gregory. 2014. 'The land governance programme database and map.' *Global Donor Platform for Rural Development*. Available at: www.donorplatform.org/land/interviews/1128-gregory-myers-of-usaid-on-the-land-governance-programme-database-and-map.html

Narula, S. 2013. 'The global land rush: Markets, rights and the politics of food.' *Stanford Journal of International Law*, 49(1): 103–175.

Nesvetailova, A., and R. Palan. 2010. 'The end of liberal finance? The changing paradigm of global financial governance.' *Millennium*, 38(3): 797–825.

Nitzan, Jonathan, and Shimshon Bichler. 2009. *Capital as Power: A Study of Order and Creorder*. London & New York: Routledge.

Osborne, Tracey Muttoo. 2011. 'Carbon forestry and agrarian change: Access and land control in a Mexican rainforest.' *The Journal of Peasant Studies*, 38(4): 859–884.

Oxfam. 2013. The new alliance: A new direction needed. *Oxfam Briefing Note*, September.

Paul, Helena, and Ricarda Steinbrecher. 2013. 'African agricultural growth corridors and the new alliance for food security and nutrition: Who benefits, who loses?' *EcoNexus*, June.

Peluso, Nancy. 2005. 'Seeing property in land use: Local territorializations in West Kalimantan, Indonesia.' *Geografisk Tidsskrift, Danish Journal of Geography*, 105(1): 1–15.

Peluso, Nancy, and Christian Lund. 2011. 'New frontiers of land control: Introduction.' *The Journal of Peasant Studies*, 38(4): 667–682.

Perrone, Nicolás Marcelo. 2013. 'Restrictions to foreign acquisitions of agricultural land in Argentina and Brazil.' *Globalizations*, 10(1): 205–209.

Peters, Pauline. 2013. 'Land appropriation, surplus people and a battle over visions of agrarian futures in Africa.' *The Journal of Peasant Studies*, 40(3): 537–562.

Ploeg, Jan Douwe van der. 2009. *The New Peasantries: Struggles for Autonomy and Sustainability in an Era of Empire and Globalization*. London: Earthscan.

———. 2010. 'The peasantries of the twenty-first century: The commoditization debate revisited.' *The Journal of Peasant Studies*, 37(1): 1–30.

Polanyi, Karl. 1957. *The Great Transformation*. Boston: Beacon Press.

Rosenberg, Justin, 2001. *The Empire of Civil Society*. New York: Random House.

Sachs, Wolfgang. 1993. 'Global ecology and the shadow of "development".' In *Global Ecology: A New Arena of Conflict*, ed. Wolfgang Sachs, 3–22. London: Zed Books.

Santos, de Boaventura. 2002. *Towards a New Legal Commonsense*. London: Butterworth.

Sikor, T. 2013. 'Introduction: linking ecosystem services with environmental justice.' In *The Justices and Injustices of Ecosystem Services*, ed. T. Sikor. London: Earthscan Publications, 1–18.

Smith, Neil. 2007. 'Nature as accumulation strategy.' In *Coming to Terms with Nature*, ed. Leo Panitch and Colin Leys. London: Merlin Press.

Storm, Servaas. 2009. 'Capitalism and climate change: Can the invisible hand adjust the natural thermostat?' *Development and Change*, 40(6): 1011–1038.

Sukhdev, Pavan, Ravi Prabhu, Pushpam Kumar, Andrea Bassi, Wahida Patwa-Shah, Thomas Enters, Gabrial Labbate, and Julie Greenwalt. 2011. REDD+ and a green economy: Opportunities for a mutually supportive relationships. *UNEP Policy Brief*, Geneva, 1–8.

Trouillot, Rolph. 1995. *Silencing the Past: Power and the Production of History*. Boston: Beacon.

Urquhart, S. 2008. 'Food crisis, which crisis? Our crisis or theirs? The battle over the world's Food supply relocates to Rome.' *Guerrilla News Network*, June 2. Available at: http://gnn.to/articles/3718/food_crisis_which_crisis

Vermeulen, S., and L. Cotula. 2010. 'Over the heads of local people: Consultation, consent and recompense in large-scale land deals for biofuels projects in Africa.' *The Journal of Peasant Studies*, 37(4): 899–916.

Vidal, John. 2010. 'How food and water are driving a 21st-century African land grab.' *The Observer*, March 7.

War on Want. 2012. *The Hunger Games: How DFID Support for Agribusiness Is Fuelling Poverty in Africa*. London: War on Want.

Weis, Tony. 2007. *The Global Food Economy: The Battle for the Future of Farming*. London: Zed.

World Bank. 2007. *World Development Report, 2008*. Washington, DC: World Bank.

World Commission on Environment and Development (WCED). 1987. *Our Common Future*. New York: Oxford University Press.

Wuethrich, B. 2013. 'When property rights systems collide.' *FOLA*, October 14. Available at: www.landcoalition.org/blog/guest-post-fola-team-wri-and-landesa

4 From transgression to normative innovation

Land conflict resolution in South Kivu, Democratic Republic of the Congo[1]

An Ansoms, with Emery Mushagalusa Mudinga, Aymar Nyenyezi Bisoka, Giuseppe Davide Cioffo, Klara Claessens

Scholarly analysis of land rights in Africa – and beyond – has recognized legal pluralism as a *de facto* phenomenon that characterizes interactions, negotiations and conflicts within the land arena. *Legal pluralism* refers to the co-existence of different normative systems and different norm-producing authorities such as the state, customary and religious authorities, economic authorities and local communities. "[It] draws attention to the possibility that within the same social order, or social or geographical space, more than one body of law, pertaining to more or less the same set of activities, may co-exist" (von Benda-Beckmann and von Benda-Beckmann 2006: 14). Within the land arena, the concept refers to "the different sets of rights and obligations concerning land and property, as these reside within multiple social fields or normative orders" (Unruh 2003: 355). These rights and obligations take the form of norms and rules that can be anchored within the official legal framework and formal jurisprudence; but also within traditions and within contemporary and evolving customary orders. Everyday practices and interactions in the land arena thus take place in a situation where different legal fields – formal and informal – coexist, interact, reinforce and compete with each other.

Scholars disagree on how to appreciate this de facto plurality of norms. One stream in the literature has pointed to the existence of a variety of normative frameworks as a constraint for development and a cause of conflicts around land property rights. Proponents of this "legal centralist" view argue that the competition between the different legal orders is confusing and causes uncertainties. Such confusion is considered to have a negative impact on tenure security, with two problematic consequences. First, less certainty with regards to one's formal land rights is likely to result in lower investments and eventually in a lower development rate (Deininger and Feder 2009; see also De Soto's (2003) arguments in favour of individual land titling). Second, the ambiguity in land rights enhances the likelihood of land conflicts to emerge and complicates the achievement of legitimate conflict settlements respected by all actors involved (Blundo 1997; Schoonmaker 1992). In fact, according to this literature, legal pluralism should be considered as a source of state fragilization as it calls into question the role

of the state as the (unified) legitimate arbitrator in land conflicts. Legal centralism is therefore defended by this literature as the precondition for sound land
management.

However, there is a second stream of literature that has embraced legal pluralism as an opportunity rather than a threat for effective and peaceful land management, arguing that the principle of plurality offers a space for manoeuvre to the
state's citizens to find innovative solutions for their problems (Macdonald 2002).
According to Macdonald, the principle of one single juridical order, guaranteed
by the state, is not a realistic hypothesis when thinking of law in multicultural
societies. The author pleads in favour of embracing the idea of legal pluralism and
highlights the crucial role of those subject to the normative frameworks in recognizing (or not) the legitimacy of juridical institutions (state and non-state) that
guarantee the respect of that very same normative framework (Macdonald 2002).
In the same way as Macdonald, Kleinhans points to the problematic assumption of
recognizing the predominant power of the state and of official law, as this seems
to dismiss all other normative orders to a statute of inferiority, non-officialness,
and semi- or pre-juridical status (Kleinhans and Macdonald 1997). According to
Jarronson (1997), it is exactly because of the pitfalls of a global legal framework
that alternative norms have emerged, based on local practices that incorporate the
specificity of the local context. Given that these alternative norms allow people
to manage their situation, it has sometimes been suggested that the state should
consider these realities as an opportunity. In this view, the state could adopt legal
pluralism as a reality and a marker of the discrepancy between the official and the
"real" legitimate local social norms. In this way, it could adapt the official law to
existing social practices to ensure that the formal legal institutions are not disconnected from local legitimation processes. This could even reinforce the legitimacy
of the state.

A third stream of literature considers legal pluralism within an institutional
perspective, as a reality with both positive and negative sides. Meinzen-Dick and
Pradhan (2002) for example plead in favour of exploring the potential of the coexistence and interaction between different legal orders. In their view, this gives
scope for processes of forum shopping in which actors "use different normative
repertoires in different contexts or forums depending on which law or interpretation of law they believe is most likely to support their claims" (Meinzen-Dick and
Pradhan 2002: 5). Practically, forum shopping allows actors to strategically opt
for those normative arrangements that best suit their goal, which creates room
for manoeuvre for poorer and less powerful actors. Cleaver (2012) goes beyond
the idea of actors' strategically choosing between various normative frameworks.
She develops the concept of institutional bricolage, which describes the process
in which "people consciously and non-consciously draw on existing social formu-
lae . . . to patch or piece together institutions in response to changing situations"
(Cleaver 2012: 10). This process of creative interpreting and re-interpreting existing normative frameworks not only contributes to a changing institutional landscape, but creates space for agency for all types of actors interacting, negotiating
and competing with each other in the land arena. Similarly, Olivier de Sardan

(2008) introduces the exploratory concept of practical norms to draw attention to "the variety of social regulation methods and real governance patterns, without prematurely grouping them into a single model or organizing them into a priori types" (Olivier de Sardan 2008: 18). These norms gain legitimacy throughout the negotiation processes within the social arena, which could and should lead to normative innovations in the formal legal framework. Indeed, both Cleaver and Olivier De Sardan share the idea that the production of normative orders is not the exclusive domain of the state, on the contrary. Actors instrumentalize other normative orders when those suit their situation better than formal legislation, and, in this way, contribute to the legitimation of those alternative normative orders.

However, while creating agency and scope for negotiation, institutional bricolage and the dynamic evolution toward the establishment of practical norms are at the same time authoritative processes, shaped by power relations that often remain invisible. Therefore, the opportunities involved in institutional bricolage are often limited for poorer and less powerful actors, whereas more powerful actors are capable of navigating more strategically. In this way, institutional bricolage can reinforce unequal outcomes and inequality. On the one hand, such inequalities can be challenged through public negotiations or through local-level contestation. On the other hand, the cost of such contesting strategies is often disproportionally high for poorer actors. Cleaver concludes that, "whilst such processes of institutional formation and functioning may be complex, multi-layered and negotiable, they result for many people in commonly inequitable outcomes. The creativity and diversity of institutional design and practice creates room for manoeuvre and new possibilities for some people but simultaneously reproduces and even reinforces social inequalities for others" (Cleaver 2012: 15). Forum shopping and institutional bricolage are thus processes that can give scope to human agency, but at the same time, the space of manoeuvre they provide is often monopolized by better-off and better-connected actors.

In this chapter, we build upon the concepts of Cleaver and Olivier de Sardan to illustrate how legal pluralism has shaped and will continue to shape interactions in the land arena in the eastern part of the Democratic Republic of Congo (DRC). In the first part, we analyze how two rounds of land reforms (1973, 2000) have failed in their aim to reduce the plurality of land arrangements and to reinforce the centrality of the state. In the second part, three cases of positive resolution of conflicts around land in the DRC are presented. We first of all sketch the ways in which the different actors involved in the conflict interact with the variety of legal frameworks in which they ground their claims (cfr. forum shopping). Then, we illustrate that institutional innovation results from the creative (re-) interpretation and transgression of existing normative frameworks. We analyze how institutional innovations claim for legitimacy through transgression based on their capacity for conflict settlement. In line with Sikor and Lund (2009), we find that actors involved in such institutional innovation through transgression often search for ex-post anchorage of their settlement within the existing normative orders (formal and/or informal) to enhance legitimacy in a more sustainable way. Finally, we discuss the way in which grassroot innovations test the limits of the existing institutions and the norms they produce, and we refer to the relevance of this finding in relation to the ongoing debates on land reform in the DRC and on the conceptualization of property rights within it.

1. Land reforms in the DRC: a failed ambition for the state's normative monopoly

Many land reform processes in post-colonial Africa took legal centralism – see previous discussion – as the point of departure. The aim of such reforms was often to homogenize the range of frameworks in which individuals could claim land rights and to reinforce the legitimacy of official institutions. In fact, the colonial period had introduced a reality of juridical dualism with the production of a formal legal framework in relation to land matters for whites and foreigners, while tolerating the existence of customary law for autochthones. Land rights and customary authorities were allowed to continue to exist inasmuch as they allowed the achievement of colonial aims (mobilization of labour force and organization of land for the extraction of economic surplus, population control, etc. (Ndaywel è Nziem 1998). In the aftermath of independence, the national elites aimed at consolidating their positions through the official state-based legitimation of their power in land matters, therefore further stating the centrality of the state as the main source of legitimacy.

This has also been the dominant ideology behind the two land reforms (in 1973 and in 2000) undertaken by the DRC. Both land reforms aimed at reducing the plurality of existing land property arrangements by reinforcing the state as the only legitimate authority to make claims on land rights and conflict resolution. However, whereas the 1973 reform was largely based upon a formal legalist perspective – based on private, individual formal property rights – the 2000 reform recognized the existence of customary arrangements and community rights as a reality to be taken into account in the reform process (Oyono 2011; Mugangu Matabaro 2008). Let us look at both reforms in more detail.

During colonial times, legal centralism was the basic principle for the definition of land rights. However, although all legislative power was derived from the Belgian administration, customary systems were left in place for what concerned "indigenous" land. However, during the Mobutu era, the co-existence of different sources of legitimacy and power was viewed as a threat and a source of conflict. During a speech in Bukavu in 1973, Mobutu explicitly mentioned that land does not belong to the customary chiefs but rather to its users: 'your lands, like your wives, don't belong to your customary chiefs [in accordance with customary law]; they belong to you [in accordance with civil law]' (*'vos terres, comme vos femmes, n'appartiennent pas à vos chefs coutumiers [conformément au droit coutumier]; ils vous appartiennent à vous [conformément au droit légal]'*). As a result, the 1973 reform and land law (n° 73–021 of July 1973) had the ambition to restructure the inherited colonial land system to drastically reduce the power of customary chiefs. Nevertheless, the reform did not succeed in dismantling normative pluralism in land rights, nor in bringing an end to the ongoing land crisis

(Oyono 2011; Mugangu Matabaro 2008), on the contrary. As a result, the plea in favour of a strong decentralization of the land administration, and the request to clarify the statute of those lands under the de facto control of customary chiefs, became louder toward the end of the 1980s (Utshudi Ona 2009).

The land reform process that started in 2000, therefore, adopted a more nuanced stance on the de facto co-existence of different normative frameworks and legitimate authorities in the land arena. As such, the 2000 reform adopted the ambition to put an end to a situation of legal pluralism as a point of departure. However, in contrast to its 1973 precedent, the 2000 law did take local practices into account, and rather aimed at inserting these practices into a legal framework that would eventually find its legitimation through the state. Local practices have thus served as an inspiration for the law. In this way, the 2000 land reform claimed to be based on principles of participation, decentralization and on the respect for human rights and the environment (RDC Ministère des Affaires Foncières 2013: 3). Nevertheless, although the 2000 reform claimed to be inspired by local practices, it still embraced the same classic approach to land rights. It assumed that land rights are to be guaranteed and legitimated through the state, in the form of the proclamation of property rights arrangements that define the relationship between an individual owner and his land. Such an approach does not take into account the variety of normative frameworks that define land rights beyond the idea of pure property rights and beyond the principle of individual rights of a person in relation to an economic asset.

2. Land conflict resolution in eastern DRC

In this paper, we move beyond these perspectives by taking a different angle to look at land dynamics in Congo. Instead of focusing on the ambitions of land reforms to frame land rights in terms of the relation between a person and his or her asset, we approach land dynamics through the ways in which they shape the relationships between persons. An ideal way of doing this is by focusing upon land conflicts and the way in which land rights (access to and/or control over land) are negotiated throughout such conflicts. In contrast to our previous work, where we concentrated on the many types of problematic land conflicts that exist within the Congolese context (see Ansoms and Hihorst 2014; Ansoms and Marysse 2011), this paper focuses on conflicts with positive outcomes in the form of (at least temporary) resolution.

The case studies presented in this article analyze the ways in which different normative frameworks are combined, transgressed and reconfigured in the process of conflict mediation and resolution. Indeed, in many cases, the normative orders in place contradict each other, or are inadequate to deal with locally-specific complex land conflicts. The absence, inadequacy or abundance of both customary and state norms does not necessarily entail passivity from the side of local actors. On the contrary, this legal uncertainty may inspire actors to discover new and unexplored paths. The transgression and the mistrust of existing norms might constitute an inventive strategy for local actors to deal with such uncertainty (Debuyst 2011; Crozier 1970). Such ingenuity might be a form of resistance to normative frameworks that are not recognized as effective or adapted to specific contexts (Kerkvliet 2009; McAllister 2012) eventually opening up possibilities for the negotiation of alternative normative frameworks. In this light, the following case studies represent situations where conflict resolution mechanisms did not find their legitimation in the central jurisdiction of state law, nor in the body of customary practices that the state recognizes as legitimate. In fact, the cases of conflict resolution we present are ad hoc solutions through transgression of pre-existing normative orders.

Our paper is based on different phases of fieldwork carried out throughout 2013 by Aymar Nyenyezi and Emery Mudinga. Semi-structured interviews were carried out with various actors involved in the land conflicts presented, as well as with mediators and observers in the field. Respondents were chosen on the basis of a social cartography of the conflicts. The analysis and the discussion of the cases are the product of the authors' collaborative work.

A. Organizing the transhumance: from norm contestation to institutional innovation

The first conflict presented here concerns a land conflict between livestock farmers and agriculturalists in Fizi (a territory in South Kivu). The conflict is framed around the management of *cattle transhumance*, defined as "the regular movement of herd [cows in this case] to given points, according to the seasonal availability of grazing areas" (Blench 2001: 12). Each year from May to September, farmers guide their livestock from the high and middle lands – where weeds have dried up and can no longer meet livestock's grazing needs – to the greener plains bordering the coast of Lake Tanganyika. This movement concerns about 200,000 cows and their herders (Kambale Nzweve 2013). While the topic was largely ignored during the colonial period, the issue of the transhumance appeared on the national policy agenda of Zaïre in the 1970s (Bucyalimwe Mararo 2001). With rising livestock numbers and the increasing number of conflicts between farmers and pastoralists, statutory authorities in collaboration with customary chiefs defined corridors for the passage of livestock to grazing fields and to water points.

According to local actors engaging in transhumance, the practice was regulated by customary law since "the beginning of time".[2] The pastoralists used to pay a usage fee to local authorities in order to access grazing spaces and water points. Known in the Ruzizi plain as *itulo*, the usage fee was the traditional method for regulating the relationships between farmers and their customary chiefs on the one hand, and pastoralists on the other hand. *Itulo* often consisted of payments in kind (i.e. cassava for farmers, gold for mine-diggers, cows for livestock farmers) to the local chief to grant access to land and to ensure the chief's protection.

However, throughout time, rising population pressure put these corridors and passages under increased pressure. In lack of common fields designated for livestock grazing, conflicts between pastoralists, farmers and customary chiefs intensified. In our interviews, various local actors suggested that since 1990, transhumance was practiced "through force", resulting in the violation of existing land rights and in confrontations between farmers and pastoralists.[3] These conflicts also exacerbated dynamics of ethnic opposition between, for example, the Banyamulenge[4] (majority of pastoralists, usually rwandophone) and the Babembe (majority of farmers and also the withholders of customary power).

The start of the Congo wars (from 1996 onward) was a real turning point in the relations between local farmer communities and livestock farmers engaged in seasonal transhumance.[5] First of all, much of the passage points became inaccessible during the wars, and large tracks of land were later appropriated by political and military elites (ADEPAE, Arche d'Alliance and RIO 2011). Second, when returning after years of absence in the aftermath of the wars, pastoralists refused to continue fulfilling their customary obligations toward the chiefs of local populations. The reticence to pay *itulo* was seen by customary chiefs as a threat to their position. Moreover, they accused pastoralists of instrumentalizing the conflict to arm themselves and appropriate land. As Kambale Nzweve (2013: 8) highlights, "pastoralists have set up armed security patrols to be ready to any occurrence, they contest the authority of customary chiefs whom are perceived as accomplices with armed groups". On the other hand, pastoralists accused customary chiefs and farmer communities of supporting *Mai-Mai* militias that threatened pastoralists and pillaged their livestock. As Kambale Nzweve (2013) points out, "these armed groups interfere with transhumance and the *itulo* arrangement linked to it. While claiming to protect community land, armed groups restrict livestock movements, they pill livestock or they directly extort money from the pastoralists, they extract the *itulo* illegitimately, assuming the role of local chiefs" (Kambale Nzweve 2013: 8).

The weakening of the *itulo* system is reflected in the changing interpretation of what this symbolic payment represents. First, pastoralists increasingly interpret the payment of *itulo* as a land purchase. As one farmer puts it: "*Today's problem is that livestock farmers think that when they pay the* itulo, *they are actually purchasing the land; and they think they paid the fee to the farmers*'.[6] Second, the role of the customary chief in the *itulo* system is increasingly called into question. Farmers on the one hand call into question the legitimacy of the customary chief to receive compensation for what they perceive as 'their' land. One of our interviewees mentioned: '*Our fields are ours, they are not grazing land. We are not obliged to let pastoralists graze their livestock. They shall ask for permission politely, they shall negotiate with us, as it is not us who receive the* itulo'.[7] Pastoralists from their side, contest the authority of customary chiefs, whom they perceive as incapable of assuring a peaceful transhumance notwithstanding receiving the *itulo*" (Kambale Nzweve 2013: 8). Even local officials seemed critical of the system: "*All that customary chiefs do is collecting the* itulo *fee, without giving pastoralists any advice or guarantee of security. They do not even have enough space for grazing, and they do not consult with farmers on who has the right to refuse access to their land. As for pastoralists, they think that once they have paid the* itulo, *they have a right to go everywhere*".[8] In fact, some Banyamulenge groups even consider the *itulo* as a form of perpetual domination by the Babembe local chiefs, guaranteeing their political and administrative power over pastoralist communities. Finally, the monetization of the *itulo* has also contributed to the erosion of its symbolic function. Some local chiefs keep the count of how many cows they ought to receive in order to successively convert them into a claim in dollars. This adds up to the impression of *itulo* having been transformed into a forceful extraction mechanism and a tool for exploitation of pastoralist communities.

Since 1996, the coins turned several times, sometimes in favour of the pastoralist communities; then in favour of farmer communities. Over the period from 1996 to 2003, the pastoralists were in a position of relative force, given their prominent role in the 1996 AFDL[9] rebellion and later with RCD[10] rebel movements in 1998. However, after the peace agreement between the rebel forces and the government in Sun City in 2003,[11] the tables turned in favour of farmer communities. Since 2006, land conflicts occurred more frequently and intensified with farmers expelling transhumants from their plots and cutting their cows' hooves. Kambale Nzweve (2013) reports how during this period, transhumance became a source of violence and uncertainty, with armed pastoralists ready to engage in confrontation on one side and farmers ready to avoid any infringement of their property rights on the other. This situation increasingly deteriorated living conditions on both sides and contributed to an overall feeling of insecurity and uncertainty.

In order to cope with this situation, a group of local pastoralists and farmers came together in local committees to find new ways of managing seasonal transhumance and the land conflicts it triggered. In 2010, at the occasion of a three-day meeting on the subject, they elaborated an "agreement on peaceful transhumance" (*accord sur la transhumance apaisée*). This agreement, signed by all stakeholders, constituted a significant innovation as it entailed the deliberate reinterpretation and transgression of key elements of all pre-existing normative frameworks. This situation is not unique to DRC. Lund, for example, explains how farmers and pastoralists in Burkina Faso try to settle land disputes. In a land dispute opposing a Fulani family to a group of farmers of the Bassindigo province, the state, instead of imposing a specific settlement upon these two conflicting parties, left the parties to develop a possibly new (but least-adapted) community norm. The agreement was then a combination of the somewhat formalist logic of the state law and the more substantial logic of community (Lund 2003).

On the one hand, the Fizi agreement restored certain parts of the pre-existing customary *itulo* system. In this way, the agreement could be interpreted as an institutional innovation that creatively interprets and reconfigures existing normative frameworks. The principle of pastoralists obtaining passage and grazing rights on land owned by farmers in return for compensation has been reaffirmed. Moreover, the symbolic and non-monetary nature of *itulo* has been restored as a basic principle, as well as the securitization of plots and wells by the pastoralists during the time of their stay. The agreement furthermore foresees the possibility for pastoralists to pay the *itulo* collectively, while local chiefs actively engage in ensuring the safety of pastoralists' livestock through the disaffiliation from armed groups. Both farmers and pastoralists agreed not to carry firearms.

On the other hand, the agreement introduced significant innovations through a deliberate transgression of certain key principles of the traditional *itulo* system.

First of all, the agreement was acted in a written document, in contrast to a tradition of oral rule transmission (and the continuous reinterpretation this involved). Second, and more importantly, the agreement implicitly called into question the exclusive power of the customary chiefs to determine transhumance rights. The agreement enacted the principle that all local groups should be involved to identify areas suitable for the passage and grazing of livestock. Moreover, a system of conflict resolution through mixed committees was established, including customary chiefs, pastoralists and farmers.

Since the agreement on peaceful transhumance was signed, it has been used as a framework for the organization of local transhumance flows and for the resolution of land-related conflicts. Its legitimacy is largely based upon the fact that the agreement has significantly reduced overt tensions between pastoralist and farmer communities. The success of the agreement also highlights the inadequacy of the state's normative framework to deal with land conflicts in relation to transhumance. Nevertheless, the agreement does not reject the state as such. In fact, despite the state's limitations, local actors have found it opportune to anchor their agreement – and the institutional innovation involved – within the existing state normative framework. In 2011, negotiations started in order to transform the agreement into a provincial regulation. Although this process has stagnated due to administrative, technical and financial constraints, it is interesting that local actors have considered it useful to search for formal legitimation of a locally negotiated arrangement that transgressed the state's legal system.

Furthermore, the agreement has also become a reference in the reform of customary systems of transhumance. The mere existence of the agreement illustrates that land conflicts between pastoralists and farmers may be settled through a deliberate transgression of existing norms, a solution constructed outside both state law and existing customary arrangements. The "agreement on peaceful transhumance" has emerged from the negotiation of new normative arrangements suitable for dealing with a changing and locally-specific environment. Interestingly, this calls into question the common assumption that actors see customary arrangements as natural, their rationality being seldom-contested, resulting in the idea that customary norms can – in the perception of local actors – not be renegotiated (Mambi Tunga-Bau 2010). The renegotiation of customary rules opens up important possibility for real democratic grassroots participation at the local level in defining mechanisms of access to land (Fung and Wright 2003).

B. Land conflicts in Kalehe: local mediation committees as an institutional coup d'état

Whereas in the first case, actors deliberately transgressed the existing customary normative system when confronted with their incapacity to deal with intense and violent land conflict; the following case discusses how local actors replaced both formal and customary mediation institutions with innovative new forms of land conflict settlement.

In recent years, the territory of Kalehe (South Kivu) has been confronted with increased tension between the *Havu* and *Tembo* (considered autochthonous to the area), and *Hutu* and *Tutsi* groups (considered as foreigners).[12] Confrontation between both sides was particularly intense in 1993, when *Tembo* militias fought rwandophone groups (largely *Hutu*). The eruption of violence strongly affected local living conditions and contributed to an overall feeling of insecurity. As a reaction to this, a group of local leaders and actors from different ethnic communities in the area decided to put in place a pacification committee in charge of promoting peace among armed groups. The peace process was hindered by the massive arrival of new waves of *Hutu* refugees in 1994, and the wars that followed in 1996 and 1998. However, in the early 2000s the committee restarted its activities in order to ensure freedom of movement for all local people in the area.

Given that intercommunity tensions often emerge around land conflicts, land issues were automatically taken up by the pacification committee. In 2009, the committee organized a meeting with the customary chiefs and the leaders of different ethnic communities (mainly Havu, Tembo, Barongeronge, Hutu and Tutsi). During these talks, representatives of each group agreed upon the overall principle of respecting each group's de facto land rights. This was not that straightforward, given that the legitimacy of "foreign" land claims by Hutu and Tutsi groups were often called into question by "autochthonous" ethnic groups in other parts of eastern DRC. In addition to the overall principle, four local mediators were identified to serve as a reference point in case of land-related conflicts. The mediators would meet every three months. Quite soon after the installment of the land conflict resolution mechanism, it proved to be too rigid and non-adapted to quickly evolving and contextually-specific local land conflicts. Therefore, ad hoc committees were installed to mediate in case of local conflicts. These committees were composed of local leaders as well as members of the local administration. According to several leaders of local organizations, the creation of these committees has proven to be rather successful, due to their participative character. The committees extract their legitimacy from their efficiency in bringing conflicting actors together through locally mediated solutions. Moreover, they ask for no compensation for their services. In this way, the committees acquired a strong popularity and credibility since their inception, echoed in several of our interviews: *"The mediation committees saved us; we've been waiting for something similar for a long time"; "It is a great thing to have someone who helps you to solve your problem without frustrating you or asking for money;" "It is thanks to those committees that my cousin recognized he was passing into my field from his".*[13]

However, the popularity of local ad hoc committees has increasingly been perceived as a trespassing of existing normative arrangements (both formal and informal) do deal with land conflicts, especially by customary chiefs as well as by the local police. In fact, before the installment of the ad hoc committees, it was the customary chiefs who mediated in case of land conflicts in the informal sphere, whereas the local police occupied a key role in the formal environment. However, both customary authorities and the police used to ask for compensation in return for their role as mediator; and through compensation, actors could often bend the mediation efforts in their favour. As one customary chief puts it: *"These committees do a great job for the people, but not for us the customary chiefs. [. . .] Since they started addressing land issues for free, they turned people away from us. [. . .] We will die of starvation because of these committees! [. . .] How do people think we will make a living if there are no conflicts to be solved?"*[14] Also members of the local police expressed their regret that they were no longer solicited in case of land conflicts, although some claimed that the committee's work made their job easier. As one policeman reported, *"It is true that we are losing out on some of the advantages we had with conflict resolution, but it is also true that we can now spend our time on many other issues".*[15] Another added, *"At present we only deal with land conflicts when damage is caused, [for example land conflicts resulting] in wounds and other violence. The committee is in charge of all other quarrels".*[16]

This case illustrates how locally established committees, emerging outside of the customary or formal institutional environment dealing with land conflicts, result from a process of deliberate transgression of existing normative orders. The police and the customary chiefs find themselves in a difficult position. On one hand their prerogatives have been usurped; on the other they cannot publicly question the legitimacy of an institution that has come out of a popular consultation. The success of such institutions could be attributed to their grassroots nature, as they were born out of a long process of discussion and negotiation embedded in locally specific dynamics. The fact that the ad hoc committees do not ask for money, together with their capacity to come to effective settlements, reinforces their credibility and legitimacy. Interestingly, civil society organizations such as the local organization Action Pour la Paix et la Concorde (APC) and the UN Habitat Programme are supporting these local initiatives, reinforcing their mediation capacities and facilitating their functioning.

C. Death of a customary chief and the absence of the state: legal innovations outside the legal framework

Whereas the previous cases concerned larger social groups, our third case study describes a very micro-level situation. Nevertheless, the larger context of this local case study is important. The *chefferie* in the Ruzizi plain is one of the three collective customary chiefdoms of Uvira territory, 75 kilometres South of Bukavu. The plain is inhabited by a number of communities practicing agriculture, such as the Bashi, Banyindu, Barega, Babembe, Barundi and Bafuliru. These groups are also found outside the Ruzizi plain, and they are part of the social configuration of the Southern Kivu Province. The Bafuliru are the largest group, and they have been in a conflict with the Barundi since colonial times. Struggles for land between customary chiefs from both sides play an important part in this conflict. The murder of the Barundi customary chief, the *mwami*, on April 25, 2012, exacerbated the conflict between the Barundi and Bafuliru in the Ruzizi plain. The signing, in September 2012, of a code of good conduct by representatives of the two communities – under the guidance of United Nation Mission in Congo (MONUSCO) as well as national and provincial authorities – did not lead to the resolution of the conflict. The disappearance of the Barundi customary chief not only complicated the situation at the higher level (Barundi – Bafuliru conflict); it also exacerbated tensions at the very local level. In fact, the disappearance of the *mwami* led to an impasse in the whole customary land governance system.

In fact, in case of land conflicts, people turn either to a jurisdictional conflict resolution mechanism or to an alternative conflict mediation mechanism. The jurisdictional solution is only available in a court of peace (*tribunal de paix*, the lowest institution in the judicial system). Although – according to the law – every area should dispose of such a court of peace, this is often not the case. As a result, people often opt for alternative land-conflict resolution methods. This alternative mechanism is activated when both parties in a conflict agree to submit themselves to a non-judicial instance to solve their issue. According to customary traditions, conflicts should be addressed to the village chief. If the village chief does not succeed in resolving the issue, the case goes up one level, to the *chef de localité* or, in last instance, to the *chef de groupement*.

These three levels (village, *localité* and *groupement*)[17] judge by customary law. The three figures are issued from customary *mwami* chief lineage, and they are supported by wise men when engaging in conflict resolution. The customary system is hereditary, meaning that power is passed from father to son – and so the role of the *chef de village, de localité* or *de groupement*. The situation changes when the chief does not die of a natural death, and when another ethnic group tries to conquer chiefdom power. Therefore, when the old chief is absent, and the struggle for power is ongoing, the tenure system experiences a void, as in the Bunanira village. This void could not be filled by state institutions that were largely absent at the local level. As one of our interviewees mentioned, *"Many people exploited this void to use land [that] was not theirs, or [that] had been previously taken from them by the authorities"*.[18]

In one of the villages of the Ruzizi plain, a school teacher of the Bafuliru tribe became a major protagonist in the set-up of a locally-embedded land conflict resolution mechanism. He observed that, *"There have always been land conflicts in the village. However, when the* mwami *died, a number of people – manipulated by the politicians, and close to the court or the government – started taking advantage of the situation and appropriating other people's land. The state was never there to solve the conflicts; the villagers do not have enough money to pay for transport to go to the tribunal and to pay court fees"*.[19]

In such a context, the teacher took the initiative to contact *"four members of the community, the serious people in the village"* to start solving land conflicts. For this school teacher, it was essential to act *"before politicians [could] come and manipulate the villagers"*: *"It is not easy to give reason or to blame in a land conflict. Some people may have a little proof of purchase on a piece of paper, others may have witnesses, and other people may have papers from the local administration . . ."* In a context where so many sources of legitimacy seem to collide with each other, the teacher chose to favour the witness of neighbours he considered "serious", as *"The problem is to know to whom a certain part of the land should go. It is difficult to trust a piece of paper from the administration, as everyone could have written it in exchange for a little tip. Similarly, customary chiefs sometimes come here and they solve conflicts giving reason to the party who buys them beer"*.[20]

Out of the 27 cases submitted to the committee guided by the teacher, 16 consisted of simple restitutions of land. The committee centered its judgment around the symbolic importance of land to come to negotiated solutions, even when one side of the conflicting parties possessed official documents from the administration. In cases where the litigants were reluctant to accept this reasoning, the committee would resort to the respective pastors from the local churches to talk them into an agreement.

In other instances, however, conflicts emerged from the purchase of land that was, unknowingly, already customary owned by someone else. According to a member of the mediation committee, the land was given back to the original owner in three such cases when one of the litigants *"already had many plots, and for just one more they did not wish to be a source of conflict for the village"*.[21] However, for the remaining six cases, land had been shared among the parties. According to the school teacher, everyone understood that the issue was not to recognize ownership according to customary or state law, given that *"authorities' decisions had engendered a situation in which there were landless people in the community"*. According to him, *"Authorities do not feed us, all they do is distributing the land which feeds us without asking themselves what the people who do not have land anymore will do. It is our duty to care about our people in this village"*.[22] Eventually, two persons from the village refused to collaborate. The school teacher explained this by the fact that the persons involved were the parents of young Bafuliri chiefdom militia: *"They are convinced that their sons have the support of the customary chiefs and that these are going to come and support them appropriating all the* (contested) *land"*.[23]

Again, as in the previous case studies, existing normative orders fell short of dealing with complex land conflicts at the local level. The death of the customary chief led to voids in the customary normative framework. At the same time, formal land conflict resolution mechanisms were unavailable at the local level. The inadequacy of the existing normative orders to deal with locally-specific complex land conflicts did not entail passivity from the side of local actors. On the contrary, this legal uncertainty inspired influential local actors to discover new and unexplored paths. A locally set-up mediation committee, composed of local natural leaders, judged land conflicts on the basis of principles of fairness and local-level compromise while ignoring previously established land rights on the basis of customary norms or formally recognized land rights. The transgression and the mistrust of existing norms constituted an inventive ad hoc strategy for local actors to deal with the voids of the existing normative frameworks.

3. Conclusion: from transgression to normative innovation

On the basis of a wide variety of case studies, we have selected these three as emblematic of the variety of situations in which alternative conflict resolution strategies, born out of grassroots initiatives, may result from the transgression of existing rules emanating from different normative frameworks. Transgression represents a means to overcome the pitfalls of established norms or to overcome a situation of legal uncertainty and social distress. Through such transgressions, new institutions are created to regulate issues of ownership and use of natural resources. Jarronson (1997) has already highlighted how alternative methods for conflict resolution are born out of the shortcomings of established mechanisms. These three cases clearly illustrate how alternative conflict resolution mechanisms may emerge out of a process of institutional bricolage (Cleaver 2012).

Following Cleaver (2002), we suggest that the alternative conflict resolution methods – issued through collective action by key local actors (to which we will turn in the next paragraph) – have given birth to socially embedded institutions "based on culture, social organisation and daily practice, commonly but erroneously referred to as informal" (2002: 13). The "agreement of peaceful transhumance" (case 1) as well as the committees set up under the initiative of local actors in Kalehe (case 2) and in Ruzizi (case 3) are institutions that are mainly the produce of two factors.

First, they emerge out of the questioning of elements from existing normative frameworks, both state-produced and customary. The activity of institutional bricolage is not limited to the adaptation and reinterpretation of the existing norms but also involves their deliberate transgression or neglect. Interestingly, legal pluralism has in these cases not been the source of uncertainty or conflict; it rather appeared as the very pre-condition for the production of normative innovations. It is exactly because local actors had the possibility to resort to different normative orders that the parties involved reached an agreement that accommodated competing interests by drawing on traditional institutions and giving them new meanings. Of course legal pluralism does not represent a method of conflict resolution per se, but without such a repertoire, collective action would not have resulted in the institutions that finally achieved an effective arrangement.

Second, the institutional structure emerging out of this process is the result of local social cleavages (ethnic or economic), power relations and serendipity, and is unique to the *milieu* in which it comes to be, which makes them socially embedded. In three cases presented, a new institutional arrangement, or a temporary ad hoc solution, was reached by means of local agency activated in pursuit of a socially desired objective. In the cases presented, differences of power and unequal relations between actors at the local level played a major role in finding a way out conflict and also resulted in land allocation that accommodated competing interests. Land allocation was not the result of rational economic choices, as mainstream institutionalists seem to argue and as modernist land reform proponents often assume (Borras 2003), but of careful local planning aimed at achieving what was perceived by the actors involved as fair. By no means do we intend to claim that collective action at the local level will always result in a "happy ending", as great power imbalances may influence the outcome of local-level negotiations about land property rights and land use. However, in complex conflict situations land does not just stand as a good to be exchanged on the market, or to be owned in virtue of a purchased title, but it does mediate the relations between different groups (farmers and pastoralists, Babembe and Hutu) who do not fit in the easy categorizations that are often necessary for state legislation.

The socially embedded nature of such a set of "new rules" also poses questions about the generalizability of local-level arrangements and the need of the state to enforce a degree of control and homogenization. On one hand, the integration of grassroots innovation into the legal system represents an opportunity, as it may provide answers to land conflicts that are grounded into the reality and complexity of social relations at the local level. On the other hand, integrating local-level innovations into wider systems may risk generalizing localized solutions, which might prove alien in different contexts. Therefore, when thinking about the land reform process at the macro-level, a certain degree of openness is needed in order to accommodate socially embedded solutions. However, an important problem may reside in the role that the transgression of established norms may play in achieving a socially desired objective. In the case of the committees in Kalehe (case 2), state authority tolerated the usurpation of some of their functions by the newly established committees. In the first case, locally-negotiated non-formal land rights were temporarily given during particular times (the transhumance season) to a particular group (the pastoralists) and in a particular form (non-monetary collective payment) on which all the parties agree upon. In our last case study, legal land titles were willingly ignored and land re-allocated or shared, with ad hoc solutions. However, when extrapolating such experience in the broader context, transgression might be perceived as a calling into question of the state's authority, and might not easily be tolerated. Such forms of bricolage, acting through transgression rather than re-composition, might be the most difficult to accommodate in a legalistic system.

In fact, centralized legalistic efforts fall short of meeting the two features of the normative innovations highlighted above: their negotiated nature to and their social embeddedness. While it may advance state control, the enforcement of property rights does little to ensure that resources and access are distributed in a way that is perceived as fair or socially desirable by parties at the local level. In a context characterized by the coexistence of multiple systems of legitimation and norm-production, the implementation of a one-size-fits-all approach may hinder people's capacity to solve land conflicts in creative ways that respond to the changes in their social and natural environments.

Notes

1 The authors would like to thank Christian Lund and Etienne Verhaegen for their valuable comments.
2 Individual interviews, Customary chiefs, Baraka/Fizi, July, 2013.
3 Individual and focus groups interviews with customary chiefs, farmers and administration officers, at Uvira and Fizi territories, July–August, 2013.
4 The Banyamulenge (sing.:munyamulenge), literally "those who come from Mulenge", a river affluent to the Rusizi) are a rwandophon group of mainly pastoralists living in Eastern DRC. They may mainly be found in South Kivu, at the border with Burundi. See also: Jean-Claude Willame (1997).
5 Interview, local chiefs, Fizi, July, 2013.
6 Interview, Farmer, Malinde/Fizi, August 2013.

7 Interview, Farmer, Katanga village, July, 2013.
8 Interview with the Provincial Inspecteur of Agriculture, Fishery and Farming-IPAPEL, Fizi, August, 2013.
9 Alliance de forces démocratiques pour la liberation du Congo, a rebel coalition led by Laurent-Désiré Kabila who took power at the end of the First Congo War (1996–1997).
10 Rassemblement congolais pour la démocratie, a rebel movement actif in eastern DRC since 1998.
11 In June 2003, the Congolese government and several major rebel groups (MLC, RCD) came to an agreement according to which power was shared in a transitional government.
12 Hutu and Tutsi groups in the region, in fact, are often rwandophones – which highlights their "foreign" character in the eyes of the Havu and Tembo.
13 Interviews, farmers, Kasheke village, August 2013.
14 Interview, Chef de groupement Mbinga Nord, August, 2013.
15 Interview, Chef de Poste, sous commissariat, Kalehe centre, August, 2013.
16 Interview, Chef de poste, sous commissariat, Nyabibwe, August, 2013.
17 *Localités* are not present in the new administrative structures of DRC. Regardless, *chef de localité* still exist in some the settings of the study. For the new administrative structure see: République Démocratique du Congo, Loi organique n° 08/016 du 07 octobre 2008 portant composition, organisation et fonctionnement des Entités Territoriales Décentralisées et leurs rapports avec l'Etat et les Provinces. See also: République Démocratique du Congo, Loi organique n° 10/011 du 18 mai 2010 portant fixation des subdivisions territoriales à l'intérieur des provinces.
18 Focus group, farmers, Bunanira, August 2012.
19 Interview, school teacher, Bunanira, August 2012.
20 Interview, school teacher, Bunanira, August 2012.
21 Interview, member mediation committee, Bunanira, August 2012.
22 Interview, school teacher, Bunanira, November 2012.
23 Interview, school teacher, Bunanira, November 2012.

Works cited

ADEPAE, Arche d'Alliance and RIO (2011) *Au-delà des groupes armés. Conflits locaux et connexions sous-régionales. L'exemple d'Uvira et Fizi (Sud-Kivu, RDC)*, Series des Grands Lacs, Uppsala, Life and Peace Institute.

Ansoms, A. and Hihorst, T. (eds.) (2014) *Losing your land: Dispossession in the Great Lakes*, Suffolk, James Currey.

Ansoms, A. and Marysse, S. (eds.) (2011) *Natural resources and local livelihoods in the Great Lakes Region: A political economy perspective*, London, Palgrave.

Blench, R. (2001) "'You can't go home again': Pastoralism in the new millennium", *Overseas Development Institute (ODI)*, www.odi.org/sites/odi.org.uk/files/odi-assets/publications-opinion-files/6329.pdf (last consulted January 8, 2016).

Blundo, G. (1997) "Gérer les conflits fonciers au Sénégal: le rôle de l'administration locale dans le sud-est du bassin arachidier", in Becker, C. et Tersiguel, P. (éds.), *Développement durable au Sahel*, Dakar and Paris, Sociétés, Espaces, Temps, Karthala, pp. 103–122.

Borras, S.M. (2003) "Questioning market-led agrarian reform: Experiences from Brazil, Colombia and South Africa", *Journal of Agrarian Change*, 3(3): 367–394.

Brabant, J. and Kambale Nzweve, J.L. (2013) *La houe, la vache et le fusil Conflits liés à la transhumance en territoires de Fizi et Uvira (Sud-Kivu, RDC): État des lieux et leçons tirées de l'expérience de LPI*, Série des Grands Lacs, Upsala, Life & Peace Institute.

Bucyalimwe Mararo, S. (2001) "Pouvoirs, élevage bovin et la question foncière au Nord-Kivu", in Marysse, S. and Reyntjens, F. (eds.), *L'Afrique des Grands Lacs. Annuaire 2000–2001*, Paris, L'Harmattan.

Cleaver, F. (2002) "Reinventing institutions: Bricolage and the social embeddedness of natural resources management", *The European Journal of Development Research*, 14(2): 11–30.

Cleaver, F. (2012) *Development through bricolage: Rethinking institutions for natural resource management*, New York, Routledge.

Crozier, M. (1970) *La société bloquée*, Paris, Ed. Seuil.

Debuyst, F. (2011) "Acteurs, strategies et logiques d'action", in Debuyst, F., Defourny, P. and Gerard, H. (eds.), *Savoirs et jeux d'acteurs pour des développements durables*, Louvain la Neuve, Academia Bruylant, pp. 115–148.

Deininger, K. and Feder, G. (2009) "Land registration, governance, and development: Evidence and implications for policy", *World Bank Research Observer*, 24(2): 233–266.

De Soto, H. (2003) *The Mystery of capital: Why Capitalism triumphs in the West and fails everywhere else*, New York, Basic Books.

Fung, A. and Wright, E.O. (eds.) (2003) *Deepening democracy: Institutional innovations in empowered participatory governance*, New York, Verso.

Jarronson, C. (1997) "Les modes alternatifs de règlement des conflits. Présentation générale", *Revue internationale de droit compare*, 49(2): 325–345.

Kambale Nzweve, J.L. (2013) "La régulation de la transhumance – un enjeux de la paix en Est de la RDC", *New Routes*, 2: 7–11.

Kerkvliet, T. (2009) "Everyday politics in peasant societies (and ours)", *The Journal of Peasant Studies*, 36(1): 227–243.

Kleinhans, M.-M. and Macdonald, R.A. (1997) "What is critical legal pluralism?", *Canadian Journal of Law and Society*, 12(25): 25–46.

Lund, C. (2003) "Conflicts and contracts in Burkina Faso: Land and local law between state and community", *Journal für Entwicklungspolitik*, 19(1): 91–106.

Macdonald, R.A. (2002) "L'hypothèse du pluralisme juridique dans les sociétés démocratiques avancées, *Revue de Droit*", *Université de Sherbrooke*, 22: 133–152.

Mambi Tunga-Bau, H. (2010) *Pouvoir traditionel et pouvoir d'Etat en République Démocratique du Congo*, Kinshasa, Médiaspaul.

McAllister, K. (2012) *Rubber, rights and resistance: The evolution of local struggles against a Chinese rubber concession in Northern Laos*, Presentation, International Conference on Global Land Grabbing II. Department of sociology, Cornell University, 17–19 October.

Meinzen-Dick, R.S. and Pradhan, R. (2002) "Legal pluralism and dynamic property rights", *CAPRI working paper n°22*.

Mugangu Matabaro, S. (2008) "La crise foncière à l'Est de la RDC", in Marysse, S., Reyntjens, F. and Vandeginste, S. (eds.), *L'Afrique des Grands Lacs. Annuaire 2007–2008*, Paris, L'Harmattan.

Ndaywel è Nziem, I. (1998) "Histoire générale du Congo. De l'héritage ancien à la République Démocratique", De Boeck et Larcier s.a., Paris et Bruxelles.

Olivier de Sardan, J.P. (2008) "Researching the practical norms of real governance in Africa", *Afrique Pouvoir et Politique*, Discussion paper n°5.

Ostrom, E. (1995) "Designing complexity to govern complexity", in Hanna, S. and Munasinghe, M. (eds.), *Property rights and the environment*, Washington, USA, Beijer International Institute of Ecological Economics and the World Bank.

Oyono, P.R. (2011) *La tenure foncière et forestière en République Démocratique du Congo [RDC]: Une question critique, des vues centrifuges. Revue compréhensive de la littérature*, Yaoundé, L'Initiative des Droits et Ressources.

République Démocratique du Congo (2008) Loi organique n° 08/016 du 07 octobre 2008 portant composition, organisation et fonctionnement des Entités Territoriales Décentralisées et leurs rapports avec l'Etat et les Provinces.

République Démocratique du Congo (2010) Loi organique n° 10/011 du 18 mai 2010 portant fixation des subdivisions territoriales à l'intérieur des provinces.

République Démocratique du Congo, Ministère des Affaires Foncières (2013) Réforme foncière. Document de programmation.

Schoonmaker, F. (1992) "Le règlement des conflits en matière de gestion des terres", in Collectif, *Land tenure, local institutions and natural resources in senegal*, Madison, Land Tenure Center, University of Wisconsin-Madison, vol. 4: 13p

Sikor, T. and Lund, C. (2009) "Access and property, a question of power and authority", *Development and Change*, 40(1): 1–22.

Unruhn, J.D. (2003) "Land tenure and legal pluralism in the peace process", *Peace & Change*, 28(3): 352–377.

Utshudi Ona, I. (2009) "La décentralisation en RDC: Opportunité pour un gestion foncière décentralisée?", in Marysse, S., Reyntjens, F. and Vandeginste, S. (eds.), *L'Afrique des Grands Lacs. Annuaire 2007–2008*, Paris, L'Harmattan.

von Benda-Beckmann, F. and von Benda-Beckmann, K. (2006) "The dynamics of change and continuity in plural legal orders", *The Journal of Legal Pluralism and Unofficial Law*, 38(53–54): 1–44.

Willame, J.-C. (1997) *Banyarwanda et Banyamulenge: violence ethniques et gestion de l'identitaire au Kivu*, Paris, L'Harmattan.

Part II

Social mobilization and the counter-movement

5 Forging a single proletariat

J. Phillip Thompson

Capitalism is typically considered to operate independently of race; race is thought to be little more than a social characteristic of a worker, and workers of a given skill level are considered interchangeable. History does not bear this out. Racial division was crucial for slavery and thus for the cotton trade, the first major capitalist industry. Cotton production was equally predicated on colonialism in Asia and expropriation of land from indigenous tribes in the Americas. None of this was possible without a powerful nation-state, massive violence and political ideologies of racism to justify these actions. Capitalism created not one but two proletariats: the first, colored (initially slave and colonial) and the second, white. Property ownership was not only a foundation of labor exploitation writ large: it helped structure divisions between the two proletariats.

At the base of all capitalism is politics, which can spawn a variety of economic logics (Crouch 2005). As the economic historian Karl Polanyi noted, humans are not economic but *political* animals: "[t]he economic factor, which underlines all social life, no more gives rise to definite incentives than the equally universal law of gravitation. . . . With man – the political animal – everything is given not by natural, but by social circumstances" (Polanyi 2014). The early period of capitalism was what historian Sven Beckert calls "war capitalism." War capitalism, necessary for slavery and colonialism, enabled the development of European and US manufacturing that in turn strengthened the capacity of Western nation-states to spread capitalism (Beckert 2014). These states would not have been possible, particularly in democratic regimes, without ongoing support from a significant part of the working class – the white proletariat. The construction of racially divided proletariats was not a natural or inevitable outcome of capitalism, but the intended consequence of social and political ideology and actions.

Differences in property status helped to separate the two proletariats. For millennia, property was conceived as an inseparable part of political, religious, and social hierarchies, and so it was for blacks prior to the US Civil War. Capitalist land grabs were also justified as "natural" using the Lockean argument that God intended land to be used for the benefit of the greatest number of people, and capitalists were more industrious utilizers than Native Americans (Wood 2012: 268). Property has more recently been considered the result of heroic individual achievement or merit. All of these conceptions of property are political; all come with embedded racial narratives to explain the separation of the two proletariats: blacks are not human at all (slavery), biologically inferior and incapable of industriousness (Jim Crow) and culturally inferior or *lumpen* (recent). At various points in history, many on the white Left endorsed each of these viewpoints, yet held to the ostensible position that there is a single proletariat, albeit one confused about its true self-interest. W.E.B. Du Bois held a radically different view, arguing that capitalism indeed divided the proletariat in two:

> [The] black proletariat is not part of the white proletariat . . . while Negro labor in America suffers because of the fundamental inequities of the whole capitalist system, the lowest and most fatal degree of its suffering comes not from the capitalists but from fellow white laborers. It is white labor that deprives the Negro of his right to vote, denies him education, denies him affiliation with trade unions, expels him from decent houses and neighborhoods, and heaps upon him the public insults of open color discrimination.
>
> (Du Bois 1995)

1. The non-racial capitalism view

To explicate Du Bois's notion of two proletariats, I begin with the traditional argument that race and capitalism are not linked. Ellen Wood, a Marxist historian of capitalism, says of worker identity and consciousness:

> Even when the "assemblage and transformation" of the labor force is complete, people are at best assembled only in productive units, factories, and so on. Their assemblage in class formations which transcend such individual units is a process of a different kind, one that depends upon their consciousness of, and propensity to act upon, a *common experience and common interests*.
>
> (Wood 1995, 2016: 91) (emphasis added)

Wood maintains that workplaces are the primary spatial locations where workers from all backgrounds develop such a common experience and interests. This view of workers' lives is incomplete. Workers have meaningful experiences in neighborhoods, schools, and churches that are, in the US at least, typically ethnically and racially distinct. Conversely, workers shop in malls that often gather far more people than workplaces, and they may feel an exhilarating sense of equality and commonality in being able to freely roam around glitzy shops choosing products to covet or buy (on credit). How do we know whether common experiences at the workplace have greater impact on workers than their common experiences in malls, or outweigh their racially distinct encounters in neighborhoods, churches, and schools? What if narratives in and of the workplace (say, by unions) are less compelling and coherent explanations of their lives than those of race, ethnic, or religious leaders? Neighborhoods and shopping centers embody property relations just as much as do workplaces, and discourse about property is ubiquitous, so why privilege workplace discourse for the formation of workers' consciousness?

Of race and gender, Wood says:

> [I]t is not so clear that racial or gender equality are antagonistic to capitalism, or that capitalism cannot tolerate them as it cannot deliver world peace or respect the environment. . . . The extraction of surplus value from wage labor-ers takes place in a relationship between formally free and equal individuals and does not presuppose differences in juridical or political status. In fact, there is a positive tendency in capitalism to *undermine* such differences, and even to dilute identities like gender or race, as capital strives to absorb people into the labor abstracted from any specific identity.
>
> . . . [I]f capital derives advantages from racism or sexism, it is . . . because they disguise the structural realities of the capitalist system and because they divide the working class.
>
> (Wood 1995, 2016: 266–267)

During the period of Jim Crow and slavery, contrary to Wood's argument, great differences in juridical and political status existed between white workers and workers of color. (Nelson 2001) Further, according to Wood, race is useful to capitalism only in so far as it disguises capitalism's true nature and divides workers. This argument presumes that it is not essential for capitalism to divide workers in this way; capitalists have other ways to subdue workers. Thus race is not a "structural reality" of capitalism. However, in the actual lived world, there is no experience of pure capitalist logic in which race (and gender) do not play a crucial dividing role. Wood creates an imaginary world of labor, "abstracted from any specific identity", in which capitalism is devoid of its deepest political contradictions. She then credits a "positive tendency in capitalism", rather than intrepid political movements *against* capitalism, for victories over the inherent racial and gender oppression structured within capitalism. Here is history turned upside down.

A contrary Marxian analysis of race was put forward by, among others, Jamaican-born British cultural theorist Stuart Hall. Hall attributed views such as Wood's to "reductionism" in analysis of capitalism. Reductionism most often takes the form of *economism*:

> a specific theoretical approach which tends to read the economic founda-tions of society as the *only* determining structure. . . . The approach . . . has little or no theoretical room left in it for ways of conceptualizing the political and ideological dimensions, let alone ways of conceptualizing other types of social differentiation such as social divisions and contradictions arising around race, ethnicity, nationality and gender.
>
> (Hall 1996: 417–418)

Hall notes that Marxists often reduce even economic study by prioritizing production relations in the workplace over other equally important forms of economic activity such as consumption, exchange and social reproduction – for example, education, healthcare, housing, shopping malls and finance. In politics, reductionism conceives of "class struggle" as between agents of the working class and agents of the capitalist elite, rather than as consisting of fluid sites of contention, complex pacts among workers, and contentious sets of alliances across economic divides (Hall 1996: 425).

Politics is constructed through discourse, and the ideas and culture informing discourse thereby acquire material force. Ideas and culture cannot be reduced to simplistic categories like "class". Human beings are historical beings, influenced by all kinds of past discourses going back to the Stone Age and forward into imaginary worlds. Hall insisted on a non-essentialist understanding of both race and class. He also maintains that the modern state is far more important and complex than Marx or Weber ever conceived of it: "The state is no longer conceived as simply an administrative and coercive apparatus – it is also 'educative and formative'," and it provides much of the moral and ethical underpinning of society" (Hall 1996: 448).

The implication of Hall's argument for traditional Marxism is significant: state policies like social security, public housing, land-use laws, public schools, legal segregation, immigration, or communication licensing may shape consciousness more than workplaces. To Hall, the "structural realities" of capitalism are not chained to the economy; how to understand and organize workers is a far more complex question than reductionism allows. While it is true that the cultural influences and institutional structures of society are bound by material and ideational capacities – this is where Marx's materialist emphasis on history and economic conditions comes in, and why Hall considers himself Marxist – beyond this, there are no limits or guarantees of what can or will happen.[1] This means that the social category of race might be constitutive of capitalism, as well as the other way around. Whether there is a single or double proletariat is a matter for empirical investigation; it cannot be dismissed a priori by a predetermined capitalist "logic".

2. Race, class and property thru the Civil War

To make the argument that capitalism operates according to a non-racial logic, many historians and social scientists have argued that the slave South was "pre-capitalist" (Genovese 1966; Wilson 1978, 1980). This gave rise to the related idea that modern racism is a lingering by-product of pre-capitalist feudal social relations and that racism will gradually disappear as social consciousness catches up with modern capitalist production relations. Subsequent scholarship on slavery and the antebellum South has undermined this notion (Hahn 1983; Johnson 2013). Slavery was thoroughly capitalist, and it was undergirded by a highly specific political and racial construct – only Africans were made slaves. Indeed, capitalism pre-dates slavery in the US; Britain originally chartered *corporations* to settle the colonies and make profits. Early settlers in the US were members of these corporations, "and the consolidation of the slave system served to transform one form of corporate elite into another" (Martinot 2003: 43). Exempting capitalism from actual early US history requires extensive myth-making that sanitizes the origins of capitalist private wealth, minimizes slavery and glosses over the pure expropriation of Native American land (Wald 1993: 26).

Blacks' social, economic and political exclusion and similar conditions in colonies are what led Du Bois to argue that capitalism structured two proletariats:

> [I]n cultured lands, the Machine and harnessed Power veil and conceal. The emancipation of man is the emancipation of labor and the emancipation of labor is the freeing of that basic majority of workers who are yellow, brown, and black.
>
> (Du Bois 1992: #30, 15)

Black labor became the foundation stone not only of the Southern social structure, but of Northern manufacture and commerce, of the English factory system, of European commerce, of buying and selling on a worldwide scale; new cities were built on the results of black labor, and a new labor problem, involving all white labor, arose both in Europe and America (Du Bois 1992: #30, 5).

We can see that Du Bois distinguished labor of color, capitalism's "foundation stone" or what I will call the "first proletariat", from US and European "all-white" labor, who, with the aid of high profits coming from super-exploitation of workers of color, were offered a "veil" of power and cultured achievement such as that found in modern cities. Moreover, capitalism offered white workers, the second proletariat, a special role in relation to the first proletariat:

> The system of slavery demanded a special police force and such a force was made possible and unusually effective by the presence of the poor whites. . . . Considering the economic rivalry of the black and white worker in the North, it would have seemed natural that the poor white would have refused to police slaves. But two considerations led him in the opposite direction. First of all, it gave him work and some authority as overseer, slave driver and member of the patrol system. But above and beyond this, it fed his vanity because it associated him with the masters.
>
> (Du Bois 1992: #30, 12)

Du Bois further argued that poor whites abandoned their own class interests in pursuit of the "American" idea that they could become future exploiters of workers of color. For Du Bois, capitalism did not emerge separate from the state or from racial categories; it depended on both. Black and white workers were never interchangeable; from the start, race was fundamental to policing and maintaining the system. The two proletariats were formed intentionally in opposition to one another, with race as the dividing line. Before rule by property elites could be challenged, the two proletariats would have to overcome this division.

Property and social identity

In the 1820s and 1830s, as capitalism developed, strong class tensions emerged between ordinary white farmers and banks. "Hugely profitable because they collected interest on loans considerably exceeding their real capital, banks seemed from the beginning threatening and fraudulent to the subsistence-oriented sector of American society" (Sellers 1991: 46). Yet, the greatest political conflicts in the US at this time were over land, especially as territory opened up west of the Mississippi River. Slave owners wanted to expand slavery westward as many decades of cultivation had depleted land on existing plantations. They came into conflict with Northerners who saw the future of the country, and of democracy, as based on small-scale entrepreneurship and ample land for ordinary citizens (Foner 1970: 316). Neither side of the conflict, however, embraced anti-racism. Those opposing expansion of slavery into the West, the Free Soilers, were typically adamant that free blacks be excluded from the territory as well.

Truly democratic whites had much to worry about: fugitive slave laws implored white citizens to hand over runaway slaves to at the risk of imprisonment – or worse. Many white abolitionists took serious personal risks to shield slaves and help them find safety in parts of northern states or Canada. In these and other ways, being white, or staying white, was thus a political/ethical choice closely connected to one's commitment to genuine democracy. Property ownership was part of this larger dilemma of whiteness; it was a realm of individual freedom only for those willing to subvert the freedom of non-white others. Du Bois thus described abolitionism as "abolition-democracy," arguing that the two things, if indeed democracy requires a minimum level of human decency, could not be separated.

Property, race, law, politics and insoluble contradictions

In America, whiteness freed whites from being made slaves. Property ownership was made conditional on race (and gender) from the beginning. Paradoxical efforts to merge slavery and democracy created policy and legal conflicts, and even burdens for some whites that ultimately helped lead to the Civil War. For example, the constitution of 1787 counted slaves as three-fifths a person for the purpose of apportioning seats in Congress. This provided whites in the South with far more voting power than other white citizens, which they then used to reduce their tax burdens relative to Northerners and to secure other advantages (Einhorn 2006).

Non-slave corporations (Northern-based) also were challenged to draw legal distinctions between themselves and slaves, the other government-sanctioned form of property ownership under the law.[2] The Southern states wanted strong state government powers over corporations in order to maintain slavery with minimal interference from abolitionists in the North. But, Jacksonian-era populists used local state power to attack privileges and corrupt deals allowing elites to aggregate even more wealth. Non-slave corporations sought to come under federal protection rather than subject themselves to the laws of populist leaning states, arguing that unpredictability among state legislatures and different treatment across state lines made it difficult to attract financing or grow businesses across regions.

Ultimately, the status of free blacks came to be at the center of this controversy: "[i]f corporations had access to the federal courts, then free blacks probably did as well. And if the court protected their rights as it did corporate rights, then the South's system of racial rule faced a grave threat" (Allen 2006: 43). Conversely, if blacks who'd bought themselves or been freed by their masters could cross state lines and enjoy the privileges of federal citizenship, why couldn't corporations? Yet, corporations making this policy argument in the face of slave-owner power in Congress were certain to lose. This conundrum led Chief Justice Taney's Supreme Court in 1857 to issue its infamous Dred Scott decision, stripping all rights from black Americans, free or not.

Dred Scott ended all hope of gradual elimination of slavery, and it heightened the determination of abolitionists to end slavery by any means necessary – including armed insurrection. This latter threat was a key source of Northern business irritation with slavery. Slavery was politically and militarily unstable, as well as legally unpredictable, and it thereby limited long-term investment and development overall.

Contrary to Wood's argument that capitalism favors anti-racism, in reality without abolitionist opposition to slavery, and without slave insurrections and escapes, there would likely have been little business opposition to slavery. For that matter, Chief Justice Taney assiduously sought to please both Southern plantation owners *and* Northern industrialists by denying blacks any rights whatsoever – thus securing corporate access to federal protection by separating them legally from black ex-slaves. It was not Northern capitalism, but the opponents of the slave industry that pushed the nation on a more democratic path – via the Civil War.

3. Opportunity lost: the Civil War was a revolutionary war for human rights over property rights

The counter-revolution that followed the Civil War has obscured, for many, the broad scope and revolutionary character of the war and Reconstruction. Freeing slaves was a major taking of property at the cost of hundreds of thousands of lives. It was for radicals an opportunity to re-found the nation on the basis of equality and to merge the two proletariats. The North passed the Thirteenth, Fourteenth and Fifteenth Amendments to alter the constitutional framework and not only ensure blacks' freedom, but to entitle *all* workers to advance economically and receive just compensation for labor (Goluboff 2007: 158). Yet Union troops and Reconstruction officials encountered deep opposition confronting the racial attitudes of white Southern workers. Discussing efforts of the Freedman's Bureau to uphold the rights of freed slaves, the head of the Mississippi Freedman's Bureau, Col. Samuel Thomas, wrote that white opinion could not

> conceive of the negro having any rights at all . . . to take property away from a negro they do not deem robbery. . . . They still have the feeling that the black people at large belong to the whites at large.
>
> (Foner 1988: 149)

Ingrained racist culture, even more than elite economic interests, stood in the way of revolutionary change. Within weeks of Lincoln's assassination by a Confederate, the newly-elevated President Johnson, a former slave-owner, granted amnesty to most Confederates, restored most confiscated lands to whites, and replaced Reconstruction officials who wanted to redistribute land to blacks with officials who wanted coercive forms of contract labor for former slaves.

These counter-revolutionary moves were accompanied by the rise of death squads directed against democratic activists in the South, which effectively stifled radical egalitarian transformation before it could take hold. With the ascent of Southern power to Congress, "about 94 percent of the federal election regulatory code built up after the Civil War would be repealed" (King and Smith 2011: 59). While slavery was not directly reinstated, property ownership was denied to freed slaves. This re-created the basic two-proletariat structure, but given that some whites were also poor and property-less and potentially inclined to unite with blacks, new rigid forms of racial segregation were instituted that sharply heightened racial distinctions between the two proletariats.

Government property distribution reinforced racial hierarchy. Large land give-aways after the war, called "homesteading", increased property ownership among whites while land distribution for blacks was blocked. In March 1865, at the close of the war, Congress passed legislation stating that to "every male citizen, whether refugee or freedman, there shall be assigned not more than forty acres of land". Congress acknowledged at the time that this policy was essential to establishing equality; slaves could not actually be "free" without property and resources. Instead they would be forced back into another kind of slave-like condition. Yet the legislation was never put into effect, undermining the Civil War victory. It left ex-slaves landless and penniless, forcing them to work as debt farmers and low-wage laborers barely distinguishable from their former enslaved condition.

Prior to the counter-revolution, in 1862, President Abraham Lincoln signed the Homestead Act, which opened government-owned land to small family farmers ("homesteaders"). The Act gave any citizen who was the head of a family 160 acres for five years, after which they had to pay only $18. Farmers could also opt to buy the 160 acres after only 6 months for $1.25 an acre. Blacks could not take advantage of the virtual land giveaways before 1866, because they were not citizens. After 1866, being penniless ex-slaves, very few had the ability to move and build a house as the program required. By 1900, settlers had obtained *80 million acres* of land through the Homestead Act. To make way for homesteaders, the federal government forced Native American tribes into reservations.

The system that emerged to keep blacks working on former plantations was sharecropping – a form of debt-internment. Since few blacks had money or access to land after slavery, most were forced to work for former slave owners. Landowners would advance them credit to buy supplies, and then pay them for bringing in the crop. However, the payment for the crop typically did not cover the cost of supplies, and sharecroppers found themselves bound to the land by debt to the landowner or local merchant. "Debt operated in the South as a way to buttress the economic and legal regime of Jim Crow. Blacks who resisted were often lynched or brutally attacked" (Dawson & Ming-Francis 2015: #2043).

4. Corporate power and counter-revolution after the Civil War

The basic structures of modern capitalism were constructed on the basis of the suppression of democratic advancements post-Civil War. As industry grew, the fight over property focused not only on land but also on wages and control of corporations. In a shocking misreading of the Fourteenth Amendment, a conservative Supreme Court decided without argument in the 1886 *Santa Clara* decision that corporations were legal persons entitled to the same protections as citizens. Eleven years later, in a case concerning the right of state governments to regulate a railroad company, the Court wrote, "corporations are persons within the provisions of the fourteenth amendment," and, "a state has no more power to deny to corporations the equal protection of the law than it has to individual citizens". The ruling was a direct blow to democratic control of corporations and led directly to the era of robber barons and monopolies. Under the new philosophy of the *Santa Clara* Court, redistributive economic justice was not judicially enforceable; it could only be pursued through democratic politics. As historian Gerald Magliocca observed, "liberty of contract was invented to give voice to renewed interest in protecting property rights, and that idea was grafted onto the Fourteenth Amendment because no other part of the Constitution could bear it" (Magliocca 2011: #2034, 150).

This new view of corporations emerged during the Court's simultaneous reasoning that racial inequality perpetrated by "private" parties, including businesses, was not prohibited by the Fourteenth Amendment; the Court maintained that the Fourteenth Amendment was only intended to protect blacks from state *governments*. The reading was both patently false and tragically ironic: the Court used a Civil War statute intended to protect former slaves to instead shield corporations from democratic accountability; it then supported extensive private and governmental racial segregation, the latter through its farcical "separate but equal" doctrine essentially to re-enslave blacks.

It was no accident that the Court issued its infamous *Plessy v. Ferguson* decision, endorsing racial segregation, on the heels of the Populist Movement. The Populist Movement, mainly of poor whites but reaching out to Southern African Americans – thereby threatening to unite the two proletariats – endangered corporate power and property. The movement already had proven its capacity to capture state and local offices when one of its key leaders, William Jennings Bryant, won the Democratic nomination for President in 1896. The reaction was swift: many states quickly established restrictions on voting, including literacy tests, grandfather clauses, poll taxes, and other measures that not only kept blacks, but also large numbers of poor whites from the polls as well.

Racial segregation was an even more powerful structural means of dividing the emerging movement. Physical separation by race became far more important for whites' identity-formation than economic status. Segregation bred racial enmity and undermined radical interracial movements time and again. Thurgood Marshall and other NAACP lawyers made just this point before the Supreme Court in the famous 1954 *Brown v. Board of Education* case that eliminated, at least formally, the "separate but equal" doctrine (Magliocca 2011: #2034, 97).

A major ideological shift accompanied the counter-revolution: the abolitionist-democratic view that the right to self-governance through a democratic process is the most basic of all rights was replaced by the conservative liberal view that private property rights trumped democracy and those who lacked property were inferior human beings. By the turn of the twentieth century, the dominant American cultural narrative framed "self-made men" such as Carnegie and Hilton as the drivers of progress. The aspiration for government was for efficiency, making it much like industry. Poverty was not a reflection of political oppression, but of personal failings. Fairness was a matter of procedure, not substance. The best place for women was in the home, not agitating for rights.

Labor unions embraced this new philosophy (Norton 1986: 55). White labor unions declared their distinction from the colored proletariat, "[b]y 1905 AFL president Samuel Gompers portrayed trade unions as agents of 'Caucasian civilization' and warned that 'if the colored man continues to lend himself to the work of tearing down what the white man has built up, a race hatred far worse than any ever known will result'" (Nelson 2001: xxxii). "The new systems justified in terms of these far-ranging racial doctrines included not only anti-black measures but similar laws and practices aimed at Mexicans in the Southwest, Asians in California, and Native Americans in many western states. They also supported the racially justified imperial conquest and governance of Filipinos, Puerto Ricans, and Pacific Islanders, and eventually the systems of race-based immigration quotas enacted in the 1920s" (D. S. King and Smith 2011: 66). In the enactment of each of these measures, labor was at the forefront leading the charge.

5. A Second opportunity lost: the new deal era

Racial exclusion weakened white labor. Witnessing the rise of corporate elites and increasing attacks on labor in 1924, the National Association for the Advancement of Colored People (NAACP) strongly urged, "that black and white labor get together . . . [or] organized labor in this country is threatened with irreparable loss"(Bois 1995: 537). The NAACP was directly on target. In 1929, the rise of corporate power led to economic ruin for millions of workers and farmers. In response, the Congress of Industrial Organizations (CIO) aggressively organized mass industrial unions. The CIO recruited blacks in the hundreds of thousands. Competition with the old (almost all-white and segregated) American Federation of Labor (AFL) unions forced the CIO to organize and grow rapidly, but the more it recruited white workers, the more difficult it was to forge a progressive program – due to white workers' resentment of black "invasion" of their neighborhoods and factories in cities like Detroit and Chicago (Sugrue 1995: #1288).

Labor organizing at this time was physically dangerous and legally hamstrung; unions desperately sought federal legal recognition of the right to organize and protection from hostile police and hired goons. Despite a US president, F.D. Roosevelt, sympathetic to labor, the South still controlled key committees in Congress; dealmaking was the only path forward. African Americans within and outside of the labor movement made three demands of their labor allies: push the president and Congress to make lynching a federal crime, bar racial segregation in their ranks and include black workers in labor protections.

The 1935 National Labor Relations Act (NLRA) had provided federal protection for labors' right to organize into unions and to bargain collectively, facilitating a large increase in union membership – from 3.7 million in 1935 to nearly 10.5 million in 1941 (Goluboff 2007: 28). But the legislation that awarded labor this victory, at the insistence of Southern Congressional leaders, excluded agricultural workers and domestic workers – most black labor, and much of Latino labor. The legislation remained mute on segregation and dropped the lynching issue entirely. Labor again rejected an opportunity to unify the two proletariats in favor of a racialized deal with Southern "Dixiecrats". Mirroring corporations' abuse of the Fourteenth Amendment in 1896, labor used Civil War-era civil rights statutes to defend white workers while excluding black and Latino labor from those protections: "Thus, the vulnerable workers who were excluded from the promise of liberty during the New Deal were precisely those workers whom that promise of liberty was supposed to protect" (Zeitlow #2041: 1706).

Black labor leader A. Philip Randolph continued the NAACP's earlier push for a *unified* labor/civil rights agenda – one that could merge the two proletariats. The NAACP's program emphasized the right for all to work, as well as comprehensive social welfare (Goluboff 2007: 109). Echoing Du Bois, Randolph accurately predicted that the ongoing split between the two proletariats would undermine CIO gains.

In 1946, Republicans gained control of Congress. They combined with Southern Democrats to pass the Taft-Hartley amendments to the NLRA, severely weakening labor protections. The amendment restricted strikes and boycotts, excluded Communist-led and other radical unions from NLRA protections – eventually leading to nearly a million workers being expelled from labor unions – and it enabled state "open-shop" laws.

The impact of Taft-Hartley and the failure of their Southern organizing caused the CIO to merge with the more conservative AFL in 1955. Over black protest, the issue of racial segregation in unions was tabled during the convention ratifying the merger. Yet, labors' refusal to support civil rights had greater implications. It allowed Southern conservatives to steer the post-war agenda: the launch of the Cold War, construction of the Marshall Plan, suppression of anti-colonial movements from the Congo to Vietnam, and the creation of a new white "middle class" fed by the GI Bill and publicly financed infrastructure jobs for whites that segregated metropolitan geographies and built black ghettos. The federal housing programs that enabled working class whites' movement into racially segregated suburbs later translated into equity in their homes that drove a spectacular racial divide in family wealth that persists to this day (Sugrue 1995: #104). These policies led directly to the Civil Rights and Black Power movements that erupted in the late 1950s.

6. The 1960s black movements

The 1960s civil rights movement continued efforts to eliminate the two-proletariat structure in favor of a racially inclusive social welfare democracy. (Hamilton and Hamilton 1997: #1200) In 1961, Martin Luther King Jr. addressed the national convention of the AFL-CIO, demanding an end to racially segregated unions and appealing for a single movement: "Together we can bring about the day when there will be no separate identification of Negroes and labor.... A dream of equality of opportunity, of privilege and property widely distributed . . ." (M. L. King 1986). Four years later, addressing the Illinois AFL-CIO, King noted that labor had lost political influence, and he warned once again that, "Where there are millions of poor, organized labor cannot really be secure."

By *civil rights* the black movement meant to address the *totality* of conditions faced by the colored proletariat: they were exploited on the job or unemployed; they were not free to vote or live where they pleased; and they were daily humiliated in public life. Black leaders viewed labor unionism as part of a broader battle for basic human rights. Randolph and King argued that black workers were especially important to the labor movement precisely because they did not limit the labor movement to wages and contracts, the usual fare of white labor's narrow business unionism. Instead, the presence of black workers pushed the labor movement to stand for a higher moral purpose – that of dignity and equality for all people in all aspects of life (M. L. King 2011, 1965: 115–117). In their view, winning on economic issues entailed uniting workers in an anti-racist movement to overturn the consciously constructed historic racial hierarchy between the two proletariats.

Echoing this view in 1968, Minnesota Senator Hubert Humphrey secured the Democratic nomination for president. Humphrey called for a domestic Marshall Plan to rebuild inner cities and create jobs for unemployed urban minorities. White labor unions were mostly antagonistic to his program: "Polls revealed that for the first time in more than thirty years organized labor was failing to give a majority of its support to the Democratic presidential candidate" (Thurber 1999: #2035, 213). George Wallace, running for president on the American Independent Party line, attacked Humphrey and stressed "law and order" and racial segregation as campaign themes. "Union backing for Wallace, columnists Rowland Evans and Robert Novak reported, was burgeoning into a 'full fledged political revolution'" (Thurber 1999: #2035, 214). Wallace won an estimated 37 percent of the labor vote, more than enough to account for Humphrey's loss to Nixon by less than a single percentage point. This was a decisive turning point and the beginning of the end of "democratic-abolitionists'" second major effort since slavery to reconstruct capitalist democracy. Nixon was quick to take note, adopting Wallace's law and order theme and constructing his own "southern strategy" to win over white workers by pledging to hold the line on Civil Rights gains. Jimmy Carter, Reagan and Bush, and later, Bill Clinton, all built on Nixon's example to varying degrees (McAdam and Kloos 2014: #1975).

7. The rise of neo-liberalism in the US

With black insurgency precluding formal legal segregation, President Nixon began to attack the federal government itself for implementing racial integration programs. Nixon maintained that he was thwarted by lawyers (the Supreme Court) and bureaucrats (federal programs) in his efforts to help what he called the "silent majority" (the white working class). Using thinly veiled racist appeals, Ronald Reagan went so far as to attack the social welfare state itself, stating in his first inaugural address that, "government is the problem." If legal segregation could no longer be upheld, the solution would be to privatize social programs such as public education or attempt to eliminate social programs altogether.

The "secure" alignment between government elites and white labor unions broke by the late 1970s. With the black movement repressed and subdued in the mid-1970s and poor whites firmly aligned politically against blacks, big capital found little need for making concessions to white labor. Douglas Fraser, President of the United Auto Workers, in resigning from President Carter's Labor-Management group in 1978, wrote: "I believe leaders of the business community . . . . have chosen to wage a one-sided class war. . . . they try to destroy us and ruin the lives of the people I represent" (Zinn and Arnove 2009: 530–533). Fraser was describing a realignment: government leaders of both parties had aligned with large corporations against both white labor unions and people of color. The racial police state was strengthened, and some poor whites found employment overseeing blacks in prisons or policing the streets in black communities.

Yet as the social welfare state came under attack, far more poor whites than blacks lost welfare state benefits. Instead of quality public education, affordable higher education, and steadily rising wages, poor whites were offered 401K self-managed retirement fund investment opportunities (tied directly to Wall Street performance) and college and credit card debt. If Wall Street crashed when they retired, as happened to many in 2008, they were simply out of luck. Those unable to afford adequate healthcare and who had home equity were encouraged to use up the equity and take on more debt to pay off their bills.

Though few poor whites made the connection between race and their declining standard of living, their worsening condition was directly related to labor's repeated rejection of black entreaties to merge the two proletariats. The rise of financial capital, decline of unions, and weakening of government support programs had everything to do with Republicans' ability to take advantage of popular white resistance to racial integration, which in turn enabled corporations to block progressive property redistribution. Neo-liberalism arose in a period of domestic reaction and backlash to civil rights advocacy in the same way that conservative liberalism ascended in 1896.

Opposed to neo-liberalism in the 1970s, and largely forgotten, was a counter-movement spearheaded by black labor leaders, the Congressional Black Caucus, progressive white social democratic congressional leaders such as Hubert Humphrey, and parts of the AFL-CIO leadership. The counter-movement was for full employment, a central black demand since the 1930s. Many black labor leaders felt that affirmative action, while needed in the short term, was too narrow to build the kind of broad coalition needed to beat neo-liberal conservatism. Senator Hubert Humphrey co-sponsored a full employment bill with a social-democratic black Congressman from California, Augustus Hawkins. During debates leading up to the bill, some black Congressmen pressed for language enabling citizens to sue the government for a job. AFL-CIO leaders killed the right-to-sue measure and opposed many of the stronger proposals, such as including youth among the protected unemployed, as had been the case in the 1960s, worrying that full employment might fill unions with black and brown workers who would not vote them back into union office (Weir 1992).

The biggest problem, however, was that the AFL-CIO also opposed wage and price controls, a more European style of solidarity wages across the workforce, arguing that wage controls would limit the ability of individual unions to bargain for wage increases. In essence, this position sought to maintain wage hierarchies within labor. Particularly damaging was the appearance before Congress of Humphrey's former ally and Johnson's former budget director Charles Schultze, who testified in 1976 that, "The stumbling block to low unemployment is inflation; the supporter of a full employment policy must of necessity become a searcher for ways to reduce the inflation that accompanies full employment" (Cowie 2010: 275).

Humphrey called Schultze's testimony a "stab in the back" from the liberal establishment – which included AFL-CIO leadership. Humphrey added:

> If the greatest free nation in the history of mankind has to get down on its knees in fear of something as abstract and as arbitrary as these so-called 'free market forces,' well, then we're through. . . . We might just as well haul down the flag, lock up the Capital, go home and admit that we don't have the courage or the imagination to govern ourselves.
>
> (Cowie 2010: 278)

Via this vital point, Humphrey, by no means considered a radical, was nonetheless asserting the primacy of self-governing democracy over so-called economic "laws."

Assuming inflation would inevitably rise with full employment also assumed that government could not convince workers to constrain wage demands or convince businesses to limit prices, because in the end everyone is a self-interested economic actor less invested in maintaining democracy and fostering equality than in maximizing personal gain (as if this were possible without collaboration of others). Humphrey was clear, echoing Polanyi, that Schultze's view, far from describing natural law or science, was merely one possible position in a political and ideological battle over democratic control of the economy. Moreover, the anti-inflation argument was tinged with racial prejudice – that the non-white poor would lack discipline and make unsustainable demands on the system.

Out of the 2008 disaster wrought by the ascent of unregulated finance and corporate-dominated policies, Barack Obama emerged. Obama's election and re-election signaled the numerical rise of the first proletariat, workers of color. But, opposition from white workers – he won only 43 percent of the white vote- limited his presidency. Obama was able to pass a weakened version of healthcare reform over strong Republican opposition, but little else. He was unable to unite white workers and workers of color despite repeated efforts.[3] In the 2016 prima- ries, the Democratic candidates, Bernie Sanders and Hillary Clinton, were having the same problem as Obama. To cast the deep and enduring racial division among workers as a mere chimera, or capitalist ideological trick, as do Wood and many on the Left, does little to explain more than 100 years of persistent racial conflict among white workers and workers of color.

8. Conclusion

Very recently the Service Employees International Union (SEIU) spearheaded a broad coalition of non-labor groups including Black Lives Matter and LGBTU groups to support a rise in the minimum wage to $15/hour through legislative action in California, New York, and several other locations. The campaign, which affected millions of workers, did not start off with this broad approach. It began as a traditional labor campaign to win collective bargaining contracts from fast food employers such as McDonalds.

Notably, the original narrow business unionism approach is precisely what Randolph and King opposed. Under criticism from worker leaders of color, the fast food campaign was transformed into the broader '"for $15", with a focus on the dignity of all people, unionized or not. Police brutality, gay rights, school inequality, and other issues concerning dignity and social recognition were high- lighted under the same banner of "Fight for $15". The shift to a civil rights/human rights frame for labor advocacy had a deliberate goal of uniting the historically divided two proletariats. Its emergence may represent the birth of a third attempt at reconstructing capitalist democracy in the US.

Unions alone have not directed these campaigns. Rather than rely on limited membership labor organizations, open access coalitions provided a broader base for the movement. Its guiding ideology has not been self-interest but awareness and inclusion of the Other – especially the colored and female poor. Rather than considering incremental material gains, such as wage hikes, to be the principal incentive for participation, some of the movement's leaders are pressing for critical independent thinking and social awareness and relationship-building among work- ers across race as the driver for change. Another facet of this changing perspective is recognition that the colored proletariat is *global*. Inclusion in the Fight for $15 of so-called "undocumented" immigrant workers has been a major turnaround for American labor. Participants in the emerging movement are beginning to recog- nize that at the bottom of the property structure is the colored global proletariat;

challenging property from below necessitates their recognition and inclusion. This understanding would portend the greatest power shift yet in American history.

Notes

1 Sizek and Karatani make this point in a different way. . . .
2 The semi-public nature of corporations is discussed in Ciepley (2013). The semi-public status of slaves is exemplified by their inclusion in the Constitution as three-fifths a person for purposes of electoral apportionment.
3 See Grabelsky and Thompson (2010) for an account of the Obama White House efforts to integrate the construction building trades.

Works cited

Allen, A. (2006). *Origins of the Dred Scott Case*. Athens, University of Georgia Press.

Beckert, S. (2014). *Empire of Cotton: A Global History*. New York, Vintage Books.

Bois, W. E. B. D. (1995). The American Federation of Labor and the Negro. In: D. L. Lewis (Ed.). *W. E. B. Du Bois: A Reader*. New York, Henry Holt & Company.

Ciepley, D. (2013). "Beyond Public and Private: Toward a Political Theory of the Corporation." *American Political Science Review* 107(1): 139–158.

Cowie, J. (2010). *Stayin' Alive: The 1970s and the Last Days of the Working Class*. New York, The New Press.

Crouch, C. (2005). *Capitalist Diversity and Change: Recombinant Governance and Institutional Entrepreneurs*. New York, Oxford University Press.

Dawson, M., & Ming-Francis, M. (2015). *The Neo-liberal Racial Order*. Political Science.

Du Bois, W. E. B. (1992). *Black Reconstruction in America*. New York: Atheneum.

Du Bois, W. E. B. (1995). Marxism and the Negro Problem. In: D. L. Lewis (Ed.). *W. E. B. Du Bois: A Reader*. New York, Henry Holt and Company.

Einhorn, R. L. (2006). *American Taxation, American Slavery*. Chicago, University of Chicago Press.

Foner, E. (1970). *Free Soil, Free Labor, Free Men: The Ideology of the Republican Party Before the Civil War*. New York, Oxford University Press.

Foner, E. (1988). *Reconstruction: America's Unfinished Revolution 1863–1877*. New York, Harper & Row.

Genovese, E. (1966). *The Political Economy of Slavery*. New York, Pantheon.

Goluboff, R. L. (2007). *The Lost Promise of Civil Rights*. Cambridge, Harvard University Press.

Grabelsky, J. and J. P. Thompson. 2010. "Emerald Cities in the Age of Obama: A New Social Compact between Labor and Community." *Perspectives on Work*: 15–18.

Hahn, S. (1983). *The Roots of Southern Populism: Yeoman Farmers and the Transformation of the Georgia Up Country 1850–1890*. New York, Oxford University Press.

Hall, S. (1996). Gramsci's Relevance for the Study of Race and Ethnicity. In: D. Morley and K.-H. Chen (Eds.). *Stuart Hall: Critical Dialogues in Cultural Studies*. New York, Verso.

Hamilton, D. C., & Hamilton, C. (1997). *The Dual Agenda: Race and Social Welfare Policies of Civil Rights Organizations*. New York: Columbia University Press.

Johnson, W. (2013). *River of Dark Dreams: Slavery and Empire in the Cotton Kingdom*. Cambridge, Harvard University Press.

Karatani, K. (2005). *Transcritique: On Kant and Marx*. Cambridge: MIT Press.

King, D. S. and R. M. Smith (2011). *Still a House Divided: Race and Politics in Obama's America*. Princeton, Princeton University Press.

King, M. L., Jr. (1986). If the Negro Wins, Labor Wins. In: J.M. Washington (Ed.). *A Testament of Hope: The Essential Writings and Speeches of Martin Luther King, Jr.* San Francisco, Harper.

King, M.L., Jr. (2011 [1965]). Labor Cannot Stand Still. In: M. Honey (Ed.). *All Labor Has Dignity*. Boston, Beacon.

Magliocca, G. N. (2011). *The Tragedy of William Jennings Bryan: Constittional Law and the Politics of Backlash*. New Haven: Yale University Press.

Martinot, S. (2003). *The Rule of Racialization: Class, Identity, Governance*. Philadelphia, Temple University Press.

McAdam, D., & Kloos, K. (2014). *Deeply Divided: Racial Politics and Social Movements in Postwar America*. New York: Oxford University Press.

Nelson, B. (2001). *Divided We Stand: American Workers and the Struggle for Black Equality*. Princeton, Princeton University Press.

Norton, A. (1986). *Alternative America: A Reading of Antebellum Political Culture*. Chicago, University of Chicago Press.

Polanyi, K. (2014). Economics and the Freedom to Shape Our Social Destiny. In: G. Resta and M. Catanzariti (Eds.). *For a New West: Karl Polanyi, Essays 1919–1958*. Malden, MA, Polity.

Sellers, C. (1991). *The Market Revolution: Jacksonian America, 1815–1846*. New York, Oxford University Press.

Sugrue, T. (1995). *The Origins of the Urban Crisis: Race, Industrial Decline, and Housing in Detroit 1940–1960*. Princeton: Princeton University Press.

Thurber, T. N. (1999). *The Politics of Equality: Hubert H. Humphrey adn the African American Freedom Struggle*. New York: Columbia University Press.

Wald, P. (1993). *Constituting Americans: Cultural Anxiety and Narrative Form*. Durham, Duke University Press.

Weir, M. (1992). *Politics and Jobs: The Boundaries of Employment Policy in the United States*. Princeton, Princeton University Press.

Wilson, W. J. (1978 [1980]). *The Declining Significance of Race: Blacks and Changing American Institutions*. Chicago, University of Chicago Press.

Wood, E. M. (2016 [1995]). *Democracy against Capitalism: Renewing Historical Materialism*. New York, Verso.

Wood, E. M. (2012). *Liberty & Property: A Social History of Western Political Thought from Renaissance to Enlightenment*. New York, Verso.

Zeitlow, R. E. James Ashley's Thirteenth Amendment. *Columbia Law Review, 112*

Zinn, H. and A. Arnove (2009). *Voices of a People's History of the United States*. New York, Seven Stories Press.

6   Urban squatters

Sonia Katyal and Eduardo M. Peñalver

The image most of us have of the person who intentionally flouts property laws is not particularly favorable. The Oxford English Dictionary, for example, defines a trespasser as a "transgressor, a law-breaker; a wrong-doer, sinner, offender" (The Oxford English Dictionary 1961: 328). In early modern England, landowners frequently left "man traps" and "spring guns" along boundary lines to discourage trespass on their lands.[1] Such violent measures were not prohibited by law until the nineteenth century.[2] And in rural areas of the United States, it is not uncommon to come across signs warning that "Trespassers Will Be Shot" (Jones 2001). The overridingly negative view of property lawbreakers in popular consciousness comports with the centrality of property rights within our characteristically individualist, capitalist, political culture (Marx 1978: 42; Glendon 1991).

The dim view of property lawbreakers is shared to a large degree by property theorists, many of whom tend to focus on the stabilizing role of property law. The importance attached to exclusivity within contemporary theories of property underscores the apparent threat to order and stability posed by property lawbreakers. Many courts and commentators have placed this right at the center of their concept of private ownership.[3] As Abraham Bell and Gideon Parchomovsky have correctly argued, one key purpose of property law is to provide stability, both for owners and for those who would engage in transactions with them (Bell & Parchomovsky 2005: 552). Property law achieves this stability in a variety of ways. One crucial way is through the criminal enforcement of existing property entitlements. Laws of criminal trespass protect the boundaries around real property established through market transactions. Laws prohibiting larceny, fraud, robbery, and burglary similarly wrap privately determined entitlements within the safety of the publicly enforced criminal law.

Without denying the importance of property's stability, we can complicate the story by highlighting the powerful, and at times ironic, role of the lawbreaker in the process of fostering the evolution of property. Our goal is therefore to rehabilitate, at least to a certain extent, the image of the intentional property outlaw, and to show how these lawbreakers have played integral roles in producing a system of property that is characterized by a complex and subtle contradiction: it is at once stable, perhaps even essentially so, and yet this seemingly ordered system at the same time masks a pervasive instability that is necessary to prevent the entire edifice from becoming outdated (Underkuffler 2003: 143; Blomley 2003: 126–133).

Our task is made easier by the fact that, despite the broadly negative view of property lawbreakers that prevails among lawyers and laypeople alike, property outlaws have repeatedly played a powerful and visible role as catalysts for needed legal change. Time and again, groups of people have intentionally violated property laws, and in a number of important instances, property law has responded by shifting to accommodate their demands, bringing them back within the fold of the law-abiding community. From the squatters and adverse possessors of the nineteenth-century American frontier to the Native American and civil rights protesters of the 1960s to the urban squatters of the 1970s and 1980s, those disenfranchised by the existing property system have frequently flouted the law in hopes of achieving their goals. Whatever one thinks about the merits of their positions, there can be no doubt that the activities of these property outlaws have been important engines for legal change.

In this chapter, we will discuss the occupation and improvement of underused (but privately owned) urban land as a strategy of resistance. In contemporary urban life, conflicts about land and space are pervasive. This is true both where land is intensively used, and therefore scarce and expensive, and where land is abandoned, and therefore abundant and (relatively) cheap. Here, using information drawn from news accounts and interviews with participants in property disobedience, we can see at work a distinctive vision of property, one that engages with land at a human level, as the place where individuals and communities form relationships and live out their lives. This vision diverges from the (dominant) conception of property that treats land as wholly commodified and delocalized – the proper subject of fully fungible investment products.

For many communities, one consequence of the dominance of the securitized conception of property was widespread blight and abandonment in the form of the collapse of the housing market in 2008. That experience transformed entire neighborhoods. The consequent epidemic of foreclosures sparked an increase in several different types of lawbreaking activity. Much of this activity illustrates the category of what we call "acquisitive outlaw", disobedience that aims to appropriate property in order to simply acquire and use it. We distinguish acquisitive outlaws from "expressive outlaws", those who engage in illegal activities mostly for expressive purposes, like the lunch counter sit-in participants in the civil rights era. We argue that even though the law tends to privilege the conduct of expressive outlaws, acquisitive outlaws offer us important pieces of value. In the last section of this chapter, we suggest that the law should attempt to avoid over-deterring and over-punishing such kinds of disobedience because of the informational and redistributive benefits these practices may offer.

1. Urban squatters: a brief, domestic history

The decades after World War II saw a massive migration of capital and people out of America's cities and into its suburbs (Jackson 1987: 190–218). This migration, far from being purely an accident of market forces, was actively encouraged and, indeed, subsidized by the federal government (*id.*). Through its creation of the interstate highway system and the discriminatory policies of the Federal Housing Administration (FHA), which would not guarantee mortgages in urban or racially integrated neighborhoods, government policy both lured and pushed investment capital out of inner cities and into outlying areas. Following in the path laid out by the FHA, private mortgage lenders simply refused to lend money for the construction or upkeep of properties within many urban neighborhoods (*id.*).

In some cases, the owners of urban residential properties did not respond to this capital drought simply by selling their real estate. In order to maximize the return on their investment, they engaged in a practice called "milking", whereby they took advantage of favorable tax treatment and extracted rents from tenants while investing as little money as possible in the upkeep of their properties (Mele 2000: 188–194). In the most run-down neighborhoods, the final stage of this process was often either "arson for profit" or the sale of the property to speculators with little interest in rehabilitating the dilapidated buildings (Mele 2000: 194). In many cases, however, the owner would simply abandon his decrepit building, in which case the property ended up in government hands as a result of tax foreclosures (Mele 2000: 191).

In the 1970s and 80s, an epidemic of urban property abandonment led to a dramatic expansion of government-owned property in cities across the country. By the 1980s, for example, New York City and Philadelphia each owned thousands of vacant buildings seized from delinquent taxpayers (Hirsch & Wood 1988: 605, 610). These abandoned buildings and vacant properties became zones of criminality (Mele 2000: 197). Crack houses and shooting galleries attracted drug users, dealers, and prostitutes, whose activities terrorized and blighted entire neighborhoods (*id.*). Landlord abandonment therefore had the perverse effect of exacerbating the very urban ills on which subsequent abandonment was predicated. The result was an ever-widening zone of urban decay and dysfunction (Mele 2000: 194).

City governments attempted to return their newly acquired property to the private sector by auctioning it to the highest bidder. In so doing, they hoped both to raise revenue and to foster private development that would, it was argued, increase the urban tax base (Mele 2000: 204–206; Hirsch & Wood 1988: 610). All too often, however, the highest bidder was a speculator who simply allowed the property to fall back into tax arrears. In New York City, for example, over 90 percent of auctioned properties were delinquent on property taxes within one year of their sale (Katz & Mayer 1985: 15, 25). When they were not auctioning the property off to speculators, city governments seemed unable to figure out what to do with the property, often simply holding it in its dilapidated state, even in the face of strong local demand for low-income housing (Seth Borgos 1986: 433–435, 438–439). In Philadelphia, for example, the city's program for distributing abandoned, city-owned houses to "homesteaders" was riddled with corruption and inefficiency, ended up being used to funnel houses toward well-connected speculators (*id.*).

A federally funded, pilot homesteading program was initiated in 1974, but it was small and primarily geared in practice toward members of the middle class.[4] The statute creating the program authorized HUD to transfer federally owned, unoccupied dwellings over to local homesteading projects, but it somewhat schizophrenically indicated that, in designing its rules for eligibility, those projects were to weigh homesteaders' need for housing and ability to bear the financial burdens of rehabilitation.[5] These dual and contradictory considerations directly reflected disagreement among the programmers' designers over the question whether homesteading should be used primarily to rehabilitate housing and boost local property tax receipts or to provide housing for the poorest citizens (Borgos 1986: 19). In its earliest years, the program helped rehabilitate only a handful of houses, most of which were occupied by people whose income placed them solidly in the middle class.

At the same time, a consensus was forming among residents of blighted communities that absentee ownership was a source of neighborhood problems and that conditions could be improved by transferring ownership from absentee landlords or the city or speculators to local residents (Mele 2000: 203). Neighborhood activists and advocates for low-income housing in cities across the country organized protests aimed at pushing governmental owners of abandoned urban properties to seek ways to convert those properties into housing for the poor. In the late 1970s and early 1980s, when conventional protests proved ineffective, several groups, most prominent among them the Association of Community Organizations for Reform Now (ACORN) initiated concerted squatting campaigns to attract attention to their demands (Mele 2000: 206; Clarity 1977: 1; Borgos 1986: 433–435; Hirsch & Wood 1988: 613–614). Unlike the squatters of the nineteenth-century American frontier, who were motivated almost exclusively by a desire to acquire property for themselves (acquisitive outlaws, in our rubric), the urban squatters of the late twentieth century acted out of an amalgamation of motives, not least of which was a desire to express their opposition to governments' failures to provide adequate options for low-income housing in the cities.

These hybrid motives are exemplified in a particularly clear way by ACORN's tactics. ACORN carefully selected squatters who were interested in becoming homeowners but who could not afford to purchase housing on the open market (Borgos 1986: 434–435). In its Philadelphia campaign, for example, many of the squatters were people who had been sharing cramped residences with relatives in public housing projects while languishing on the waiting list for the city's corruption-ridden homestead program (Borgos 1986: 435). ACORN warned squatters that their actions were illegal, though (in ACORN's view) morally justified, and that there was no guarantee they would end up owning the home in which they squatted. Squatters were required to sign a "squatter's contract" in which they pledged to participate in "meetings, rallies, and other activities" organized by ACORN to pressure the city to reform its homesteading program. Squatters also had to obtain signatures from 75 percent of the neighbors of the abandoned property to demonstrate neighborhood support for their action. Finally, on the day the squatting was to begin, ACORN always alerted the media and held a rally, which often featured local ministers and even elected public officials.

The official responses to modern urban squatting movements varied widely. President Carter's Secretary of Housing and Urban Development, Patricia Harris, described squatters in Philadelphia as "no better than shoplifters" (Borgos 1986: 433). The President of the Philadelphia City Council called the squatting movement the "beginning of anarchy" (*id.*). Most mayors denounced squatters and refused to deal with them. Squatters were often arrested and their homes demolished (Hirsch & Wood 1988: 613). Seth Borgos describes the hostile reaction of most public officials to ACORN's 1982 squatting campaign:

> City and federal authorities cracked down hard in some locations. Squatters were arrested in Pittsburgh and St. Louis; a HUD Area Office manager led a midnight raid on a squatter's house in Dallas; the St. Louis Land Reutilization Authority filed a $500,000 civil suit against ACORN and the leaders of its squatting group.
>
> (Borgos 1986: 439)

In many cases, however, squatters were able to get government property owners to grant title in the occupied housing to squatters (Borgos 1986: 433). Half of the 200 squatters who participated in Milton Street's 1977 squat in HUD-owned housing in Philadelphia, for example, obtained title to the properties they occupied (*id.*).

More significantly, some squatting campaigns led to the creation of city-run homesteading programs targeting low-income residents. New York City, for example, ultimately responded to illegal squatting movements by establishing a legal system for urban homesteading on abandoned, city-owned properties (*see* Hirsch & Wood 1988: 615; *see also* Malve von Hassell 1996: 26). In New York's Lower East Side, for example, 28 buildings have been fully renovated and acquired by tenants through the city's homesteading program (Von Hassell 1996: 26). Similarly, ACORN's 1979 squatting campaign in Philadelphia led to the reform of that city's troubled urban homesteading program and inspired similar squatting efforts across the country (Borgos 1986: 435–437).

In 1982, an ACORN squatting campaign, which included the construction of a tent city on the ellipse in Washington, DC, pushed to shift federal policy away from its prevailing schizophrenia and toward an exclusive focus on homesteading as a means of providing low-income housing (Borgos 1986: 440–441). The visibility of ACORN's protests led to congressional hearings, and in 1983, the federal program was reoriented toward lower-income homesteaders (Housing & Urban Recovery Act of 1983, Tit. III, 97 Stat. 1196). The federal program remained small, however, and never accounted for more than a tiny percentage of federal housing efforts (Rohe 2007: 444).

2. Analysis: two outlaw trajectories

Despite the limited nature of their practical successes, the greatest achievement of the urban squatting movements in the 1970s and 1980s was in the domain of public opinion. As a method of protest, urban squatters were extremely photogenic (Borgos 1986: 442). Their activities consistently attracted media attention, most of it favorable. The image of squatters attempting to reclaim abandoned property through their own labor was appealing to American audiences, notwithstanding a general political climate in the early 1980s that typically manifested itself as hostility toward poverty-relief programs (*id.*). Even politicians who opposed urban squatters have often acknowledged the "romantic" power of their actions (Leuck 1996: B3 (quoting Mayor Giuliani)). Urban squatters were therefore extremely effective at keeping the problem of low-income housing on the political agenda, even winning a few modest legislative victories at a time when the tables were stacked heavily against them.

According to Hans Pruijt, a Dutch scientist, contemporary squatting displays a variety of different modalities: (1) deprivation-based squatting; (2) squatting as an alternative housing strategy; (3) entrepreneurial squatting, such as setting up a community center or small business; (4) conservational squatting, for example, in Amsterdam when a number of squatters took over properties to protect their historical character; and (5) political squatting, like the Israeli Committee Against House Demolitions in the West Bank, which blocks bulldozers who are sent to demolish Palestinian homes (Pruijt 2013a: 19 and 21).

Pruitt's taxonomy, we would argue, is exemplary in its disaggregation of the variety of activities that fall under the broad aegis of squatting. But in thinking about how the law should respond to squatters, a distinction that focuses on the differences between acquisitive lawbreaking and expressive lawbreaking may be additionally useful. For ease of discussion, we posit that intentional lawbreakers fall somewhere along a continuum of motivations, ranging from self-regarding, appropriative violations of property rights on one end, to more other-regarding, expressive violations of property rights on the other.

A. Between acquisitive and expressive lawbreaking

"Expressive" lawbreaking, which corresponds loosely – though imperfectly – to the category traditionally called "civil disobedience",[6] seeks to send a strong message about the perceived injustice of existing property arrangements. "Acquisitive" lawbreaking, in contrast, involves actions that are oriented primarily toward direct appropriation. Here, the dominant motivating factor might be to gain immediate access or procure a certain good, as opposed to making a general statement about the appropriate scope of property rights in such instances. The key difference between the expressive and acquisitive categories is the distinction between intentional lawbreaking that generates immediate and substantial benefits for the lawbreaker and intentional lawbreaking that generates no such immediate benefits but that instead self-consciously aims at achieving (or generating support for) a larger legal goal.

Of course, in drawing this distinction, we recognize that self-interest and expression often can seem like inseparable halves of the same whole; nevertheless, we think it is appropriate to draw some descriptive and normative distinctions between the two, recognizing, of course, the need for caveats and the presence of borderline cases. Even within the category of acquisitive lawbreaking, we would argue that today's urban squatting movements raise a number of questions that complicate the normative solutions that law currently offers us. For example, should the law draw a distinction between the organizations that design and create squatting campaigns, like ACORN, and the end users or consumers that are the principal beneficiaries of these activities? Which figure demonstrates more culpability, as a legal matter – the organizers of the squatting campaigns or the ones who are actually squatting for their daily housing and sustenance? In this sense, we might draw a line between the principal squatters, the putative beneficiaries of a squatting campaign, and those that contribute to the squatting – by creating the campaigns and conditions for the activities to unfold. Each group displays aspects of both acquisitive and expressive lawbreaking.

Consider, as an example, the Anti-Eviction Campaign, a group in Chicago that was founded in 2009 and that frees up abandoned properties by fixing up the buildings and moving homeless people into vacant homes.[7] According to the US Postal Service, around tha time, there were 62,000 vacant homes in Chicago – and the cost to the city of going into these homes, fixing them up, and then reselling them was prohibitive (Austen 2013). (In one case, the city spent $350,000 to repair a house that couldn't be sold for less than half that amount) (*id.*). Even though the city fixed up over 800 of these properties, only 91 of them have been sold. Instead of leaving them empty and abandoned, the Anti-Eviction Campaign movement provides a means to prevent further blight by enabling homeless families and responsible individuals to occupy these homes by refurbishing them and adding to these communities. Is the Anti-Eviction Campaign the principle lawbreaker? Or is it the individual families and others who actually occupy homes? How, if at all, should the law distinguish between the two?

Moreover, as Pruitt's taxonomy demonstrates, not all urban squatting movements are as consistently and overtly expressive in their practices as groups like ACORN or even the Anti-Eviction Campaign. Some movements, for example, such as the Homes Not Jails movement in San Francisco engage in covert squatting that simply aims to get the homeless indoors (see Corr 1999: 20). At times, Homes Not Jails combines these covert squats with symbolic squats to draw public attention; even though it has never gained title to a property, the immense media coverage and public sympathy that they drew led to a law in San Francisco that prohibited landlords from vacating their property and allowed the city to acquire those buildings for the homeless (*id.*).

In contrast, other squatters, particularly those in continental Europe or those in North America influenced by the European squatting tradition, have viewed squatting almost as a form of artistic expression or play rather than a form of overtly political dissent.[8] These "artistic occupations," often refer to a host of practices that are motivated more by expressive purposes, rather than self-interested, acquisitive purposes. According to Alan Moore, an art historian, artists are used to working in alternative economies – gift and exchange, volunteer based, attribution economies that operate outside of our traditional market-based system of wage labor (Moore 2012). Many artists, therefore, engage in squatting activities that are simultaneously expressive and acquisitive in nature – ranging from whole scale "free cities" of artists in Copenhagen and Holland to New York's ABC NO RIO, which started as an occupation of a vacant city-owned commercial property for an art exhibition that continued through 30 years of tenancy until final full legalization in the early 2000s (Moore 2012: 3–4). Or, consider 59 Rue de Rivoli in Paris, a building that had been abandoned for 15 years before artists took it over in 1999 and began using the space for performances. When the ministry of culture found that it drew 40,000 visitors a year, they decided to buy the building, renovate it and legalize it for the artists themselves. There are now a dozen such venues in Paris (Moore 2012: 10).

Moore argues that these artistic occupations might be considered to be "a kind of repossession by the dispossessed working and creative classes, targeting the surplus properties set aside for speculative purposes that have resulted from the process" of gentrification that has recently unfolded in cities across America (Moore 2012: 2). Something similar might be said, as well, about other urban squatting movements, many of which blend artistic occupations with some degree of consumptive activity – and demand a rethinking of the concept of urban squatting.

Another area that straddles the boundaries between expressive disobedience and acquisitive disobedience is the guerrilla gardening movements that have also taken place in recent times. The term "guerrilla gardening" was coined by an artist, Liz Christy, who noticed in the 1970s that tomato plants were growing out of rubbish, and so she began scattering seeds in empty urban spaces (Brooks & Marten 2005). Eventually, this culminated in the dedication of a vacant lot on Bowery and Houston in Manhattan for community-garden status, which effectively began the Green Guerrilla movement (*id.*). The movement echoes themes that can be traced back to the diggers in England who fought for common land and a right to grow food in neglected spaces (Haynes 2011). Some guerrilla gardeners operate covertly; others operate more visibly in an attempt to convince a private property owner or city to dedicate the land for the purpose.[9] Nevertheless, their motivations are often both consumptive (both in the sense of self-interested consumption and the provision of food for others to consume) and expressive in nature, driven perhaps by a desire to create pressure for legal change.

In Los Angeles, for example, an LA resident named Ron Finley became frustrated about having to drive over half an hour to buy fresh produce, and began planting a vegetable garden in the space between the sidewalk and the street outside of his home (Hochman 2013; Kettman 2013). When the city prohibited him from doing so, he founded a group called LA Green Grounds that enlisted hundreds of volunteers planting produce in overlooked urban areas. Under the media's gaze, Finley turned attention back to the city, which he argued owned 26 miles of vacant lots that could host countless vegetable plants. Eventually, Finley's activities led to the city enacting a protective provision to allow for fruits and vegetables to be planted along sidewalks.[10]

All of the strategies discussed here – urban squatting, guerrilla gardening, and artistic occupations tend to turn the notion of property disobedience on its head.

As we can see, some of the reasons for these activities can be expressively politi-cal, some aesthetically oriented, and some, consumptively oriented because they focus on the generation of goods (housing, access to food, etc.) to satisfy immedi-ate necessities. Because they often contain elements of expressive political activ-ity as well as consumptive activity, they challenge the dominant conception of the trespasser. At the same time, the acquisitive nature of the activity suggests that their motivations are not always purely expressive in nature. We argue that the appropriative strategies of resistance that we discuss have provided a valuable means of dissent from the dominant conception of property while simultaneously transforming the damaged reality that conception has left on the ground. Far from viewing property as a purely fungible asset, these individuals demonstrate that access to land can be a vital ingredient for strengthening communities while lim-iting the role of land as a purely market based instrument of development. In addition, incidents of occupation raise deep questions about the function of these groups as viable and perhaps valuable responses when urban policy fails. Because so many of these movements have foregrounded productive, legal changes, it becomes incumbent on us to contemplate the optimal response the law should take when these events surface. How should the law – specifically criminal law – respond to incidences of productive legal activity? The next section explores this question.

B. Utilitarian and rights-based theories of law enforcement

For the purposes of our analysis, we will accept the common characterization of the dominant theories of law enforcement and punishment as either broadly utili-tarian or rights-based (*see generally* Kahan 1996: 594). By the former, we mean theories that view the purpose of punishment as yielding optimal levels of crimi-nality by creating disincentives that self-interested potential criminals will take into account in deciding whether the possible rewards of a criminal act outweigh the risk of punishment (Kahan 1996: 603; Bibas & Bierschbach 2004: 105). In the classic view, the ultimate goal of deterrent punishment ought to be something very close to zero incidence of the proscribed criminal behavior (Hylton 1996: 198). Some contemporary theorists have suggested a similar goal, at least as an (admittedly impossibly expensive) ideal (see, e.g. Coleman 1980: 314). Most recent utilitarian discussions, however, have abandoned the goal of zero crime in favor of punishment that seeks to achieve an "optimal" level of crime by forc-ing criminals to internalize the social costs of crime, including both the harm to victims and the costs of law enforcement (Klevorick 1980: 292–293). Typically, the process of calculating the optimal level of utilitarian punishment is described as one involving some variation on a mathematical calculation linking, among other things, the likelihood that a criminal will be caught with an aggregation of the harm to victims and enforcement costs generated by the sort of criminality in which she is engaged (*see* Becker 1968: 201; Hylton 1996: 198–199; Polinsky & Shavell 1979: 880).

In contrast, by referring to rights-based theories of punishment, we refer to theories that identify the purpose of punishment as rooted in moral theories about culpability and just desert (*see* Bibas & Bierschbach 2004: 107; Kahan 1996: 601–602). In contrast to the forward-looking utilitarian approach, the rights-based position centers not on the consequences of outlaw conduct but rather on the punishment the offender deserves in light of the moral character of his conduct.[11]

While we decidedly do not intend to take sides between these two approaches, our description of the appropriate legal response to property outlaws must vary depending on which theory one prefers. Our argument is premised on the general notion that certain categories of property outlaws are less culpable (or, in deterrent terms, create less social harm or perhaps even create some social benefits) than ordinary criminals. Accordingly, we analyze a variety of ways in which both utilitarian and rights-based theories of law enforcement can (and at times actually do) take into account the productive aspects of disobedience in order to preserve the inherent dynamism that it introduces within property law.[12]

a) Acquisitive outlaws in utilitarian perspective

In the forward-looking prism of utilitarianism, the law is rightfully reluctant to incentivize disorder by loosening the punitive sanctions associated with property lawbreaking. In the absence of high transaction costs, utilitarians generally regard encroachments on property rights as socially wasteful rent seeking. Indeed, this analysis forms the principal basis for the most common utilitarian arguments against theft (Tullock 1967: 231; McChesney 1993: 227–228). Nevertheless, the case for involuntary transfers of property can be quite strong when there is reason to believe that the lawbreaker places a higher value on the property in question than the true owner and when there is some obstacle to a consensual transfer between the parties. People who have nothing (or very little) will have limited means to express in market transactions the value they place on shifts in entitlements (Schwab 1989: 1178–1179). Consequently, involuntary transfers may be one of the few options available to them. The difficulty lies in identifying situations where the lawbreaker truly does value the property more than the owner and in which the long-run effects of permitting occasional violations of the default rule against involuntary dispossession will not swamp the benefits created by permitting the transaction (*see* Hasen & McAdams 1997: 370).

Our argument is that these calculations, whether framed in terms of general or specific deterrence, fail to consider or recognize the productive informational and redistributive potential of some kinds of legal transgression in spurring property law's evolution. Consider the example of urban squatting, which often draws attention to the ways in which local communities respond to economic blight and also provide housing and other necessities for disenfranchised groups. By overlooking these potentially useful functions, utilitarian models of punishment are likely to call for levels of punishment that over-discourage or preclude certain forms of lawlessness without recognizing that some elements of property lawbreaking may be more socially productive than others.

What is the value of property lawbreaking that utilitarian theorists have overlooked? Two categories are particularly significant. First, there may in certain situations be value in the outlaw's directly redistributive conduct. We refer to this broad category of utility gains as "redistributive value". As scholars have observed, property law contains several doctrines that permit forced transfers under certain circumscribed conditions where they are especially likely to be efficient (Epstein 2003: 98–100; Fennell 2006: 1038). Second, in cases of persistent, widespread lawbreaking, citizen behavior communicates vital information to the state, indicating that some element of a property law may be out of date or unjust in some respect that the political process has ignored. We refer to this signaling function provided by outlaw conduct as its "informational value". The information generated by outlaw conduct can, under the right circumstances, convince the state to reevaluate its commitment to an unjust status quo.

Adverse possession law already provides a useful illustration of this tension at work. In that context, the lawbreaker's long-term use (and improvement) of the property, combined with her risk of civil and criminal sanctions, will in many cases constitute strong *prima facie* evidence that she places an exceptionally high value on the property (*see* Fennell 2006: 1040). When these factors are coupled, as adverse possession requires, with a lackadaisical response by the true owner, the law achieves a high degree of confidence that the possessor values the property more than its absentee owner. The relative ease with which property owners can protect their rights and the heavy burdens placed on adverse possessors diminishes the ancillary costs of creating such a mechanism for forced transfers.

But situations in which the rigorous requirements for adverse possession are met are not the only circumstances where the law might be justified in inferring that the lawbreaker places a higher value on property than its true owner does and in which the ancillary effects of recognizing the lawbreaker's claim fail to tip the balance. Traditional adverse possession law gains confidence from the failure of the true owner to step forward and enforce her property rights, thereby indicating that she places abnormally low value on the property. Comparable confidence may arise, however, when there is good reason to think that the non-owning claimant values the property at an abnormally *high* level in the absence of any countervailing evidence that the true owner places similarly exceptional value on the property. This might occur, for example, when the distribution of property rights is extremely skewed: the true owner is very wealthy, the acquisitive outlaw is very poor, and the presence of other conditions, like survival or a broader conception of necessity, weigh in favor of a legal reevaluation of entitlements. On a cold night, at least as a purely subjective matter, the homeless man almost certainly values the sheltered entrance to a large shopping center more highly than even the most attentive owners value their right to exclude him. He simply cannot communicate his preference in a way intelligible within a system of monetary valuation and consensual transactions.

Apart from the direct redistributive value that results from certain involuntary transfers, pervasive and persistent acquisitive outlaw conduct can generate important and valuable information about the existence of possibly inefficient legal allocations of property rights. Concentrations of lawbreakers clustered around discrete legal entitlements might suggest that transaction costs or wealth effects are standing in the way of what would otherwise be an efficient transfer of rights.

In England, for example, it was common in the twentieth century for outdoors enthusiasts to trespass on private land as they rambled over the countryside. Such acquisitive outlaw conduct went on for decades, sometimes accompanied by expressive (or intersectional) forms of disobedience, until it caught the attention of the Labour Party, which ultimately responded by altering the nature of land-owners' rights to exclude ramblers from "open" rural lands that did not implicate concerns for privacy (Shoard 1999; Stephenson 1989). Particularly when their conduct is pervasive and protracted, acquisitive outlaw behavior generates an informational value above and beyond any redistributive value it may have. This informational value, however, has been largely disregarded in utilitarian discussions of nonconsensual transfers.

Of course, in the case of acquisitive outlaws, like many urban squatters, the quality of that information is undermined by the self-interested nature of the out-law's behavior. In the context of market transactions, an offer to give something up in order to consummate the purchase gives us fairly reliable information about the value the acquiring party places on a shift in legal rights, though this infor-mation is distorted by wealth effects.[13] In the case of a forced transfer, however, we cannot tell from the outlaw's conduct the extent to which she values a shift in entitlements, whether for the limited purpose of the specific transaction in question or more broadly through systematic legal change. The truth of two (at least) plausible assumptions, however, would reinforce the informational value of persistent, widespread outlaw conduct. First, in a well-functioning society, it is likely that most citizens possess an intrinsic willingness to obey the law, a will-ingness that is particularly pronounced when the law faithfully reflects broadly shared values (Tyler 1990: 65; Zimring & Hawkins 1973: 97). And this seems true irrespective of the private gains citizens might derive from breaking the law, particularly when they perceive that the law is fair and is widely obeyed by their fellows (Tyler 1990: 22; Kahan 1996: 603–604). This assumption is not meant to deny the reality that some people may actually resemble the Holmesian "bad man". For these, cold considerations of deterrence will be paramount (Wright et al. 2004: 205–206). Barring a widespread breakdown in the social order, how-ever, most people will opt for market mechanisms of acquiring property, and widespread lawlessness will convey important information. Second, consistent with the findings of behavioral economists, most people are less eager to pursue someone else's property than they are to keep something they already possess (Aigler 1924: 406).

The combination of these two factors suggests that, as an initial matter, the behavioral balance is tipped in favor of departing from existing allocations of property only through legal, market-based transactions. That bias in turn suggests that when large numbers of people persistently engage in illegal actions aimed at shifting property entitlements away from the status quo, they are likely to be acting in response to fairly powerful incentives or objections. Widespread failure to resort to the market within a particular subgroup, or an intentional and coordi-nated strategy to shun the market, will therefore often suggest some sort of market failure or widely perceived injustice.[14]

None of this discussion is meant to suggest that we are unmindful of the potential costs involved. As rule utilitarians have frequently pointed out, any government decision to permit violations of general laws against forced transfers risks creating negative spillover effects that could easily swamp out any short-term gains achieved by a specific forced redistribution. The long-term negative side effects of permitting the activities of individual acquisitive outlaws could take several forms: first, permitting outlaws to either temporarily or permanently retain the property they seize might well encourage property owners to resort to violence to protect their property from the poor or to reduce productive investment in their property out of fear of losing it;[15] second, tolerating forced acquisitions in one case might erode the general deterrent effect of the criminal law and encourage further acquisitive behavior in broadly analogous situations by opportunists with less compelling claims than the original lawbreakers;[16] and, third, permitting lawbreakers to profit from their actions could more generally undermine respect for the rule of law.[17]

Of particular concern is the possibility that, over the long run, the general deterrent effects of permitting certain forced transfers will generate harmful feedback effects that actually magnify the harm caused by the illegal act, repercussions that would negatively affect the utility maximizing results from a forced transfer. For example, numerous adherents to the urban "Broken Windows" theory of criminal behavior have repeatedly hypothesized about the crime-amplifying effects of visible disorder.[18] Permitting some forced transfers might conceivably contribute to such a feedback process, especially if the forced transfers were concentrated around neighborhoods already suffering from the effects of pervasive disorder.

Further, if the pressure for the particular type of forced transfer within a community is broad enough, legalizing the transfer may *increase* order and respect for the rule of law and for property rights by bringing the official law into greater conformity with people's sense of justice and fairness.[19] For example, among squatting communities in the American West, the perception that federal land policy was patently unfair and unworthy of obedience threatened to undermine squatters' respect for the rule of law more broadly.[20] Bringing the law of land distribution into conformity with the widely held views of the local community – by ratifying squatters' (illegal) appropriations – converted a group of outlaws into a group with something at stake in protecting the (modified) property system.

A similar intuition appears to underlie the arguments made by Hernando de Soto with respect to the benefits of granting title to squatters in Lima, Peru (de Soto 1989: 23–26). In Peru, where the mass of people are cut off from property ownership by their own poverty, residents have frequently resorted to concerted land invasions to occupy underutilized land, both public and private (*id.*: 19–22). As de Soto observes, "people are capable of violating a system which does not accept them, not so that they can live in anarchy but so that they can build a different system which respects a minimum of essential rights" (*id.*: 55). De Soto observes that 69 of 100 houses built in Lima in 1985 were constructed on unlawfully occupied land (*id.*: 23). Under the circumstances de Soto describes of widespread rejection of the existing distributive order, ratifying the conduct of property outlaws – or accommodating them by creating a formalized process by which they can accomplish the goal of ownership – is ultimately an order-enhancing, not an order-destroying, strategy.

Other observers of squatter communities throughout the developing world have commented on their impressive, albeit largely informal, orderliness. Robert Neuwirth argues that Rio's squatter communities (*favelas*) are safer and more orderly than the formal communities they border. He quotes one resident as claiming that "[t]here is no risk doing business in the favelas. You have more risk with a store in Ipanema [a well-off beachfront neighborhood] than in [the favela of] Riocinha . . . In the favela, the community protects itself" (Neuwirth 2006: 256–257). Neuwirth ultimately concurs with de Soto and others who have argued that – for better or for worse depending on one's orientation – once their claims are recognized, squatters become fierce defenders of their property rights and, by extension, supporters of the legal order from which they were formerly excluded. The simultaneous radicalism and conservatism of squatters explains why they have so frequently been attacked by commentators on both the left and the right: they are suspect to the right because their squatting begins in an act of defiance of the established legal order; and they are suspect to the left because, when most successful, their act terminates by reinforcing the very systems of private ownership they initially transgressed (*see id.*: 295–297).

For analogous reasons, how others respond to a system of forced sharing will depend on the precise means by which that sharing is accomplished. Not all law-breaking, even of the acquisitive (or intersectional) variety, need contribute to a sense of widespread disorder that would undermine broader crime-control efforts. Unlike the broken windows approach, an act of appropriation may actually contribute to visible *order*.[21] Squatters in the American West created elaborate (and ordered) systems of informal law to protect their investments should their legality some day be recognized.[22] Similarly, de Soto has observed that organized squatters in Peru often keep meticulous land records indicating who "owns" which parcel and take great pains to defend their informal property rights against owners and "ordinary criminals" (de Soto 1989: 27–29). The highly organized nature of much urban squatting in the United States in the 1980s likewise may well have worked to *displace* the preexisting disorder generated by extensive urban abandonment.[23] Urban squatters were fixing broken windows, not breaking them.[24] It is perhaps for this reason that neighborhood residents were typically supportive of squatting efforts, notwithstanding their illegality.[25]

b) Acquisitive outlaws in a rights-based perspective

It is commonplace within theories of civil disobedience to distinguish between conscientious disobedients, who violate laws with the self-conscious purpose of drawing attention to the injustice of the laws they oppose, and mere criminals motivated by greed or selfishness. Dworkin's theory of civil disobedience, for example, actively privileges conscientious lawbreakers (who overlap substantially with our own category of expressive lawbreakers) over other types of criminals (*see* Dworkin 1985: 108–110, 1977: 206–216). Indeed, for him, the principal difference between the most justified and least justified forms of civil disobedience turns on the degree of intensity with which the disobedient citizen views the law as unjust (Dworkin 1985: 107–108). Accordingly, on his view of civil disobedience, many of the people we have called acquisitive lawbreakers would not fare particularly well. Their subjective motivation, while often a mystery, frequently appears to be little more than a self-interested desire to acquire property rights currently in the hands of others.

The central message sent by the acquisitive lawbreaker's actions is that another person owns something that she wants (or needs) for herself but that she will not (or cannot) purchase in a voluntary transaction. In most cases, this desire for the property of another will be unworthy and unjustified, and society correctly responds to the lawbreaker's behavior by punishing her for her transgression. But, as we have shown, at times external conditions might call into question, or at least lead us to soften, our reflexive tendency to penalize the lawbreaker.

In contrast with Dworkin, we believe that the justification of an act of acquisitive lawbreaking can turn on the objective content of the law and the facts on which the law itself operates, and not just on the subjective attitude of the lawbreaker herself. In so doing, we draw on a long, though neglected, tradition within Western thought. Early Christian thinkers, for example, viewed the failure of the rich to share with the poor as tantamount to theft (*see* Charles Avila 1983: 55). Thomas Aquinas built on this tradition, arguing that when a poor person takes what he needs from the "superabundance" of another, he is simply taking that to which he is already morally entitled and, as a consequence, he does not commit the crime of theft.[26] More recently, Jeremy Waldron has endorsed a redistributive principle that "[n]obody should be permitted ever to use force to prevent another man from satisfying his very basic needs in circumstances where there seems to be no other way of satisfying them" (Jeremy Waldron 1993: 240–241). Within modern criminal law, analogous intuitions appear to underlie the justificatory doctrine of necessity, although in practice the doctrine has been so hemmed in by qualifications and exceptions as to make it virtually inoperative in circumstances of economic need.

It is important to note that, unlike the dominant theories concerning civil disobedience, the subjective attitude of the acquisitive outlaw with respect to the justice of the violated law is not the most relevant factor in this analysis. Calling the lawbreaker's action an act of selfishness, even if true, does not necessarily undermine its justification under these necessity inquiries. Instead, what matters is whether, as a question of objective distributive justice, she took what she badly *needed* from the superabundance of another in such a way that her actions avoided an even greater evil. Someone in dire need is certainly not justified in taking from someone else in dire need. The outlaw's subjective view regarding the objective injustice of the existing property distribution, however, is not the crucial factor.[27]

There are, obviously, many pragmatic reasons for preferring legislative solutions to distributive problems over the often unreflective self-help of the acquisitive outlaw (*see* Waldron 1993: 243–245). From a rigidly rights-based point of view, these consequences are not an appropriate consideration in answering the narrow question of the justice of an individual outlaw's behavior when the legislature has failed to act. All things being equal, however, even a nonutilitarian could favor the rectification of the injustice that justifies the outlaw's behavior through the most efficient means possible (*see id.*: 244: "The welfare state is a way of ensuring that no one should ever be in such abject need that he would be driven to violate otherwise enforceable rules of property."). Accordingly, even someone who is not a thoroughgoing utilitarian about the purposes of punishment can appreciate the informational value generated by acquisitive outlaws, because the information they generate might point toward previously overlooked distributive injustices in need of legislative attention.

Even assuming the justice of acquisitive actions under the most extreme circumstances of need, the more interesting question is whether there is an argument that the category of justified acquisitive conduct extends beyond the situation of the person in immediate need of sustenance for her physical survival. We limit ourselves to the observation that there are plausible theories of distributive justice that would be amenable to permitting some additional room for self-help beyond the extreme case of, say, imminent starvation. In large part, the question turns on the breadth of one's definition of *necessity*. Many people would admit the validity of some acquisitive actions in order to fulfill basic human needs but then argue for an extremely narrow understanding of "need" as encompassing only those items necessary to sustain physical survival.[28]

In an affluent society like ours, the number of people who might need to engage in criminal violations of property laws in order to stave off imminent physical harm attributable to poverty is likely to be very small, though not trivial.[29] But in a highly unequal society in the developing world, the numbers will be much larger (*see, e.g.* de Soto 1989: 19–22). Worldwide, roughly a billion people live on land that is not their own, many of them in conditions of extreme deprivation.[30] As one commentator has put it, "[t]he overwhelming majority of the world's one billion squatters are simply people who came to the city, needed a place to live that they and their families could afford, and, not being able to find it on the private market, built it for themselves on land that wasn't theirs."[31]

In addition to these situations of dire need in both the developing and developed world, many theorists have argued for a broader understanding of needs. Thinkers as diverse as Aristotle,[32] Adam Smith,[33] John Ryan (Ryan 1906: 72–74, 126–127) and, more recently, Amartya Sen[34] have, for example, agreed that the category of human needs extends well beyond the basket of goods necessary to stave off starvation and exposure. In particular, they have focused on the intuition that, as social animals, human beings' legitimate "needs" include the property necessary to facilitate a minimally acceptable degree of participation in the social life of their respective communities.[35] Given the differences in material circumstances of various communities and, accordingly, the different material preconditions for effective social participation, this understanding of necessity is likely to yield different concrete definitions of need for differently situated societies.[36]

As Smith put it in his *Wealth of Nations*, the category of "necessaries" includes "whatever the custom of the country renders it indecent for creditable people, even of the lowest order, to be without" (Smith 1776: 821). Smith gives the example of leather shoes, a commodity that might be viewed as a luxury or perhaps as an eccentricity in other cultures, but that was a minimum requirement for even the most basic level of social respectability in Smith's England (*id*.: 822). Building on Smith's culturally relative definition of needs, Sen has proposed a definition of poverty that considers the material commodities necessary to permit a person to both survive physically and to participate, at least at some minimal level, in the social life of the community (Sen 1984: 336–337).

If we employ this metric while shifting our attention away from subsistence economies, the commodities necessary to participate minimally in the life of a community are likely to expand (*see id*.: 336: "For a richer community . . . the nutritional and other physical requirements . . . are typically already met, and the needs of communal participation . . . will have a much higher demand in the space of commodities and that of resources."). Presumably in some communities, a loincloth, some tools or weapons, and a makeshift shelter would be sufficient to be a member of the community in good standing. A comparable list for life in the twenty-first century United States would include substantial quantities of clothing, a fairly sophisticated shelter with indoor plumbing and access to various utilities (electricity, gas, telephone service), a series of functional household appliances, and an effective means of transportation.[37]

As a community becomes more affluent, the list of commodities needed to participate in community life tends to expand. This is why items that were once regarded as luxuries, such as indoor plumbing, are now considered to be minimal requirements of habitability and why, notwithstanding its onetime status as a luxury item, we are justified in continuing to refer to housing that lacks indoor plumbing (and even to much housing that has it) as unacceptably "poor".[38]

To a limited extent, existing law recognizes the importance of this expanding list. For example, landlord-tenant law permits tenants to engage in self-help, though, for example, refusing to pay rent or deducting the cost of certain essential repairs from rent, when landlords fail to maintain properties at an adequate level.[39] And the circumstances that would justify such a refusal to pay rent encompass features of residential property, such as running water and heat that would have been viewed as housing luxuries a century ago.[40] Unfortunately, the legal protection of an individual's ability to affirmatively receive most of these services is inadequately protected by existing law.[41]

Extending Sen's context-specific definition of "need" to the question of self-help, one could plausibly argue that the propertyless person might be entitled to take for herself from the property of others reaches somewhat beyond that necessary to sustain physical existence and includes at least some of those commodities needed to permit a minimal participation in the life of the community. This assertion sounds fairly radical in the abstract. Nevertheless, doctrines like the implied warranty of habitability, adverse possession, and necessity suggest that self-help redistribution is already accepted, in a circumscribed way, by current property doctrine. The necessity doctrine, for example, need not encompass every element of the expanded list of needs. After all, on most accounts, the entitlement protected by the doctrine does not guarantee the right to avoid any need at all, but only "dire" or some similarly qualified need. Still, a broader understanding of human need would justify expanding the prerequisites for an assertion of necessity beyond a showing of imminent physical harm, and may be worth considering as a pathway to future legal reform.

3. Conclusion

The intentional violation of property law plays an important, though underexamined, role in the development of property doctrine. The behavior of property outlaws of all sorts provides a particularly effective mechanism by which those who are left out of the system of private ownership can challenge and change that system from the outside. The descriptive story, we would argue, demonstrates that these communities, far from being lawless, devoid of order or regulatory impulse, can become sophisticated avenues for legal reform. Urban squatting campaigns have been able to draw attention to the harms of underused urban property. In many cases, their work has been instrumental in reshaping the political landscape of urban neighborhoods. While such intentional lawbreaking has been deployed as a strategy of legal change in a variety of areas, it has been particularly influential in the context of property law, within which an emphasis on stability ensures that property doctrine will often fall out of step with the needs of contemporary society. Property scholars should be attentive to the criminal enforcement of property laws and the ways in which that enforcement may unfairly punish or overdeter property outlaws' activities.

Notes

1 *See* Stephenson (1989, 89) (discussing the use and dangers of these devices); *see also* Ilott v. Wilkes (1820) 106 Eng. Rep. 674, 676–77 (K.B.) (deciding a case arising out of injuries inflicted on a trespasser by a property owner's spring gun).
2 *See* Spring Guns and Man Traps Act, 1828, 7 & 8 Geo. 4, c. 18, § 12 (Eng.).
3 *See* Lingle v. Chevron USA Inc., 544 U.S. 528, 539 (2005) (describing the right to exclude as "perhaps the most fundamental of all property interests"); Loretto v. Teleprompter Manhattan CATV Corp., 458 U.S. 419, 435 (1982) ("The power to exclude has traditionally been considered one of the most treasured strands in an owner's bundle of property rights."); *see also* Merrill (2000: 970–974) (discussing the idea of "exclusion" as "the hallmark of property").
4 The federal program was based on Section 810 of the Housing and Community Development Act of 1974. *See* 88 Stat. 649, 734. Section 810 required that special consideration be given to a homesteader's capacity to make the required improvements to the property, a criterion that ultimately tipped the balance of the program in favor of moderate income families (Mele 2000: 188–194; Borgos 1984: 19).
5 *See* 88 Stat. 649, 734.
6 We do not use the term "civil disobedience" so as to avoid any confusion about the broader scope of our discussion, which encompasses lawbreaking activity that would not normally be understood as civil disobedience.

7 Information regarding the Anti-Eviction Campaign can be found at: http://chicagoanti eviction.org/. Examples of their campaign efforts can be found at: http://start2.occupyour homes.org/partnerships/chicago-anti-eviction-campaign.

8 *See, e.g.*, Foundation for the Advancement of Illegal Knowledge (1994: 29–45) ("Squatters were artists because they moved into empty space to play in it, and on no account to 'furnish' it.").

9 People's park in Berkeley is one example of a public park that originally grew out of a guerrilla gardening project; there's an organization called Greenaid that uses gumball machines to produce clay balls with seeds that are then tossed or planted in areas that might be beautified by flowers; today – almost every major city has some sort of guerrilla gardening movement. In London, after a pub frequented by Amy Winehouse burned down, hedging was replanted cut in the shape of Amy's beehive hairdo (Sullivan & Eaton 2007; Nguyen & Reed 2010; Mooallem 2008).

10 The Los Angeles Department of Public Works passed the "Edible Landscapes" ordinance, Council File 13–0478, on October 24, 2013 by unanimous vote. Los Angeles Municipal Code §§ 62.161–62.169 will be revised to allow owners or occupants of residentially zoned properties ability to install plant materials within parkways in front of their properties without the need to obtain a permit.

11 The "rights-based" category obviously includes an enormous diversity of approaches to criminal punishment. For our limited purposes, we intend the category to refer broadly to all nonutilitarian approaches.

12 The risk is present whether one adopts a more formalist approach in which the outlaw is viewed as having broken an existing legal rule, with the law sometimes changing in response, or a more pluralist, the "alt-law"), merely insists upon her own interpretation of the extant law, which the organs of official legal interpretation sometimes adopt as their own. Within the formalist framework, we would describe the law as having adopted a new rule in response to the outlaw's defiance of the old one. Within a pluralist framework, we would describe the alt-law as having provided the occasion for official clarification of an ambiguous legal norm. In both case, however the outlaw/alt-law faces the same risk of punishment should she find herself on the losing side of the argument. Accordingly, whether styled as outlaw or alt-law conduct, our point about the need for flexibility in the (official) law's response remains the same.

13 Ronald Dworkin highlights the problems posed by this measure of value when he poses the hypothetical of a "poor, sick man [who] needs medicine and is therefore willing to sell a favored book, his sole source of pleasure, for the $5 the medicine costs. His neighbor is willing to pay $10 to have the book . . . because he is the famous (and rich) grandson of the author, and if he autographs the book he can sell it for $11." (Dworkin 1986).

14 Tom Tyler has argued in a similar vein that willingness to break the law correlates strongly with views about the justice of society's distribution of wealth as well as views about legal legitimacy (Tyler 1990: 96, 107–108).

15 In part, this failure to invest might result from something analogous to the "demoralization" that Frank Michelman famously identified as one of the likely consequences of uncompensated government takings (Michelman 1967: 1165, 1214). In part, however, it might also result from genuine uncertainty about the contours of property rights within a regime that would ratify the actions of acquisitive outlaws (see, e.g. Smith 2005: 69, 88–91).

16 See Southwark v. Williams, 2 All E.R. 175, 179 (A.C. 1971) (arguing that permitting forced transfers based on claims of need would lead to claims by "others who would imagine that they [are] in need" or who "would invent a need" in an attempt to fit themselves within the rule).

17 Id. at 180 (arguing that "in the interest of law and order itself," courts must adopt a narrow interpretation of the necessity doctrine).

18 The Broken Windows thesis was first raised in Wilson and Kelling (1982: 29) ("[I]f a window in a building is broken *and is left unrepaired*, all the rest of the windows will

soon be broken . . . . [O]ne unrepaired broken window is a signal that no one cares, and so breaking more windows costs nothing."). The body of literature supporting the thesis is large, rapidly growing, and somewhat controversial (*see, e.g.,* Skogan 1990: 9–14 (discussing how crime can be caused by disorder); Ellickson (1996: 1165, 1171, 1182) (arguing that public crime and public begging will lead to disorder through additional crime); Stelle Garnett (2005: 1075, 1083) (arguing that eliminating disorder will curb crime as people see others behave lawfully); Kahan (1996: 349, 394) (concluding that a major factor in a person's decision to commit a crime is whether other people are committing crimes). *But see* Harcourt and Ludwig (2006: 271, 314–316) (concluding, after empirical analysis, that increased police attention to eliminate disorder and misdemeanor violations does not reduce crime); Harcourt (1998: 291, 386–389) (stating that the Broken Windows policy in New York has not played a significant role in reducing crime rates).

19 *See* Tyler (1990: 96, 107–108) (noting that fair procedures have a legitimizing effect on legal authorities); Zimring and Hawkins (1973: 220–221) (noting that the threat of punishment for behavior widely viewed as justified within a particular community can lead to an overall deterioration of respect for the rule of law).

20 *See* Gates (1968: 235) (stating that, during the 1830s, squatters were indirectly encouraged to take more land when the government forgave past squatters).

21 *See* Kahan (1996: 369) (emphasizing that it is "visible" disorder that undermines community efforts to control crime). Property owners' responses to such appropriation, however, might well contribute to such visible signs of disorder.

22 *See* Singer (2006: 25–26) (quoting Hurst 1956: 3–5).

23 *See, e.g.,* Mele (2000: 197) (observing that abandoned urban properties became zones of criminality); Borgos (1986: 428–429, 433–436) (describing neighborhood support for ACORN Housing's squatting actions, which helped to clean up otherwise derelict housing).

24 A similar story can be told about the Green Guerrillas, 1970s activists who trespassed on abandoned, rubble-strewn properties in New York City to create community gardens. See Mele (2000: 208–210); Liz Christy Community Garden (2007) (describing the creation of one community garden in New York by the Green Guerrillas).

25 *See* Mele (2000: 208) (noting that squatters and homesteaders enjoyed community support).

26 *See* St. Thomas Aquinas (*in* Baumgarth & Regan 1988: 187) ("It is not theft, properly speaking, to take secretly and use another's property in a case of extreme need because that which a man takes for the support of his life becomes his own property by reason of that need.").

27 This is not to say that the lawbreaker's subjective intent is absolutely irrelevant. *See, e.g.,* Berman (2005: 681, 701–704) (discussing the problem of mistaken necessity).

28 This is apparently also the position of the Catholic Church. *See* Catechism of the Catholic Church (2007, para. 2408) (stating that it is not a violation of the Seventh Commandment to steal property in cases of urgent necessity).

29 A search of public records and news reports for the past decade turns up nearly 100 reported homeless deaths from exposure, a figure that almost certainly undercounts the actual number. *See* Spreadsheet of Homeless Deaths (on file with authors). For newspaper articles describing deaths of homeless persons due to exposure, see Casey (2005: 1B), Garland (2005a: B8, 2005b: B1), and Moore and Hutchinson (2005: 5).

30 *See* Neuwirth (2006: 9). By 2030, some observers estimate that one in four people on earth will be squatting.

31 *Id.*

32 *See* Nussbaum (1988: 145, 149–150, 157) (describing Aristotle's view that all people should be given the necessary resources to "liv[e] well").

33 *See* Smith (1776: Bk. V, ch. ii, pt. 2) (arguing that an increase on taxes of necessary items must be accompanied by an increase in wages to compensate).

34 *See* Sen (1984: 325–345) (describing the merits of an absolutist approach to poverty).

35 *See* Waldron (1993: 246–247) (arguing that there may be a moral duty for welfare provision).
36 *See id.* at 247 ("The goods . . . that are necessary for basic interaction with others may vary from society to society; but it may well be true that in each society those goods are so important to the social side of human existence that men and women will . . . strive for them").
37 For an example of the "necessity" of telephone service, see Julia Sommerfeld (2003: B3).
38 This explains why arguments that the poor are materially well off in comparison to the poor of the last century often come off as incurably obtuse. In addition, the notion of a shifting list of commodities necessary to participate in community life is consistent with the observations by behavioral economists that people exhibit strong preferences regarding their relative position in society with respect to certain "positional goods" such that they are willing to forego a degree of absolute consumption in order to retain a favorable relative ranking. For a clear summary of this finding, see Frank (2005: 137).
39 *See* Singer (2006: 716–718) (discussing actions tenants are entitled to take when landlords fail to maintain their property).
40 *See id.* at 715 (describing circumstances that can give rise to this right of self-help).
41 The protection provided by landlord-tenant law, for example, only applies to parties who have already successfully established a contractual landlord-tenant relationship. It says nothing about an affirmative entitlement to any of these goods apart from such a preexisting relationship.

Works cited

Legal texts

Housing & Urban Recovery Act of 1983, Stat. 1196.
Spring Guns and Man Traps Act, 1828, 7 & 8 Geo. 4, c. 18, (Eng.).

Case law

Ilott v. Wilkes, (1820) 106 Eng. Rep. (K.B.).
Lingle v. Chevron USA Inc., 544 U.S. (2005).
Loretto v. Teleprompter Manhattan CATV Corp., 458 U.S. (1982).
Southwark v. Williams, 2 All E.R. (A.C. 1971).

Doctrine

Aigler, Ralph W. 1924. The Operation of the Recording Acts. *Mich. L. Rev.*, vol. 22, 405.
Aquinas, St. Thomas. 1988. Summa Theologiae II-II, at Q. 66, art. 7, *reprinted in* On Law, Morality, and Politics (William P. Baumgarth & Richard J. Regan eds.).
Austen, Ben. 2013. The Death and Life of Chicago. *New York Times Magazine* (May 29), available at www.nytimes.com/2013/06/02/magazine/how-chicagos-housing-crisis-ignited-a-new-form-of-activism.html?pagewanted=all.
Avila, Charles. 1983. *Ownership: Early Christian Teaching*. London: Sheed and Ward.
Becker, Gary S. 1968. Crime and Punishment: An Economic Approach. *Journal of Political Economy*, vol. 76: 1–54.
Bell, Abraham & Gideon Parchomovsky. 2005. A Theory of Property. *Cornell Law Review*, vol. 90: 531–616.
Berman, Mitchell N. 2005. Lesser Evils and Justification: A Less Close Look. *Law & Philosophy*, vol. 24: 681–703.

Bibas, Stephanos & Richard A. Bierschbach. 2004. Integrating Remorse and Apology into Criminal Procedure. *Yale Law Journal*, vol. 114: 85–148.

Blomley, Nicholas. 2003. Law, Property, and the Geography of Violence: The Frontier, the Survey, and the Grid. *Annals of the Association of American Geographers*, vol. 93, no. 1 (Mar., 2003), pp. 121–141.

Borgos, Seth. 1984. The ACORN Squatters' Campaign. *Social Policy*, vol. 15: 17–26.

Borgos, Seth. 1986. Low-Income Homeownership and the ACORN Squatters Campaign. In: Rachel G. Bratt et al. (eds.), *Critical Perspectives on Housing*. Philadelphia, PA: Temple University Press.

Brooks, Steve & Gerry Marten. 2005. *Green Guerillas: Revitalizing Urban Neighborhoods With Community Gardens*, EcoTipping Points Project (June 2005), available at www. ecotippingpoints.org/our-stories/indepth/usa-new-york-community-garden-urban-renewal.html.

Casey, Juliet V. 2005. Homeless in Las Vegas: On a Mission of Mercy. *Las Vegas Review Journal* (August. 15).

Catechism of the Catholic Church Para. 2408, available at www.vatican.va/archive/catechism/p3s2c2a7.htm#II (last visited March 23, 2007).

Clarity, James F. 1977. Philadelphia's Poor Taking over Houses to Fight City Decay. *N.Y. Times* (June 11).

Coleman, Jules L. 1980. Crimes, Kickers, and Transaction Structures. In: J. Roland Pennock & John W. Chapman (eds.) *Nomos XXII: Property*. New York: NYU Press.

Corr, Anders. 1999. *No Trespassing! Squatting, Rent Strikes, and Land Struggle Worldwide*. Boston, MA: South End Press.

de Soto, Hernando. 1989. *The Other Path: The Invisible Revolution in the Third World*. New York: Basic Books.

Dworkin, Ronald. 1977. *Taking Rights Seriously*. Cambridge, MA: Harvard University Press.

Dworkin, Ronald. 1985. *A Matter of Principle*. Cambridge, MA: Harvard University Press.

Dworkin, Ronald. 1986. *Law's Empire*. Cambridge, MA: Harvard University Press.

Ellickson, Robert C. 1996. Controlling Chronic Misconduct in City Spaces: Of Panhandlers, Skid Rows, and Public-Space Zoning. *Yale Law Journal*, vol. 105: 1165–1266.

Epstein, Richard A. 2003. *Skepticism and Freedom: A Modern Case for Classical Liberalism*. Chicago: University of Chicago Press.

Fennell, Lee Anne. 2006. Efficient Trespass: The Case for "Bad Faith" Adverse Possession. *Northwestern University Law Review*, vol. 100: 1037–1095.

Foundation for the Advancement of Illegal Knowledge, Cracking the Movement: Squatting Beyond the Media. 1994. Retrieved from: https://www.amazon.com/Cracking-Movement-Squatting-Beyond-Autonomy/dp/0936756756

Frank, Robert H. 2005. Positional Externalities Cause Large and Preventable Welfare Losses. *The American Economic Review*, Vol. 95, No. 2, Papers and Proceedings of the One Hundred Seventeenth Annual Meeting of the American Economic Association, Philadelphia, PA, January 7–9, 2005 (May, 2005), pp. 137–141.

Garland, Greg. 2005a. Helping the Helpless. *Ariz. Republic* (September 7).

Garland, Greg. 2005b. Two Homeless Dead after Overnight Exposure. *Baltimore Sun* (December 4).

Garnett, Nicole Stelle. 2005. Relocating Disorder. *Virginia Law Review*, vol. 91: 1075–1134.

Gates, Paul W. 1968. *History of Public Land Law Development*. Washington, DC: Wm. W. Gaunt & Sons.

Glendon, Mary Ann. 1991. *Rights Talk: The Impoverishment of Political Discourse*. New York: The Free Press.

Harcourt, Bernard E. 1998. Reflecting on the Subject: A Critique of the Social Influence Conception of Deterrence, the Broken Window Theory, and Order-Maintenance Policing New York Style. *Michigan Law Review*, vol. 97(2): 291–386.

Harcourt, Bernard E. & Jens Ludwig. 2006. Broken Windows: New Evidence from New York City and a Five-City Social Experiment. *University of Chicago Law Review*, vol. 73: 271–320.

Hasen, Richard L. & Richard H. McAdams. 1997. The Surprisingly Complex Case against Theft. *International Review of Law & Economics*, vol. 17(3): 367–378.

Haynes, Flora. 2011. Is Guerrilla Gardening a Form of Vandalism or Conservation?. *Conservation Jobs* (November 18), available at www.conservation-jobs.co.uk/49992/is-guerrilla-gardening-a-form-of-vandalism-or-conservation/.

Hirsch, Eric & Peter Wood. 1988. Squatting in New York City: Justification and Strategy. *New York University Review of Law and Social Change*, vol. 16(4) (online).

Hochman, David. 2013. Urban Gardening: An Appleseed with Attitude. *New York Times* (May 3), available at www.nytimes.com/2013/05/05/fashion/urban-gardening-an-appleseed-with-attitude.html?pagewanted=all.

Hurst, James Willard. 1956. *Law and the Conditions of Freedom in the Nineteenth-Century United States*. Madison: University of Wisconsin Press.

Hylton, Keith N. 1996. Optimal Law Enforcement and Victim Precaution. *Rand Journal of Economics*, vol. 27(1): 197–206.

Jackson, Kenneth T. 1985. *Crabgrass Frontier: The Suburbanization of the United States*. New York: Oxford University Press.

Jones, M. 2001. Trespassers Will Be Shot, and More Family Fun. *Blessings for Life*, available at http://blessingsforlife.com/southernliving/trespassers.htm.

Kahan, Dan M. 1996. What Do Alternative Sanctions Mean? *University of Chicago Law Review*, vol. 63: 591–653.

Katz, Stephen & Margaret Mayer. 1985. Gimme Shelter: Self-Help Housing Struggles within and against the State in New York City and West Berlin. *International Journal of Urban & Regional Research*, vol. 9(2): 15–46.

Kettman, Matt. 2013. How Guerrilla Gardening Can Save America's Food Deserts. *Smithsonian.com* (June 20), available at www.smithsonianmag.com/food/how-guerrilla-gardening-can-save-americas-food-deserts-1464414/?all.

Klevorick, Alvin K. 1980. On the Economic Theory of Crime. Originally published in *Criminal Justice*, vol. 27: 289–309, reprinted in *Nomos XXII: Property* (J. Roland Pennock & John W. Chapman, eds.).

Leuck, Thomas J. 1996. Police Evict Squatters from Three City-Owned Tenements in the East Village. *N.Y. Times* (August 14).

Marx, Karl. 1978 [1843]. On the Jewish Question. In: Robert C. Tucker (ed.), *The Marx-Engels Reader* (2nd ed.). New York: W. W. Norton & Company.

McChesney, Fred S. 1993. Boxed In: Economists and Benefits from Crime. *International Review of Law & Economics*, vol. 13(2): 225–231.

Mele, Christopher. 2000. *Selling the Lower East Side: Culture, Real Estate, and Resistance in New York City*. Minneapolis: University of Minnesota Press.

Merrill, Thomas W. 2000. The Landscape of Constitutional Property. *Virginia Law Review*, vol. 86(5): 885–1000.

Michelman, Frank I. 1967. Property, Utility, and Fairness: Comments on the Ethical Foundations of "Just Compensation" Law. *Harvard Law Review*, vol. 80(6): 1165–1258.

Mooallem, Jon. 2008. Guerrilla Gardening. *New York Times* (June 8), available at www.nytimes.com/2008/06/08/magazine/08guerrilla-t.html?pagewanted=print.

Moore, Alan W. 2012. *Art + Squat = X* 8 (June 15) (unpublished manuscript from Lecture at Universidad Complutense de Madrid), available at www.academia.edu/2558355/_Art_Squat_X_unpublished_2012.

Moore, Robert F. & Bill Hutchinson. 2005. The Killer Chiller. *Daily News (New York)* (January 19).

Neuwirth, Robert. 2006. *Shadow Cities: A Billion Squatters, a New Urban World.* London: Routledge.

Nguyen, My Tam & Amanda Reed. 2010. Greenaid: Seedbombing for the Modern Guerilla Gardening Movement. *WorldChanging.com* (July 27), available at www.worldchanging.com/archives/011420.html.

Nussbaum, Martha. 1988. Nature, Function, and Capability: Aristotle on Political Distribution. In: Julia Annas & Robert H. Grimm (eds.), *Oxford Studies in Ancient Philosophy* (Supp. 1988). Oxford University Press.

The Oxford English Dictionary. 1961.

Polinsky, A. Mitchell & Steven Shavell. 1979. The Optimal Tradeoff between the Probability and Magnitude of Fines. *The American Economic Review*, vol. 69: 880–891.

Pruijt, Hans. 2013a. The Logic of Urban Squatting. *International Journal of Urban and Regional Research*, vol. 37(1): 19–45.

Pruijt, Hans. 2013b. Squatting in Europe. In: Squatting Europe Kollective (eds.), *Squatting in Europe: Radical Spaces, Urban Struggles.* Wivenhoe, New York, and Port Watson: Autonomedia, 17–60, available at www.minorcompositions.info/wp-content/uploads/2013/03/squattingineurope-web.pdf.

Rohe, William A. 2007. Expanding Urban Homesteading. *Journal of the American Planning Association*, vol. 57: 444–455.

Ryan, John. 1906. *A Living Wage: Its Ethical and Economic Aspects.* London: Macmillan.

Schwab, Stewart. 1989. Coase Defends Coase: Why Lawyers Listen and Economists Do Not. *Michigan Law Review*, vol. 87(6): 1171–1198.

Sen, Amartya. 1984. *Resources, Values, and Development.* Oxford: Basil Blackwell.

Shoard, Marion. 1999. *A Right to Roam.* Oxford: Oxford University Press.

Singer, Joseph W. 2006. *Property Law: Rules, Policies, and Practices* (4th ed.). New York: Aspen Publ.

Skogan, Wesley G. 1990. *Disorder and Decline: Crime and the Spiral of Decay in American Neighborhoods.* San Francisco: University of California Press.

Smith, Adam. 1937 [1776]. *The Wealth of Nations* (Edwin Cannan, ed.). London: Random House.

Smith, Henry E. 2005. Self-Help and the Nature of Property. *Journal of Law, Economics and Policy*, vol. 1(1): 69–107.

Sommerfeld, Julia. 2003. Voice-Mail Service for Homeless Will Expand. *Seattle Times* (September 8).

Stephenson, Tom. 1989. *Forbidden Land: The Struggle for Access to Mountain and Moorland* (Ann Holt, ed.). Manchester, UK: Manchester University Press.

Sullivan, Ron & Joe Eaton. 2007. Guerrilla Gardeners Treat the Earth with Great Gusto. *SFGate.com* (May 30), available at www.sfgate.com/homeandgarden/thedirt/article/Guerrilla-gardeners-treat-the-earth-with-great-2590456.php.

Tullock, Gordon. 1967. The Welfare Costs of Tariffs, Monopolies, and Theft. *Western Economic Journal*, vol. 5(3): 224–232.

Tyler, Tom R. 1990. *Why People Obey the Law.* New Haven: Yale University Press.

Underkuffler, Laura S. 2003. *The Idea of Property: Its Meaning and Power.* Oxford: Oxford University Press.

von Hassell, Malve. 1996. *Homesteading in New York City, 1978–1993*. New York: Praeger Publ.

Waldron, Jeremy. 1993. *Liberal Rights: Collected Papers 1981–1991*. Cambridge: Cambridge University Press.

Wilson, James Q. & George L. Kelling. 1982. Broken Windows. *Atlantic Monthly* (March).

Wright, Bradley R.E., Avshalom Caspi & Terrie Moffitt. 2004. Does the Perceived Risk of Punishment Deter Criminally Prone Individuals? Rational Choice, Self-Control, and Crime. *Journal of Research on Crime & Delinquency*, vol. 41(2): 180–213.

Zimring, Franklin E. & Gordon J. Hawkins. 1973. *Deterrence: The Legal Threat in Crime Control*. Chicago: University of Chicago Press.

7 Land and territory

Struggles for land and territorial rights in Brazil

Sérgio Sauer and Luís Felipe Perdigão de Castro

In 2014, the national congress of the Landless Rural Workers' Movement (MST) brought together over 15,000 peasants in the capital Brasilia to mark its thirtieth anniversary. The MST emerged as part of the political process of re-democratization after 1984. Its mobilizations renewed land occupations and came to deeply influence agrarian struggles in Brazil, reinvigorating a struggle over land predate the MST that was initially led by social movements that were persecuted and eventually destroyed by the dictatorship following the 1964 *coup d'etat* (Welch and Sauer 2015). The MST was not alone, however, in replacing land at the center of social struggles in Brazil, and land occupations were not the only form such struggles for land took. Instead, a long list of social actors and subjects, actions, and demands for territorial rights have contributed to this struggle over the past 30 years (Sauer and França 2012; Sauer 2011; Martins 2002).

Despite having the same Latin root in Portuguese, the terms *land* and *territory* have quite a different common understanding in Brazil, and *land struggles* have been seen as distinct from demands for territorial rights (Sauer 2011). Land struggles, which fit into a broader Latin American history (Petras and Veltmeyer 2001), are closely related to the demands and struggles of peasants, or landless rural workers. The Brazilian Constitution of 1988 reinforced such an understanding, as it established that land that does not fulfill its social function – limited to the meaning of "unproductive" land – must be expropriated for agrarian reform. Territorial claims are dealt with in distinct articles of the Constitution, which recognizes the territorial rights of indigenous peoples and Quilombola communities (rural communities of afro-descendants of former slaves). Thus, the Constitution distinguishes between territory and land, two notions that correspond to different sets of claims and related to different constituencies (Sauer 2011).

The social demands and political claims for land are constantly face strong opposition from a powerful agribusiness sector, which promotes a model of agricultural production based on land concentration, monocultures for export, and the expansion of agricultural frontiers. This "economy of agribusiness" (Delgado 2013) has been heavily financed by governmental programs and incentives (including loans and tax exemptions) and supported by public investments in infrastructures, all of which promoted ". . . an economic model rooted in the intensified exploitation of natural and agricultural resources" (Baletti 2014: 6).

The combination of "an intensified export-oriented model of extractive develop-ment" with "a progressive social agenda based on the reduction of poverty" – a combination described as "neo-extractivism" in Baletti's (2014) terms, and that others have referred to as "neo-developmentalism" (Boito and Berringer 2014) – has recently led to increasing private appropriation of land, social conflicts, and environmental degradation (Sauer 2018). Reaffirming property as an absolute right, this rationale openly denies territorial rights to rural social groups, simulta-neously denying their achievements and renewing a discussion of the meaning of property and tenure rights of land in Brazil (Sauer and França 2012).

This chapter first adopts a historical perspective to reflect on the process of land concentration and on the impacts of this process on the denial of land rights (Sec-tion 1). It then analyzes how the outcomes of social struggles are reflected in the 1988 Brazilian Constitution and legal system, including the social-environmental function of land and different property and tenure regimes (Section 2). The result is a rainbow of social and cultural relations to land, which the Brazilian legal system partially acknowledges, but which also goes hand in hand with the reality of disputes and struggles for land rights (Section 3). In such disputes, the core argument is that varied social and cultural categories, popular claims for land, and different practical ways of accessing and controlling territories create space for debate over the existence of different types of properties and tenure rights and regimes beyond those outlined in legislation.

1. Land concentration, conflicts, and conquered territories in Brazil

Land ownership in Brazil is highly concentrated, and it is this concentration that is the most important historical cause of land conflict and struggles for land in the country. Though such concentration dates back to colonial days, it was aggravated after the 1960s with the implementation of the Green Revolution, an economic plan put forth by the dictatorship (1964–1984) to increase agricultural produc-tion. Faced with strong popular demands for agrarian reform, the dictatorship responded with political repression of social mobilizations and the persecution of popular leaders – many of whom were arrested and tortured – and the creation of financial incentives to expand the so-called agricultural frontiers to the Amazon and Cerrado regions (Martins 1994). The governmental incentives for the expan-sion of agricultural frontiers aimed to facilitate the occupation of "empty spaces" and thus, it was hoped, to minimize conflicts caused by popular demands for land (Sauer 2018).

In economic terms, large investments accompanied the implementation of the Green Revolution. Agricultural modernization was achieved by capitalizing large estates, which were granted access to credit and tax breaks, thus creating condi-tions for the acquisition of innovative inputs (hybrid seeds, chemical fertilizers) and mechanized agricultural implements (tractors, chainsaws, harvesters) (Mar-tins 1994). Through subsidized credit and tax breaks, the government favored large property-holders. Productivity growth and increased production followed

(Sauer 2010). But this strategy also intensified the concentration of land owner-ship, driving the displacement of millions of people in a rural exodus or forced shift toward the agricultural frontier (Martins 1994).

The main result of this has been, according to official 2006 Agricultural and Livestock Census data (IBGE 2009), that estates of less than ten hectares – although they represent 47 percent of the total number of farm units – occupy only 2.7 percent of the total rural area, or 7.8 million hectares. Estates larger than a thousand hectares represent only 0.91 percent of the total number of estates, but they encompass more than 43 percent of the total area, holding an estimated 146.6 million hectares (Sauer and Leite 2012). Aside from this unequal land distribu-tion, there were around 3.1 million families without land (landless peasants[1]) in 2003, following the definition of "rural workers without access to land" (MDA 2005: 17). Such landless families – combined with other social groups such as Indigenous people, Quilombolas communities, rubber tappers, extractive com-munities, coconut breakers, river dwellers, fishing communities, among others traditional communities that rely on the "commons"[2] – has contributed to a strong social demand for a more equitable access to and use of land and territorial rights (Sauer and Leite 2012), at the same time contributing to different perspectives in approaching land and "redefining" property rights in Brazil.

This historical agrarian concentration is further reinforced by the increas-ing demand for land resulting from investments by national and multinational agribusinesses for commodity production and/or land speculation (Sauer 2018; Fairbairn 2014). There have also been large investments made by extractive and mining companies (for the production of non-agricultural commodities); they too have been supported by governmental incentives with the intention of expanding agricultural frontiers and increasing Brazilian competitiveness on world markets (Baletti 2014). Combined with cattle raising, wood extraction, and the building of infrastructure, this process brings new land into (monoculture) production – especially for grains, mainly soy – and it has further fueled speculation over land, or "land grabbing" (Sauer and Leite 2012; Sauer 2018).

What we are witnessing is not just an economic process of growth, but the reproduction of a predatory, exploitative logic causing significant concentration of land and wealth. To many, the notion of agribusiness summarizes this whole process.[3] It is based on a pact of political power, involving large agro-industrial capital, a system of public credit to agriculture and agro-industries, property, and the State (Delgado 2013). This "economy of agribusiness" (Delgado 2013) goes beyond a pure economic strategy to "ideologically build a hegemony from the top, [involving] large landholdings, agro-industrial chains closely linked to the foreign sector, and the bureaucracies of the State", enabling "the accumulation of capital under the scope of these sectors melded by public funds" (Delgado 2013: 62). Thus, as part of an agro-strategy (Almeida 2011), it is a system justified by narratives linked to food-supply needs, food security, and to "environmental gov-ernance" as "the condition of possibility for neo-extractivism" (Baletti 2014: 7).

This economy of agribusiness has become a central feature of Brazil's eco-nomic logic in recent years, rooted both in "the capture and overexploitation of natural comparative advantages" (Delgado 2013: 64) and land appropriation (or land grabbing) for the production of agricultural and non-agricultural commodities and in speculation (Fairbairn 2014). Among other consequences of such an economy there is an exacerbation of territorial disputes or "conflicts over competing models of development and territories" (Fernandes *et al.* 2012: 37). Its rationale includes the denial of basic rights, such as the territorial rights of indigenous groups and other traditional communities, and an exacerbation of conflicts for and disputes over land and territory (Almeida 2011).

However, these processes of expropriation and concentration have occurred historically amidst resistance and ongoing struggles by social movements and rural populations (Fernandes *et al.* 2012). Such struggles resulted in the conception and implementation of a series of public policies and governmental programs that not only responded to social demands for land, but also reshaped notions of property and tenure rights (Sauer 2012).

Despite, or perhaps in response to, governmental incentives given to large landowners and the modernization of agriculture, agrarian movements intensified their grassroots mobilizations and struggles for land starting in the 1980s. Led by the MST, land occupations spread across the country (Martins 1994), resulting in a number of governmental land policies, specifically that of agrarian settlements (Sauer 2017). According to official data of INCRA (2018), an estimated 98 million hectares of land have been expropriated or bought to settle around one million landless families (Sauer 2017).

Though land occupations are the leading form of struggle for land access, other means of struggle have been developed in parallel, in particular through the resistance of indigenous and the Quilombola communities.[4] According to official data of Incra (2015), 124 Quilombola territories were titled – 139 titles went to 207 communities, including 12,906 families – between 1995 and 2012. In constitutional terms, these territories and land are held under collective or communitarian tenure, ensuring land rights to these communities. Also, there are a total of 690 territories officially recognized as indigenous land by the National Foundation of Indigenous People (Funai). These lands occupy an area of 112,984,701 hectares, which means that 13.3 percent of Brazilian national territory is set aside for indigenous people (Funai 2015).

Even though these numbers have been highly contested both by social movements and by scholars, they represent important social and political achievements that affect land access and use as well as land rights. Aside from gaining access to around 25 percent of the Brazilian territory (see Table 7.1), such struggles have resulted in a series of conceived and implemented public policies and governmental programs that have not only responded to the social demands for land and rights but also reshaped notions of land property and tenure rights, a consideration that has resulted in different territorial arrangements:

This struggle for land has built, revealed, and even reshaped social identities, instituting "new" social and political subjects. A similar process also took place in struggles for environmental protection with the creation of the "conservation units of sustainable use" (Almeida 2006) and the extractive reservations

Table 7.1 Territorial arrangements related to different struggles and land use

Territorial arrangements	Number of projects	Hectares	% of Brazilian territory
Settlements of landless families	9.127	85,291,180	10,0
Conservation units of sustainable use	141	30,184,984	3,5
Indigenous Land	690	112,984,701	13,3
Quilombola territories	124	995.009	0,11
Total		229,415,874	26,9

Sources: INCRA (2018, 2015), Funai (2015), ICMBio (2014).

(RESEX), following the struggles and resistance of groups in the Amazon, of which the rubber tappers are the best known (Gallois 2004). According to official data, there were 141 sustainable use areas in 2014, encompassing over 30 million hectares for different sustainable uses and tenure (ICMBio 2014).

This range of struggles for land embodies various strategies for (re)claiming, creating, and recreating territories and has resulted in a profound reshaping of property and tenure regimes. Despite all legal and institutional restrictions and enclosures,[5] and especially due to opposition and threats by agribusiness representatives, there is an ongoing struggle and demand for land, especially by indigenous people, Quilombola, and other "traditional" communities relying on communally owned land for their ways of living and culturally creating territories (Sauer 2012).

Figure 7.1 illustrates the territorial achievements made by different social subjects and movements, encompassing different forms of access, use, control, and tenure of land. Such achievements are not necessarily officially recognized or written as part of property laws. Thus, there are ongoing processes of building social and political identities through a process of self-definition of traditional communities[6] that involve demands transcending the rights of land property (Sauer 2012). Self-definition assuming a social identity is closely linked to historical land use practices and constitutes a fundamental criterion for the recognition of rights (Almeida 2011). Moreover, the struggle for access to land itself – besides guaranteeing social well-being and improving living conditions – creates places for self-determination related to "liberation and emancipation" (Sauer 2012: 98). As such, land is seen as a place of life, "not restricted to the struggle for access necessarily via real property rights. It should be considered a wider institutional space of struggles, which includes other forms of access, linked to the land struggle as a place of social justice" (Castro 2013: 44).

Popular claims for land and historical processes of self-determination thus transcend struggles to access and control of means of production. They are processes of construction on social and political subjects, which recreate socioenvironmental relations and transform rural areas, building territories (Almeida 2011; Fernandes *et al*. 2012) and often subverting the notion of property itself. The search for land "as a place of life" (Sauer 2010) should be considered as a

Figure 7.1 Lands and territories in Brazil, according to status
Sources: INCRA (2018, 2015), Funai (2015), ICMBio (2014).
Prepared by Ralph de Medeiros Albuquerque – Mader/FUP.

struggle in a broader institutional space that includes hybrids and multiple forms of access and use. Thus, property, tenure, and tenancy rights also reflect the "new aspects and perspectives, from Brazilian rural world, bringing old and new dilemmas and including demands for dignified and sustainable access to land" (Castro 2013: 11). Land struggles interface with property and tenure rights, which are managed – and in some cases, reshaped – according to the interests, views, and demands arising from the socio-political identities and social movements.

2. Social struggles and the constitution: the social-environmental function of land

In spite of the repression and the persecution of the 1960s to the 1980s, agrarian conflicts and demands for land remained on the national political agenda.

Local rural unions, popular leaders, and pastoral agents mobilized and organized peasants – particularly rural dwellers living on the agricultural frontiers – who remained on the land in resistance to those trying to expel them (Sauer 2010). Though most of the pastoral agents worked under the coordination of the Pastoral Commission on Land (CPT), the CPT was not alone: local rural unions and associations continued to operate in spite of repression and persecution, although their actions and resistance were restricted to the local level (Welch and Sauer 2015). The National Confederation of Workers in Agriculture (CONTAG), founded in 1963, also demanded land reform, basing its demands on the argument that the 1964 Land Statute should be implemented, thus reinforcing an "institutional" means of social pressure (Medeiros 1993; Welch and Sauer 2015).

There were new political opportunities for popular mobilization in the late 1970s. Together with the political amnesty granted in 1979 – allowing the return of many political leaders from exile – this resulted in the creation of several popular organizations like the Workers Party (PT), in 1979 and the Central Workers' Organization (CUT) in 1983 (Sauer 2010). In building new organizations and rebuilding old political parties, such as the Communist and the Socialist Parties, popular mobilizations kept demands for land on the political agenda (Deere and Medeiros 2007). This process resulted in the creation of the MST, officially established in 1984 (Stédile and Fernandes 1999), consolidating the land struggle through massive camping and land occupations (Sauer 2013; Martins 1994).[7]

In street demonstrations and rallies demanding democracy, these popular mobilizations "raised expectations regarding the possibility of agrarian reform" (Deere and Medeiros 2007: 83), which was seen as a mechanism by which political democratization would be achieved (Sauer 2010). Thus, the first civilian government had to formulate the National Plan for Agrarian Reform (PNRA) in 1985, promising to meet the demands that 1.4 million landless families be settled on land in a four-year period. The government of José Sarney (1985–1989) ultimately failed to fulfill this goal, however. Led by CONTAG and the Brazilian Association for Agrarian Reform (ABRA), the social mobilizations and demands then shifted their focus to the Constituent Assembly, which was elected in 1986 to write a new Constitution (Welch and Sauer 2015; Martins 1994).

As the elected Congress was expected to draw up the new Constitution, there were demands made for mechanisms that would allow for popular participation, achieved by an instrument called "popular amendment" (Sauer 2012). Rural social movements actively participated in the process, specifically by way of one popular amendment that gathered 1.2 million signatures to support the inclusion of agrarian reform in the text of the draft Constitution (Martins 1994). Following an intense dispute in the National Congress, the Constitution included a provision that property shall fulfill its "social function" (Article 5, XXI). With regards to rural properties, Article 184 of the 1988 Constitution establishes that the State shall expropriate any land that is not fulfilling its social function for agrarian reform (Sauer 2010). In addition, Article 186 of the Constitution stipulates that land property shall be dependent upon collective rights to life, not just on private rights (Marés 2003). The social function of land is considered to be fulfilled when it: (1) is rationally and adequately used; (2) makes an appropriate use of natural resources and ensures the preservation of the environment; (3) is in compliance with provisions governing labor relations and when, (4) its exploitation or use favors the well-being of owners and workers (Article 186).

The Brazilian Constitution could be labeled an "environmental constitution" with "evident social appeal" (Marés 2003; Tartuce 2014), where the right to private property is made subordinate to its social function (Castro 2013; Sauer and França 2012). The Constitution is written in the same spirit as the 1964 Land Statute, using notions of environment and sustainability to replace old legal terms, such as "satisfactory levels of productivity" with the expression "rational and adequate use" (Marés 2003: 194).

Article 225 of the Constitution also established environmental rights, originating in the notion of the environment as a common good, or a "good of common use", stating that "everyone has the right to an ecologically balanced environment" and "imposing both to public power and to society the duty of defending and preserving it for present and future generations". The constitutional mandate imposes a duty toward the environment, not only on public authorities but on each individual[8] (Sauer and França 2012: 295). As such, land must fulfill not only a social function, but a social-environmental function (Sauer and França 2012: 295). The "rational and appropriate use" should not be interpreted based exclusively on the notion of productivity (Article 185, II) – an interpretation that would confuse and distort the concept of social function (Martins 1994; Marés 2003).

This social-environmental function is an important constitutional innovation in the legal sphere. Yet, it has been challenged by historical land concentration and reduced to its economic and productive aspects, or land as means and place of production (Sauer 2013). The rational and appropriate use of land has been interpreted by its economic dimension in the 1993 Law no. 8,629, as well as by judicial decisions in which the only criterion used for land expropriation for agrarian reform is an assessment by the National Institute of Colonization and Agrarian Reform (INCRA) as to whether the land is or is not put to productive use (Sauer 2013).

In the drafting disputes, intentionally carried out by the representatives of private land owners in 1988 (Martins 1994), Article 185, Item II (Brasil 2014) introduced the notion of "productive land" into the constitutional text (Marés 2003). Such an insertion was "doubly misleading", as it has led to "full ambiguity in the definition of property subject to expropriation" (Martins 1994: 90). While confirming the social function of land (Art. 186), the Constitution also provided a protection from expropriation (Marés 2003: 194). This device has been interpreted and used in reverse, leading to a situation in which "if the land does not fulfill its social function, but is considered productive, it cannot be expropriated" (Marés 2003: 119). Thus, more than merely ambiguous, the notion that land should be "productive" "allowed an interpretation and legal practice fully reversing the constitutional spirit" (Sauer and França 2012: 297).

The notion of productive land provided the basis for judicial decisions and administrative actions in which productivity of any property acts suffices to protect it from any expropriation and seeing the social-environmental function of property as merely programmatic (Marés 2003; Alfonsin 2003).[9] As the private land owners managed to press the thesis that productive property is not subject to expropriation for agrarian reform, many have argued that the political process of 1987–1988 resulted in a defeat for the agrarian social movements, since they struggled to include land reform in the Constitution (Martins 1994). The legal practices and constitutional interpretations reduced the social function to its economic dimension, severely restricting the possibilities to carry out an agrarian reform in Brazil.

These reductive interpretations reinforced distinctions between concepts of land (means of production) and of territory (place of livelihood and of cultural and social identity). This distinction has been further enhanced by other constitutional articles, such as the recognition of the territorial rights of Quilombola communities (Article 68 of the Constitutional Provisions Acts – ADCT[10]) and indigenous groups (Article 231). These articles are based in an "original right" related to tradition, and indigenous or Quilombola territories are considered "traditionally occupied land" (Sauer 2011; Marés 2003), without any relation to a productive or economic dimension.

Consequently, the constitutional interpretation emphasizing production and productivity has led to a differentiation between the notions of land – seen only as a means and place of production – and territory as a place or land of identity, of self-recognition, and of historical occupation, etc. Such a distinction has ended up giving different meanings to struggles for land on one hand (often reduced to occupations of unproductive land as done by agrarian social movements) and for territorial rights on the other,[11] as well as to the resistance of traditional communities to the invasion of their lands (Sauer 2010: 298).

Besides the legal and political limitations imposed on the social-environmental function of land, Brazilian social, political and economic models have historically been based on large land ownership. They have taken on new dimensions throughout history, but have not changed significantly due to constant rearrangements of power and the formation of new political alliances between sectors of the industrial and financial ruling class and the rural oligarchy (Martins 1994).

It is important to acknowledge that, even in those cases of achievement through agrarian settlements, land rights are still under dispute. The landless families gained access to and use of the plots, but the land is still under a title issued to INCRA. Thus, the settlements are public land – a kind of usufruct by the families – and the debate over titling is ongoing. After the impeachment of President Dilma Rousseff, Michel Temer issued a Provisional Measure in 2016, approved by the Congress as Law no. 13.465 of 2017, allowing the individual titling of the plots of the settlement projects as private properties, removing the control of INCRA (Sauer and Leite 2017). Social movements – particularly the MST – are against this law, opposing the issue of individual titles, since it will end in privatization of the settlement projects. Historically, the social movements have supported a particular version of titling referred to as "real concession of use" or "concession right of use" (as part of "use with collective and social interest"), which is conceived of as permanent tenure and use – including the inherited or handed-down right – but without rights of disposal or sale (Tartuce 2014; Diniz 2010).

However, the struggles are not restricted to the demand for land access and use and the control of territories. There are also conflicts targeting political exclusion and social marginalization, which have been present in the modernization process, alongside increasing agricultural production (Martins 2002). These struggles therefore are eminently political, not just economic in nature: they are struggles for land, citizenship, social inclusion and democracy (Sauer 2010). Consequently, social mobilizations, struggles and the achievements of peasants, landless families, Quilombola and traditional communities, indigenous people and rural populations must be seen as part of social processes of "reinvention" of the countryside in Brazil (Sauer 2010). The struggle for land materializes this re-creation, adding new elements and perspectives to life in rural areas, creating new perspectives on use, access, property and the tenure of land (Almeida 2011; Sauer 2012).

3. Land accesses and uses: property and tenure regimes

The right to property is an institutional law with deep constitutional roots, stated as a fundamental right (Diniz 2010; Tartuce 2014; Costa 1998). Using the classic divisions of civil law, property is considered a "real right" that guarantees the legal faculties "of using, enjoying, disposing and recovering something" (Diniz 2010: 848). It is also "a power provided by the social group for using property taken as physical and moral goods of life" (Bevilaqua 2003: 127). According to Article 1228 of the 2002 Civil Code, "property rights must be exercised in accordance with their economic and social purposes and so that they are preserved in accordance with the provisions of a special law, the flora, the fauna, the natural beauty, ecological balance, and historical and artistic heritage while avoiding air and water pollution".

There are other real rights – such as usufruct, surface, servitude, use, special use concession for housing purposes, concession right of use, among others – but property is *par excellence* the paradigmatic one (Tartuce 2014: 900). The reference to property rights includes secondary rights species. Tenure does not fit in this list of real rights, as it is the externalization of power and control over a thing. It is, therefore, "the factual domain that a person carries over a thing" (Tartuce 2014: 861). According to Article 1996 of the Civil Code, a tenure right is that of that person who is exercising, fully or not, a property right. Thus, the person has the appearance of being the owner, while he or she is not legally the owner.

The discussion about property and tenure rights surpasses legal categories and goes beyond the understanding of land rights as a literal notarized title or judicial act but, in a broader sense, as procedures and rights that have been called into dispute. Thus, land struggles have caused variations in land access, use, enjoyment, disposal and the recovery of things, especially "goods of the physical and moral life" (Bevilaqua 2003: 127). The axiological and social breadth of land claims recognize that property and tenure rights are regulated in the legal world, but that they are being reinvented and realized through social and political disputes. Therefore, different property and tenure regimes are affected and reshaped by social relations, and their limits and practices move between formal (or written) rights, hybrid forms and customary norms. Social categories and different uses of land have resulted in collective property, permanent tenure, temporary tenure and a common-use system for cropping. There are collective (or communitarian) uses of common land, open use of water resources and other concessions, such as free lending (Bevilaqua 2003).

There are also "mix regimes" that overlap communitarian traditional use of land, such as environmental preservation units, and indigenous land or land managed by Quilombola or other traditional communities (Almeida 2006: 60). In all situations, the 1988 Constitution provides usufruct and tenure rights to indigenous people. A land, traditionally occupied by an indigenous group, constitutes a State property (Article 20, XI, of the Constitution), while the tenure and usufruct of land resources, such as soil, animals, plants, rivers and lakes (Article 231, §2) are part of indigenous rights. Articles 20 and 231 confirm the permanent character of the tenure recognized to indigenous peoples and the exclusive usufruct they benefit from.

Traditional occupation has some benefits offered specifically to indigenous populations, including the collective use of land resources and the permanent and continuous use of the physical and cultural spaces over successive generations. Pure usufruct rules are unsatisfactory, however, since according to civil standards they are always temporary, strictly personal and not transferable (Bevilaqua 2003). Indigenous rights cannot be defined by these rules, creating not only a special kind of land use, the "indigenous usufruct", but also a specific way of affectation with "constitutional allocation to specific purposes" (Farias and Rosenvald 2008: 577).[12]

The indigenous tenure regime is even more peculiar, since it is not related to just any land, but to the land "traditionally occupied" with ties to historical claims and struggles around ethnic identity and recognition. After the process of identification, recognition, demarcation and ratification (processes regulated by Decree 1775 of 1996), the resulting regime provides indigenous territory with a usufruct of the land and its resources. The land thus demarcated has the nature of a federal public good, but at the same time it is the source of private, continuous and collective tenure rights (Farias and Rosenvald 2008). This intricate arrangement is not a legal formulation, nor is it an ideal or permanent solution. It is instead a legal regime "built from reality" (Souza Filho 2010: 121) and the outcome of territorial disputes, cultural symbols and ethnical struggles.

Special tenure and usufruct regimes are also the result of lands that serve non-uniform purposes. In the same territory, there are lands that serve different purposes with complementary uses, such as indigenous occupation and environmental protection. These uses generate different rights, like land "occupied on a permanent basis" by indigenous people or a traditional community, but also indispensable to "environmental preservation" and essential to "physical and cultural reproduction" (Gallois 2004: 37). Tenure or use regimes coexist with different spatial logics, since "it is not the nature of the indigenous societies to establish precise (geographic) boundaries for their territories and ways of living" (Oliveira Filho 1996: 9). Formally recognizing land as an indigenous territory results in an ethnic and cultural appropriation, which leads to a new concept of tenure, distinct from the (classic) State's ownership. Thus, there is a tension between the notion of "indigenous land" – as part of political and legal processes conducted by the State – and of "indigenous territory". The latter is constituted as part of the internal social, political and ethnic-cultural processes, created in a relationship between a certain (ethnic) group and its place of life or territory (Gallois 2004: 39).

Besides indigenous rights, Article 68 of the Constitutional Provisions Acts (ADCT) ensures the land ownership of Quilombola communities. Based on Decree no. 4887/2003, Quilombola ownership is established by federal administrative procedures,[13] including an administrative act allowing the INCRA to demarcate, title and register the land, establishing the limits of the territory (Costa 1998). Quilombola ownership of land is granted by collective titling, issued in the name of the legal community association. Additionally, the land is affected by clauses of imprescriptibility and protection from seizure (Normative Instruction, no. 57 of 2009). On the other hand, if a Quilombola territory or any other traditional community land is located in an environmentally protected area, national security area, national border strip or on indigenous land, there will be a coexistence to ensure the sustainability of the communities and reconciliation with public interests (Almeida 2006).

It is important to note an even more specific regime for functional, used land, especially the concept of conservation units of sustainable use. Federal Law no. 9.985, of 2000, implementing Article 225 of the Constitution, establishes the National System of Conservation Units (SNUC). The SNUC establishes criteria and standards for the creation and management of environmental conservation units in federal, state and local levels of governments. According to this system, environmental preservation areas (or conservation units) include "fully protected areas" – "untouchable" territories such as national forests and parks – and "sustainable use areas" (or the conservation units of sustainable use) that include human dwelling and use (Calegare *et al.* 2014).

Conservation units of sustainable use were created to reconcile conservation with the sustainable use of nature, regulating human presence in protected areas (Calegare *et al.* 2014).[14] Seven categories regulate human presence in the territories, allowing use of traditional populations through management forms with low impact to nature of already occupied land (zoning with proper management of forest remnants and the enforcement of environmental laws). These different categories of conservation units of sustainable use include the Extractive Reserve (Resex), which is the most well-known (Calegare *et al.* 2014), as well as the Sustainable Development Reserve (RDS), the Unit for Sustainable Use and others that offer full environmental protection. These are under the management of the Chico Mendes Institute for Conservation of the Biodiversity (ICMBio) aiming to oversee the management and governance of territories, linking traditional knowledge to conservation goals while respecting culture, territorial rights, and the use of natural resources by traditional populations (Calegare *et al.* 2014: 123).

Aside from the conservation concerns, there are also several land use modalities that have been created to combine human occupation with environmental protection. In response to the demands and struggles of local movements, particularly in the Amazon, the government recently created the Sustainable Development Project (PDS), the Forest Settlement Project (PAF) and the Agro-extractive Settlement Project (PAE). Despite their differences, they all coexist under the national agrarian reform program and are placed under the management of INCRA with the purpose of combining land use and environmental projection (Sauer and França 2012).

Again, there are many cases of overlapping uses and purposes for lands, and the solutions have resulted in a great complexity of property and tenure rights. There is the possibility of "double affectation", resulting in a re-categorization of the legal regime for environmental protection as sustainable use and in "shared management" of the territory (Figueiredo 2013). Double affectation and shared management involve special forms of access, use and exploitation of the land, requiring plans for traditional use, terms of commitment, zoning instruments and terms of conduct adjustment (Figueiredo 2013).

Since the 1988 Constitution, struggles and claims for land and the advent of "several collective identities have become a legal precept to legitimize territorialities in specific ethnic constructions" (Almeida 2006: 28).[15] Property and tenure boundaries have unfolded into regimes that show profound differences in terms of claims, access, use and enjoyment, as well as control and disposal of the land. The social and cultural differences are not recognized only through socio-environmental function, nor are they restricted to legal classifications. Different forms of living and dwelling on land – as they are related to land use, work, living practices, celebrations, festivals and other cultural practices – could fall as part of "Brazilian cultural heritage" and considered "goods of material and immaterial nature", including ways or modes of "creating, doing and living", according to the Constitution (Article 216, II of the Constitution). Possibilities and perceptions of property and tenure that were conceived as multiple regimes exist as variations in the legislation and in social practices. They make reference to social (and ethnic) identities and memories of various groups that are as part of the country's "cultural heritage" (Gallois 2004).

4. Conclusion

Historically, the concentration of land, and more recently the increasing of demand for land and the expansion of agricultural frontier in the Amazon and Cerrado regions, have been the main causes of conflicts, struggles and claims for territorial rights in Brazil. These struggles (involving different political subjects and social actors) resulted in legal innovations, in particular the adoption of the socio-environmental function of land by the 1988 Brazilian Constitution. Despite all remaining problems and conflicts, and the ongoing disputes related to land and territorial rights, these struggles and claims resulted in victories and achievements through recognition or creation of agrarian reform settlements, indigenous lands, Quilombola territories and sustainable use protected areas.

These different ways of access, uses and control (or management) of land allow for the construction of social and ethnic identities of rural workers (or peasants or even family farmers), indigenous people, Quilombola and other traditional communities like rubber tappers, extractive communities, and Babaçu nut breakers, among others – indeed, the relationship to land is a crucial component of such identities. These different accesses and relations to territories are (re)shaping land rights, beyond legal changes in property regimes; they are affirming the existence of different properties and tenure regimes.

Propriety and tenure regimes are based on the existing legal framework, but they go beyond the legal aspects, especially because of the social dynamics and adaptations, resistances and reinvention of accesses and uses of land, constructing territories. Different social and cultural groups, in struggles to access and use land, invent and recreate property and tenure rights, putting law into question, or at least, creating "hybrid figures" that transcend the purism of strict formal measures. Different access, use and control of land, including community and cooperation projects, combining agricultural and extractive activities (agro-extractive activities), popular management of natural resources, and various other economic, social, and environmental uses demand different regulations and rights, forcing legal notions and formal concepts of property to be rethought.

The multiplicity of land relationships, kinships, territorialities, ancestralities, traditions and cultural practices of a social identity and political subject are fundamental factors for inventing and reinventing places with respect to property and tenure rights. Such diversity has been reflected in regimes that may vary on a case-by-case basis and that transcend the purism of legal forms by creating hybrid figures (Castro 2013). They are characterized by the cultural diversity, creativity and adaptation capacities of social groups, which show that the law, territorial rights and land are spaces of multiple disputes, claims and struggles (Sauer 2012).

The struggles, achievements and accesses to land are crucial social processes that create territory, highlighting a relationship with land as beyond a means and place of production. The involved subjects claim rights that transcend notions of private property, in which property, tenure and other forms of access are not restricted to an economic notion. Summarizing, there are ongoing struggles to move out from a "legal monoculture" of property law to socio-biodiverse practices of cultural accesses, uses, controls and tenures of land, leading to self-determination and to the constitution of rights to land and territories of life in Brazil.

Notes

1 Martins (2002: 326) stated that social categories such as "peasantry" and "peasant" do not represent all "the rural subjects", since they are "differentiated in terms of background, culture, and class". We agree that different territorial practices are at play here, each deserving specific conceptual and legal treatments. However, the author may be

going too far in his criticism condemning the social movements, particularly the MST for an attempt "to amalgamate" the rural population "into a uniform 'Brazilian peasantry' with a uniform political interest" (Martins 2002: 327).

2 Brazil issued the Decree No. 6040 in 2007, defining traditional peoples and communities as those "culturally differentiated groups, who recognize themselves as such and who have their own forms of social organization, occupying and using territories and natural resources as conditions for their cultural, social, religious, ancestral and economic reproduction, using knowledge, innovations and practices generated and transmitted by tradition" (*Decreto 6040. Política Nacional de Desenvolvimento Sustentável dos Povos e Comunidades Tradicionais*, Article 3, available at www.planalto.gov.br/ccivil_03/_ato2007-2010/2007/decreto/d6040.htm).

3 According to Fernandes *et al.* (2012: 37), the hegemonic narratives put the agribusiness as "a totality, a self-contained system composed of financial sources, scientific knowledge, technological innovation, hired labour, agricultural production, animal husbandry, industrial processing, and marketing".

4 According to Decree 4.887 of 2003, Quilombola community is the ethnic-racial group, self-identified as such based on black African ancestry, built historically as resistance to oppression, with traditional territorial relations, mainly the land used to guarantee its physical, social, economic and cultural reproduction.

5 In spite of the important achievements, there remains much to be done, since there are over a thousand processes pending in the INCRA. This Institute is asked to recognize land rights of more than 21 thousand Quilombola families, whose traditional occupation of land encompasses an area of 19.541.000 hectares. Also, while 98.5 percent of the already demarked territory is located in Amazon, indigenous peoples' rights are severely threatened in areas all over the country.

6 Legally, "the key element of the definition of *traditional community* is the *self-definition* or *self-recognition* as a socially differentiated group with an identity of its own and a close relation to a specific territory and land" (Sauer 2012: 94). The struggles on which such self-definition depend are not restricted to keeping "traditional peasant values" (for further discussion, see Sauer 2012).

7 The MST's mobilizations and massive land occupations (Stédile and Fernandes 1999) are central in the discussion on land and territory. Though the MST did not invent land occupations as a means of resistance, but its occupations became more organized and massive, forcing responses from the government and transforming local struggles into a national-level political issue (Martins 1994; Sauer 2010).

8 This constitutional innovation has become a trend in subsequent legislation, since the Civil Code of 2002 also comprised the social-environmental function (Article 1228).

9 The Law no. 8,629 of 1993 establishes two indicators for evaluating land productivity; the "degree of land use" (GUT) and the "degree of exploration efficiency" (GEE), and the property is "productive" if it achieves both, with no clear references to other constitutional dimensions or aspects of the social function (Sauer 2011).

10 Roughly, these ADCTs are constitutional transition rules, in which "there is no division of matter into Titles, Chapters and Sections", and the different subjects and themes are treated in a "residual form" (HORTA 1995: 321).

11 The territory is a continuum of "practical" and "functional" political and economic domain, but also a "cultural and symbolic appropriation" (Haesbaert 2012: 96). Beyond just a function or tenure, it is both real and symbolic in different combinations of tenure, use and control, and it is "intimately linked to how people use land as they are themselves organized in space and how they give meaning to the place" (Haesbaert 2010: 22).

12 Almost all indigenous people lost large portions of their territories in Brazil, fragmented into plots, invaded and expropriated, in spite of their "original right" over their lands, according to the Constitution. In several cases, demarked land is invaded

generating new claims and conflicts (Gallois 2004: 39), but, as mentioned before (see Table 1), there are over 112 million hectares of officially recognized and demarked as indigenous land.

13   With a delay of 15 years, Article 68 was finally implemented by Decree no. 4.887/2003. However, since 2004, this Decree was under legal challenge by agribusiness representatives, but the Supreme Court ruled and reaffirmed its constitutionality in 2018. There are also over 215 different constitutional amendments pending in the Senate and/or Chamber of Deputies, aiming to transfer to the National Congress the responsibility for recognizing and demarcating traditional communities' lands.

14   Unfortunately, this system did not solve all the problems, since the creation of environmental protected land has "also generated evictions of local population, which caused conflicts with the local social groups and fostered supporting mobilizations by the civil society" (Calegare *et al.* 2014: 123).

15   The diversity of property, tenure, access, use, control, and possession has been consolidated by state legal measures like the "backyard fields" for communitarian pastures in Bahia; the coastal fishing communities and river dwellers and fishing communities; extractive groups of the Amazon forest; the common and communitarian uses of land – the so-called faxinais – in the Paraná; the "Free Babaçu palm" law in Maranhão, among other regulations and legal decisions (Almeida 2006: 28).

References

Alfonsin, J.W. 2003. *O acesso à terra como conteúdo de direitos humanos fundamentais à alimentação e à moradia.* Porto Alegre, Sérgio Antonio Fabris.

Almeida, A.W.B. 2006. Quilombolas, Quebradeiras de Coco Babaçu, Indígenas, Ciganos, Faxinaleses e Ribeirinhos: movimentos sociais e a nova tradição. *Revista Proposta*, vol. 29, n. 107/108, 25–38.

Almeida, A.W.B. 2011. A reconfiguração das agroestratégias: novo capítulo da guerra ecológica. In: Sauer, S. and Almeida, W. (orgs.). *Terras e territórios na Amazônia: demandas, desafios e perspectivas.* Brasília, Editora da UnB, 27–44.

Baletti, B. 2014. Saving the Amazon? Sustainable soy and the new extractivism. *Environment and Planning A*, vol. 46, 5–25.

Bevilaqua, C. 2003. *Direito das Coisas.* Brasília, Senado Federal.

Boito, A. and Berringer, T. 2014. Social classes, neodevelopmentalism, and Brazilian foreign policy under presidents Lula and Dilma. *Latin American Perspectives*, vol. 41, 94–109.

Calegare, M.G.A., Higuchi, M.I.G. and Bruno, A.C.S. 2014. Traditional peoples and communities: From protected areas to the political visibility of social groups having ethnical and collective identity. *Ambiente & Sociedade*, vol. 17, n. 3, 115–134.

Castro, L.F.P. 2013. *Dimensões e lógicas do arrendamento rural na agricultura familiar* (Master thesis). Universidade de Brasília, Brasília.

Costa, W.M. 1998. *O Estado e as políticas territoriais no Brasil.* São Paulo, Contexto.

Deere, C.D. and Medeiros, L.S. 2007. Agrarian reform and poverty reduction: Lessons from Brazil. In: Akram-Lodhi, A.H., Borras, S.M., Jr. and Kay, C. (eds.). *Land, poverty and livelihoods in an era of globalization: Perspectives from developing and transition countries.* London and New York, Routledge, 80–118.

Delgado, G. 2013. Economia do agronegócio (anos 2000) como pacto do poder com os donos da terra. In: *Revista Reforma Agrária.* Brasília, ABRA, special edition, 61–68.

Diniz, M.H. 2010. *Código Civil Anotado.* São Paulo, Ed. Saraiva.

Fairbairn, M. 2014. 'Like gold with yield': Evolving intersections between farmland and finance. *The Journal of Peasant Studies*, vol. 41, n. 5, 777–795.

Farias, C.C. and Rosenvald, N. 2008. *Direitos Reais*. Rio de Janeiro, Lumen Juris.

Fernandes, B.M., Welch, C.A. and Gonçalves, E.C. 2012. *Land Governance in Brazil. Framing the Debate Series*, no. 2, Rome, ILC.

Figueiredo, L.M. 2013. Populações tradicionais e meio ambiente: espaços territoriais especialmente protegidos com dupla afetação. In: Vitorelli, E. (org.). *Temas Aprofundados do Ministério Público Federal*. Salvador, Juspodivm, 263–293.

FUNAI – Fundação Nacional do Índio. 2015. *Terras Indígenas no Brasil*. Brasília, Funai. www.funai.gov.br/index.php/indios-no-brasil/terras-indigenas.

Gallois, D.T. 2004. Terras ocupadas? Territórios? Territorialidades? In: Fany, R. (org.). *Terras Indígenas & Unidades de Conservação da Natureza*. São Paulo, ISA, 37–41.

Haesbaert, R. 2010. Território e multiterritorialidade: um debate. *GEOgraphia*. www.uff.br/geographia/ojs/index.php/geographia/article/view/213/205.

Haesbaert, R. 2012. *O mito da desterritorialização: do fim dos territórios à multiterritorialidade*. Rio de Janeiro, Bertrand Brasil.

Horta, R.M. 1995. *Estudos de Direito Constitucional*. Belo Horizonte, Del Rey editora.

IBGE – Instituto Brasileiro de Geografia e Estatística. 2009. *Censo agropecuário 2006*. Rio de Janeiro, IBGE. www.ibge.gov.br/home/estatistica/economia/agropecuaria/censoagro/default.shtm.

ICMBio – Instituto Chico Mendes de Conservação da Biodiversidade. 2014. *Unidades de Conservação no Brasil*. Brasília, ICMBio. www.icmbio.gov.br/portal/unidades-de-conservacao.

INCRA – Instituto Nacional de Colonização e Reforma Agrária. 2015. *Quilombos no Brasil*. Brasília, INCRA. www.incra.gov.br/quilombola.

INCRA – Instituto Nacional de Colonização e Reforma Agrária. 2018. *Informações gerais sobre os assentamentos da Reforma Agrária*. Brasília, INCRA. http://painel.incra.gov.br/sistemas/index.php.

Marés, C.F. 2003. *A função social da terra*. Porto Alegre, Sergio Antonio Fabris Ed.

Martins, J.S. 1994. *O poder do atraso: Ensaios de sociologia da história lenta*. São Paulo, Ed. Hucitec.

Martins, S.J. 2002. Representing the peasantry? Struggles for/about land in Brazil. *Journal of Peasant Studies*, vol. 29, n. 3–4, 300–335.

Medeiros, L.S. 1993. *Reforma agrária: concepções, controvérsias e questões*. Rio de Janeiro, CPDA/UFRRJ. http://www.oocities.org/spaprado/reformaagrariaquestoes.html.

MDA – Ministério do Desenvolvimento Agrário. 2005. *II Plano Nacional de Reforma Agrária: paz, produção e qualidade de vida no meio rural*. Brasília, INCRA.

Oliveira Filho, J.P. 1996. Viagens de ida, de volta e outras viagens: os movimentos migratórios e as sociedades indígenas. *Revista Travessia*, vol. 9, n. 24, 5–9.

Petras, J. and Veltmeyer, H. 2001. Are Latin American peasant movements still a force for change? Some new paradigms revisited. *Journal of Peasant Studies*, vol. 28, n. 2, 83–118.

Sauer, S. 2010. *Terra e modernidade: a reinvenção do campo brasileiro*. São Paulo, Expressão Popular.

Sauer, S. 2011. Considerações finais: apontamentos para a continuidade do (em)debate territorial. In: Sauer, S. and Almeida, W. (orgs.). *Terras e territórios na Amazônia: demandas, desafios e perspectivas*. Brasília, Editora da UnB, 411–422.

Sauer, S. 2012. Land and territory: Meanings of land between modernity and tradition. *Agrarian South: A Journal of Political Economy*. Sage, vol. 1, n. 1, 85–107.

Sauer, S. 2013. Reflexões esparsas sobre a questão agrária e a demanda por terra no século XXI. In: Stédile, J.P. (ed.). *A questão agrária no Brasil: debate sobre a situação e perspectivas da reforma agrária na década de 2000.* São Paulo, Expressão Popular, 167–187.

Sauer, S. 2017. Rural Brazil during the Lula administrations agreements with agribusiness and disputes in Agrarian policies. *Latin American Perspectives*, online first, 1–19.

Sauer, S. 2018. Soy expansion into the agricultural frontiers of the Brazilian Amazon: The agribusiness economy and its social and environmental conflicts. *Land Use Policy*, vol. 79, 326–338.

Sauer, S. and França, F.C. 2012. Código Florestal, função socioambiental da terra e soberania alimentar. *Caderno CRH*, vol. 25, n. 65, Salvador, May/August, 285–307.

Sauer, S. and Leite, A.Z. 2017. Medida Provisória 759: Descaminhos da reforma agrária e legalização de terras no Brasil. *Retratos de Assentamentos*, vol. 20, n. 1, 14–40.

Sauer, S. and Leite, S.P. 2012. Agrarian structure, foreign investment in land, and land prices in Brazil. *The Journal of Peasants Studies*, vol. 39, n. 3–4, 873–898.

Souza Filho, C.F.M. 2010. *O Renascer dos Povos Indígenas para o Direito.* Curitiba, Juruá.

Stédile, J.P. and Fernandes, B.M. 1999. *Brava gente: A trajetória do MST e a luta pela terra no Brasil.* São Paulo, Fundação Perseu Abramo.

Tartuce, F. 2014. *Manual de direito civil.* Rio de Janeiro, Forense; São Paulo, Método.

Welch, C.A. and Sauer, S. 2015. Rural unions and the struggle for land in Brazil. *The Journal of Peasant Studies*, vol. 42, n. 6, 1109–1135.

8 The right to land and territory

New human right and collective action frame[1]

Priscilla Claeys

The commodification of natural resources, and especially the conversion of land into a product that can be bought, sold, leased or exchanged on markets, is one of the founding characteristics of capitalism (Bernstein 2010, 23). Marx and Polanyi, for example, showed that the enclosure of land played a key role in the development of capitalism in England in the sixteenth and seventeenth centuries (Vergara-Camus 2012, 1153). Today, an increasing proportion of the common resources upon which rural communities depend is being commoditized. This historical process of commodification is far from complete however: in many parts of the world, the establishment of private property rights on the land, enshrined in law and enforced by the state, is not yet a reality. It is challenged by social actors, particularly in the rural South (Bernstein 2010, 98–102), but also in the North (Transnational Institute 2013).

The pressures on the land seem more numerous every day, as the result of urbanization, tourism, industrialization or mining. In addition, land has been transformed into an opportunity for transnational investment, as shown by the growing number of large-scale acquisitions of land, a phenomenon widely documented since the 2007–2008 food crisis and reinforced by the financialization of agriculture (Clapp 2014). States have played an active role in this process, often facilitating the appropriation of nature through legislative reforms to encourage companies, pension funds and other states to invest in land (Künnemann and Monsalve Suárez 2013, 129).

The gradual appropriation of nature has had devastating consequences for the rural world. At the heart of the global food crisis, the transnational agrarian movement La Via Campesina (LVC) denounced "the ferocious offensive of capital and of transnational corporations (TNCs) to take over land and natural assets (water, forests, minerals, biodiversity, land, etc.), that translates into a privatizing war to steal the territories and assets of peasants and indigenous peoples" (Vía Campesina 2008b). Resistance against the appropriation of nature, especially land, has been at the center of La Via Campesina's struggles since its inception in 1993 (Vía Campesina 1996). One of the objectives of food sovereignty, the movement's principal demand, is to ensure that the rights to use and manage lands, territories, waters, seeds, livestock and biodiversity are in the hands of those of us who produce food (Monsalve Suárez 2012).

This contribution offers a critical examination of the emergence of the "right to land and territory", both as a collective action frame deployed by transnational peasant movements and as a new human right in international law. It explores the various ways in which agrarian movements are using the human rights framework to question the establishment of "absolute private property rights" over land, and restore "political limits on access to, and exploitation of, land and resources" (Vergara-Camus 2012, 1137). It argues that peasant movements are claiming a new human right to land through a combination of institutional and extra-institutional channels, in an effort not only to achieve increased protection of peasants' land rights (against and by the state), but also to advance an alternative conception of human rights that resonates with their worldviews and allows for the development of food sovereignty alternatives, including outside the state.

This article integrates insights from the sociology of rights, sociology of social movements and rural sociology. It is based on more than 115 semi-directed interviews of leaders and members of the transnational food sovereignty movement, and notably with La Via Campesina activists in Mexico, Guatemala, Nicaragua, Canada, France, Belgium and Indonesia, and on participant observation at more than 65 meetings with agrarian activists in the previously mentioned countries as well as in Haiti, Nepal, India, the Democratic Republic of the Congo, Bolivia and various United Nations (UN) bodies, notably the Committee on World Food Security (CFS) and the Human Rights Council (HRC), between April 2008 and November 2014.

After describing how La Via Campesina (LVC) activists have used the human rights framework to formulate land claims (1), this article discusses activists' efforts to achieve the recognition and protection of land rights, both through institutional channels (2), and at the grassroots level (3). It focuses on two UN processes where LVC has succeeded in generating debate on land rights and contributed to generating new international norms dealing with access to resources: the Human Rights Council and the Committee on World Food Security. It ends with a discussion of the various frames that are currently deployed by La Via Campesina activists in ongoing land struggles (4) and offers some concluding thoughts (5).

1. La Via Campesina, land struggles and human rights framing

The transnational movement La Via Campesina includes more than 164 national and sub-national organizations from 79 different countries, as of the last International Conference of June 2013. It developed in the early 1990s as farmers from various organizations from Central and South America, North America, Asia and Europe started sharing experiences and set to create a network to articulate a common response to the wave of neoliberal reforms that had struck their regions in the 1980s, leading to a drastic decline in their livelihoods (Desmarais 2007). Over the last twenty years, LVC activists have mobilized around a range of issues including agricultural trade liberalization and the World Trade Organization (WTO), genetically modified organisms (GMOs), agrarian reform and development projects (dams, mining concessions, nature reserves), strongly contributing to the visibility of the global justice movement (Pleyers 2010). More recently, LVC has turned its attention to issues of climate justice (Bullard and Müller 2012), agro-ecology (Rosset and Martínez-Torres 2012), land and resource grabbing and the articulation of all three.

Access to land was a key theme of the parallel forum to the World Food Summit in 1996, which saw the participation of several La Via Campesina activists. In 1999, LVC launched the Global Campaign for Agrarian Reform (GCAR), in partnership with the international human rights organization Foodfirst Information and Action Network (FIAN) that defends the right to food worldwide. The GCAR denounced the land titling policies of the World Bank and its "market assisted land reform" programmes for privatizing land and leading to the reconcentration of the land. On the occasion of the WTO ministerial summit of Seattle, the same year, the network called for the right of each country to "prohibit imports in order to protect domestic production and to implement Agrarian Reform providing peasants and small to medium-sized producers with access to land" (Vía Campesina 1999). In the years following, LVC engaged in dialogue with other constituencies – nomadic pastoralists, fisher folk and indigenous peoples – on the various meanings and functions attached to the land, for example on the occasion of the Land, Territory and Dignity Forum organized in the margins of the 2006 International Conference on Agrarian Reform and Rural Development (ICARRD) (Rosset 2013). It also tried to define its own vision of agrarian reform, integrating lessons learned from past agrarian reform processes and linking the land issue to the broader issues of food sovereignty and the environment (Borras 2008).

The issue of access to land has become even more central after the food crisis of 2007–2008, in a context increasingly marked by land grabbing and climate change. Gathered at the occasion of the World Summit on Food Security organized by FAO in June 2008, LVC and other social organizations, demanded that an end be put to the "new enclosure movement" that converts "arable, pastoral, and forest lands for the production of fuel" (International Planning Committee for Food Sovereignty (IPC) 2008). As anticipated by Borras, the major policy battle around land policy today is being fought around the twofold issue of "formalization" of land rights and "privatization" of remaining public lands (Borras 2008, 281). The terms of the global land reform debates have radically changed, forcing La Via Campesina to think beyond land reform, and the GCAR to reassess its strategy. This, in essence, was the objective of the International Workshop and Seminar "Agrarian Reform and Defense of Land and Territory in the 21st Century: The Challenge and the Future" organized by the movement in Indonesia in 2012 (Vía Campesina 2012). At the heart of the discussions were the need to expand the scope of the GCAR to better take into account the issue of access to land in the North, the specific challenges faced by indigenous peoples in the defence of their territories, and how to react to resource grabbing and counteragrarian reform processes.

To build a common agenda for a widely diverse (politically, economically and culturally) membership and to overcome North-South divisions, LVC has widely relied on human rights "framing". The movement has framed its main organizational frame, food sovereignty as a new collective right (Claeys 2012b) – the right of peoples "to define their own food and agriculture systems" (Nyéléni Food Sovereignty Forum 2007b) – and, to a large extent, has framed its struggles over access to land and control over resources as human rights issues. Framing – the production of "meaning" for participants and their opponents – is one of the main activities of social movements: it is used to diagnose certain situations as problematic, propose solutions and call activists to action. The "rights master frame"[2] has been mobilized by a wide range of movements (Benford and Snow 2000), for it facilitates the international exportation of claims (Agrikoliansky 2010) and helps formulate demands in a way that does not put forward particular or sectorial interests (Mooney and Hunt 1996). These factors help explain the appeal of the rights master frame for LVC activists, who faced the challenge of having to articulate demands emerging from widely different local, cultural, political and social contexts.

Human rights framing was at the core of the Global Campaign for Agrarian Reform (GCAR).[3] La Via Campesina and FIAN International jointly framed land claims in terms of rights in an effort to articulate agrarian issues and human rights law and methodologies (Borras 2008). Exchanges between the two networks led, in the first years of the campaign, to the collective elaboration of what could be described as a "right to agrarian reform" frame, although the term was not formally used. Efforts to give life and content to this right soon revealed important differences in how the two networks conceived of human rights. For LVC, the objective of the GCAR was to defend the right to produce, to resist the creation of land markets by the World Bank, to demand recognition of the social function of the land and to preserve/promote collective forms of land use/tenure (Vía Campesina 2006). For FIAN International, which had documented numerous land conflicts since its creation in 1986, and had supported local communities in their struggle for the land, mostly through letter campaigns, the challenge was twofold. It was, first, to emphasize that excluding food producers from accessing the productive resources that they rely on was a human rights violation, and, second, to conceptualize the implementation of redistributive land reforms as an obligation of states (Windfuhr 2000).

From a framing perspective, these two objectives were somewhat in tension and their articulation was no easy task. To highlight the importance of securing access to land to ensure the livelihood of rural communities, FIAN deployed a "right to feed oneself " frame (Künnemann 1984), in particular in its communications to the general public and potential allies. This frame aimed at pushing for an agrarian interpretation of the right to food and at clarifying that the right to food was not to be understood as the right to be fed. In its communications to states, however, FIAN always made explicit reference to the right to food as recognized by the UN, and almost systematically recalled the obligations that derived from the International Covenant on Economic, Social and Cultural Rights (ICESCR). The "right to food" frame enabled the organization to remind states of their commitments under international human rights law and imbued the demands it made of states with the legitimacy of internationally agreed language.

This strategy proved partly successful, as it allowed FIAN to use the law to push for a progressive interpretation of it.[4] Thanks to its "right to feed oneself" frame, for example, FIAN managed to influence normative developments of the right to food in ways that recognize its agrarian dimensions.[5] At the same time, the "right to feed oneself" frame can be considered as a "failed frame" (Heitlinger 1996) in the sense that it lacked resonance. It was brought to the attention of La Via Campesina organizations in the early 1990s, but was, interestingly, not picked up by LVC activists, despite its striking proximity with the then-emerging "right to food sovereignty" frame. It was later dropped by the organization, in favour of the more universal "right to food" frame, which was perceived as able to better capture the nutritional dimensions of the right to food and the specific needs of the urban poor. The former Secretary General of FIAN comments: "You cannot replace the right to food with the right to feed oneself. . . . Via Campesina uses the point of view of producers . . . but they do not see themselves as having to solve this. . . . [T]he right to feed oneself was dropped from FIAN's vision and documents".[6]

While FIAN defended access to land as an essential component of the right to food, La Via Campesina did not confine its claims to the limits set by international human rights law. Rather, it framed its demands in terms of rights that did not enjoy legal recognition and were in that sense new, such as the "right to produce", the right "to be a peasant", and the "right to land and territory". Such claims indicated a departure from the social-democratic conception of rights (Stammers 1995) that is at the heart of the right to food and indicated the emergence of an alternative conception of human rights, characterized by a strong focus on the concept of responsibility and an emphasis on the interdependence of human beings and nature/their environment (Claeys 2012a). This excerpt from the synthesis report of the Nyeleni 2011 Food sovereignty European Forum is illustrative of this:

> Reclaiming the right to our Commons. We oppose and struggle against the commodification, financialisation and patenting of our commons, such as: land; farmers', traditional and reproducible seeds; livestock breeds and fish stocks; trees and forests; water; the atmosphere; and knowledge. Access to these should not be determined by markets and money. In using common resources, we must ensure the realisation of human rights and gender equality, and that society as a whole benefits. We also acknowledge our responsibility to use our Commons sustainably, while respecting the rights of mother earth. Our Commons should be managed through collective, democratic and community control.
>
> (Nyéléni Food Sovereignty Forum 2007a)

2. Institutional strategies to demand new (land) rights at the international level

La Via Campesina has sought recognition of new human rights dealing with access to land and resources in two international arenas: the Human Rights Council (HRC), where LVC has obtained that negotiations take place on a "Declaration on the Rights of Peasants and Other People Living in Rural Areas", and the Committee on World Food Security (CFS), where LVC has engaged in discussions on how to best secure tenure of land and support reinvestment in small-holder agriculture. Elsewhere, I have discussed the institutional trajectory of the new right to food sovereignty, with an emphasis on international trade and the right to participate in policy-making (Claeys 2015). This contribution focuses on the right of peoples to land and territory, leaving aside other important developments with regard to rights and resources, such as the recognition of farmers' rights over their seeds and biodiversity, notably at the FAO through the International Treaty on Plant Genetic Resources for Food and Agriculture (Batta Bjørnstad 2004).

One could wonder why LVC has put efforts into the creation of new human rights, whilst most movement activists perceive existing human rights as difficult to realize and almost impossible to enforce. Why not focus on implementation? Why not make (better) use of national, regional and international human rights protection mechanisms? For years, this issue was at the heart of tensions between LVC activists and human rights experts[7] who were concerned that the "proliferation" of new rights would threaten the consistency of the human rights framework (Alston 1984).

I argue that peasant movements have engaged in the creation of new human rights at the international level (Bob 2010) because such processes allow for "new interpretations and reconfigurations of meanings" to emerge (Idrus 2010, 91) and provide an arena where contestation can take place. Indeed, the two norm-setting processes I discuss later, both at the HRC and at the CFS, are indicative of the ability of agrarian movements to create and seize "legal opportunity structures" understood as a specific set of circumstances allowing a social movement to push through legal change (Israël 2003). The creation/seizing of such opportunities is important to analyze in view of what local and national peasant movements may experience or perceive as their inability to bring change in national settings. As other scholars have shown, failure to achieve the enforcement of state laws is often what drives activists to go global (Nash 2012). Peasant activists may decide to support international processes in the hope that these will help achieve goals set at the national level.[8] Indonesian activists, for example, hope that the Declaration on the Rights of Peasants will support their demands for agrarian reform in Indonesia (Konsorsium Pembaruan Agraria KPA 2013). Engagement in intergovernmental processes is therefore often characterized by a tension between the demand to be included as citizens (legal inclusion) and resistance against the state, a tension that has been well documented in the case of indigenous peoples' rights (Idrus 2010).

A. The Declaration on the Rights of Peasants at the Human Rights Council

The Declaration on the Rights of Peasants, adopted by LVC at its International Conference in Maputo in 2008, places a strong emphasis on land issues. Article 4 on the "right to land and territory", claims a wide range of new rights for peasants, such as:

- the "right to own land, collectively or individually, for their housing and farming";
- the "right to toil on their own land, and to produce agricultural products, to rear livestock, to hunt and gather, and to fish in their territories";
- the right to "manage, conserve and benefit from the forests";
- the right to "reject all forms of acquisitions of land and land conversion for economic purposes"; and
- the "right to security of tenure and not to be forcibly evicted from their lands and territories."

(Vía Campesina 2008a)

The first version of the Declaration on the Rights of Peasants was developed in 1999 in Indonesia. The Peasants' Rights Charter, as it was then called, was originally discussed by farmers, academics and NGO activists, in the framework of a participatory research project on integrated pest management conducted by the International Institute for Environment and Development (IIED) in the late 1990s. At the time, the main concern of farmers was to denounce the green revolution and corporate takeover of agriculture (Fakih, Rahardjo, and Pimbert 2003), but land issues were also at the forefront. In 2002, the Indonesian agrarian organization SPI brought the draft Declaration to the attention of the other member organizations of LVC in the region. The Declaration was later put on the agenda of the international working committee of LVC on human rights.

In recent years, LVC has actively worked to bring the Declaration to the Human Rights Council with the support of human rights experts and NGOs such as FIAN International and Centre Europe Tiers Monde (CETIM). These efforts have borne fruit. On September 23, 2012, the Council adopted a resolution on the "Promotion of the human rights of peasants and other people living in rural areas" sponsored by Bolivia, Cuba and South Africa. An inter-governmental working group was created with the mission to negotiate, finalize and submit to the Council a final draft Declaration, taking as basis for discussion the text proposed by LVC (Human Rights Council 2012) with some adjustments to improve the structure and make it more consistent with UN language (Golay 2009).

At the first session of the working group, in July 2013, experts were invited to discuss various aspects of the proposed Declaration, and states had the opportunity to express their views. On November 12, 2014, an informal consultation was held during which civil society[9] participants insisted on the need to ensure that the instrument protects not only peasants, but all people working in rural areas, and on the importance of guaranteeing access to resources. At the second session in February 2015, a new draft Declaration was presented by Ambassador Angelica Navarro of Bolivia, with a view to overcoming opposition by some HRC member states. In order to do this, the new draft uses agreed language wherever possible, i.e. it builds on recent developments in international human rights law, as well as advances in other relevant international fora, to formulate the new rights (to land, seeds, decent livelihoods) listed in the Declaration. This approach proved to be a decisive factor finally allowing the Declaration to be supported by a majority of the member states in the Human Rights Council, and finally, in December 2018, to be adopted by the United Nations General Assembly.[10]

The assertion of new rights to resources was the major stumbling block in the negotiations. For LVC, the rights to land, seeds, biodiversity and fair prices were to be central elements of the Declaration. For states reluctant to recognize new human rights for peasants, such as the European Union member states or the United States, the proposed right to land and right to seeds were amongst the most controversial because of the collective nature of the rights claimed, because their indeterminate content departs from existing standards and because of the challenges that their implementation would represent. These rights have also been criticized for being associated with and imposing a certain type of development model (Golay 2015).

B. Land issues at the Committee on World Food Security

In parallel, LVC has invested new arenas of global governance, such as the Committee on World Food Security (CFS), to actively contribute to the development of new international standards related to land issues, to a large extent grounded in human rights (McMichael 2014). Since its reform in 2009, the CFS has emerged as a central policy platform at the UN to address issues of food security, agriculture and nutrition. The CFS is an interesting arena due to the alternative governance model it offers (Duncan 2015). It includes as members and participants not only states, but also international financial institutions, international organizations, the private sector, philanthropic foundations and civil society.

The CFS represents a new institutional space within which peasant movements can formulate their claims. Through the "civil society mechanism (CSM)",[11] LVC has actively participated in the negotiations of Voluntary Guidelines on Responsible Governance of Tenure of Land, Fisheries and Forests in the Context of National Food Security (VGGT), which were endorsed by the CFS in May 2012. It has also been involved in the negotiations of Principles for Responsible Agricultural Investment (PRAI), which were adopted by the CFS in October 2014 in response to the phenomenon of land grabbing.

Most members of the Civil Society Mechanism positively assess progress made so far within the CFS, despite the fact that debates are often perceived as too technical and disconnected from on-the-ground realities. To many, participation in the negotiations on the VGGT demonstrated that civil society involvement in international standard-setting can make a difference, as it enabled the recognition of the "legitimate tenure rights" of rural communities over the lands and territories they depend on for their livelihoods (Paoloni and Onorati 2014). According to the VGGT, states should recognize and respect these rights, including informal and customary rights, and protect land rights holders in the context of land transfers, large-scale investments in land, and programmes designed to adapt to and mitigate the impacts of climate change. States should also facilitate land reform processes where necessary (Committee on World Food Security (CFS) 2012). Civil society efforts are now turning to the implementation of the

VGGT in national contexts, notably through the setting-up of multi-stakeholder dialogue platforms. How the VGGT will be implemented and interpreted by state actors in the years to come will determine whether the development of new international standards on land tenure has a positive impact on land tenure security on the ground.

Participation in the PRAI process, however, proved less successful. In the initial phase of the negotiations, civil society participants felt satisfied that they were able to use the process to promote an alternative development vision, grounded in peasant-based agro-ecological production and local food systems and markets. When the principles were finally adopted, however, at the forty-first session of CFS, civil society participants walked out in protest, complaining that the principles failed to recognize the central role of small-scale producers and workers, instead placing the emphasis on facilitating large-scale investment. Members of the Civil Society Mechanism also regretted that the principles failed to offer protection against land grabbing and were not sufficiently grounded in international human rights standards (Civil Society Mechanism 2014). The principles nevertheless reaffirm the importance of respecting legitimate tenure rights.

C. Toward a right to land and territory in international law?

Progress so far and ongoing discussions on land issues, both within the Human Rights Council and the Committee on World Food Security, suggest the existence of a window of opportunity for the recognition of a new human right to land (De Schutter 2010a). The idea has made some notable advances in recent years. In its 2007 report to the Human Rights Council, the Special Rapporteur on the right to housing, Miloon Kothari, recommended that the right to land be recognized in international law. The Special Rapporteur on the Right to Food, Olivier De Schutter, in its 2010 report to the General Assembly recommended that international human rights bodies consolidate the right to land and clarify "the issue of land as a human right". The rapporteur also called on states to implement land redistribution programmes wherever there is a high degree of land ownership concentration (De Schutter 2010b).

Following intense internal discussions, FIAN International has also called for the formal recognition of a right to land (FIAN 2009), which the organization defends as a necessary response to land grabbing. For FIAN, the explicit recognition of a right to land would enable questioning the legal doctrines inherited from the colonial era (which grant states the almost absolute power to dispose of the soil and do not effectively protect informal or customary land rights), as well as political reforms aimed at promoting the privatization and commodification of the land such as titling programmes. The new right to land would be defined as the "right of every human being to access – individually or in community – local natural resources in order to feed themselves sustainably, to house themselves and to live their culture" (Künnemann and Monsalve Suárez 2013). It is not framed as a right to property and it does not refer to rights to buy or sell land, nor it is a right to make profit with land; it is limited to its use for communities and individuals feeding themselves and nurturing their cultures; it does not provide a right to far away land as the lands meant under the right to land are local.

The emergence of the right to land is particularly interesting to study because it highlights the role of transnational peasant movements as "makers of legal change" (Rajagopal 2003a). Acknowledging the influence that the rights-based claims advanced by La Via Campesina activists have had on the various frames used by her organization, a member of the International Secretariat of FIAN, goes as far as arguing that: "the right to land itself could be the result of the interaction and mutual influence between the right to food network and the food sovereignty movement".[12]

While it can be argued that UN Special Rapporteurs and international human rights organizations such as FIAN have defended a new right to land in response to social movements' claims, it is interesting to note that the institutionalization of a new "right to land and territory" (beyond the land component of the Declaration of the Rights of Peasants) has not been a top priority for peasant movements. In order to defend access to land and control over territories, La Via Campesina has mostly sought to mobilize collective action repertoires (Tilly 1986) that strengthen its ability to act as a social movement (Rosset and Martinez 2005), rather than use institutional repertoires. The GCAR, for example, has not engaged with many institutions beyond some individuals and departments within the FAO and IFAD (Borras 2008).

3. Non-institutional strategies: the defense of lands and territories

While La Via Campesina has pursued the recognition of new human rights in international settings, the movement has also deployed the human rights framework in support of food sovereignty struggles at the local, sub-national and national levels. If some of these struggles seek to achieve institutional change (Claeys 2014), many LVC member organizations have, in recent years, deployed more oppositional and defensive strategies in an effort to bring social change "from below". Struggles to resist the appropriation of land and nature, protect biodiversity and seeds, promote agro-ecology (Altieri, Funes-Monzote, and Petersen 2011) and develop alternative food networks (Renting, Marsden, and Banks 2003) all place a strong focus on grassroots mobilization. These struggles are characterized by a strong distrust of the capacity of state institutions to produce social change and by a preference for sub-political forms of action (Scott 1985). They may be framed in human rights terms, but are not necessarily geared toward the state as primary enforcer. Rather, their primary purpose is to "reclaim control" through a focus on alternative production and consumption practices. The following excerpt from the 2007 Nyéléni Forum provides a good insight into this increasingly resonant collective action frame:

> We will fight against the corporate control of the food chain by reclaiming control over our territories, production, markets and the ways we use food.
> (Nyéléni Food Sovereignty Forum 2007b)

The concept of territory plays an increasingly important role in these multifaceted struggles aimed at reclaiming control. As expressed by this activist member of the *Confédération paysanne* in France: "How to reclaim our territories? Occupy the space? This is what is at stake".[13] The defense of territories has long been at the heart of indigenous peoples' resistance (Daes 2001). What is new is the growing resonance of the concept of territory within La Via Campesina – which includes several indigenous peoples' organizations – and the food sovereignty movement at large. The recognition of indigenous peoples' "rights to their lands, territories and resources" in the 2007 UN Declaration on the Rights of Indigenous Peoples is likely to have created such a new framing opportunity. Indeed, legal developments often offer new frames for social movements to deploy (Bereni and Chappe 2011).

The notion of territory runs counter to the capitalist transformation of the local into a "non-place" (Ploeg 2008, 269). It helps rethink the organization of our food system in terms of interconnected territorial units. In Guatemala, where the World Bank uses "territorial restructuring" to facilitate control over land and labour and enable the development of extractive industries, indigenous acts of "territorial resistance" open spaces and places for "territorial sovereignty" (Holt-Giménez 2007). In the European context, the French term *terroir* describes a particular and vital relationship between a place or a specific region, quality products, producers and consumers (Petrini 2001). The territory embodies a story, the relationship to a place, a commitment to a social and cultural context, as exemplified by the use of the notion of territory in urban land rights struggles (Sauer 2012) and "right to the city" movements (Harvey 2008), GM-free regions in Europe and elsewhere, or food standards developed from below (Friedmann and McNair 2008).

Based on these different sources of inspiration, LVC is seeking to articulate notions of land and territory in a powerful frame that not only captures evolving peasant representations and practices, but also incorporates the ongoing struggles of other (potentially) allied social groups. The articulation of land and territory represents a challenge at numerous levels: the diversity of social actors and the various relations that different categories of land users have to land, territory and space; the important variations that exist across local, cultural and historical contexts; and the distinct levels of recognition of the rights of various groups in international human rights law. For example, the principle of free, prior and informed consent (FPIC) that has been recognized for indigenous peoples is increasingly seized by other groups to defend their land against appropriation. The proposal to extend FPIC to rural communities[14] was made during the negotiations of Voluntary Guidelines on the Governance of Tenure of Land, Fisheries and Forests, at the CFS, notably by the UN Special Rapporteur on the right to food. Yet, such a demand was not supported by indigenous peoples' representatives, who feared that this would weaken the implementation and defense of their granted rights.

Such an articulation will also need to move beyond the stereotypical connotations associated with land and territory. As shown by Sauer, territories tend to be associated with notions of self-determination and autonomy, whilst lands tend to be seen as productive resources. Yet, many lands have symbolic and social dimensions and are increasingly seen as central to achieving peasant autonomy, while not all territories are traditional nor free from exploitation for income generating purposes (Sauer 2012). Similarly, the use of the term *territories* tends to be associated with resistance, whereas a growing body of literature on land rights in Asia, where palm oil development has seriously encroached on indigenous land, shows that the "resistance-domination framework" (Idrus 2010) is insufficient to analyze the complex dynamics at stake, including intra-community divisions, ambivalent relations toward the state, and eagerness of some community members to enter business ventures or reap the benefits of such opportunities (Barney 2004).

The ongoing dialogue between peasants and various other rural constituencies has already generated a new conception of agrarian reform from a territorial (and food sovereignty) perspective. Such a conception seeks to ensure that agrarian reform does not truncate the rights of other users of the land and emphasizes that the purpose of land and territory is "reconstructing and defending community". A number of open questions still need to be addressed, however, such as how to confront patriarchy and how best to advance women's rights (through communal or individual land rights), which mode of tenure is best able to resist appropriation, and how to build self-determination and autonomy from that perspective (Rosset 2013).

4. Which reference frame for future land struggles?

In recent years, LVC member organizations have faced the arrival of new issues on the international agenda, such as the food crisis, reinvestment in agriculture, climate change and land grabbing. In this context, "land is becoming the new common denominator " (in the words of an activist from Habitat International Coalition interviewed at the 2009 World Summit for Food Security), and the "food sovereignty" frame needs to make more room for land rights issues. At the same time, the "right to agrarian reform" frame is losing resonance, despite efforts to give it a renewed meaning. As emphasized by a member of the Secretariat of FIAN International I interviewed, "farmer organizations increasingly use the concept of territory", especially in their "struggles against megaprojects", but "the concept of agrarian reform does not speak to indigenous peoples", especially as they "may be adversely affected by the redistributive land reforms".[15] The demand for agrarian reform seems less appealing and appropriate to the current context, although it remains important. As pointed out by Borras and Franco, land reform is primarily targeted at the redistribution of already privatized resources, as in the case of the *latifundia* in Latin America. The contemporary wave of land grabbing, to the contrary, constitutes an attack on "non-private" lands because they take place where the land has been redistributed (e.g. Brazil, Mozambique, the Philippines and India) or in areas that are not covered by private institutional arrangements (such as public or communal lands) (Borras and Franco 2012).

Will LVC, which just celebrated its twentieth anniversary, succeed in elaborating a new and potent frame for land struggles in the years to come? To resonate, this frame will need to manage the articulation of a) local, national and global struggles over the land; b) peasant, other rural, indigenous and urban claims on the land; and c) institutional and sub-political land struggles. Two broad categories of frames – food sovereignty and peasants' rights – appear to coexist at the moment, from which the future organizational frame for land struggles is likely to emerge. While it is difficult to anticipate the extent to which these frames will resonate with other constituencies engaged in agrarian struggles, it appears at this stage that both the "land sovereignty" and the "right to land" frames could potentially become powerful in the future, though for different reasons.

On one hand, the "food sovereignty frame", which has played a key role in the emergence and consolidation of the LVC movement, could evolve so as to further incorporate increasingly important land struggles. Efforts to link agrarian reform and food sovereignty have already been made, as illustrated by some frames used by the movement, such as "agrarian reform in the context of food sovereignty" (International Planning Committee for Food Sovereignty (IPC) 2006) or "agrarian reform-based food sovereignty" (Borras and Franco 2012). This frame could be invigorated by the proposal made by Borras and Franco[16] to frame land claims in terms of land sovereignty in order to unify demands (for example across North and South) and integrate the "notions of space, ecology, territory, identity and belonging in a way that is both sustainable and accounts for access to, use of, and control over land " (Borras and Franco 2012, 6). Such a frame could become influential if it succeeds in incarnating what McMichael has called the "emergent ontology of land sovereignty" that is "dedicated to the restoration of natural and social rights to reproduce humanity adequately and ecologically", and, indeed, in taking us "beyond the era of nation-state building, where counter-movements were concerned with labour, gender, and civil rights in the modern state" (McMichael 2014).

On the other hand, the "peasants' rights" frame could gain support and resonance within the movement and beyond, if negotiations on an International Declaration on the Rights of Peasants at the UN are seized as an opportunity to generate serious and wide-ranging public debate on control over natural resources. This frame could become particularly powerful if the emerging "right to land and territory" is recognized with the support of the human rights community as a human right. Not only could the right to land and territory embody the symbolic meanings carried by La Via Campesina's "right to produce" and FIAN's "right to feed oneself", but it could also establish itself as a way for local and national movements engaged in struggles to defend and control lands and territories, to re-establish a political limitation on "absolute private property"(Vergara-Camus 2012).

5. Conclusion

Access to land has been at the heart of La ViaCampesina's struggles over the last two decades. To resist the appropriation of land and nature, the movement has claimed a new human right to land and territory, both at the grassroots and in international settings. It has deployed the right to land as a collective action frame in local struggles and sought to make it relevant to various and evolving contexts, movement activists and potential allies. The movement has also pursued the recognition of land as a human right at the UN, demonstrating its ability to create legal opportunities and act as maker of legal change.

By engaging in the very definition of human rights, LVC and other agrarian movements are calling for an inclusive public deliberation on the future of the peasantry and the allocation of natural resources. In so doing, they insist that the value of human rights lies not in their supposed universality but in their very contestability: only through global public dialogue can we make sure that human rights are relevant and can be considered universal (Whiteside and Mah 2012). They also remind us that, if the contribution of epistemologies from the South is crucial to the reconfiguration of human rights "from below" (Rajagopal 2003b; Santos and Rodríguez-Garavito 2005), such a reconfiguration needs to account for ongoing social struggles over rights and resources (Newell and Wheeler 2006).

Notes

1 An earlier version of this paper was published in French under "Droit à la terre et contrôle des territoires. Du rôle du droit dans les luttes agraires", in *Au-delà de l'accaparement. Ruptures et continuités dans l'accès aux ressources naturelles*, L. Silva-Castañeda et al. (dir), coll. Ecopolis, Bruxelles, Peter Lang, 2014, p. 135–154. It was later published in English in the *Revue interdisciplinaire d'études juridiques* (R.I.E.J.), 2015, vol. 73, and it is reproduced her with permission. The author is grateful for the various comments she received from all the different reviewers.
2 If most frames are "organizational" or specific to a particular social movement, some frames are shared by a large number of movements, because they are more inclusive, more flexible, and because they resonate. This allows them to function as "master frames". The "rights master frame" was initially mobilized by the civil rights movement, and has been deployed in many social struggles articulated in terms of rights, such as welfare rights, women's rights, the rights of migrants, gay and lesbian rights and indigenous rights. See (Benford and Snow 2000).
3 An assessment of the achievements and limitations of the GCAR is beyond the scope of this paper. See (Borras 2008).
4 This is exemplified by article 11(2) of the ICESCR, which was used by FIAN activists to justify the existence of an obligation to implement agrarian reforms: "the States Parties to the present Covenant [. . .] shall take [. . .] the measures [. . .] which are needed [. . .] to improve methods of production, conservation and distribution of food by making full use of technical and scientific knowledge, by disseminating knowledge of the principles of nutrition and by developing or reforming agrarian systems in such a way as to achieve the most efficient development and utilisation of natural resources [. . .]" (International Covenant on Economic, Social and Cultural Rights, art. 11(2)).
5 General comment 12 defines availability as "the possibilities either for feeding oneself directly from productive land or other natural resources, or for well functioning distribution, processing and market systems that can move food from the site of production to where it is needed in accordance with demand" (General Comment 12 on the right to adequate food (art. 11) of the UN Committee on Economic, Social and Cultural Rights (E/C.12/1999/5)).
6 Interview by the author, Heidelberg, June 23, 2009.
7 Interview by the author, Geneva, July 3, 2009.
8 This effect has been described by Keck and Sikkink as the "boomerang" pattern of influence: domestic NGOs bypass their state and search out international allies to try to bring pressure on their states from outside. While research conducted by Keck and Sikkink focuses on transnational advocacy networks and the impacts of transnational

campaigns on the domestic context, many parallels can be drawn with the expected outcomes of engaging in norm-setting at the international level. See (Keck and Sikkink 1998) M. KECK and K. SIKKINK, *Activists Beyond Borders: Advocacy Networks in Transnational Politics*, Ithaca, Cornell University Press, 1998.

9 La Via Campesina, the International Federation of Rural Adult Catholic Movements (FIMARC), the World Forum of Fisher People (WFFP), the International Union of Food Workers (IUF), CETIM and FIAN.

10 Details are provided in the introductory chapter by Olivier De Schutter and Balakrishnan Rajagopal.

11 The Civil Society Mechanism (CSM) operates in an autonomous and self-organized fashion and ensures the participation of 11 constituencies (small farmers, fisherfolk, landless, urban poor, agricultural workers, women, youth, indigenous peoples, consumers and NGOs) from 17 different sub-regions according to specific procedures. La Via Campesina sits in a number of working groups, where themes such as land, agricultural investment, gender or nutrition are discussed.

12 Interview by the author, Heidelberg, June 23, 2009.

13 Peasant woman of the Confédération paysanne, speaking at the General Assembly of the Confédération paysanne which was held in Montreuil on May 4, 2010.

14 The extension of the consent principle to other rural communities is also defended by human rights experts. See (Gilbert 2013).

15 Interview by the author, Heidelberg, June 24, 2009.

16 The authors place land sovereignty within the rights master frame. They define land sovereignty as "the right of working peoples to have effective access to, use of, and control over land and the benefits of its use and occupation, where land is understood as resource, territory, and landscape".

Works cited

Agrikoliansky, Eric. 2010. "Les Usages Protestataires Du Droit." In *Penser Les Mouvements Sociaux. Conflits Sociaux et Contestations Dans Les Sociétés Contemporaines*, 225–243. Paris: La Découverte.

Alston, Phillip. 1984. "Conjuring up New Human Rights: A Proposal for Quality Control." *The American Journal of International Law* 78 (3): 607–621.

Altieri, Miguel, Fernando R. Funes-Monzote, and Paulo Petersen. 2011. "Agroecologically Efficient Agricultural Systems for Smallholder Farmers: Contributions to Food Sovereignty." *Agronomy for Sustainable Development (INRA and Springer-Verlag)*.

Barney, Keith. 2004. "Re-Encountering Resistance: Plantation Activism and Smallholder Production in Thailand and Sarawak, Malaysia." *Asia Pacific Viewpoint* 45 (3): 325–339. https://doi.org/10.1111/j.1467-8373.2004.t01-1-00244.x.

Batta Bjørnstad, Svanhild-Isabelle. 2004. "Breakthrough for 'the South'? An Analysis of the Recognition of Farmers' Rights in the International Treaty on Plant Genetic Resources for Food and Agriculture. FNI Report 13/2004." Fridtjof Nansen Institute.

Benford, R. D., and David A. Snow. 2000. "Framing Processes and Social Movements: An Overview and Assessment." *Annual Review of Sociology* 26: 611–639.

Bereni, Laurence, and Vincent-Arnaud Chappe. 2011. "La Discrimination, de La Qualification Juridique à l'outil Sociologique." *Politix*, 94 (February): 7–34.

Bernstein, Henry. 2010. *Class Dynamics of Agrarian Change*. Agrarian Change and Peasant Studies. Initiatives in Critical Agrarian Studies. Halifax: Fernwood Publishing and Kumarian Press.

Bob, Clifford. 2010. *The International Struggle for New Human Rights*. Philadelphia, PA: University of Pennsylvania Press.

Borras, Saturnino. 2008. "La Vía Campesina and Its Global Campaign for Agrarian Reform." *Journal of Agrarian Change* 8 (2–3): 258–289.

Borras, Saturnino, and Jennifer C. Franco. 2012. "A 'Land Sovereignty' Alternative? Towards a Peoples' Counter-Enclosure (Discussion Paper)." TNI Agrarian Justice Programme.

Bullard, Nicola, and Tadzio Müller. 2012. "Beyond the 'Green Economy': System Change, Not Climate Change?" *Development* 55 (1): 54–62.

Civil Society Mechanism. 2014. "Civil Society Statement on Rai | PAN AP." October 15, 2014. www.panap.net/campaigns/land-food-rights/international-advocacy-and-instruments/2498.

Claeys, Priscilla. 2012a. "Vers Des Alternatives Au Capitalisme Néolibéral Par Une Conception Alternative Des Droits Humains? L'expérience Des Organisations Paysannes." In *Le Courage Des Alternatives (Christoph Eberhard, Ed.)*, Cahiers d'Anthropologie du droit. Laboratoire d'anthropologie juridique de Paris UMR de droit comparé-Paris I, 103–120. Paris: Karthala.

———. 2012b. "The Creation of New Rights by the Food Sovereignty Movement: The Challenge of Institutionalizing Subversion." *Sociology* 46 (5): 844–860.

———. 2014. "Vía Campesina's Struggle for the Right to Food Sovereignty: From Above or From Below?" In *Rethinking Food Systems. Structural Challenges, New Strategies, and the Law (Lambek, Claeys, Brilmaeyer and Wong, Eds.)*, 29–52. Dordrecht: Springer.

———. 2015. "Food Sovereignty and the Recognition of New Rights for Peasants at the UN: A Critical Overview of La Via Campesina's Rights Claims over the Last 20 Years." *Globalizations* 12 (4): 452–465.

Clapp, Jennifer. 2014. "Financialization, Distance and Global Food Politics." *Journal of Peasant Studies* 41 (5): 797–814.

Committee on World Food Security (CFS). 2012. "Voluntary Guidelines on the Responsible Governance of Tenure of Land, Fisheries and Forests in the Context of National Food Security." FAO, United Nations.

Daes, Erica-Irene A. 2001. "Prevention of Discrimination and Protection of Indigenous Peoples and Minorities. Indigenous Peoples and Their Relationship to Land. Final Working Paper (E/CN.4/Sub.2/2001/21)." Commission on Human Rights, United Nations.

De Schutter, Olivier. 2010a. "The Emerging Human Right to Land." *International Community Law Review* 12 (3): 303–334. https://doi.org/10.1163/187197310X513725.

———. 2010b. "Report of the Special Rapporteur on the Right to Food Presented to the 65th General Assembly of the United Nations [A/65/281], 'Access to Land and the Right to Food'." United Nations.

Desmarais, Annette Aurélie. 2007. *La Vía Campesina: Globalization and the Power of Peasants*. Halifax; London; Ann Arbor, MI: Fernwood Pub.; Pluto Press.

Duncan, Jessica. 2015. *Global Food Security Governance: Civil Society Engagement in the Reformed Committee on World Food Security*. S.l.: Routledge.

Fakih, Mansour, Toto Rahardjo, and Michel Pimbert. 2003. "Community Integrated Pest Management in Indonesia. Institutionalising Participation and People Centred Approaches." IEED and IDS.

FIAN. 2009. "Recognize Land as a Human Right. Sellout of Agricultural Lands Will Aggravate Food Crisis (Press Release)." *FIAN*. December 10, 2009. www.fian.org/news/press-releases/recognize-land-as-a-human-right-sellout-of-agricultural-lands-will-aggravate-food-crisis/?searchterm=access%20to%20land%20resources.

Friedmann, Harriet, and Amber McNair. 2008. "Whose Rules Rule? Contested Projects to Certify 'Local Production for Distant Consumers'." *Journal of Agrarian Change* 8 (2 and 3): 408–434.

Gilbert, Jeremie. 2013. "The Right to Freely Dispose of Natural Resources: Utopia or Forgotten Right?" *Netherlands Quarterly of Human Rights* 31 (2): 314–341.

Golay, Cristophe. 2009. "Les Droits Des Paysans. Cahier Critique N°5." Centre Europe Tiers-Monde (CETIM).

———. 2015. "Negotiation of a United Nations Declaration on the Rights of Peasants and Other People Working in Rural Areas. In-Brief No. 5." Geneva Academy.

Harvey, David. 2008. "The Right to the City." *New Left Review* 53 (October): 23–40.

Heitlinger, Alena. 1996. "Framing Feminism in Post-Communist Czech Republic." *Communist and Post-Communist Studies* 29 (1): 77–93.

Holt-Giménez, Eric. 2007. "Development Report No 16: LAND–GOLD–REFORM The Territorial Restructuring of Guatemala's Highlands." Food First/Institute for Food and Development Policy. www.foodfirst.org/en/node/1770.

Human Rights Council. 2012. "Resolution on the Promotion of the Human Rights of Peasants and Other People Working in Rural Areas (A/HRC/21/L.23)." United Nations.

Idrus, Rusaslina. 2010. "From Wards to Citizens: Indigenous Rights and Citizenship in Malaysia." *PoLAR: Political and Legal Anthropology Review* 33 (1): 89–108.

International Planning Committee for Food Sovereignty (IPC). 2006. "For a New Agrarian Reform Based on Food Sovereignty! Final Declaration of the 'Land, Territory and Dignity' Forum (Porto Alegre)." https://www.foodsovereignty.org/

———. 2008. "No More Failures-as-Usual! Civil Society Statement on the World Food Emergency (Rome)." https://www.foodsovereignty.org/

Israël, Liora. 2003. "Faire Émerger Le Droit Des Étrangers En Le Contestant, Ou l'histoire Paradoxale Des Premières Années Du GISTI." *Politix* 16 (62): 115–143.

Keck, Margaret, and Kathryn Sikkink. 1998. *Activists Beyond Borders: Advocacy Networks in Transnational Politics*. Ithaca: Cornell University Press.

Konsorsium Pembaruan Agraria KPA. 2013. "UN Declaration on The Human Rights of Peasants Can Encourage Implementation of Agrarian Reform in Indonesia." April 2013. www.kpa.or.id/?p=1516&lang=en.

Künnemann, Rolf. 1984. "The Human Right to Food: A Strategy for an International Network." In *The Right to Food: From Soft to Hard Law. Report of the International Conference Organized by the Netherlands Institute of Human Rights in Cooperation with the Norwegian Human Rights Project and the Christian Michelsen Institute, Norway, from 6–9 June 1984, Utrecht*, 90–103. Utrecht: Netherlands Institute of Human Rights (SIM).

Künnemann, Rolf, and Sofía Monsalve Suárez. 2013. "International Human Rights and Governing Land Grabbing: A View from Global Civil Society." *Globalizations* 10 (1): 123–139.

McMichael, Philip. 2014. "Rethinking Land Grab Ontology." *Rural Sociology* 79 (1): 34–55. https://doi.org/10.1111/ruso.12021.

Monsalve Suárez, Sofia. 2012. "The Human Rights Framework in Contemporary Agrarian Struggles." *Journal of Peasant Studies*, 1–52.

Mooney, Patrick H., and Scott A. Hunt. 1996. "A Repertoire of Interpretations: Master Frames and Ideological Continuity in U.S. Agrarian Mobilization." *The Sociological Quarterly* 37 (1): 177–197.

Nash, Kate. 2012. "Human Rights, Movements and Law: On Not Researching Legitimacy." *Sociology* 46 (5): 797–812.

Newell, Peter, and Joanna Wheeler. 2006. *Rights, Resources and the Politics of Accountability*. Claiming Citizenship. London and New York: Zed Books Ltd.

Nyéléni Food Sovereignty Forum. 2007a. "Synthesis Report. Nyéléni Forum for Food Sovereignty." https://nyeleni.org/spip.php?article290

———. 2007b. "Declaration of Nyéléni." https://nyeleni.org/spip.php?article290

Paoloni, Lorenza, and Antonio Onorati. 2014. "Regulations of Large-Scale Acquisitions of Land: The Case of the Voluntary Guidelines on the Responsible Governance of Land, Fisheries and Forest." *The Law and Development Review* 7 (2): 32.

Petrini, Carlo. 2001. *Slow Food: The Case for Taste*. New York: Columbia University Press.

Pleyers, Geoffrey. 2010. *Alter-Globalization: Becoming Actors in the Global Age*. Cambridge: Polity Press.

Ploeg, Jan Douwe van der. 2008. *The New Peasantries: Struggles for Autonomy and Sustainability in an Era of Empire and Globalization*. London and USA: Earthscan.

Rajagopal, Balakrishnan. 2003a. *International Law from Below: Development, Social Movements, and Third World Resistance*. Cambridge: Cambridge University Press.

———. 2003b. *International Law from Below: Development, Social Movements, and Third World Resistance*. Cambridge: Cambridge University Press.

Renting, Henk, Terry K. Marsden, and Jo Banks. 2003. "Understanding Alternative Food Networks: Exploring the Role of Short Food Supply Chains in Rural Development." *Environment and Planning* 35 (3): 393–411.

Rosset, Peter. 2013. "Re-Thinking Agrarian Reform, Land and Territory in La Via Campesina." *Journal of Peasant Studies* 40 (4): 721–775.

Rosset, Peter, and Maria Elena Martinez. 2005. "Participatory Evaluation of La Vía Campesina." The Norwegian Development Fund and La Via Campesina.

Rosset, Peter, and Maria Elena Martínez-Torres. 2012. "Rural Social Movements and Agroecology: Context, Theory, and Process." *Ecology and Society* 17 (3). www.ecologyandsociety.org/vol17/iss3/art17/.

Santos, Boaventura de Sousa, and César A. Rodríguez-Garavito. 2005. *Law and Globalization from Below: Towards a Cosmopolitan Legality*. New York: Cambridge University Press.

Sauer, Sérgio. 2012. "Land and Territory: Meanings of Land between Modernity and Tradition." *Agrarian South: Journal of Political Economy* 1 (1): 85–107.

Scott, James C. 1985. *Weapons of the Weak: Everyday Forms of Peasant Resistance*. New Haven, CT: Yale University Press.

Stammers, Neil. 1995. "A Critique of Social Approaches to Human Rights." *Human Rights Quarterly* 17 (3): 488–508.

Tilly, Charles. 1986. *La France Conteste*. Paris: Fayard.

Transnational Institute. 2013. "Land Concentration, Land Grabbing and People's Struggles in Europe." TNI Agrarian Justice Programme.

Vergara-Camus, Leandro. 2012. "The Legacy of Social Conflicts over Property Rights in Rural Brazil and Mexico: Current Land Struggles in Historical Perspective." *Journal of Peasant Studies* 39 (5): 1133–1158.

Vía Campesina. 1996. "The Right to Produce and Access to Land. Food Sovereignty: A Future without Hunger (Statement at the Occasion of the World Food Summit, Rome, Italy)." https://nyeleni.org/IMG/pdf/1996_Declaration_of_Food_Sovereignty.pdf

———. 1999. "Seattle Declaration: Take WTO out of Agriculture." https://viacampesina.org/en/seattle-declaration-take-wto-out-of-agriculture/

———. 2006. "Commentary on Land and Rural Development Policies of the World Bank. Working Document. Global Campaign for Agrarian Reform." February 14, 2006. http://viacampesina.org/en/index.php/main-issues-mainmenu-27/agrarian-reform-mainmenu-36/83-commentary-on-land-and-rural-development-policies-of-the-world-bank2.

———. 2008a. "Declaration of Rights of Peasants, Women and Men." https://viacampesina.org/en/wp-content/uploads/sites/2/2011/03/Declaration-of-rights-of-peasants-2009.pdf

———. 2008b. "Declaration of Maputo (Declaration of the 5th International Conference of Via Campesina, Maputo, Mozambique)." https://viacampesina.org/en/declaration-of-maputo-v-international-conference-of-la-via-campesina/

———. 2012. "Bukit Tinggi Declaration on Agrarian Reform in the 21st Century." July 14, 2012. http://viacampesina.org/en/index.php/main-issues-mainmenu-27/agrarian-reform-mainmenu-36/1281-bukit-tinggi-declaration-on-agrarian-reform-in-the-21st-century.

Whiteside, Noel, and Alice Mah. 2012. "Human Rights and Ethical Reasoning: Capabilities, Conventions and Spheres of Public Action." *Sociology* 46 (5): 921–935.

Windfuhr, Michael. 2000. "Agrarian Reform: A Human Rights Obligation. Paper Presented to the International Conference on Agrarian Reform and Rural Development (ICARRD) Tagaytay City, Philippines." FIAN International.

Part III

Shaping alternatives

From commodification to rebuilding
the commons

9 Facilitating the commons inside out

Hanoch Dagan and Tsilly Dagan*

Commons property is a true challenge to the law, especially in a legal context that respects individual mobility, which is key to freedom and autonomy. While a tragedy of the commons is not inevitable, the sustainability – let alone flourishing – of the commons is far from obvious either. But the rewards of the latter trajectory are critical: a successful commons property can generate significant economic benefits, due to its intrinsic advantages of economies of scale, risk-spreading, specialization and synergy. These benefits multiply in the context of social commons property regimes that function as the loci and engines of meaningful interpersonal relationships; indeed, they at times even become constitutive elements of commoners' identities. This essay explores examples of governance mechanisms for the collective management of resources as well as tax tools for collective production that can support the success of these social commons property regimes. These legal devices, which set (respectively) the internal rules of the game and provide external incentives, both counter the potentially destructive dynamics of the commons property and help preserve the non-commodified aspects of its owners' community.

1. The challenge

A familiar property tale depicts the commons as an impossible regime or, more precisely, as one that inevitably fails, at least once demand pressures on the resource are high enough (Hardin 1968; Demsetz 1967). Yet this proposition is refuted in *Governing the Commons*, Elinor Ostrom's definitive synthesis of case studies of well-functioning commons property regimes (1990). Ostrom demonstrates that resources that are owned or controlled by a finite number of people who manage them together and exclude outsiders are not doomed to tragedy. *Governing the Commons* further distills the institutional arrangements that distinguish between cases of long-enduring commons and cases of failures and fragilities.[1] If there is a tragedy of the commons, then, it cannot be about supposedly inevitable tragic outcomes of commons property.

As the theory of *The Liberal Commons* demonstrates (Dagan and Heller 2001), the putative tragedy lies in the common presupposition of both foes of the commons (typically neoclassical economic-legal theorists) and friends (typically political scientists and some new institutional economists) that commoners' cooperation and success are not possible without strong limitations on exit. This implies a choice – and certainly a tragic one – between the economic and social benefits to be derived from a commons and the most fundamental liberal commitment to individual autonomy. But even this dilemma is not inevitable. A strong right of exit indeed exacerbates the incentives for opportunistic behavior commons property seems to invite; yet if the law is properly guided by the liberal commons model, it can dissolve this tragedy and enable commoners to capture the economic and social benefits from cooperative use of a scarce resource without sacrificing the commitment to free exit.

This essay focuses on a challenge peculiar to commons property in land. Our starting point is the observation made by the organizers of this symposium, that we are witnessing a growing "trend toward increased commodification" of land that ill-fits "the needs of the rural and urban poor in developing regions" (Balakrishnan and De Schutter 2014). Accordingly, we discuss cases in which land is not only an economic asset but also a locus of community or rather the medium (amongst others) by which a group of users constitutes itself as a community. In these cases, cooperation is a good, in and of itself, in addition to being an important facilitator of economic success. This means that owners in such a group share a joint commitment and may even perceive themselves as members of a "plural subject" (Gilbert 1996: 8). Commons settings are particularly suitable for furthering such close (even intimate) interpersonal relationships because certain tasks, like the common management of a given resource, serve as an opportunity to enrich and solidify the interpersonal capital that grows from cooperation, support, trust and mutual responsibility.[2] In some settings, such as certain religious, ideological and cultural communities, the commons resource may even constitute (or lie at) the center of a way of life that profoundly affects the commoners' self-identity (Gray 1997: 109–111; Riley 2000: 194).

In what follows, we will explore some of the legal devices that can support the success of these predominantly social liberal commons. We do not disregard the significance of the economic gains from cooperation (notably, economies of scale and risk-spreading), nor do we marginalize the value of individual autonomy within such communities. Rather, we acknowledge – in line with the liberal commons model – that efficiency and autonomy are both valuable and can significantly add to the social benefits of the commons. (Economic success tends to strengthen trust and mutual responsibility; a liberal right to exit ensures that members' self-identification with the community does not erase their individual identity.) We therefore take the injunction of productivity and the commitment to free exit as side constraints and investigate the means by which the law can – within these constraints – best contribute to the flourishing of such communities and to the non-commodified aspect of the commons.

Fostering predominantly social liberal commons is a complex and ambitious mission. It requires attention to the material incentives necessary to counter the potentially destructive dynamics of the commons. But at the same time, it entails resisting a conceptualization of the interactions between the community and its members – as well as amongst the members *inter se* – as market transactions. "The norms structuring market relations," explains Elizabeth Anderson, "have five features that express the attitudes surrounding use . . .: they are impersonal, egoistic, exclusive, want-regarding, and oriented to 'exit' rather than 'voice'" (1993: 145). These norms are crucial for "the production, circulation, and valuation of economic goods," and furthermore, they "embody the economic ideal of freedom" (145). But their imperialistic tendencies threaten to undermine the other-regarding nature of vital non-market domains, such as intimate relations, professionalism and politics (1993; Radin 1996).[3] In our non-ideal world, where complete noncommodification is often harmful, preserving the intrinsic good of these non-market domains often requires mixed or hybrid strategies such as incomplete commodification, where commodified and noncommodified understandings coexist (Radin 1996: chapter 7; Fisher and Dagan 2011).[4]

The law can support the governance of the commons and the commoners' collective activities and help preserve their noncommodified features by both setting the internal rules of the game and providing external incentives, notably through the way these activities are taxed. We do not purport to cover here the entire array of devices that could be suited to this task. Rather, we present certain examples of governance mechanisms for the collective management of resources and of tax tools for collective production. Many of the details we provide may be specific to the particular legal contexts in which they function (the Continental legal regimes of co-ownership and the unique tax regime governing the collective *kibbutz* communities in Israel); and we do not mean to imply that they should be simply cut and pasted into other contexts. We do believe, however, that they can illustrate the significant role the law plays in constituting viable social liberal commons and the arsenal of devices at the law's disposal to facilitate their flourishing.

2. Governance

The name of the game in any successful liberal commons regime – the precondition to generating the economic and social gains of cooperation – is (partial) realignment of the parties' interests. This is a challenging task in a liberal environment given the (justified) availability of exit, which exacerbates the parties' vulnerability and thereby threatens the possibility of trust and reciprocity. To contend with this challenge, social liberal commons contain – as the liberal commons theory prescribes – a governance regime for decisions regarding consumption and investment, management and allocation. These governance regimes are complex and include three types of techniques for partially realigning stakeholders' interests: internalizing externalities around individual use and investment decisions, democratizing a set of fundamental management decisions by shifting authority from individual to group control and de-escalating tensions around entry and exit.[5]

The multiplicity of mechanisms available for each of these three tasks is neither chaotic nor unprincipled. Rather, the particular property configuration that serves as the default for the property institution at hand is, by and large, aligned with the underlying "character" of that institution. Thus, in predominantly economic property institutions, the law tends to conceptualize the parties as "absentee investors," interested in maximizing their profits with minimal daily involvement (Hansmann and Kraakman 2000: 423–425). Concerns about potential conflicts of interest in the sphere of individual consumption and investment decisions – that is, about how to internalize costs of over-use and under-investment – are therefore typically allayed by limiting individual access to the resource. Potential conflicts of interest in the sphere of democratizing management decisions, in turn, are likely to be mediated by setting hierarchical and formal procedures. And in the sphere of de-escalating tensions during transactions, there is little internal control, because market transactions provide ample policing against the external effects of stakeholders' decisions.

Our focus lies elsewhere, of course: in predominantly social liberal commons. With these property institutions, stakeholders are increasingly understood – by themselves and by others – to be active participants in a joint endeavor, members in a purposive community. Thus, concerns about over-use and under-investment can no longer be alleviated by limiting access. The law must instead detail a sphere of "individual dominion" – a realm of decisions regarding consumption and investment that a member can make on her own. In this realm, the potential abuses of over-use and under-investment would be regulated by setting accounting rules that protect against such opportunism. Furthermore, in the sphere of more fundamental managerial decisions, hierarchies – at least in liberal legal environments – are unacceptable. Where the economic aspect of the joint resource is tangential to its role as a focal point of a community's self-identification, participatory procedures are warranted. The closer a property institution is to the social pole, the greater the emphasis on voice – the more likely, in other words, that we will find a republican governance regime in which joint management is not only a means to the end of maximizing yield, but also a forum and medium of community-building. Finally, in predominantly social types of property institutions, the market does not provide sufficient protection against the external effects of stakeholders' transactional decisions. The more social the institution, the greater the risk of opportunistic exit and entry. Accordingly, the more social the institution, the more collective control we see over exit and entry. Supporting predominantly social property institutions requires legal mechanisms that police opportunistic exit and preempt opportunistic entrants.

To demonstrate these features, we turn now to a brief survey of the main rules of co-ownership in Continental legal systems, focusing specifically on the German tradition (Germany, Austria, Switzerland and, in this context, Israel[6]), which is particularly supportive of social liberal commons.

* * *

Consider the three basic rules of Continental systems regarding individual dominion. The first rule relates to the concern of over-use, which can be triggered by the dynamics of the commons. Certain commons property regimes can, and often do, create detailed regulations restricting and channeling use, tailored to the specific resource and its particular environmental, economic, and social circumstances and imposing corresponding escalating punishments (Ostrom 1990: 71–74, 94–100; McKean 1992: 256, 272–275). Formal law, however, is less likely to provide a successful default regime of direct regulation that is sufficiently contextual and dynamic. And indeed, a more effective legal intervention is to address over-use indirectly (Dagan and Heller 2001: 583–584) by prescribing – as the Continental traditions do – that every commoner is liable to the other commoners for the fair market value of every use-calculated pro rata, that is: according to ownership share (Israel Land Law § 33, 1959, 23 L.S.I. 288 (1968–1969)).[7]

Supplementing this is another rule in the Continental tradition, which prohibits, as in common law systems, a co-owner from making use of the resource in a way that interferes with its reasonable use by other co-owners.[8] The salient difference is in the details of the implementation of this vague (and, therefore, mostly inspirational) prohibition specifically when joint use is impossible or unreasonable. The approach German law takes is supportive of the liberal commons: use by one co-owner is permitted only when it does not interfere with a similar use (even if not actual) by other co-owners (Langhein 1996).[9] This rule encourages the parties in such circumstances to reach a cooperative and efficient solution (such as rental to a third party), rather than engaging in a strategic game where each co-owner seeks the right to exclude the others.[10]

The flip side of over-use is under-investment, which the structure of the commons seems to invite due to the potential for freeriding. To address this issue, German and Israeli law allow a commoner who invests in the maintenance and management of the commons resource to claim immediate pro rata contribution from each of the other commoners but disallow recovery for improvements[11] whose value is less clearly shared by all commoners (Dagan and Heller 2001: 587–588). This relatively broad provision for immediate reimbursement for non-contestable (reasonable) collective goods bestowed upon the land – the second basic rule of Continental co-ownership law in the sphere of individual dominion – discourages the sort of under-investment that can undermine the success of any commons and demoralize any community (Arneson 1982: 621–622). Furthermore, such a regime of immediate contribution – as opposed to a regime that prescribes contribution only upon partition[12] – assumes that dissolution is not a satisfying first or best solution but should be a last-resort solution.

Thirdly, the legal regimes in the Continental tradition distribute the net fruits and revenues of the commons property on the basis of the commoners' shares in that property. Moreover, even where these revenues are not produced by all the commoners but by one (or a few) of them, the laboring commoner does not get to keep the net profits in their entirety. Rather, in addition to fair market value for the use of their shares, the other commoners receive at least a slice of the generated net profits.[13] Adopting this rule represents a preference for ameliorating overuse and for inculcating a sense of community over policing against under-investment (Dagan and Heller 2001: 589; Compare Berger 1979: 1021–1022).

At first glance, these three rules may seem frustratingly impractical because of their high administrative costs. But a more charitable reading suggests that these accounting mechanisms are not intended to serve commoners on a daily basis. Commoners are generally unlikely to resort to these legal devices – as opposed to informal social norms of rough mental accounting – on a regular basis and not only because it would be costly: rather, people often perceive recourse to law as unnecessary, unneighborly and even hostile in ongoing relationships of cooperative interaction, mutual trust and group solidarity (Ellickson 1991: 56, 60–64, 69, 76, 234–236, 274). The role anticipated for the Continental co-ownership doctrines is quite different. They are supposed to function in the background of the parties' relationship and intended to supply a formal "safety net" against the excessive exploitation of any one party by another if the commons breaks down. In this way, the mere existence of these rules allows commoners, without taking prohibitive individual risks, to enjoy the benefits of trusting one another (Dagan and Heller 2001: 578–579, 585). And just as trust secures success, so does success reinforce trust – a virtuous circle in which trust, as Philip Pettit claims, "builds on trust" and can "grow with use" (1995: 209–210).

* * *

While rules regarding individual use and investment decisions are not trivial, the more significant way in which Germanic legal regimes support the commons lies in their architecture of group self-governance. These systems allow majority rule a wide jurisdiction and reserve a relatively small domain for unanimity. German law, for example, allows for majority rule in decisions "corresponding to the character of the common object" and requires unanimity only for "essential alteration[s] of the object" (§ 745 BGB).[14]

Majority rule is key to curbing holdouts and anti-commons tragedy as well as to helping commoners capture the economic and social benefits of a viable commons. Such a democratic regime gives the group the power to attune the management and use of the commons resource to changing environmental, economic and social circumstances. It also ensures voice for each individual commoner, encouraging commoners to opt for voice first and use exit as only a final recourse; this facilitates group deliberation, which is a means of socialization and cultivating collective commitments. These cooperation-enhancing qualities produce a relatively broad majority-rule jurisdiction. Theoretically, majority rule should be available for decisions that tend to increase the size of the pie, and unanimity ought to be required only to protect against the risk of minority exploitation, namely: when decisions merely redistribute within a same-sized pie. The more restrictive threshold of the German tradition, which rests on the founding commoners' expectations as to how the property will be used, could reflect caution over possible court error as to the utility of conflicting uses in complicated disputes (Dagan and Heller 2001: 590–594, 615–616).

Democratic self-governance requires supportive procedural norms, both informal and formal. In successful commons regimes, Margaret McKean reports (1992: 258, 260–261), commoners "convene regularly in a deliberative body to make decisions about opening and closing the commons," set harvest dates, decide "rules governing the commons" and "adjudicate conflicts" amongst themselves.

These bodies, as she describes them, seem to operate typically along republican democratic lines. Not only is power decentralized so that there is no hierarchy dividing leadership (even if elected) from "citizens," but significant emphasis often tends to be placed on collective deliberation. To ensure adherence to the group's decisions, deliberative bodies take into account the views of *all* eligible users of the commons. Thus, although formally majoritarian, these bodies usually engage in consensual decision-making (Ellickson 1993). Democratic governance operates as a background rule, while daily decision-making, in the absence of deep dissent, is governed by a social norm of unanimity. This background/ operational split legitimates and promotes consensus but does not create a formal anti-commons structure, with its attendant tragedy (Dagan and Heller 2001: 594).

The Continental co-ownership regimes foster such republican governance of participatory democracy, which is, of course, an important institutional mechanism for community-building. Under German law, for example, each co-owner has the right to "adequate" participation in the decision-making process, which includes access to adequate information and a right to adequate consideration of one's opinion in the process (§ 744 Nr. 1 BGB; Langhein 1996: 163–164). Israeli law requires disclosure and consultation in decision-making and that parties engage in the consultation open-mindedly; it further provides that any violation of these requirements will render the majority decision void.[15] These procedural safeguards are significant because they may ease parties' concern that other co-owners will maneuver behind their backs. To support cooperation amongst parties, the judiciary is further enlisted to resolve disputes by "provid[ing] solutions that permit [parties] to end their quarrels and to get on with their lives" (Smith 1991: 71). And where no such reconciliation is possible, a court is likely to order dissolution of the commons, because for hostile parties, co-ownership and co-management of commons resources are bound to end in tragedy. Finally, the prescription of open-minded consultation is difficult to enforce because the majority can often adhere in a purely superficial way. Yet it could nonetheless facilitate republican social norms by providing commoners with guidelines for conduct and judgment they each can expect the others to generally follow in a social context governed overall by cooperation and mutual trust (Dagan and Heller 2001: 595).

* * *

Finally, even rules regarding the end-game of the commons may help ameliorate opportunism, which is – especially where the law is committed, as it should be, to safeguarding every commoner's right of exit[16] – the nemesis of successful commons property. One such rule applied in the legal systems we analyze allows for a cooling-off period by enforcing party agreements that restrain exit (both through alienation of one's share and through partition) for a limited time period. This is generally achieved by only invalidating agreements to restrain alienation if they exceed a set number of years or by subjecting restraint beyond a limited period of time to judicial scrutiny.[17] A cooling-off period ensures that a decision to exit is informed (rather than emotional) and sincere (rather than strategic). Allowing such temporary restraints on exit can also serve as a catalyst for mutual trust and cooperation. For even relatively brief "grace periods" that delay exit generate an inertia of repeat interactions, which, in turn, leads parties to view their relationships as though they were of endless or unknown duration and, therefore, to adopt a tit-for-tat strategy that fully "rational" parties would adopt only in indefinite games (Dagan and Heller 2001: 599–600).[18]

Ensuring distributive equality upon partition also supports the success of the commons. Legal systems in the Continental tradition use two methods to achieve this goal. The first is scrupulously fair distribution of the value of the property on partition. Thus, where partition in kind – which is generally the preferred form of division[19] – applies, each party is ensured its fair share through the mechanism of owelty payments.[20] A second mechanism, which is used in German law, is to limit partition in kind to situations in which owners will receive identical value in a physical partition. German law provides further security against unfair distribution of the physical portions by prescribing that, following partition, the parts are distributed by lot (§ 752 BGB). "Partial partition" is allowed only upon the unanimous consent of the commoners (Langhein 1996: § 749 ¶ 53). This seemingly harsh requirement is justified because allowing a subset of commoners to carve out a share through physical division absent general consent would likely cause injury to the remaining commoners, who may be left with a larger share of a smaller and less valuable piece of property (Dagan and Heller 2001: 617–618).

3. Taxation

Thus far, we have discussed the internal affairs of the commons and the significant role of the law in providing background rules that protect against opportunism, facilitate cooperation, and entrench norms of interpersonal trust. We now turn to one of the bluntest forms of external incentive that the law can provide: the tax treatment of landed communities. Contrary to its usual depiction in impersonal, business-oriented terms, we will show that tax can provide incentives that support noncommodified interaction amongst members of such communities.

Indeed, income tax is traditionally viewed as a vehicle for collecting and allocating the costs of government in an equitable and efficient manner (Murphy and Nagel 2002: 12; Greatz and Schenk 2002: 25–27). But in addition to realizing these goals, tax also reflects, as well as shapes, a particular vision of our personal identities, of our social interactions, and of the communities we belong to.[21]

Consider identity first. Income tax law embodies a particular conception of the self and the social roles of taxpayers in various contexts. When, for example, the law acknowledges some differences amongst taxpayers (e.g. a person's disability, her childcare expenses or her support of dependent relatives) while ignoring others, it reinforces a certain conception of a taxpayer and disregards – at times, even undermines – alternative conceptions. In so doing, it draws on some image of an archetypical individual taxpayer while simultaneously participating in its construction. These assumptions are not merely expressive. They entail real-life consequences and, therefore, impact taxpayers' real-life choices and, indirectly, their perceptions of themselves and others.

Secondly, income taxation plays a unique role in shaping social interactions. To begin with, since tax influences individuals' choices, when a sufficient amount of taxpayers change their choices, social meanings may also change along with social norms. As a result, tax can also impact the ways in which taxpayers function within their families, communities and workplaces.[22] Tax may likewise affect the composition, size and nature of the communities that taxpayers form. A seemingly technical regulation (e.g. disallowing the deduction of commuting expenses) could encourage the formation of communities centered around workplaces rather than, say, family connections. Furthermore, income taxation operates under particular, often implicit, assumptions regarding the nature and meaning of the social institutions it impacts. Some of these institutions are integral to a person's identity: her family, residential community, the philanthropic institutions she contributes to and communities she belongs to. Guided by these assumptions, tax law, whether explicitly or implicitly, is engaged in shaping these social institutions and structures. Not only does it provide economic incentives (positive and negative) in relation to particular social ideas, actions and behaviors, but it also has an expressive function: it both reflects and molds our perceptions of which behaviors, communities and interactions are to be considered normative and, therefore, acceptable and which are not (or less so).

Particularly relevant for our purposes is that the way in which tax treats certain networks of support and voluntary schemes of redistribution could determine the level and form of this redistribution, promote some social institutions and discourage others. Take, for example, the tax treatment of interactions within families: tax often ignores services provided amongst family members and may allow a deduction for the financial support of dependent children, while including in the tax base financial support provided to other relatives (say, support of a disabled relative, which is not deductible).

The analysis that follows illustrates this powerful (but too often ignored or marginalized) function of tax law. Our particular interest is tax policy's interaction with communities, specifically the noncommodified aspect that makes a subset of communities particularly unique. We will focus on three core contexts where we find tax law's intervention particularly significant: one, tax law can provide incentives or disincentives for the actual formation of certain communities. Secondly, it also affects the division of labor between the state and communities in bearing responsibility for the social safety net and redistribution in general, thereby shaping members' allegiance to their communities and their sense of belonging and solidarity. Thirdly, and most relevant to our discussion, tax law participates in constituting the distinction between market and non-market interactions (both in society at large and within communities) by targeting certain income-producing activities and veering away from non-market interactions (for example, the non-taxation of imputed income, gifts and housework).

Just as the Continental law of co-ownership was our test case for how supportive governance mechanisms can facilitate the commons, the unique taxing regime applied to the Israeli *kibbutz* is the test case in our inquiry into the impact of a supportive taxation regime. The *kibbutz* is – or at least used to be predominantly[23] – a community governed by the maxim "from each according to his ability, to each according to his needs." *Kibbutz* members hold and manage jointly all property (means of production, housing and other consumer durables), and its benefits are distributed equally, with no direct link between the work an individual performs or any other contribution she makes to communal life and the distributed benefits. Private property holding is generally prohibited, and all income, including the salaries of members who work outside the *kibbutz*, goes into the common purse. At the same time, there is collective provision of members' needs (such as food, clothing, housing, education and health), through either the services of other *kibbutz* members or a collective system of production and consumption. This constitutes what is known as the "mutual guarantee" amongst all *kibbutz* members. Thus, what could be interpreted in any other context as a series of quid-pro-quo barter transactions amongst the *kibbutz* members is a set of non-market interactions in the *kibbutz* context, given its ethos of equality, fraternity and mutual assistance (Dagan and Margalit 2014).

In its divergence from the surrounding environment, the *kibbutz* in its traditional form presented a challenge to the state's income taxation regime. Should tax law support these unique features of the *kibbutz* by setting a separate taxing regime for the *kibbutz*? How should tax law treat interactions amongst *kibbutz* members? And should it allow for – perhaps even encourage – its private scheme of redistribution?

* * *

Because goods and services are distributed amongst the *kibbutz* members as per their needs and in accordance with the *kibbutz*'s financial capacities, the services *kibbutz* members receive from the community are not, almost by definition, remuneration for the services they provide (or vice versa). But whereas the *kibbutz* is clearly not a framework of strictly commercial relationships, it is also no stranger to the material realm: from its inception, the *kibbutz* constituted the main economic framework for meeting its members' material needs. In recognizing this uniqueness, the Israeli tax system has traditionally accorded special treatment to *kibbutzim*: it taxes *kibbutz* business activities (e.g. agriculture, industrial enterprises and tourism), but refrains from taxing services provided by members to other members, at either the *kibbutz* level or individual member level. In fact, *kibbutz* members are not taxed at all. The *kibbutz* is the only entity taxed, although its liability is determined according to its individual members' tax rates.

Under this system, there are two stages to calculating the *kibbutz*-level tax. The first stage involves the calculation of the *kibbutz*'s income, as an independent entity, from all branches of its business activities, including the income of members who work outside the *kibbutz*. In the second stage, the (theoretical) tax liability of members for their allocated income is calculated by attributing to them equal shares of the *kibbutz*'s taxable income. At this stage, the credits, personal deductions and other individual member benefits are also taken into account in the tax liability calculation. Members, however, do not actually bear this tax liability personally, but rather, the *kibbutz* pays the aggregate of taxes calculated for its members. Thus, the *kibbutz* is essentially taxed as an upside-down, flow-through entity, where the entity, rather than its members, is taxed.[24]

Three prominent features emerge in this taxation system: the *kibbutz* is treated as a unique type of incorporation; economic interactions within the *kibbutz* are not classified as (taxable) transactions; and there is equal attribution of the *kibbutz* income amongst its members. All three of these features both acknowledge and facilitate the exceptional nature of the traditional *kibbutz*.

* * *

To understand this, consider first the fact that unlike the two-stage taxation system applied to companies or the flow-through taxation of partnerships, *kibbutzim* are taxed as the sum of all their individual members. Were the *kibbutz* regarded as just a garden-variety commercial entity, it would be treated as though it purchases services from its members and sells services to member and non-member customers. In traditional tax law, this would yield two levels of taxation: the one at the *kibbutz* level (taxing income from sale of services and allowing the deduction of purchase costs) and the other at the level of the individual members (taxing income from the sale of their services). However, Israeli tax law does not regard *kibbutz* members to be employees of the *kibbutz*, nor the services they receive to be analogous to shareholder or partner profits.

Thus, the *kibbutz*'s provision of its members' needs is not deemed income for its members (as either wages or profit distribution), nor is it tax-deductible for the *kibbutz*. Instead, the incomes of both the *kibbutz* and its members are taxed jointly at the *kibbutz* level, as a single unit, much like a family rather than a company. Despite being a corporation, the *kibbutz* is taxed along with its members at only one level, with the *kibbutz* paying income tax not only on the profits it makes but also for the value of goods and services it provides to its members (C.C. (Hi.) 1013696/, *Kibbutz Beit Zera v. Gen. Federation of Labor in Israel*, 2000 Isr. D.C. 5762(2), 385: 433). Yet in contrast to other flow-through entities (such as partnerships), the taxation is at the corporation level and not the individual level. The applicable tax rates, however, are individual progressive rates rather than corporate rates, and – unlike companies – the *kibbutz* can enjoy individual member credits and exemptions (e.g. childcare and disability credits and exemptions).

* * *

Abstracted from its communal context, the daily life of the traditional *kibbutz* is saturated with barters between members. These could be viewed (from a market perspective) as simple "give-and-take" transactions in which the *kibbutz* functions as a clearinghouse. Thus, for example, whereas some *kibbutz* members work at its plant in the manufacture of products to be sold on the market and thereby contribute to the collective income, other members work in the collective *kibbutz* kitchen preparing and serving meals for all members and thereby provide internal services.

Yet as noted, Israeli tax law has traditionally refrained from taxing such interactions amongst *kibbutz* members as barter transactions, just as it refrains from
taxing, say, the value of services a taxpayer provides to her family members.
Not taxing the reciprocal services of *kibbutz* members – refusing to conceptualize them as the provision of a service for a benefit – reflects and reinforces their
understanding as non-market interactions. By the same token, the law ignores
the array of mutually provided services through which members' needs are met,
however great they are and irrespective of the extent of their contribution to the
collective good (Refael and Efrati 1986: 368). Accordingly, when members provide one another with early childhood education, laundry services, kitchen services, gardening, maintenance and the like, the consumption resulting from these
services is not taxed at either the *kibbutz* level or individual member level.[25] And
again, not treating these interactions as a complex system of barter transactions –
opting instead to take them as part of a cooperative sharing of goods and services
based on joint ownership of resources – reflects tax law's embrace of the *kibbutz*'s
distinctive noncommodified character.

* * *

Lastly, recall that the *kibbutz* is taxed at the collective tax rate of its members
(including progressive taxation and credits) and not the corporate tax rate; thus,
the *kibbutz* is implicitly conceptualized, for tax purposes, as purely the representative of its members. Attributing to the *kibbutz* the tax benefits for which its individual members are eligible rests on the premise that those individuals share, in
equal part, the *kibbutz* income.[26] Although this income is not actually distributed
amongst the members, this is no mere legal fiction. Rather, this working assumption accommodates – indeed, even embodies and fosters – the *kibbutz*'s traditional
egalitarian ideology, under which all members have equal rights.

4. Conclusion

Commons property is a true challenge to the law, especially in a legal context
that respects – as we think should be the case – individual mobility, which is key
to freedom and autonomy.[27] While a tragedy of the commons is not inevitable,
the sustainability – let alone flourishing – of the commons is far from obvious.
But the rewards of the latter trajectory are critical: a successful commons property can generate significant economic benefits, due to its intrinsic advantages
of economies of scale, risk-spreading, specialization and synergy. These benefits
multiply in the context of social commons property regimes that function as the
loci and engines of meaningful interpersonal relationships; indeed, they at times
even become constitutive elements of commoners' identities.

For a liberal polity that celebrates autonomy-enhancing choice and is thus committed to structural multiplicity, providing a platform for these types of property
institutions is as crucial as cultivating other, more individualistic property institutions, such as the fee simple absolute (H. Dagan 2012). In contending with the
challenge of the commons, particularly the social commons on which we focused

here, the law needs to be sensitive to both material incentives and expressive implications of this institution. The two contexts we explored may be localized and their specific features not suited to all cases. Yet we believe that they highlight the range of instruments available to the law in carrying out its task and the subtle ways in which they can be used to assist commoners in overcoming collective action problems, developing trust and social capital and preserving the integrity of their noncommodified relationships.

Notes

* The authors are grateful to Rashmi Dyal-Chand and participants of the MIT *Property from Below* Conference for helpful comments.
1 Even heterogeneous sets of individuals may overcome the commons difficulties with the help of proper institutional innovation and design, such as the ones Ostrom identifies, although if they do not develop shared values, they will eventually fail (1992).
2 Compare Netting 1976: 143n13.
3 [[Endnote data missing]]
4 For other non-binary mechanisms along the market – non-market spectrum, see Fisher and Dagan 2011 (arguing that the binary choice between alienability and inalienability is over-simplistic and presenting a detailed framework of intermediate alienability techniques, thereby exposing the modularity of alienability and facilitating creative ways for its use to promote a wide array of normative goals).
5 This paragraph and the two following ones draw heavily on Dagan and Heller (2005).
6 Although in many respects, Israel is usually considered a common-law jurisdiction, the Israel Land Law is part of a codification that was heavily influenced by the Continental tradition. See Shachar (1995: 5–6).
7 See also the Louisiana Civil Code, article 806 (West Supplement 2000).
8 See § 828 Allgemeines Bürgerliches Gesetzbuch (ABGB) (Austria); Code civil article 815–9 (France); § 743 Nr. 2 BGB (F.R.G.); Israel Land Law § 31(a)(1); see also Louisiana Revised Statutes Annotated article 802.
9 For the diametrically opposite American rule, which the text implicitly criticizes, see Dagan and Heller (2001: 611).
10 If joint use is impossible, the disposition of the property is determined by agreement of all the commoners; if this is impossible too, a majority vote can determine the use of the property, and compensation for the benefits of this use must be paid to the nonusing owners, § 745 BGB. Swiss law is similar in this regard (Meier-Hayoz 1966).
11 For Germany, see § 748 BGB, translated in The German Civil Code (Forrester, Ilgen and Goren 1975: 122), which states, "Each participant is bound as against the other participants to bear the burdens of the common object and the costs of maintenance, management, and common use in proportion to his share." See also Langhein (1996: 219) (indicating that there is no compensation for improvements). This rule also holds in Israel, Land Law § 32.
12 As American law by and large provides. See Dagan and Heller (2001: 612).
13 For Israel, see Land Law § 35, and C.A. 274/82, *Yotzer v. Yotzer*, 39(1) P.D. 53, 55–56 (Israel). For similar rules in Germany and Austria, see § 839 Allgemeines Bürgerliches Gesetzbuch (ABGB) (Austria); §743 Nr. 1 Bürgerliches Gesetzbuch (BGB) (F.R.G.); Langhein1996.
14 See similarly § 833–35 ABGB (Austria); ZGB article 647 (Switzerland); Sbirka Zakonu (Sb.) article 139 (Czech Republic); Astikos kodix articles 789, 792–793 (Greece); Polgari Torvenykonyv (PTK.) articles 140, 144 (Hungary); Codice civile articles 1105–1106, 1108 (Italy); Minpo articles 251, 252 (Japan); Land Law § 30 (Israel).

15 See respectively *Zol Bo Ltd.*, 37(4) P.D. 737; C.A. 458/82, *Vilner v. Golani*, 42(1) P.D. 49.
16 On exit and property, see Alexander and Dagan (2012: 147–153, 158).
17 In Israel, the time limit on agreements restraining alienation is five years, Israel Land Law 1969 § 34(b); the time limit on agreements restraining partition is left to the discretion of the court – after three years, the court may order partition despite the agreement if the court deems it just to do so, Israel Land Law § 37(b). Many Continental regimes limit agreements to restrain partition to five years, see e.g., Code Civil article 815 (Belgium); Code Civil article 815 (France), as does Japan, Minp❍ article 256. In Louisiana, parties may agree to restrain alienation and partition for a period of up to fifteen years. Louisiana Revised Statutes Annotated § 9:1112 (West 1991). Some provisions in the Germanic systems relating to agreements to restrain exit go too far in supporting the flourishing of the commons and threaten the liberal premises upon which desirable commons regimes are based. See Dagan and Heller (2001: 618–619).
18 A more controversial means along somewhat similar lines is the right of first refusal, provided for, for example, under French law and in French-influenced civil codes. See e.g., Code Civil articles 814–815 (France); Sb. article 140 (Czech Republic). For a preliminary analysis, see Dagan and Heller (2001: 601).
19 See e.g. § 843 ABGB (Austria); Israel Land Law §§ 39, 40, 1959, 23 L.S.I. 288 (1968–1969); ZGB article 651(2) (Switzerland). The preference given to partition in kind usually implies that it applies unless it would *seriously* compromise the value of the property distributed amongst the parties C.A.1017/97, *Ridlevitch v. Moda'i*, 52(4) P.D. 625 (Israel).
20 See Code Civil articles 833 (Belguim); Code Civil articles 830 (France); Israel Land Law § 39(b); ZGB article 651(3) (Switzerland).
21 The three following paragraphs draw heavily on T. Dagan (2006); T. Dagan (2009).
22 Thus, for example, not taxing the work of a stay-at-home spouse while disallowing a deduction for hired help creates an incentive for single-earner families and thereby entrenches a certain convention regarding the family. Similarly, disallowing the expenses of disabled individuals or their employers in adapting their workplaces could discourage the inclusion of the disabled in society in general.
23 In recent years, many *kibbutzim* have undergone a transformation to become "renewing *kibbutzim*," which apply a differential wages system. This system links members' economic contribution to the *kibbutz* "common" coffers to the remuneration they receive from the *kibbutz*. This is supplemented by what is known as a "community tax," whereby *kibbutz* members who earn relatively higher wages contribute a portion of their salary to the funding of, primarily, communal services and the *kibbutz*'s mutual aid obligations. For a discussion of the tax implications of this intermediate form of community, see Dagan and Margalit (2014).
24 See Income Tax Ordinance (New Version), 1961, §§ 54–58 (Israel); Income Tax Circular 6/2003 Traditional Kibbutzim Taxation § 2 (Israel); Gliksberg (2007).
25 This treatment of services provided internally by *kibbutz* members differs from the treatment of services purchased by the *kibbutz* from external service providers (which are taxed at the *kibbutz* level).
26 See Income Tax Circular 52, § 2.3.1 (Israel).
27 Mobility, to be sure, challenges many other important features of our collective life as well. See T. Dagan (2013).

Works cited

Alexander, G. S. and Dagan, H. (2012) *Properties of Property*, New York: Wolters Kluwer Law & Business/Aspen Publishers.
Anderson, E. (1993) *Value in Ethics and Economics*, Cambridge: Harvard University Press.
Arneson, R. J. (1982) 'The Principles of Fairness and Free-Rider Problems', *Ethics*, 92: 616–633.

Balakrishnan, R. and De Schutter, O. (2014) Property from Below: Rethinking Use of Land and Related Natural Resource. Concept Note for the Conference "Rethinking Property", Massachusetts Institute of Technology (MIT).

Berger, L. (1979) 'An Analysis of the Economic Relations between Cotenants', *Arizona Law Review*, 21: 1015–1030.

Dagan, H. (2012) 'Pluralism and Perfectionism in Private Law', *Columbia Law Review*, 112: 1409–1448.

Dagan, H. and Heller, M. A. (2001) 'The Liberal Commons', *Yale Law Journal*, 110: 549–623.

Dagan, H. and Heller, M. A. (2005) 'Conflicts in Property', *Theoretical Inquiries in Law*, 6: 37–58.

Dagan, T. (2006) 'Commuting', *Virginia Tax Review*, 26: 185–244.

Dagan, T. (2009) 'Itemizing Personhood', *Virginia Tax Review*, 29: 93–136.

Dagan, T. (2013) 'The Tragic Choices of Tax Policy in a Globalized Economy', in Y. Brauner and M. Stewart (eds.) *Tax, Law and Development*, Cheltenham: Edward Elgar Publishing.

Dagan, T. and Margalit, A. (2014) 'Tax, State, and Utopia', *Virginia Tax Review*, 33: 549–578.

Demsetz, H. (1967) 'Toward a Theory of Property Rights', *American Economic Review*, 57: 347–359.

Ellickson, R. C. (1991) *Order without Law: How Neighbors Settle Disputes*, Cambridge: Harvard University Press.

Ellickson, R. C. (1993) 'Property in Land', *Yale Law Journal*, 102: 1315–1400.

Fisher, T. and Dagan, T. (2011) 'Rights for Sale', *Minnesota Law Review*, 96: 90–140.

Forrester, I. S., Ilgen, H.-M. and Goren, S. L. (trans.) (1975) *The German Civil Code*, South Hackensack: F.B. Rothman.

Gilbert, M. (1996) *Living Together: Rationality, Sociality, and Obligation*, Lanham: Rowman & Littlefield Publishers.

Gliksberg, D. (2007) 'Taxation, Economic Growth, and the Kibbutzim Movement', *Taxes*, 21(3): A-30 (in Hebrew).

Gray, A. (1997) *Indigenous Rights and Development: Self-Determination in an Amazonian Community*, Providence: Berghahn Books.

Greatz, M. J. and Schenk, D. H. (2002) *Federal Income Taxation: Principles and Policies*, 4th edn, New York: Foundation Press.

Hansmann, H. and Kraakman, R. (2000) 'The Essential Role of Organizational Law', *Yale Law Journal*, 110: 387–440.

Hardin, G. (1968) 'The Tragedy of the Commons', *Science*, 162: 1243–1248.

Langhein, G.-H. (1996) (Commentary) in Horn, N. (ed.) *J. von Staudingers Kommentar zum Bürgerlichen Gesetzbuch*, 13th edn, Berlin: Sellier de Gruyter.

McKean, M. A. (1992) 'Success on the Commons: A Comparative Examination of Institutions for Common Property Resource Management', *Journal of Theoretical Policies*, 4: 247–281.

Meier-Hayoz, A. (1966) 'Das Eigentum (Property Rights)', *Berner Kommentar: Das Sachenrecht*, Bern: Stämpfli Verlag.

Murphy, L. and Nagel, T. (2002) *The Myth of Ownership: Taxes and Justice*, New York: Oxford University Press.

Netting, R. M. (1976) 'What Alpine Peasants Have in Common: Observations on Communal Tenure in Swiss Village', *Human Ecology*, 4: 135–146.

Ostrom, E. (1990) *Governing the Commons: The Evolution of Institutions for Collective Action*, Cambridge: Cambridge University Press.

Ostrom, E. (1992) 'Community and the Endogenous Solution of Commons Problems', *Journal Theoretical Politics*, 4: 343–351.

Pettit, P. (1995) 'The Cunning of Trust', *Philosophy and Public Affairs*, 24: 202–225.

Radin, M. J. (1996) *Contested Commodities: The Trouble with Trade in Sex, Children, Body Parts and Other Things*, Cambridge: Harvard University Press.

Refael, A. and Efrati, D. (1986) *Income Tax Law*, Tel Aviv: Schocken Publishing (in Hebrew).

Riley, A. R. (2000) 'Recovering Collectivity: Group Rights to Intellectual Property in Indigenous Communities', *Cardozo Arts and Entertainment Law Journal*, 18: 175–226.

Shachar, Y. (1995) 'History and Sources of Israeli Law', in A. Shapira and K. C. DeWitt-Arar (eds.) *Introduction to the Law of Israel*, The Hague: Kluwer Law International.

Smith, S. D. (1991) Reductionism in Legal Thought, 91 COLUM. L. REV. 68, 71.

Legislation

Austria

§§ 828, 839, 843, *ABGB*.

Belgium

Code Civil, articles 815, 833.

Czech republic

Sb, article 139.

France

Code Civil, articles, 815–819, 830.

Germany

§ 748, *BGB*.

Greece

Astikos kodix, articles 789, 792–793.

Hungary

PTK, articles 140, 144.

Israel

Income Tax Circular 2003/6 *Traditional Kibbutzim Taxation*, §§ 2, 2.3.1.
Income Tax Ordinance (New Version), 1961, §§ 54–58.
Israel Land Law, §§ 30, 31(a)(1), 32–33, 34(b), 35, 35(b), 39–40.
Land Law 5729–1969.

Italy

Codice Civile, articles 1105–1106, 1108.

Japan

Minp❍ articles 251–252, 256.

US

Louisiana Civil Code, articles, 802, 806 (West Supplement 2000).
Louisiana Revised Statutes Annotated, § 9:1112 (West 1991).

West Germany

§§ 743, 744, Nr. 1, *BGB*.

Switzerland

ZGB, articles, 651(2)–51(3), 752.

Cases

Israel

C.A. 1017/97, *Ridlevitch v. Moda'i*, 52(4) P.D. 625.
C.A. 274/82, *Yotzer v. Yotzer*, 39(1) P.D. 53.
C.A. 458/82, *Vilner v. Golani*, 42(1) P.D. 49.
C.A. 623/71, Gan-Boaz v. Englander, 27(1) P.D. 334.
C.A. 810/82, *Zol Bo Ltd. V. Zeida*, 37(4) P.D. 737.
C.C. (Hi.) 10136/96, *Kibbutz Beit Zera v. General Federation of Labor in Israel*, 2000 Isr.
   D.C. 5762(2), 385.

10 Urban commons, property, and the right to the city

Sheila R. Foster

It is by now a truism that the world is urbanizing at an unprecedented rate, as more and more people migrate to cities and metropolitan areas (World Bank 2015; UNDESA 2014). This is particularly evident in the Global South. Less of a well-known or publicized fact is that many of the most populous cities are also host to some of the highest levels of glaring inequality in at least a generation (Brow-Snow and Pavan 2013; Kristina and Robert-Nicaud 2014). The rising level of urban inequality has significant ramifications for how we think about cities and the governance and distribution of their resources, particularly land and other physical assets. It has also given rise to progressive urban reform efforts exemplified by the movement (both grassroots and intellectual) for the "right to the city" and the emerging movement on the "urban commons." (Harvey 2003; Soja 2010; Foster and Iaione 2016).

The movement for the right to the city and the push to recognize urban commons both endeavour to reclaim democratic (and collective) control over decisions about how the city develops and to promote greater access of urban space and resources for urban inhabitants, particularly the more vulnerable and marginalized. Both movements and discourses operate on the ground level as well as in the policy arena. Activists occupy vacant or abandoned and underutilized land and structures (Alexander 2015; Quarta and Ferrando 2015), and advocate for public policies (some of which have been adopted) to open up access to city land, urban space, housing, and other material and nonmaterial resources to a broader group of urban inhabitants.[1] Yet the movements operate, at least on the surface, from within different juridical and conceptual lenses.

The "right to the city" movement operates from within a human rights framework. As critical urban geographer David Harvey has recently articulated, the right to the city embodies far more than a right of individual or group access to the city's resources; rather, the right has its roots in the human right to make and remake the world that we live in (Harvey 2012).[2] In an era in which most of us will live in cities, it is a "right to change and reinvent the city" and a right to that which is produced by those whose labours produce and reproduce the city (Harvey 2012: 4 and 137). The right to the city thus extends to "all of those who facilitate the reproduction of daily life" and "seeks a unity from within an incredible diversity of fragmented social spaces and locations" (Harvey 2012: 137).

Reinventing the city also requires endowing urban inhabitants with the "collective power" over the processes of urbanization and in decisions about urban space (Harvey 2012: 4–5, 137; Purcell 2002: 102; Lefebvre 1996).

The language of the "commons," on the other hand, is rooted within a collective property-based framework that calls into question the privatization and commodification of city space and urban goods and resists the threat of enclosure of those goods by economic elites (Harvey 2012; Webb 2014; Blomley 2008). The commons stakes out claims to a host of urban resources – from city streets to parks and neighborhood infrastructure, to vacant and abandoned land and buildings – and even to the city itself as constituting resources that should be shared and/or more accessible to a broad range of urban inhabitants and users (Blomley 2008). The urban commons, including the city as a commons, are also spaces ripe for new forms of collaborative and polycentric governance in which urban inhabitants are central actors in managing and governing city life and urban resources (Foster and Iaione 2016). Thus, much like the right to the city, efforts to recognize the existence of urban commons have significant implications for how cities are currently managed and governed.

As such, rather than giving rise to any fundamental tension, these two movements and discourses fundamentally reinforce each other.[3] This chapter endeavours to further underscore the link between right to the city and the urban commons by suggesting that the language and discourse of the "commons" is an important means to realize or instantiate the right to the city but from within a property rights framework. The strengthening of private property rights (and indeed privatization more generally) is most often seen as undergirding the dominance of market-based and "neoliberal" policies that displace urban populations (Harvey 2004). Yet clearly property rights can and do serve other functions, including promoting solidarity between individuals and communities as well as attending to distributive concerns. Property scholars in the United States have forcefully asserted, for example, that property rights can and do extend to the protection of reliance interests in property based on long established relationships or customs (Singer 1988) and to the protection of the relationship between "personhood" and property (Radin 1982). As this chapter argues, the discourse and movement of the urban commons is oriented toward recognizing and allocating property rights and protection not only to particular city spaces and resources, but also to the relational interests and generative potential that individuals and communities have in particular city spaces or urban resources.

1. Property rights as a progressive tool

At the core of most systems of property law is the problem of distribution, or allocation, of goods and resources in a community (political, social or otherwise).[4] The centrality of property law to allocation of essential goods and resources is true not just for those who are already owners of property, but also for non-owners – including short or long term users and others who might have an interest in a particular property or resource but do not hold legal title to it. As such, the concept of the "bundle" of property rights recognizes that there exists a constellation of rights – including the right to ownership, access, use, etc. – through which we allocate various kinds of property entitlements, and these allocations in turn structure the relative rights of individuals to the goods and resources that they need to survive and flourish (Baron 2014: 57–101). As Gregory Alexander and Eduardo Peñalver explain, "whenever we discuss property, we are unavoidably discussing the architecture of community and of the individual's place within it" (Alexander and Peñalver 2009).

Property rights go to the heart of questions of economic and social inequality, and this is especially true in the current era in which the gap between the haves and have nots is steadily increasing. David Super, for example, poignantly argues that property law has an important role in addressing widespread economic inequality by protecting those goods most essential to the well-being of a broad swath of society, rather than just protecting the goods that are disproportionately held by the wealthy.[5] As long as large segments of the population lack the security that property rights provide, he argues, many social problems will remain quite intractable.[6] He suggests that longstanding concepts from property can be applied to recognize and protect the most important assets of low-income and other vulnerable people, which include not only tangible assets but also relational interests in community and social ties of low-income and vulnerable populations subject to dispossession and dislocation (Super 2013: 1800, 1821–1825; Foster 2006: 527–582).

The recognition that property can and does serve not only economic ends but also a "social function" is the subject of comparative analysis of property law regimes throughout the world by legal scholars.[7] The social function of property concept poses a number of challenges to the liberal conception of property rights: it acknowledges that individuals are interdependent and not isolated, that this interdependence affects property rights, and thus that property rights can serve more than just individual interests.[8] Based on the interdependence and solidarity of individuals in a particular society, the social function of property doctrine dictates that property rights have internal limits – not just external ones – on what an owner can do with her property and requires the individual's property to be used to productive ends in service to the community (Foster and Bonilla 2011: 105, 1007). The state can thus intervene when the owner is not acting in a manner consistent with the obligations interpreted as falling within the scope of the social function of property principle.

The social function of property principle has been incorporated within a significant number of European and Latin American legal systems[9] and has been instrumental in the political struggle that has occurred in some countries to achieve a fairer distribution of land. In Latin America, for example, the social function of property has been invoked to justify the agrarian and urban reform projects developed in several countries in the region (Ankerson and Ruppert 2006). It is also incorporated in Brazil's federal law implementing the right to the city framework, which establishes that the development of urban land (either in the formal or informal sector) should be determined not only by its exchange value but also by the "social use value" of the land surrounding the area to be developed (Fernandes 2006).

There is not a comparable "social function of property" doctrine in the United States and indeed it is fair to say that the core of the right to property in US law is embedded in the classical liberal idea that an owner has an absolute right to exclude and by default possesses all the "sticks" in the bundle of property rights. Nevertheless, progressive legal scholars like Gregory Alexander have argued that there exists, at least on the margins of American property law, a "social obligation norm" that entails an owner's obligation to utilize property in service to her community (Alexander 2009). To be sure, the social obligation norm in American law has much plasticity – i.e. in its thinnest version it entails simply an obligation of property owners to contribute, through taxation, to the provision of public goods like law enforcement and schools; at its thickest, it may require the owner to contribute those benefits and goods that the community reasonably regards as necessary for its members' development of those human qualities essential to their capacity to flourish as moral agents (Alexander 2009: 753; Dagan 2007: 1255–1273). For instance, a thick version of the social obligation norm might arguably support eminent domain (or state appropriation) to transfer title of under-utilized or abandoned private properties to community-controlled land trusts or other forms of collective user- management of urban land or property for the purpose of providing affordable housing and other community goods.

One well-discussed example of a city utilizing its eminent domain power in this manner is the example of the Dudley Street Neighborhood Initiative (DSNI), a nonprofit community organization founded to revitalize their neighborhood, one of the poorest and most desolate in Boston. Enabled by the city's delegation of authority to the group to exercise the power of eminent domain to assemble vacant lots in the town to construct an "urban village" – consisting of affordable housing, shopping, open green space ("a town common") and a community center (see generally Medoff and Sklar (1994: 128–139) (describing DSNI and the history of the Dudley Street neighborhood) and Taylor (1995:1061–1086)). DSNI knew that foreclosing on each of the scattered individual private properties would be too time consuming and instead persuaded the city to grant its newly established affiliate, Dudley Neighbors Inc. (DNI) status as an "urban redevelopment corporation", giving it the power to acquire by eminent domain vacant land within the Dudley Triangle and to place it in a community land trust. This allowed DNI to oversee the development of affordable housing (as well as community facilities and open space) on land that was formerly constituted of fragmented vacant lots and to govern the "urban village" that they developed in order to preserve it as an affordable and accessible commons for future generations.[10]

2. The commons as a property concept

Different forms of community-developed or managed land fit into the category of common property or commons. When we talk about the commons, or common property, it is important at the outset to separate collective forms of property ownership from commons stewardship. Some forms of "common property" refer to property co-owned by a group of individuals (or a collective) and may include commonly shared spaces – such as community gathering spaces, parks or other recreational amenities – accessible to individual owners and users. The primary example of this type of common property – or "common interest communities" – is condominium complexes, cooperatives and even gated communities. Although owned in "common", this kind of property arrangement in most respects follows the logic of, and operates like, private property by endowing owners with full rights of exclusion. As such, any shared communal spaces are "open" only to those who hold an ownership interest or other legal entitlement (i.e. to access or use) in the resource. At the same time, the resource is "closed" to non-owners and those without any legal entitlement who can be completely excluded from the common resource. As one property scholar described it, these may be "commons on the inside" but operate very much like "private property on the outside" (Rose 1988).

In contrast, one way to think about the traditional "commons" is to think of it as the residual category of property that is neither privately owned nor state owned (Heller 2001). In other words, traditional commons property is something in which everyone has rights of *inclusion* and no one has rights of *exclusion*. Indeed, this is the idea behind Garret Hardin's classic *Tragedy of the Commons* in which "freedom in the commons" brings "ruin to all" in the sense that unlimited access to resources inevitably leads to overconsumption and complete destruction of the resource (Hardin 1968). Hardin's *Tragedy* occurs in the context of the quintessential open-access commons – an open pasture in which each herdsman is motivated by self-interest to continue adding cattle for grazing the land until the combined actions of the herdsmen results in overgrazing, depleting the shared resource for all herdsmen.

Hardin's open access commons describes most accurately the natural world, the resources to which we all have access and are able to use or consume – including air, water, land, forests and the like. These resources are traditionally open, often exhaustible, and thus are vulnerable to overconsumption. For this reason, some scholars and policymakers have invoked the *Tragedy of the Commons* to argue that a system of private property rights is superior to a state control to prevent the tragedy of the commons in land and other natural resources, rejecting the government regulatory solution as inefficient and ineffective (Siden 2007).

The public trust doctrine, in which the state holds an open access commons in trust in order to manage and sustain it for future generations, is another means to avoid the tragedy of the open commons – i.e. to protect these resources from overconsumption or exploitation (from either state or private interests). Many years ago Joseph Sax revived the ancient Roman law concept, "the public trust doctrine," in which the title to many forms of natural commons – i.e. environmentally sensitive lakes, beaches, rivers, forests and wetlands – is vested in the state to hold in perpetuity for the public (Sax 1970). The public trust doctrine ensures that the public has access to these common resources. It also gives legal "standing" to members of the public to bring a lawsuit to prevent the government, the manager of the trust, from selling or exploiting the resource for commercial profit or for strictly private gain.

The public trust doctrine was also historically applied by courts in the nineteenth century to some open access urban resources – such as city streets, public squares, roadways, etc. – which courts routinely protected against the pressure to legislatively appropriate or devote to nonpublic purposes during an era of intense industrialization (Kaplan 2012; Selvin 1987). Although, in more recent years the public trust doctrine as applied to urban resources has been limited or abolished by American courts,[11] some states continue to apply the doctrine to public parks and city streets.[12] In addition, some historic city structures and landmarks are also considered to be held in public trust, usually by legislation, and protected from sale or destruction.[13]

There is third option for managing open-access and exhaustible (or vulnerable) resources from overconsumption or degradation that neither depends on state stewardship nor private property rights. As illustrated by the groundbreaking work of Elinor Ostrom, the Nobel Prize winning American political economist, it is possible for "common pool resources" to be user-managed under certain circumstances. Ostrom identified groups of users who were able to cooperate to create and enforce rules for utilizing and sharing natural resources – such as grazing land, fisheries, forests and irrigation waters – using "rich mixtures of public and private instrumentalities" but without privatizing the resource or submitting it to exclusive state management (Ostrom 1990). Like other forms of limited-access commons, users establish rules for utilization of the resource and set limits on how many and what type of users are allowed to utilize the resource (Ostrom 1990: 26).[14] Unlike common interest communities, however, there is no private property, or privatization of the resource, and thus no alienable right of exclusion.

3. The urban commons as a collective claim to the city

Let's return for a moment to Hardin's open pasture, where any person can bring his or her cattle on to the open land without any limits. In reality, very few resources in the world, and in particular in the urbanized world, exist as truly open access resources in the sense that they are unrestricted or unregulated. Many natural resources – the air, the water, national parks, etc. – are regulated by international or national (and in some cases local) laws that control and limit pollution levels, resource extraction and the kinds of uses and users allowed to use or exploit them. Similarly, urban land and space is heavily regulated by planning and zoning rules that control the location, density and uses allowed in a city or town. Even parks and other open squares are regulated by usage rules, and some cities even ban the homeless and other undesirable populations from using open spaces for sleeping and other activities.

If completely open, unrestricted commons no longer (or rarely) exist anymore, how do we identify the contemporary urban commons? Increasingly, scholars and activists across the world (and some courts and legislatures) locate the commons in heavily regulated, and even private, spaces. Not unlike Elinor Ostrom's work illustrating the possibility and reality of user-managed and stewarded common pool natural resources, the urban commons is found throughout much of the urban landscape in user-managed and cooperatively governed shared resources, such as parks and neighborhood streets. In previous work, I identified a number of small- and large-scale urban resources – neighborhood streets, parks, gardens, open space, among other goods – that are being collaboratively managed by groups of heterogeneous users (and other stakeholders), with minimal involvement by the state (local government) and without granting those users private property rights in the resource (Foster 2011). These include community gardens, business improvement districts (BIDs) and community improvement districts (CIDs), neighborhood park groups and park conservancies and neighborhood foot patrols. The emergence of collaboratively managed urban resources resembles Ostrom's user-managed commons examples, and illustrates that, under certain conditions, local communities can autonomously decide on and enforce the rules for sharing and managing urban common pool resources, and in the process, developing and maintaining self-governing urban commons institutions (Foster 2011: 104, 107).[15]

Urban commons can also be constitutive of a host of local tangible and intangible resources – abandoned buildings or vacant land, urban infrastructure, neighborhood culture, historic structures, etc. – in which urban residents have a strong common interest or stake and that are currently under exclusive public or private ownership or control. In these circumstances, particular urban commons are identified by their relationship to the urban community – whether on the scale of a block, neighborhood or city – and are rooted in their normative relationship to the community. What gives the urban commons its value, as Martin Kornberger and Christian Borch argue, is the function of the human activity and network in which the resource is situated (Borch and Kornberger 2015). The value generated by transforming vacant urban structures into a public or community good – say a community garden, an urban farm, affordable housing, or cooperatively managed community assets – is said to outweigh (or at least heartily compete with) the value that these structures would retain under their existing use, whether they remained vacant or sold on the market by the legal owner (whether the city or a private party). This is not a cold utilitarian calculus according to which the value that maximizes overall social welfare prevails. Rather, "value is the corollary of proximity and density which are both *relational* concepts"; the value of a resource that is collectively produced results from human activity and is contingent on the ability of people to access and use the resource (Borch and Kornberg 2015: 7–8).

Characterizing a particular urban resource as a "commons" is thus a way of claiming that the resource should be open (or opened) and accessible to the public, or some segment of the public, to preserve (or to generate) collective goods for the community or public (culture, housing, arts, public services, etc.) (Bresnihan and Byrne 2015: 36–54; Huron 2015: 963–979). Unlike Hardin's tale of tragedy, in which adding an additional person to an open access resource *subtracts* value from the resource, opening up access to abandoned or vacant property instead can *enhance* its value to the community. For instance, Carol Rose found that some British courts considered as "inherently public property" even some privately owned resources where the public customarily used the space or land for gatherings or other activities valued by the community (Rose 1986). These courts vested in the "unorganized" public the right to use property, or rather to open it up or keep it open and accessible, even over the private landowner's objection, on the basis of the customary public use of the land. These courts considered the customary use by the public a signal of the special social value or emotional investment for the community, such that the more individuals engaged or participated in the activity the more valuable it became for that community.

Rose called this the "Comedy of the Commons" because the point is not that opening the resource to the public creates the opportunity for individuals to rival each other to consume the resource, but instead it creates the opportunity allow more of the public to participate (e.g. "the more the merrier"), thus "reinforce[ing] the solidarity and well-being of the whole community" (Rose 1986: 767–770).[16] As she points out, this vesting of property rights by British courts in the "unorganized public" rather than in a "governmentally-organized public" also suggest the means by which a commons may be self-managed by groups of the public who use it and depend on it, as an alternative to exclusive ownership by either individuals or exclusive management by governments (Rose 1986).[17]

As such, the emerging conception of the urban commons is not based simply on the description of some urban resources as shared in common or open. Nor is it specifically concerned with the problem or tragedy of overconsumption. Rather, the claims to the urban commons involve more forthrightly the question of distribution and, specifically, of how best to "share" the finite resources of the city among a variety of users and a broader class of users than is permitted by current urban growth and consumption patterns. As evidenced by "occupy" movements in the United States and abroad, commons activists resist the threat of some urban resources being rendered inaccessible to the public or enclosed by virtue of exclusive public or private appropriation and control of these resources (Alexander 2015: 245, 248); Bailey and Mattei 2013: 965–1013; Bailey and Marcucci 2012: 396–405). Exclusive public or private management and control tends to monopolize these resources, preventing the kind of sharing and pooling consistent with the idea of a commons as an open access resource.[18] In many cases, activists occupy and squat in foreclosed, empty or abandoned homes or structures as a means to convince municipalities to clear title and transfer these homes and units to collective forms of ownership such as either limited-equity apartments or long-term affordable rentals held by land trusts.[19] While not always using the language of the "commons," these contemporary "property outlaws"[20] are very much aligned with the idea of the commons: the collaborative creation, production or maintenance of a range of urban resources – both material and immaterial – by and for urban users and residents.

4. Urban "commoning" and the right to the city

Although the literature on the "right to the city" is voluminous, what many scholars and policymakers fundamentally embrace is that urban inhabitants should have an increased voice in local decision-making processes and exercise greater control over the forces shaping city space.[21] What is the scale and scope of enhanced participation and governance of urban development by urban inhabitants is not always clear from the literature.[22] However, as Mark Purcell has argued in his close reading of Lefebvre, the right to the city should be interpreted, at least in part, as a struggle to "de-alienate" urban space and to "reintegrate" it into the web of social connections among urban inhabitants, activating inhabitants to participate in the collective stewardship of urban life and to manage the production of urban space themselves:

> [Lefebvre] talks about this de-alienation in terms of appropriation. His idea of the right to the city involves inhabitants appropriating space in the city . . . . to take it to oneself, to make it one's own. . . . Property rights, for Lefebvre, are an *expropriation* of urban space. . . .
>
> In a way, appropriation is an act of reorientation. It reorients the city away from its role as an engine of capital accumulation and toward its role as a constitutive element in the web of cooperative social relations among urban inhabitants. It is in this sense that Lefebvre speaks about the struggle between exchange value and use value, between the city as site of accumulation and the city as inhabited. . . . What he calls "the urban" . . . nurtures use value and the needs of inhabitants. It is a space for encounter, connection, play, learning, difference, surprise, and novelty. The urban involves inhabitants engaging each other in meaningful interactions, interactions through which they overcome their separation, come to learn about each other, and deliberate together about the meaning and future of the city. These encounters make apparent to each inhabitant their existence in and dependence on a web of social connections . . .
>
> This image of inhabitants encountering each other and actively appropriating spaces points to another indispensable element of the right to the city: participation . . . Lefebvre calls for "real and active participation", the pervasive activation and mobilization of inhabitants . . . Participation means inhabitants increasingly coming to manage the production of urban space themselves. As they engage in real and active participation, their own collective power is revealed to them, and they increasingly understand themselves as capable steward of the urban and its collective life . . . As inhabitants become activated and come to manage the city themselves, they are effectively appropriating the city and the production of its space. They are taking control of the conditions of their own existence. They are making the city their own again.

> (Purcell 2013: 150)

In a very concrete way, the participation and active urban citizenship manifested in the right to the city also describes what Peter Linebaugh has called "commoning" – social practices of users in the course of managing shared resources and reclaiming the commons.[23] All over the world we can see urban residents claiming urban land or structures through "communing" activities – not just by occupation of vacant land or underutilized buildings, but also by constructing community gardens and urban farms and creating co-operative and co-managed live and work spaces. These practices reflect the idea that the urban commons is socially produced; that it is created, used, preserved and managed by some collection of the urban public. In this sense, the urban commons both depends upon and fosters the kind of social relationships among urban inhabitants, as well as between inhabitants and the resource, that Lefebvre indicates is at the heart of the "right to the city". One challenge that urban commons (and urban commoning) raises, however, is how to harness the collective capabilities and social capital of urban residents – the networks of residents who build and strengthen working relationships over time through trust and voluntary cooperation – to engage them more deeply in "city-making" (Frug 2001).

5. Conclusion: the city as a commons

As Christian Iaione and I have argued, beyond particular urban commons, such as land on which a community garden is managed by its users or a building that is cooperatively governed to provide live and work spaces, the city *itself* is a commons (Foster and Iaione 2016). This particular claim – to the city as a commons – gains traction from the idea that the city is not only a shared resource but also a collaborative space ripe for new forms of polycentric governance in which urban inhabitants are central actors in managing and governing city life and urban resources – ranging from open spaces and buildings to neighborhood infrastructure and digital networks. The city as a commons embraces some fundamental tenets, including the idea that the city is an open resource where all people can share public space and interact, that the city exists for widespread collaboration and cooperation, that the city is generative and produces goods for human need and human flourishing and that the city (as a public authority) is a partner in creating conditions where urban commons can flourish.

The city as a commons thus confronts the following questions: how might we scale up the idea of collective management of the commons from smaller urban resources (a vacant lot, an underutilized building, a neighborhood, urban open space or infrastructure, etc.) to the city itself as a resource in need of another management and governance regime? What are the possibilities of bringing more collaborative and polycentric governance structures to decisions about how city space and urban resources are used, who has access to them, and how they are shared and allocated among a diverse and differentiated urban population? How might we move beyond the Leviathan state toward a facilitator, or enabling, state in which the management of our collective resource (the city) involves a governance regime without a dominant center but rather one in which all urban inhabitants have an opportunity to be part of an autonomous center of decision making as co-partners, or co-creators, coordinated and supported by the public authority.

The right to the city has to mean, as its adherents agree, the right to *governance* of the city by its inhabitants. But what this governance looks like in practice is something that is still being experimented around the world in a variety of cities and urban contexts. From an urban commons perspective, as Christian Iaione and I have argued (Foster and Iaione 2016), governing the city as a commons means institutionalizing various forms of collaborative decision-making tools and processes to form something more akin to a polycentric system of local decision-making.[24] To do this, the state or public authority needs fairly significant reform to create and enable meaningful opportunities for user-initiated and collaborative co-management of urban resources. It requires, in fact, a redesign of local politics and policies to allow a wider range of urban actors to become part of an autonomous center of decision and to realize activities for the urban commons, coordinated (but not controlled) by the public authority. The role of the State becomes that of providing the various actors with the necessary tools and resources, as well as connecting the several networks of actors so that they become "capable of making mutual adjustments for ordering their relationships with one another within a general system of rules where each element acts with interdependence of other elements"(Ostrom 1999).

The city as a commons approach thus embraces commons-based experimentation that promotes inclusive development and city-making practices, as well as new forms of collective urban welfare provisioning. One example that Christian Iaione and I give of this kind of experimentation is the ongoing process of establishing Bologna, Italy as a "co-city." As part of this process the city of Bologna adopted and implemented a regulation that empowers residents and others to collaborate with the city to undertake the "care and regeneration" of the "urban commons" across the city through "collaboration pacts" or agreements.[25] The regulation also provides for the transfer of technical and monetary support to the collaboration, contains norms and guidance on the importance of sustaining common resources, maintaining the inclusiveness and openness of the resource, of proportionality in protecting the public interest, and directing the use of common resources toward the "differentiated" public. The specific applications of the Bologna regulation are now undergoing implementation as the city has recently signed over 250 pacts of collaboration, which are tools of shared governance. The regulation and other city public policies foresee other governance tools inspired by the collaborative and polycentric design principles underlying the regulation.

The Bologna regulation and the related Bologna co-city program[26] are illustrative of the kinds of experimentalist, adaptive, iterative governance and legal tools that allow city inhabitants and actors (i.e. social innovators, local entrepreneurs, civil society organizations and knowledge institutions willing to work in the general interest) to enter into co-design processes with the city leading to local polycentric governance of an array of common goods in the city. This process of commons-based experimentalism re-conceptualizes urban governance along the same lines as the right to the city, creating a juridical framework for city rights. Through collaborative, polycentric governance-based experiments we can see the right to the city framework be partially realized – e.g. the right to be part of the creation of the city, the right to be part of the decision-making processes shaping the lives of city inhabitants, and the right of inhabitants to shape decisions about the collective resources in which all urban inhabitants have a stake.

Notes

1 The "right to the city" has been incorporated into Brazil's Constitution and City Statute. *See* Constituição Federal [C.F.] [Constitution] arts. 182–183 (Braz.); E.CID., Lei

No. 10.257, 10 de Julho de 2001, Diário Oficial Da União [D.O.U.] 11.7.2001 (Braz.) (*see e.g.* UNESCO and UN-HABITAT (2009), and European Council Of Town Planners (2003)). The City of Bologna in Italy passed a much celebrated regulation on the care and regeneration of the urban commons (Comune di Bologna 2014).

2 Similarly, for Henri Lefebvre, who first coined and explicated the "right to the city," the right is more than just a right to the space and material resources of the city. He described it as the "right to urban life" – the right of urban inhabitants to produce and create the perceived, conceived, and lived space of the city (Lefebvre 1996; Purcell 2002: 99–108).

3 This point has been made but not always fully articulated. Foster & Iaione noted that the commons claim is "importantly aligned" with the right to the city claims (Foster and Iaione 2016: 288). *See* Susser and Tonnelat (2013: 105–132) connecting right to city with urban commons.

4 See Waldron (1988) describing the problem of allocation as the central concern of property law.

5 See Super (2013:1773–1896), arguing in part for property law to honor and protect reliance interests in certain benefits and goods, per Charles Reich's classic thesis on the subject.

6 As Super (2013: 1792–1793) argues, "broader access to the security that comes with property rights could go a long way toward addressing many of this country's salient problems . . . security that allows [low-income and low-asset people] to make the most advantageous use of those resources they have . . . ."

7 *See, e.g.*, Foster and Bonilla (2011: 1003–1015) including contributions from American and Latin American scholars exploring the doctrine's applications in Latin America and comparing it with similar "social obligation" norms in American property law (referring to Alexander 2006; and Pindell 2006: 435–79).

8 *See* Foster and Bonilla (2011: 1003–1008) tracing the idea of the social function of property to the French jurist León Duguit.

9 See, for example, the German Constitution of 1949, Article 14(2): Grundgesetz Für Die Bundesrepublik Deutschland [Grundgesetz] [GG] [Basic Law], art. 14, § 2, *translation at* www.gesetze-im-internet.de/englisch_gg/; The Italian Constitution, Article 42(2): Art. 42, Costituzione [Cost.] (It.), *translation at* www.refworld.org/docid/3ae6b59cc. html; The Mexican Constitution, Article 27: Constitución Política de los Estados Unidos Mexicanos [C.P.], art. 27, Diario Oficial de la Federacíon [DOF] 5 de Febrero de 1917; the Colombian Constitution, Article 58: Constitución Política De Colombia [C.P.] art. 58; and the Brazilian Constitution: Constituição Federal [C.F.] [Constitution] art. 5, XXIII (Braz.).

10 With the help of additional private and public funding, including a federal Housing and Urban Development (HUD) grant (secured with the help of the City), DSNI/DNI ultimately acquired about twenty-eight of the original thirty acres of vacant land in the Dudley Triangle and has steered the development of hundreds of permanently affordable housing units, six public green common spaces, two community centers, an urban farm, refurbished schoolyards, and numerous playgrounds.

11 Most modern courts and commentators consider the doctrine to be effectively confined to natural resources having some nexus with navigable waters (*see* Klass 2006: 699–754); and *Fencl v. City of Harpers Ferry*, 620 N.W.2d 808, 814 (Iowa 2000) ("We think these underpinnings of the public trust doctrine have no applicability to public streets and alleys. Simply stated, an alley is not a natural resource."))

12 *See e.g. Friends of Van Cortlandt Park v. City of New York*, 750 N.E.2d 1050, 1053–54 (N.Y. 2001) ("our courts have time and again reaffirmed the principle that parkland is impressed with a public trust, requiring legislative approval before it can be alienated or used for an extended period for non-park purposes."); *AT&T Co. v. Arlington Heights*, 156 Ill. 2d 399, 409 (Ill. 1993) (rejecting the efforts of two home-rule municipalities to profit by renting or leasing land beneath city streets to a telecommunications

provider and holding that "municipalities do not possess proprietary powers over the public streets. They only possess regulatory powers. The public streets are held in trust for the use of the public.")

13 *See e.g.* Connecticut General Statutes § 22a-19a (2012) (providing that historic structures are protected from unreasonable destruction and that to gain protection plaintiff must demonstrate "that the conduct of the defendant, acting alone or in combination with others, has or is likely unreasonably to destroy the public trust in such historic structures . . . . ")

14 Ostrom's study focused on small-scale resources affecting a relatively small number of persons (fifty to 15,000) who are heavily dependent on the resource for economic returns.

15 Although, as I pointed out, these are not always unproblematic institutions from the standpoint of distributional equity, democratic legitimacy and social inclusion and certainly should not be embraced uncritically.

16 She also added that: "In an odd Lockeanism, the public *deserved* access to these properties, because 'publicness,' nonexclusive open access, created their highest value." (Rose 1986: 767–770).

17 She also noted that these property rights claims lacked the exclusivity that normally accompanies individual property rights entitlements. Rose (1986: 711).

18 This "occupy" or "take back the land" movement is a response to the displacement of homeowners and tenants brought on by the confluence of the housing/mortgage crisis and the forces of gentrification (see Katz 2014).

19 *See e.g.* Moynihan (2015) reporting on a successful effort in New York City in which squatters occupied what was an abandoned city-owned tenement and which the City eventually turned over to the squatters with 10 other buildings they had taken over.

20 *See* Peñalver and Katyal (2010) (using "property law breaking" to intentional civil disobedience to challenge existing property laws).

21 According to Purcell (2013: 141–154): "most agree that it is the everyday experience of inhabiting the city that entitles one to a right to the city, rather than one's nation-state citizenship".

22 *See* Purcell (2002) noting that Lefebvre is clear that the decision making role of *citidans* – urban inhabitants – must be *central*, but that he is not explicit about what that centrality would mean, nor does he say clearly that decisions that produce urban space should be made entirely by inhabitants.

23 Linebaugh (2009) (noting that "there is no commons without commoning" and noting that the practice of commoning can provide "mutual aid, neighborliness, fellowship, and family with their obligations of trust and expectations of security.")

24 The polycentric approach to governance was first proposed by Vincent Ostrom, Charles Tiebout, and Robert Warren to connote "many centers of decisionmaking which are formally independent of each other" but which "may function in a coherent manner with consistent and predictable patterns of interacting behavior." (Ostrom, Tiebout and Warren 1961: 831–842).

25 The regulation provides that "[t]he City periodically advertizes the list of spaces, buildings or digital infrastructures which could be target of actions of care and regeneration, specifying the goals to be pursued through the collaboration with active citizens." (see Comune di Bologna 2014).

26 Further described in Foster and Iaione (2016: 347–349).

Works cited

Alexander, G. S. (2006) *The Global Debate over Constitutional Property: Lessons For American Takings Jurisprudence 1–2.* Chicago, IL: University of Chicago Press.

Alexander, G. S. (2009) The Social-Obligation Norm in American Property Law. *Cornell Law Review*, vol. 94: 745–819.

Alexander, G. S. and Peñalver, E. M. (2009) Properties of Communities. *Theoretical Inquiries in Law*, 10: 127–160.

Alexander, L. T. (2015) Occupying the Constitutional Right to Housing. *Nebraska Law Review*, vol. 94: 45–301.

Ankerson, T. T. and Ruppert, T. (2006) Tierra y Libertad: The Social Function Doctrine and Land Reform in Latin America. *Tulane Environmental Law Journal*, vol. 19: 69–120.

Bailey, S. and Marcucci, M. E. (2012) Legalizing the Occupation: The Teatro Valle as Cultural Commons. *South Atlantic Quarterly*, vol. 112: 396–405.

Bailey, S. and Mattei, U. (2013) Social Movements as Constituent Power: The Italian Struggle for the Commons. *Indiana Journal of Global Legal Studies*, vol. 20: 965–1013.

Baron, J. B. (2014) Rescuing the Bundle of Rights Metaphor in Property Law. *University of Cincinnati Law Review*, 82: 57–101.

Blomley, N. (2008) Enclosure, Common Right and the Property of the Poor. *Social Legal Studies*, 17: 311–331.

Borch, C. and Kornberger, M. (eds.) (2015) Introduction: Urban Commons. In *Urban Commons: Rethinking the City 6–7*. New York: Routledge.

Bresnihan, P. and Byrne, M. (2015) Escape Into the City: Everyday Practices of Commoning and the Production of Urban Space in Dublin. *Antipode*, vol. 47: 36–54.

Brow-Snow, N. and Pavan, R. (2013) Inequality and City Size. *The Review of Economics and Statistics*, vol. 95(5): 1535–1548.

Comune di Bologna (2014) *Regulation on Collaboration between Citizens and the City for the Care and Regeneration of Urban Commons*. Bologna: LabGov, Retrieved from: http://comune.bologna.it/media/files/bolognaregulation.pdf [Accessed 08/18/2016]

Dagan, H. (2007) The Social Responsibility of Ownership. *Cornell Law Review*, 92: 1255–1273.

European Council of Town Planners (2003) *The New Charter of Athens 2003*, Retrieved from: www.ectp-ceu.eu/ images/stories/download/charter2003.pdf [Accessed 08/25/2016]

Fernandes, E. (2006) Updating the Declaration of the Rights of Citizens in Latin America: Constructing the 'right to the city' in Brazil. In *International Public Debates: Urban Policies and the Right to the City*. Paris: UNESCO.

Foster, S. (2006) The City as an Ecological Space: Social Capital and Urban Land Use. *Notre Dame Law Review*, vol. 82: 527–582.

Foster, S. (2011) Collective Action and the Urban Commons. *Notre Dame Law Review*, 87: 57–133.

Foster, S. and Bonilla, D. (2011) Symposium: The Social Function of Property: A Comparative Perspective. *Fordham Law Review*, vol. 80: 1003–1015.

Foster, S. and Iaione, C. (2016) The City as a Commons. *Yale Law and Policy Review*, vol. 34: 281–349.

Frug, G. E. (2001) *City Making: Building Communities without Building Walls*. Princeton, NJ: Princeton University Press.

Hardin, G. (1968) The Tragedy of the Commons. *Science*, vol. 162: 1243–1248.

Harvey, D. (2003) The Right to the City. *International Journal of Urban and Regional Research*, vol. 27(4): 939–941.

Harvey, D. (2004) The 'New' Imperialism: Accumulation by Dispossession. *Socialist Register*, vol. 40: 63–87.

Harvey, D. (2012) *Rebel Cities: From the Right to the City to the Urban Revolution*. New York, NY: Verso.

Heller, M. A. (2001) The Dynamic Analytics of Property Law. *Theoretical Inquiries*, vol. 2: 75–95.

Huron, A. (2015) Working with Strangers in Saturated Space: Reclaiming and Maintaining the Urban Commons. *Antipode*, vol. 47: 963–979.

Kaplan, I. (2012) Does the Privatization of Publicly Owned Infrastructure Implicate the Public Trust Doctrine? Illinois Central and the Chicago Parking Meter Concession Agreement. *Northwestern Journal of Law and Social Policy*, vol. 7: 136–169.

Katz, M. M. (2014, July 1) Occupying Empty Houses and Airwaves to Fight Foreclosures in Boston. *Creative Time Reports*, Retrieved from: http://creativetimereports. org/2014/07/01/editors-letter-july-august-2014-occupy-houses-fight-foreclosures-in-boston-john-hulsey/ [Accessed 08/23/2016]

Klass, A. B. (2006) Modern Public Trust Principles: Recognizing Rights and Integrating Standards. *Notre Dame Law Review*, vol. 82: 699–754.

Kristina, B. and Robert-Nicaud, F. (2014), Survival of the Fittest in Cities: Urbanisation and Inequality. *The Economic Journal*, vol. 124(581): 1371–1400.

Lefebvre, H. (1996) *Writings on Cities* (E. Kofman and E. Lebas, trans.), Oxford, Oxfordshire: Wiley-Blackwell.

Linebaugh, P. (2009) *The Magna Carta Manifesto: Liberties and Commons for All*. Berkeley, CA: University of California Press.

Medoff, P. and Sklar, H. (1994) *Streets of Hope: The Fall and Rise of an Urban Neighborhood*. Boston: South End Press.

Moynihan, C. (2015, July 17) Umbrella House: East Village Co-op Run by Squatters. *New York Times*, Retrieved from: www.nytimes.com/2015/07/19/realestate/umbrella-house-east-village-co-op-run-by-former-squatters.html?_r=0 [Accessed 08/23/2016]

Ostrom, E. (1990) *Governing the Commons: The Evolution of Institutions for Collective Action*. New York, NY: Cambridge University Press.

Ostrom, V. (1999) Polycentricity. In *Polycentricity and Local Public Economics* (Michael McGinnis ed.). Ann Arbor, MI: University of Michigan Press.

Ostrom, V., Tiebout, C. M. and Warren, R. (1961) The Organization of Government in Metropolitan Areas: A Theoretical Inquiry. *American Political Science Review*, vol. 4: 831–842.

Peñalver, E. M. and Katyal, S. K. (2010) *Property Outlaws: How Squatters, Pirates and Protestors Improve the Law of Ownership*. New Haven, CT: Yale University Press.

Pindell, N. (2006) Finding a Right to the City: Exploring Property and Community in Brazil and in the United States. *Vanderbilt Journal of Transnational Law*, vol. 39: 435–479.

Purcell, M. (2002) Excavating Lefebvre: The Right to the City and Its Urban Politics of the Inhabitant. *GeoJournal*, vol. 58: 99–108.

Purcell, M. (2013) Possible Worlds: Henri Lefebvre and the Right to the City. *Journal of Urban Affairs*, vol. 36(1): 141–154.

Quarta, A. and Ferrando, T. (2015) Italian Property Outlaws: From the Theory of the Commons to the Praxis of Occupation. *Global Jurist*, vol. 15(3): 261–290.

Radin, Margaret J. 1982. Property and Personhood, 34 Stanford Law Review 957 (May 1982).

Rose, C. M. (1986) The Comedy of the Commons: Custom, Commerce, and Inherently Public Property. *University of Chicago Law Review*, vol. 53: 711–781.

Rose, C. M. (1988) The Several Futures of Property: Of Cyberspace and Folk Tales, Emission Trades and Ecosystems. *Minnesota Law Review*, vol. 83: 129–182.

Sax, J. L. (1970) The Public Trust Doctrine in Natural Resource Law: Effective Judicial Intervention. *Michigan Law Review*, vol. 68: 471–566.

Selvin, M. (1987) *This Tender and Delicate Business: The Public Trust Doctrine in American Law and Economic Policy 1789–1920*. New York, NY: Garland Publishing.

Siden, A. (2007) The Tragedy of the Commons and the Myth of a Private Property Solution. *University of Colorado Law Review*, vol. 78: 533–612.

Singer, J. W. (1988) The Reliance Interest in Property. *Stanford Law Review*, vol. 40: 611–751.

Soja, S. (2010) *Seeking Spatial Justice*. Minneapolis, MN: University of Minnesota Press.

Super, D. (2013) A New, New Property. *Columbia Law Review*, vol. 113: 1773–1896.

Susser, I. and Tonnelat, S. (2013) Transformative Cities: The Three Urban Commons. *Focal: Journal of Global and Historical Anthropology*, vol. 66: 105–132.

Taylor, E. A. (1995) The Dudley Street Neighborhood Initiative and the Power of Eminent Domain. *Boston College Law Review*, vol. 36: 1061–1086.

UNDESA (United Nations, Department of Economic and Social Affairs, Population Division) (2014) *World Urbanization Prospects: The 2014 Revision, Highlights*, Retrieved from: https://esa.un.org/unpd/wup/Publications/Files/WUP2014-Highlights.pdf [Accessed 08/12/2016]

UNESCO and UN-HABITAT (2009) *Urban Policies and the Right to the City*, Retrieved from: http://unesdoc.unesco.org/images/0017/001780/178090e.pdf [Accessed: 08/27/2016]

Waldron, J. (1988) *The Right to Private Property*. Oxford, Oxfordshire: Clarendon Press.

Webb, D. (2014) Urban Common Property: Notes Toward a Political Theory of the City. *Radical Philosophy Review*, vol. 17: 371–394.

World Bank (2015) *Urban Population (% of Total)*, Retrieved from: http://data.worldbank.org/indicator/SP.URB.TOTL.IN.ZS [Accessed 08/12/2016]

11 When land is inalienable

Territorial transformations and peasants' property rights in Mexico

Antonio Azuela

There is a growing concern for the "commodification of nature". Environmental degradation and disintegration of community life (particularly in rural settings) are seen as closely related to that process. Not surprisingly, inalienability, that is the social prohibition that certain things circulate as ordinary commodities, becomes a value in itself. This paper is an exploration of what can happen when the rule of inalienability is part of the law during a long period of time.

The Mexican agrarian reform was one of the main outcomes of the revolutionary movement of 1910–1917 and lasted for almost nine decades. When it came to an end with the neoliberal reforms of 1992, 53 percent of the national territory had been distributed to (or recognized as property of) some 30,000 agrarian communities. It was different from agrarian reforms in other countries not only due to its reach, but also because of the fact that it created a form of collective legal subject that owned the land with the prohibition to transfer it. The inalienability of peasants' lands became a central component of the Mexican post-revolutionary state. However, Mexico has undergone profound territorial changes. Demographic growth, urbanization and a growing pressure from world markets upon natural resources have changed the conditions under which land is appropriated and utilized. In what follows, I will try to identify the main features of the changing meaning of inalienability in the context of those transformations.

First, I will describe the transformation in the way inalienability has been defined, justified and discussed in Mexican public (and legal) discourse. Then I will offer an overview of the transformations that have occurred at the level of property relations, as part of wider historical changes in the relationship between society and territory. My main argument is that the meaning of inalienability depends on the (changing and extremely diverse) nature of property relations that develop around it.

1. Changing reasons for inalienability

It is difficult to find in other parts of the world a form of property like that of Mexican *ejidos* and *comunidades* (which I will call generally agrarian communities, or ACs) in which the inalienability of land has been a long-lasting rule established through state law. While inalienability can be found as part of property arrangements in many rural societies, it has generally been considered as a residue of a "pre-modern" world; it is only recently that collective/inalienable property regimes have been recognized as part of official legal systems. In contrast, for most of the twentieth century, ACs were at the very core of the Mexican post-revolutionary state. It was commonplace to say that they were the "favorite children" of that state, due to the fact that they drew a large part of their legitimacy from their ability to achieve social justice through land distribution.

The 1917 Constitution established the basis for a two-tiered agrarian reform: on the one hand, *pueblos* (as indigenous communities were called since colonial times) that had lost their lands during the nineteenth century were given the right to get the lands back through a process of *restitution*. The legal entity that holds such lands is called a *comunidad*. On the other hand, villages with unmet land needs were given the right to have access to it through a "provision" (*dotación*) procedure. These lands would be taken from large landholdings and transferred to peasants as *ejidos*.[1] When land distribution came to an end in 1992, approximately 52 percent of the national territory was owned by some 30,000 agrarian communities. Nine out of ten of them were ejidos and the rest were *comunidades*.

Until the mid-1930s, inalienability was seen as a *temporary* condition (Kourí, 2002; Gordillo, 1988). Peasants were considered unable to deal with full property titles, which called for legal protection from the market forces. This was part of an evolutionist theory that inspired the drafters of the 1917 Constitution (Molina-Enríquez, 1922, 1978 [1909]). It would be necessary for peasants to "evolve" to a certain level before they could be recognized as full property owners.

It was during the 1930s that the *ejido* and the *comunidad* were established as permanent forms of property, i.e. as normal and legitimate landholding systems for the peasantry.[2] The *ejido* even became a global icon in an era when intellectuals from many countries were turning their heads to Mexico as a project of social reform that contrasted with the rise of totalitarianism in other parts of the world (Tannenbaum, 1929; Simpson, 1937). Two aspects of the new property regimen took shape in those years. First, groups of peasants had legal personhood. Second, even if that corporation was recognized as legal owner of the land, such ownership was subject to three restrictions: property rights were *inalienable* (i.e. they could not be sold or transferred in any way); *imprescriptible* (peasants' property could not be lost through adverse possession) and *inembargable* (no authority could order the transfer of those rights to a third party in, for example, a foreclosure procedure).

This agrarian property regime provided legitimacy to the post-revolutionary state through land distribution, but at the same time it made peasants subordinate actors of the political system. Inalienability served both to protect their property rights and to reproduce their political subordination (Bartra, 1985; Ibarra-Mendívil, 1989; Gordillo, 1988; Warman, 2001).

By the 1950s, the "evolutionist" explanation had become untenable, and nobody would dare saying (at least in public) that ACs lands were inalienable because peasants were like incompetent children who needed the government's protection. Thus a new argument for inalienability appeared by mid-century: peasants started to be seen as stewards of a national patrimony. Urban elites (seeing themselves as acting in the name of society at large) vested upon peasants the mission of holding the land for the benefit of all. Land was "given" to them in exchange of "feeding" the country. An imagined social pact in which peasants would be symbolically linked to the nation through the land would give a new, and particularly strong, meaning to inalienability. The prohibition to sell the land was no longer a result of their incompetence but the corollary of their role as stewards of the nation's patrimony.

Public intellectuals invented a legal notion that became a credible way of representing peasants' property, even if it was wrong in strictly legal terms. The idea was that peasants did not own the land; the latter was said to be national property and peasants would only have "usufruct" rights. This legal formula has been repeated by virtually all social scientists (both Mexicans and non-Mexicans)[3] even if it was false from a strictly legal point of view.[4] However it became extremely popular outside legal circles because the dignity of the agrarian regime was at the same time the dignity of the nation. The symbolic link between nation and peasantry depended on the inalienability of their land.

This idea of the "social pact" that had been put in circulation by public intellectuals for decades was shattered in 1992 when president Carlos Salinas embarked on the most ambitious of all neo-liberal reforms so far: changing the Constitution so that 1) distribution of land came to an end, 2) *ejidos* were given the right to alienate their lands, and 3) peasants who decided to continue as *ejidos* or a *comunidads* would be able to cultivate some of their lands individually (as they had done for centuries) but they had the obligation to maintain forested areas as common property.

Reactions to the reform varied. The general feeling was that the *ejido* had come to an end, and there was a fierce debate about the legitimacy of the reform. Followers of economic liberalism celebrated with their usual association of individual ownership and a basic condition for economic development. In turn, for the left, the reform was a betrayal of the so-called post-revolutionary social pact. The hopes of the neoliberal reformers (that markets would "flourish" with higher productivity and economic growth, as in Téllez, 1993) were at the same time the fears of the opponents (that the commodification of land would lead to the dismantling of ACs, as in Calva, 1993). None of this happened. Instead, it was a series of territorial transformations that were not in the agenda of (both sides of) "rural development" that produced new meanings for inalienability.

2. Territorial transformations and the changing meaning of inalienability

The intellectual debate about the inalienability of rural land is one thing, but the way it actually works in local contexts is something different. I will now try to show the meaning that inalienability (and its demise in 1992) has had in actual property relations, i.e. in the experience of communities, their members and other social actors. Rural societies have undergone profound transformations in the last decades. In particular, new pressures for natural resources – the same pressures that are changing the face of the planet – are at the center of the changing meaning of inalienability of rural land in Mexico.

To begin with, even if some new land markets appeared, such as those in urban peripheries, massive sales did not occur as had been predicted from every quarter. Moreover, two-and-a-half decades after the reform, there is more, not less, land in the hands of agrarian communities in the country. The number of *ejidos* and *comunidades* went from 29,983 to 31,518 (i.e. more than 1,535 new ACs were created), and the total number of land owned by them increased by almost 2.7 million hectares (Robles-Berlanga, 2008).

We must distinguish between three processes related to the appropriation of land and other natural resources in ACs' lands: the emergence of "collective consumption" goods within rural communities, the re-appropriation by rural communities of natural resources held as common property, and the demands of communities' land and other natural resources by a variety of "external" social actors such as cities and mining companies.

A. Urbanization and collective consumption

Urbanization is usually understood as "the increase of the population in urban agglomerations in relation to that in rural areas". However, there is also the "urbanization of the rural world", in the sense that rural communities increasingly depend on public goods that, historically, had been distinctive of urban life. This has been long recognized (Lefevbre, 1968), and Mexico has been no exception. Anyone who visits a rural village will notice that many houses have electricity and running water, some roads have public lighting, there are a couple of soccer or baseball courts, an elementary school and a modest dispensary where an MD or a nurse provide basic medical services once a week.

This does not mean to say that such public goods are enough to satisfy the needs of the entire population. But they have introduced a new component into rural life: collective consumption. These goods are different from the traditional rural "commons" (pastures, forests, fisheries): they are expensive infrastructures that demand management skills and rules that are hard to negotiate. Those goods and services (or their absence) have changed social life in ACs in a fundamental way, as problems of *collective consumption*.[5] The traditional concerns related to rural land have not disappeared, but they are part of a wider agenda that includes who gets and who pays for water pipes, medical services, street lamps and so on. Because their provision and their management are complicated, those goods have become a fundamental part of the (micro) politics of *ejidos* and *comunidades*.

In the public imagination, ACs epitomize a rural world that is separated from the urban – a world with a moral texture that defines itself precisely in opposition to city life. However, nowadays the urbanization of rural life implies a growing interaction between rural and urban communities. With more than 40 percent of the workforce in rural communities outside the "primary sector", people living in ACs constantly move from one place to another.[6] There is also a constant movement of water, electric power and vehicles in all directions. All this creates new conflicts and tensions between ACs and municipal governments.

The only form of local government that the Mexican Constitution recognizes is the *municipio*. All ACs are within the territory of a *municipio* – there are 2,457 of them in the country.[7] The municipal government sits in the main town of the municipal territory and, in general, is so poor and weak that it hardly manages to serve and to govern that particular town. Historically, the presence of a municipal authority in the rest of its territory did not go beyond basic law and order functions. Urbanization has changed this. Because ACs have access (or have built for themselves) many of their public goods without the involvement of the municipal authorities, there are growing conflicts between the organizations. Water is the typical example. After decades in which ACs have managed their own (largely artisanal and informal) systems of water supply, municipal governments are trying to gain control of them, arguing that it is part of the powers that the nation's Constitution explicitly bestows on them. Thus there are growing tensions across the country between ACs and *municipios* for the provision of services – and the collection of their fees.

It is not an exaggeration to say that ACs have become a *de facto* fourth level of government (Melé, 2011), to the extent they do not only "administer" land as the property of a group of individuals, but they rule over many aspects of social life in their territories.[8] Only constitutional lawyers are unwilling to recognize this political reality – just because the text of the Constitution portrays ACs as simple landowners.

Also, there is a growing gap between *ejidatarios* (i.e. those with full membership rights within the *ejido*) and the rest of the citizens who live in the same village. Agrarian legislation recognizes *avecindados* (roughly: "neighbors") as individuals who settle in an *ejido* in order to make a living out of some "useful" occupation (the barber and the butcher are the typical examples) thus contributing to the welfare of the community. Such idyllic representation, however, does not compensate for the fact that *avecindados* have never had (both before and after the 1992 reform) the same rights as *ejidatarios*. They may acquire a plot of land in the village, but they do not have access to the communal assembly in which *ejidatarios* make the decisions that affect the whole community. In the early stages of agrarian reform, *ejidatarios* in those assemblies used to deal with their (mostly agrarian) problems. Nowadays they spend more time discussing the public goods and services of the community, and *avecindados* are generally excluded from that space. This form of exclusion is aggravated by the fact that *ejidatarios* become a minority when, as it happens, population grows. Thus there is a divide between those who own the land (*ejidatarios*) and those who are simple residents.[9] In a way, when it comes to local politics in rural Mexico, citizenship depends on property.

Beyond local variations (Torres-Mazuera, 2014), this represents a form of social exclusion that comes from the very heart of the *ejido* system. Although it had been registered since the early 1970s (Hernández-Ornelas, 1973), more focused research on the subject did not start until the 1990s (Azuela, 1995; Leonard and

Velázquez, 2003; Goldring, 1998; Torres-Mazuera, 2009). Nowadays, even the most enthusiastic defenders of the *ejido* system recognize that, at least in some instances, it has been the source of social exclusion (Merino, Ortiz, and Martínez, 2013: 64).

What does all this have to do with inalienability? In a wider historical perspective it is easy to see that urbanization came after land distribution had been completed, so that *ejidos* had time to coalesce as corporate organizations. For decades, the rule of inalienability of land, even if it was frequently broken in practice,[10] played an important role in sustaining their continuity as organizations. This does not mean to say that inalienability as a legal rule was, *per se*, the direct and only cause of the consolidation of *ejidos*; rather, such rule was a fundamental component of *corporatism* as a form of "subordinate inclusion" in the political system, which is the key to explain such consolidation. When *ejidos* became urbanized, they were already consolidated corporate entities prepared to deal with collective consumption problems collectively.

Thus the urbanization of rural life has changed the material conditions of the relations between *ejidatarios* and society at large. In the relations between them and newcomers, such division has grown even more acute, as they control collective goods that did not exist when rural life was "bare and simple". Urbanization has strengthened *ejidos* and has given a new meaning to their property rights; in particular, it has brought with itself new reasons for *ejidatarios* to remain as a group that interacts externally with public authorities (mainly municipalities) and internally with non-*ejidatarios* (mainly *avecindados*). If originally the *ejido* was a means for social inclusion (i.e. access to rural land), with urbanization it has become a means of social exclusion of social actors who were not in the picture of post-revolutionary Mexico. All along, inalienability was at the center of the system.

B. The traditional commons: new forms of appropriation

While urbanization has changed social life in rural communities, it has not meant the demise of the more traditional "commons". Forests and wildlife resources have been the subject of new forms of re-appropriation by ACs, which have given a new and (this time a positive) meaning to collective property rights over land – and a different role of inalienability.

Nowadays, Mexico appears as a global model of *community forestry*, as many of its agrarian communities have ". . . achieved unusual maturity doing what communities in the rest of the world are only beginning to explore: the commercial production of timber" (Bray and Merino-Pérez, 2005: 3).[11] This was not part of the original design of ACs in the post-revolutionary period. Agrarian reform had a strong bias toward agriculture and (later) toward cattle production (Warman, 2001). By and large, forest management by communities was not part of the agrarian reform. In spite of those policies, the fact is that land distribution did not only include agricultural land but also forested areas. Nowadays, more than 60 percent of all forests in Mexico belong to ACs (Madrid, et al. 2009).

For decades, there was a fundamental contradiction in government policies toward ACs and forests. On one hand, millions of forested hectares were recognized or granted as AC property as part of land distribution; on the other, permits and concessions for forest management were given to individuals and corporations, not to ACs. Nowadays it seems remarkable that, even if legislation did not deny ACs property rights to their forests, there was a widespread belief that forests were national property. I have already mentioned that, outside legal circles, many public intellectuals and social scientists thought that AC lands were national property. This had an apparent foundation in administrative practice since, for decades, large concessions were given to private companies without allowing ACs to embark on forest projects. ACs who owned the land were given only a small rent (known as *derecho de monte*).

There was a complex interaction between three different policies: land distribution (which included vast tracks of forests), conservation through national parks and forest bans and productive forestry (Boyer, 2007; Wakild, 2011; Urquiza, 2014). Until the 1980s, the government did not recognize ACs as apt enough to make a productive use of their forests.[12] However, since then ACs in the states of Veracruz and Oaxaca started to demand that forest concessions in their lands were not renewed, and permits were granted to them in order to take forest production on their own (Bray, 1991; Chapela, 2008; Klooster and Ambinakudige, 2005). After years of social mobilization and legal battles, public policies began to change. A new model of forest management emerged, in which agrarian communities assumed control of their resources. At the beginning of this century, experts could say that ". . . many Mexican forest communities are already managing for sustainable landscapes that have been designed by both grassroots action and government policy over many decades" (Bray and Merino-Pérez, 2005: 23). Far from losing their forests, ACs have gained greater control over them.

Wildlife management is another example of a massive (re)appropriation of natural resources by ACs under neoliberalism. Until the late 1990s, federal legislation regulating hunting[13] declared all wild fauna as national property. Since then, new environmental policies were directed toward empowering local communities for the use of wildlife, and in 2000[14] a new legislation granted those who own the land priority to embark on projects of sustainable use of flora and fauna in their lands. There has been an increase in the surface covered by wildlife management projects in Mexico from 1997 to 2011. As of that year, some 8,000 projects covered 15 percent of the national territory, and more than one half of them are in the hands of ACs.

Taken together, community forestry and wildlife management represent a successful (re)appropriation by ACs of their natural resources. It may seem paradoxical that a common property regime gets stronger in neoliberal times, but the truth is that, to the extent neoliberal ideology emphasizes the role of property rights, it should be no surprise that ACs, as property owners, have become the first users and supporters of such laws and policies.

The question of social exclusion takes here a different meaning to the one that was described before regarding urbanization. For the followers of Elinor Ostrom and the "institutional development and analysis" (IDA) framework, one of the conditions for the sustainable use of a "common-pool resource" is that owners must be able to *exclude* other potential users from having access to the resource (Gibson, McKean and Ostrom, 2000). Exclusion acquires here a positive meaning. In contrast, in the case of goods and services of collective consumption, because they are basic needs for every resident, exclusion creates conflict and, in the end, undermines the legitimacy of ACs' rights – even if that legitimacy deficit is only experienced at the local scale.

Again, the inalienability of land has been a fundamental historical condition for the current situation, but it has changed its meaning with a transformation of property relations. In the long post-revolutionary period it did not matter what communities had to say; inalienability helped to preserve their territorial integrity. By the time inalienability was abolished and communities were granted the right to sell their lands away, the process of (re)appropriation of natural resources such as forests was well on its way. Nowadays, to the extent ACs have (re)appropriated some of their common resources, nobody talks about selling them; the question is how to use them in a profitable and sustainable way.

C. Third parties' claims on resources on communities' lands

There is a third set of territorial issues that has changed the meaning of inalienability and, more generally, the material conditions for the exercise of ACs' property rights. Some of the resources located within the territories of ACs are claimed by social actors who are not (and will not become) members of the community. This includes a wide variety of situations, of which I will only describe two: land for the poor in the urban peripheries and mining claimed by multinational corporations. It may seem odd to put in the same category such disparate social actors, but my aim here is to make visible the many ways in which "external" demands for resources within ACs lands complicate their relationship with wider processes of territorialization.

Apart from the emergence of public goods and services in rural communities that was explained before, there is a process of urbanization related to ACs' lands: urban agglomerations that as part of their territorial expansion absorb agrarian communities located in their peripheries (Varley, 1989, 1998; Azuela, 1989; Schteingart, 1989; Connolly and Cruz, 2004). Although the total amount of ACs lands that have been lost to urban growth is small compared to their total extension (less than 2 percent after 80 years of urban growth), it is never good news that communities that strived to obtain their land as part of the agrarian reform have to disappear under a never-ending urban expansion. However, when one examines the way *ejido*[15] lands have been urbanized, things look more complex.

Before 1992, urbanization of *ejido* lands occurred as follows. As urban growth approached the lands of an *ejido*, peasants were ready to (or they did not have a choice but to) sell to urban dwellers plots that would then become an "irregular settlement". Because *ejido* lands were inalienable, developers in the formal sector did not, in general, venture in buying them – they could always buy land from private individuals. So *ejidatarios* could only sell their land to poor families because only they were ready to enter into an informal transaction.[16]

After all, it was a benign system: the government tolerated thousands of illegal transactions in which the urban poor did not obtain formal rights, precisely because land was inalienable and transactions were considered "nonexistent". But in the end there was a regularization program, as a result of which urban settlers obtained property titles. In three decades more than 1.5 million titles were issued across the country.[17] Compared to the conflicts that irregular urbanization has prompted in other Latin American cities, the system worked well, as it involved a form of state mediation between peasants and urban dwellers in which neither group was seriously harmed.

By abolishing the rule of inalienability, the 1992 reform changed the conditions for the urbanization of *ejido* lands. As it was easy to anticipate (Azuela, 1993), once *ejidos* were able to sell their lands in the formal market, they would have the opportunity to make deals with private developers (at higher prices compared to what the urban poor could afford), and they did just that. Although the "old style" of irregular urbanization has not disappeared (Connolly, 2012), a new urban development model has flourished. We have seen the emergence of housing developments that have been criticized for their distant location and their lack of connection with schools and jobs. None of this is the *ejidos'* responsibility, and developers are the ones who get the lion's share of land rents. However, the fact is that *ejidos* are selling their lands to new agents at higher prices, and this has reduced the possibilities of the urban poor to have access to a place to live.

The reform has also changed the conditions of land tenure regularization in settlements created through (illegal) land sales. *Ejidos* are now hiring lawyers to offer settlers deals for which they are charging much higher rates (Salazar, 2012). If before 1992 the urbanization of *ejido* lands was a "benign" arrangement, the neoliberal reforms have strengthened *ejidos* at the expense of social actors who require their lands for a basic need (indeed a fundamental right) such as housing.

In other words, as long as it was in force, the rule of inalienability did not prevent the formation of a land market – even if it was irregular. Indeed, it played a paradoxical role: while it did prevent *ejidos* from selling land to private developers in the formal sector, the urban poor did have access to land through an illegal (but harmless) market. Once "irregular settlements" were established, inalienability was the legal condition for the government's mediation between *ejidatarios* and urban settlers. The 1992 reform made possible a formal land market from which the urban poor are in a more vulnerable situation than in the times of inalienability. In short, when *ejido* land has been required to meet a social need, *ejidatarios* have ended up on the strong side of an unequal social relation.

Let us now consider the other extreme: resources located in *ejido* lands that are demanded by powerful social actors. Mining is no doubt the cause of the most acute conflicts in rural Mexico and in Latin America (Delgado, 2010; Paz, 2012; Svampa and Antonelli, 2010; Aranibar, 2010). Traditional mining made it possible to distinguish between surface rights and subsoil rights – with the support of the "regalian" doctrine that Mexico inherited from Spanish law (Díaz y

Díaz, 2014; Herrera and González, 2004). Those who obtained mining concessions just had to negotiate with the owners of the surface access to the minerals through leasing agreements in exchange for rent. With open-pit mining and more intensive use of chemicals and water, contemporary mining has a much greater impact. "Leasing" land is a bad joke when, after finishing the extraction, companies return it with an enormous crater. Land, as the "object" of the transaction, simply disappears, not to speak of the environmental impacts that affect local communities in the first place. There is such an unequal exchange between ACs and mining companies (Garibay, 2009) that David Harvey's concept of "accumulation by dispossession" is entirely pertinent here (Harvey, 2009). Moreover, the rule of inalienability seems totally irrelevant in front of the powerful interests that prevail in the access to mineral resources.

I have intentionally put together two themes in which "external" social actors claim a natural resource within ACs (land for the urban poor and mining for transnational corporations), in order to emphasize the variety of situations in which ACs' territories become relevant for society at large. In an exchange on ACs lands, communities can be the weak part or the strong one depending on the circumstances. There is a wide array of situations between those extremes: infrastructures that transport water to urban agglomerations frequently involve a conflict between peasants' rights and urban populations; ACs' land with archaeological sites becomes an issue when government authorities do not have the power to enforce heritage legislation in front of strong *ejidos* (Rodríguez-Herrera, 2000); genetic capital is the source of conflicts in which the frontier between the public and the private realms get blurred (Hayden, 2003); even the wind becomes an asset in regions where companies embark on aeolic farms.

I have tried to show that, beyond the dichotomy of inalienability versus marketability, it is important to identify different sets of transformations in the way land and other resources are appropriated in order to understand the specific context in which inalienability becomes relevant.

Now how does all this appear in the public sphere two decades after the reform? Apart from a fragmented and very limited academic production, public voices are far from recognizing the complexity of the territorial transformations I have just sketched here. However, a new and rather obvious parameter has emerged that regulates the discussion of the *ejido* and the *comunidad*: sustainability. While there are still those who defend (or criticize) the system with the old arguments and tropes, "environmentality" sets the basis for the new regime. Nobody puts into question that it is *their* land, forests and wildlife; the question now is whether they are able to make a sustainable use of them. On one hand, the old prejudice against community property appears under the scientific gaze of the "tragedy of the commons". For some observers the collective ownership of *ejidos* and the *comunidades* is, by definition, the condition for a misuse of natural resources. And once these observers find out that there are problems in the place of ACs within environmental policies or in their relationship with municipalities, they jump to the conclusion that these forms of property should simply be abolished (Quadri, 2007).

On the other hand, defenders of the *ejido* system claim that it is precisely its collective character that creates the conditions for the sustainable use of natural resources (Toledo, 1997). This is part of a new chronotope[18] that has been labeled as the "participatory indigenous community" (Dumoulin, 2007) that circulates globally as the new way of finding a place for peasant (and particularly indigenous) communities within a wider project of sustainability.

This debate may look like a simple echo of the divide between communitarians and classical liberals. However, anthropological approaches suggest that they are both consistent with neoliberalism (Das and Poole, 2004; Domínguez, 2011) to the extent that they are grounded in the idea of autonomous subjects that do not need any assistance from the state. No matter how those positions are interpreted, the fact is that both of them ignore the complex processes of territorialization within which communities exercise (or not) their rights and, in particular, the multiple ways in which they can be excluded or can exclude social actors with legitimate (or not) demands from the access and/or use of their natural resources.

3. Conclusion

In this chapter, I have made a distinction between property as rights and property as a social relation. Such distinction makes it possible to see that the social implications of inalienability in the case of Mexican agrarian communities (ACs) have been determined by the kind of property relations that prevail in different contexts – not by the rule of inalienability *per se*. This includes the possibility that the power involved in those relations is so strong that the rule of inalienability becomes irrelevant. That is what happens in two extremes: when mining corporations override communities in situations that can be labeled as "accumulation by dispossession", but also when communities have gained such control over their territories that they do not even consider selling their lands.

Between those extremes the relevance of inalienability has varied depending on the dynamics of property relations. I have explored three sets of issues to illustrate this: first, the growing importance of goods of collective consumption has deepened the division between members with full rights within ACs and other citizens that reside in villages and have to share those goods from a subordinate position.

Second, many ACs have undertaken the (re)appropriation of their natural resources (particularly forests and wildlife). Excluding other potential users has been a prerequisite for this success but, on the whole, that has not weakened the legitimacy of their property rights. The 1992 reforms that ended inalienability did not alter that process. Moreover, agrarian communities are now stronger than in the post-revolutionary era.

Third, when it comes to resources that are the property of ACs, or are located within their territories, property relations become even more complex and diverse when external actors demand such resources. I have shown this diversity in two contexts. On one hand, private companies that demand resources such as minerals located within communities' territories constitute a real threat to their territorial integrity and a serious environmental risk. On the other hand, when communities are located in urban peripheries, the urban poor are among those who demand their lands – not for a profit but in order to meet their basic need for housing. If before the 1992 reforms, the urban poor could manage to obtain access to a place to live in ACs lands, nowadays communities' rights generate the same kind of exclusion as those of individual landowners.

Inalienability has also been an issue in the public sphere, in the debates about the meaning and justification of the *ejido* and the *comunidad* as forms of property typical of the post-revolutionary era. I have suggested that, by mid century, there was a clear and strong chronotope that allowed Mexican elites to locate peasants in the wider polity: peasants had the land *forever*, as stewards of the nation. The most cherished parts of the territory were in their hands in exchange for feeding the nation and taking care of the land. Inalienability was the cornerstone of a narrative that gave peasants a legible and respectable place in the national polity. This hypothesis should be discussed against recent developments in anthropological approaches to inalienable possessions (Weiner, 1992; Ferry, 2002, 2005; Rozental, 2014, 2016). But it would help to understand why the 1992 reform that took inalienability out of the law books was so scandalous. The sacred link between peasants and nation had been broken, and fears of disintegration of agrarian communities dominated the public sphere.

Two decades later, agrarian communities are stronger, not weaker, than before. Nobody thinks that they do not own their lands, and the public debate around them has shifted toward the question of sustainability. The new divide is predictable: neoliberals say that collective property must be transferred to individuals or expropriated (to create national parks and so on), and they have the argument of the "tragedy of the commons". On their part, communitarians argue that no restraints should be imposed upon communities.

Intellectual debates are important to the extent they take place in the public sphere and they may influence policy making – and sometimes even law making. In turn, legal rules have a life of their own, and it is always possible that they are appropriated by social actors in local contexts. The interplay of what happens in those different scales is a challenge for future research on this subject from the viewpoint of legal geography (Braverman et al., 2014; Valverde, 2014). However, the point is that both sides in the debate about ACs in Mexico ignore the variety and the complexity of property relations that I have tried to describe. Communitarians refuse to see the different forms of social exclusion that certain forms of exercise of ACs' rights have produced, while neoliberals refuse to see the promising results of community management of forests and wildlife.

No doubt, the analysis I present here is sketchy and fragmented. The way forward is a more robust conceptual elaboration of the idea of territory and territorial transformations in socio-legal scholarship. Exploring the uses and misuses of inalienability and other rules will only make sense when a more dense view of territorial processes, with a combination of an anthropology of inalienable possessions and law-and-geography, approaches. For the moment, it suffices to recognize that the social meaning of *inalienability* cannot be derived from its mere existence as a legal rule. It is the always unpredictable dynamic of property relations that will define what happens when land is inalienable.

Notes

1 The complicated history of the word *ejido* can be summed up as follows. It comes from the latin *exitus*, and since medieval times referred to lands for common use located at the outskirts of a village or a town. It was only in the post revolutionary era that it ended up meaning the community that owns land as a result of the agrarian reform and its property regime (Kourí, 2015).

2 Although the *comunidad* was not abolished, it was seen as a "residual" category; it more profitable in political terms to "give out" the land through *ejidos* than to recognize existing rights to *pueblos*.

3 The list include illustrious names such as Kirsten Appendini (2001: 8), Armando Bartra (1985), David Bray, Leticia Merino-Pérez and Deborah Barry (2005: 4), Manuel Castells (1981), Rayond Craib (2004), Gustavo Gordillo (1988), Elizabeth Ferry (2005), Vicente Lombardo-Toledano (1962), Claudio Lomnitz (2001), Paula López Caballero (2007), Jean Meyer (2004), Monique Nuijten (1992), Daniel Nugent and Ana María Alonso (2002), Arturo Warman (2001).

4 One of the finest pieces of legal thinking on property in Mexico (Morineau, 1947) endorsed the same doctrine. See also Manzanilla-Schaffer, 1962).

5 I use the expression in the sense of the now classical urban sociology of Manuel Castells, Edmond Preteceille and others.

6 This does not mean to say that there are no "isolated communities" left; but they are far from being the majority of the rural world.

7 Without considering regional variations (which are huge) this means that, in average, there are 12.4 *ejidos* in each municipality, occupying the 53 percent of their territories and concentrating most of their rural population.

8 A seemingly irrelevant question is who authorizes building a new church in a village. The answer will always be "the community", not the municipal government. Think of the relevance of this for those who do not follow the religion of the majority in the assembly and want to build a church.

9 The rural population of Mexico is about 25 million, but there are only 2.5 million *ejidatarios* with full rights.

10 There have always been small-scale land sales, but they did not lead the disintegration of the *ejido*, as the buyer eventually took the place of the seller as a member of the *ejido*.

11 See also Alatorre-Frenk (2000).

12 It is interesting to learn, however, that contrary to a generalized belief, the intellectual leaders of forestry policies in the post revolutionary period did envision the use of forests by peasants. For Miguel Ángel de Quevedo see Urquiza, 2014. For Enrique Beltrán, see Beltrán (1964).

13 *Ley Federal de Caza*, or Hunting Federal Act 1950.

14 *Ley General de Vida Silvestre* or General Act for Wildlife, 2000.

15 Due to lack of information about *comunidades* in this subject, I will refer only to the urbanization of *ejido* lands.

16 Tenure regularization programs were so "regular", that they created the confidence that informal transactions in the end would become formal. So they contributed to the "institutionalization" of the (however irregular) urbanization of *ejidos*.

17 The legal mechanism in this program was the use of eminent domain "against" *ejidos*. No *ejidatario* was ever prosecuted for illegally selling his land; and in the end they

even obtained a small compensation for the expropriation of their lands – a compensation that was paid with the (small) price that settlers had to pay for their titles.
18 I use Mikhail Bakhtin's concept of chronotope in the sense that has been suggested by Mariana Valverde (2014).

Works cited

Alatorre-Frenk, G. (2000) *La construcción de una cultura gerencial democrática en las empresas forestales comunitarias*. Mexico: Procuraduría Agraria/Juan Pablos.

Appendini, K. (2001) *Land Regularization and Conflict Resolution: The Case of Mexico*. Document prepared for FAO, Rural Development Division, Land Tenure Service. Mexico: El Colegio de México, December.

Aranibar, A. M. (Ed.) (2010) *Conflictos mineros: una realidad actual en América Latina y el Caribe*. La Paz: Gecomin.

Azuela, A. (1989) *La ciudad, la propiedad privada y el derecho*. Mexico: El Colegio de México.

Azuela, A. (1993) "La reforma del régimen ejidal y el desarrollo urbano" in Cámara de Diputados LV Legislatura/Comisión de Asentamientos Humanos (Eds.) *El Artículo 27 y el desarrollo urbano*. México: Cámara de Diputados del Congreso de la Unión.

Azuela, A. (1995) "Ciudadanía y Gestión Urbana en los Poblados Rurales de Los Tuxtlas" *Estudios Sociológicos* 13, 39, September.

Bartra, A. (1985) *Los herederos de Zapata. Movimientos campesinos posrevolucionarios en México*. Mexico: Era.

Beltrán, E. (1964) *La batalla forestal. Lo hecho, lo no hecho, lo por hacer*. Mexico: Editorial Cultura.

Boyer, C. (2007) "Revolución y paternalismo ecológico: Miguel Ángel de Quevedo y la política forestal en México, 1946–1940" *Historia Mexicana* 42, 1, pp. 91–138.

Braverman, I. et al., (Eds.) (2014) *The Expanding Spaces of Law: A Timely Legal Geography*. Stanford: Stanford University Press.

Bray, D. B. (1991) "The Struggle for the Forests: Conservation and Development in the Sierra de Juárez" *Grassroots Development* 15, 3, pp. 13–25.

Bray, D. B. and L. Merino-Pérez (Eds.) (2005) *The Community Forests of Mexico: Managing for Sustainable Landscapes*. Austin: The University of Texas Press.

Calva, J. L. (1993) *La disputa por la tierra*. Mexico: Fontamara.

Castells, M. (1981) *Crisis urbana y cambio social*. Mexico: Siglo Veintiuno Editores.

Chapela, F. (2008) *Revisión retrospectiva del desarrollo de la UZACHI*. Mexico: Era.

Connolly, P. (2012) "La urbanización irregular y el orden urbano en la Zona Metropolitana del Valle de México de 1990 a 2005" in Salazar, C. E. (coord.) *(I)rregular. Suelo y mercado en América Latina*. Mexico: El Colegio de México.

Connolly, P. and M. S. Cruz (2004) "Nuevos y viejos procesos en la periferia de la Ciudad de México" in Aguilar, A. G. (Ed.) *Procesos metropolitanos y grandes ciudades. Dinámicas recientes en México y otros países*. Mexico: Cámara de Diputados LIX Legislatura/UNAM/Conacyt, pp. 445–473.

Craib, R. (2004) *Cartographic Mexico: A History of State Fixations and Fugitive Landscapes*. Durham and London: Duke University Press.

Das, V. and D. Poole (2004) *Anthropology in the Margins of the State*. Santa Fe: School of American Research Press.

Delgado, G. (2010) *Ecología política de la minería en América Latina. Aspectos políticos, legales y medioambientales de la mega minería*. Mexico: UNAM/CEICH.

Díaz y Díaz, M. (2014) *Ensayos sobre la propiedad.* Mexico: UNAM/Instituto de Investigaciones Juridicas.

Domínguez-Mejía, M. I. (2011) "La consolidación de un Nuevo orden estatal en el Pacífico Colombiano: titulación colectiva y nuevas identidades negras en Buenaventura" en Agudo-Sanchíz A. y M. Estrada-Saavedra (Dir.) *(Trans)formaciones del estado en los márgenes de América Latina. Imaginarios alternativos, aparatos inacabados y espacios trasnacionales.* Mexico: El Colegio de México, Universidad Iberoamericana.

Dumoulin Kervran, D. and A. Michel (2007) " La communauté indienne participative: de quelques usages dans la politique mexicaine " in Neveu, C. (Ed.) *Cultures et pratiques participatives, une perspective comparative.* Paris: Harmattan, pp. 233–253.

Ferry, E. E. (2002) "Inalienable Commodities: The Production and Circulation of Silver and Patrimony in a Mexican Mining Cooperative" *Cultural Anthropology* 17, 3, pp. 331–358.

Ferry, E. E. (2005) *Not Ours Alone: Patrimony, Value, and Collectivity in Contemporary Mexico.* New York: Columbia University Press.

Garibay, C. y A. Balzaretti Camacho (2009) "Goldcorp y la reciprocidad negativa en el paisaje minero de Mezcala, Guerrero" *Desacatos*, 30, May–Aug, pp. 91–110.

Gibson, C., McKean, M. and E. Ostrom (2000) *People and Forests: Communities, Institutions and Governance.* Cambridge: MIT Press.

Goldring, L. (1998) "Having your Cake and Eating It Too: Selective Appropriation of *Ejido* Reform in Michoacán" in Cornelius, W. A. y D. Myhre (Compiladores) *The Transformation of Rural Mexico. Reforming the Ejido Sector.* San Diego: University of California.

Gordillo, G. (1988) *Campesinos al asalto del cielo: De la expropiación estatal a la apropiación campesina* (No. DERAJ-168). Mexico: Siglo Veintiuno Editores.

Harvey, D. (2009) "The 'new' imperialism: accumulation by dispossession" *Socialist Register*, 38, 38.

Hayden, C. (2003) *When Nature Goes Public: The Making and Un-Making of Bioprospecting in Mexico.* California: University of California Press.

Hernández-Ornelas, P. (1973) *Autoridad y poder social en el ejido. Un estudio sobre las bases políticas del México rural.* Mexico: Instituto Mexicano de Estudios Sociales.

Herrera, I. and E. González (2004) *Recursos del subsuelo, siglos XVI al XX.* Mexico: UNAM/Océano.

Ibarra-Mendívil, J. (1989) *Propiedad agraria y sistema político en México.* Mexico: Miguel Angel Porrúa.

Klooster, D. and S. Ambinakudige (2005) "The Global Significance of Mexican Community Forestry" in David, B. and L. Merino-Pérez (Eds.) *The Community Forests of Mexico: Managing for Sustainable Landscapes.* Austin: The University of Texas Press.

Kourí, E. H. (2002) "Interpreting the Expropriation of Indian Pueblo Lands in Porfirian Mexico: The Unexamined Legacies of Andrés Molina Enríquez" *Hispanic American Historical Review* 82, 1.

Kourí, E. H. (2015) "La invención del ejido" *Nexos*, 455, January, pp. 54–61.

Lefevbre, H. (1968) *Le droit à la ville.* Paris: Editions Anthropos.

Leonard, E., Quesnel, A. and E. Velázquez (2003) *Políticas y regulaciones agrarias. Dinámicas de poder y juegos de actores en torno a la tenencia de la tierra.* Mexico: Ciesas/IRD/Miguel Angel Porrúa.

Lombardo-Toledano, V. (1962) "La reforma agraria en México: sus obstáculos y los objetivos actuales" (Ponencia presentada en la Mesa Redonda que sobre el tema organizó la Asociación Cultural "Isidro Fabela", 20-VIII-1965) en Schaffer, V. M. (Ed.) *Reforma agraria mexicana*. Mexico: Universidad de Colima.

Lomnitz, C. (2001) *Deep Mexico, Silent Mexico: An Anthropology of Nationalism*. Minneapolis: University of Minnesota Press.

López Caballero, P. (2007) *Récits des origines, variations identitaires et conflits pour la légitimité politique à Milpa Alta, Mexico DF (XVIIe-XXIe siècle). Ethnographier l'Etat et historiciser l'ethnicité*. Ph.D. Dissertation, École Des Hautes Études En Sciences Sociales, Paris.

Madrid, L., et al. (2009) "La propiedad social forestal en México" *Investigación Ambiental* 1, 2, pp. 179–196.

Manzanilla-Schaffer, V. (1962) *Reforma agraria mexicana*. Mexico: Universidad de Colima.

Melé, P. (2011) *Transactions territoriales. Patrimoine, environnement, et actions collectives au Mexique*. Tours: Presses Universitaires François Rabelais.

Merino, L. and A. E. Martínez (2013) "El campo forestal mexicano y las comunidades forestales" in Merino-Pérez, L. y G. Ortiz-Merino (Eds.) *Encuentros y desencuentros. Las comunidades forestales y las políticas públicas en tiempos de transición*. México: Instituto de Investigaciones Sociales/Miguel Ángel Porrúa.

Merino, L., Ortiz, G. and A. E. Martínez (2013) "La Producción Forestal" in Merino-Pérez, L. y G. Ortiz-Merino (Eds.) *Encuentros y desencuentros. Las comunidades forestales y las políticas públicas en tiempos de transición*. México: Instituto de Investigaciones Sociales/Miguel Ángel Porrúa.

Meyer, J. (2004) *La Revolución Mexicana*. México: Tusquets.

Molina-Enríquez, A. (1922) "El espíritu de la Constitución de Querétaro" en *Boletín de la Secretaría de Gobernación I*, Núm. 4. Mexico: Secretaría de Gobernación.

Molina-Enríquez, A. (1978) *Los grandes problemas nacionales*. Mexico: Ediciones Era.

Morineau, O. (1947) *Los derechos reales y el subsuelo en México*. México: Fondo de Cultura Económica.

Nugent, D. and A. M. Alonso (2002) "Tradiciones selectivas en la reforma agraria y la lucha agraria: cultura popular y formación del estado en el *ejido* e Namiquipa" in Joseph, G. and D. Nugent (Eds.) *Aspectos cotidianos de la formación del estado. La revolución y la negociación del mando en el México moderno*. Mexico: Era.

Nuijten, M. (1992) "Local organization as organizing practices" in N. Long and A. Long (Eds.) *Battlefields of Knowledge: The Interlocking of Theory and Practice in Social Research and Development*. London and New York: Routledge.

Paz, M. F. (2012) "Conflictos socio ambientales, cultura política y gobernanza: la cooperación bajo sospecha" in Guzmán, M., Durand, L. y F. Figueroa (Eds.) *La naturaleza en contexto. Ecología política en México*. México: UNAM/CRIM.

Quadri, G. (2007) "Abolir el *ejido*?" in *El Economista*, Noviembre 29.

Robles-Berlanga, H. (2008) *Saldos de las reformas de 1992 al artículo 27 constitucional*. Mexico: Cámara de Diputados/CEDRSSA.

Rodríguez-Herrera, D. (2000) *Ley Agraria y protección del patrimonio arqueológico*. Mexico: Procuraduría Agraria/Casa Juan Pablos.

Rozental, S. (2014) "Stone Replicas: The Iteration and Itinerancy of Mexican Patrimonio" *Journal of Latin American and Caribbean Anthropology* 19, 2, pp. 331–356.

Rozental, S. (2016) "In the Wake of Patrimonio: Reconstituting the Fragments of History in San Miguel Coatlinchan" *Anthropology Quarterly* 89, 1, pp. 157–196.

Salazar, C. E. (2012) "Los ejidatarios en el control de la regularización" in Salazar, C. (Coord.) *(I)rregular. Suelo y mercado en América Latina*. Mexico: El Colegio de México.

Schteingart, M. (1989) *Los productores del espacio habitable. Estado, empresas y sociedad en la Ciudad de México*. México: El Colegio de México.

Simpson, E. (1937) *The Ejido: Mexico's Way Out*. Chapel Hill: The University of North Carolina Press.

Svampa, M. y M. Antonelli (2010) *Minería trasnacional, narrativas del desarrollo y resistencias sociales*. Buenos Aires: Editorial Biblos.

Tannenbaum, F. (1929) *The Mexican Agrarian Revolution*. Washington, DC: Brookings Institute.

Téllez, L. (1993) *Nueva legislación sobre tierras, aguas y bosques*. Mexico: Fondo de Cultura Económica.

Toledo, V. M. (1997) "Sustainable Development at the Village Community Level: A Third World Perspective" in Fraser, S. (Ed.) *Environmental Sustainability: Practical Global Implications*. Boca Raton: St Lucie Press.

Torres-Mazuera, G. (2009) "La territorialidad rural mexicana en un contexto de descentralización y competencia electoral" *Revista Mexicana de Sociología* 71, 3, July/September.

Torres-Mazuera, G. (2014) *La común anomalía del ejido posrevolucionario. Disonancias normativas y mercantilización de la tierra en el sur de Yucatán*. Mérida: CIESAS-Peninsular.

Urquiza, H. (2014) *Ciencia forestal, propiedad y conservación para el desarrollo nacional. Los estudios y trabajos ambientales de Miguel Ángel de Quevedo: Una historia de su influencia en las políticas de conservación de las cuencas hidrológicas (1890–1940)*. Ph.D. Thesis in History, Universidad Nacional Autónoma de México, Mexico.

Valverde, M. (2014) "Time Thickens, Takes on Flesh: Spatiotemporal Dynamics in Law" in Braverman, I., et al. (Eds.) *The Expanding Spaces of Law: A Timely Legal Geography*. Stanford: Stanford University Press.

Varley, A. (1989) "Propiedad de la revolución? Los *ejidos* en el crecimiento de la ciudad de México" en *Revista Interamericana de Planificación* 22, 87 y 88, July–Septembver y October–December.

Varley, A. (1998) "The Political Uses of Illegality: Evidence from Urban Mexico" in Fernandes, E. and A. Varley (Eds.) *Illegal Cities: Law and Urban Change in Developing Countries*. London: Zed Books.

Wakild, E. (2011) *Revolutionary Parks: Conservation, Social Justice, and Mexico's National Parks, 1910–1940*. Tucson: The University of Arizona Press.

Warman, A. (2001) *El campo mexicano en el siglo XX*. México: Fondo de Cultura Económica.

Weiner, A. (1992) *Inalienable Possessions: The Paradox of Keeping While Giving*. Berkeley: University of California Press.

12 Conclusion

The revival of the "commons" and the redefinition of property rights

Olivier De Schutter and
Balakrishnan Rajagopal

The essays collected in this volume describe the growing resistance towards the commodification of land, and the corresponding "counter-movement" towards a revival of community-based understanding of land and resources. This reaction is directed against a sanctification of a Western understanding of property rights that has increasingly become the global norm. The contemporary revival of the "commons", however, manifests itself in two separate forms. In this chapter, we first summarize each of these branches. We argue that these two approaches are complementary rather than antagonistic: although starting from different premises and relying largely on different methodologies, they both serve to strengthen the argument in favor of empowering the community of users to define for themselves the rules by which they shall be governed in the management of their resources.

In section 2, we examine the contribution of international law to this revival of the "commons". On the one hand, recent advances in international law provide legitimacy to the recognition of customary and collective forms of tenure, thus providing a powerful counter-narrative to the strong push towards titling of property that was characteristic of development efforts starting in the 1990s. On the other hand, international law may also provide a framework to ensure that the self-determination of local communities (their ability to design the rules according to which they shall manage resources on which they depend) is not abused, and that it shall not lead to the reproduction of patriarchal, plutocratic, racial or ethnic or other related patterns of domination.

Finally, section 3 draws some lessons from these developments for a renewed understanding of property which can help anchor the insights based on international law. Against the "overcommodification" of property, in which the social purpose of property is negated, we argue for understanding property as an institution that should be redesigned to serve social justice. A first step towards achieving this objective would be to support social innovations that, in all world regions, are reinventing property. This volume is, we hope, a modest contribution towards this end.

1. The revival of the "commons": two branches

A. The political economy approach to the management of common-pool resources

A first important contribution to the contemporary revival of the "commons" comes from the political economy of the management of natural resources. In the 1960s, at the height of the developmentalist ideology, the general view was that users of natural resources would behave as rational economic agents, eager to maximize their individual utility and driven by a short-term urge to increase their revenue. It was on this utilitarian anthropology that Garrett Hardin founded his pessimistic view about the viability of shared resources, what he famously referred to as the "tragedy of the commons" (Hardin 1968; see also Gordon 1954; Demsetz 1967; and Carruthers and Stoner 1981). Since the 1990s however, a large number of studies have demonstrated that, under certain conditions, local communities are capable of managing common resources and might even do so in ways that are more sustainable and more effective than if such management were left either to individual owners following a process of privatization or to the state. These communities, after all, are ideally positioned to design the governance system that is best suited to the local conditions. In such cases, members of the community will normally perceive the rules they set as highly legitimate. Since community members will have contributed to shaping the governance regime, they are likely to have a strong incentive in contributing to the enforcement of the rules. And to a large extent, as the rules will be designed with a view to improving the situation of the community as a whole rather than that of individual members, they may be shaped in order to minimize negative externalities and to preserve the long-term viability of the resource, thus improving sustainability.

These ideas were popularized in 1990 in a book-length publication based on the studies done by Elinor Ostrom and her collaborators on the management of common-pool resources within the Workshop in Political Theory and Policy Analysis at Indiana University (Ostrom 1990). Later contributions followed, illustrating the fecundity of the hypothesis (see, for instance, Agarwal 2001; Cox et al. 2010). At the heart of these approaches is the idea that individuals should not be seen as locked into a setting in which competition for the use of the resource is inevitable. Instead, provided the right institutional conditions are present, individuals can move toward cooperative solutions. Whereas the management of natural resources is generally seen through the paradigm of the Prisoner's Dilemma, in which selfish rational behavior by each individual can only lead to collectively sub-optimal solutions (justifying therefore the imposition of top-down regulations to force efficient outcomes), the examples studied by Ostrom show that, if given the opportunity to set their own rules, communities may be able to act better (more efficiently, more legitimately and more sustainably) than the state, whereas, in the paradigm guiding the work of Mancur Olson (1965), for instance, "the prisoners in the famous dilemma cannot change the constraints imposed on them by the district attorney".

> Not all users of natural resources are similarly incapable of changing their constraints. As long as individuals are viewed as prisoners, policy prescriptions will address this metaphor. [The alternative, however, is to] address the question of how to enhance the capabilities of those involved to change the constraining rules of the game to lead to outcomes other than remorseless tragedies.
>
> (Ostrom 1990: 7)

Ostrom's approach remains limited in one important way. It is premised on the idea that there are certain types of resources – common-pool resources (CPR) – that, due to their specific characteristics, are well suited to being governed by users' communities. A common-pool resource is defined as "a natural or man-made resource system that is sufficiently large as to make it costly (but not impossible) to exclude potential beneficiaries from obtaining benefits from the use" (Ostrom 1990: 30). The analysis of Ostrom moreover focuses on relatively circumscribed situations – situations in which, in particular, "the CPR is itself located within one country and the number of individuals affected varies from 50 to 15,000 persons who are heavily dependent on the CPR for economic returns" (Ostrom 1990: 26); in which "CPR appropriators have no power in a final goods market [by forming cartels to fix prices, for instance]" and in which, finally, the actions of the appropriators do not have "significant impact on the environment of others living outside the range of their CPR" (Ostrom 1990: 31). These are important limitations. At face value, they would seem to suggest that CPRs are a particular type of good, vaguely comparable to "club goods" in the typology of goods derived from Paul Samuelson's distinction between private and public goods, as later refined by James Buchanan (Samuelson 1954; Buchanan 1965) and illustrated in Figure 12.1 that follows. CPRs, indeed, are productive resources that produce units that, if appropriated by some, cannot be appropriated by others (in that sense, the consumption of the goods produced by the resource is rival), but from which users can be excluded (so that the members of the community may at a reasonable cost reserve to themselves the exploitation of the resource).

Elinor Ostrom herself would disagree with this characterization. Instead, together with her partner Vincent Ostrom (Ostrom and Ostrom 1977) and in writings she authored alone (Ostrom 2010), she instead tends to classify CPRs among "common goods", again remaining within the classification economists use to categorize different categories of goods as illustrated in the following typology:

		Subtractibility of use	
		High	Low
Difficulty of excluding potential beneficiaries	High	Common goods: lakes, fisheries, forests, etc.	Public goods: national defense, public infrastructures (unless a toll is imposed), etc.
	Low	Private goods: food, clothing, housing, etc.	Club goods: infrastructures subjected to payment of a toll, private clubs, etc.

Figure 12.1 A typology of goods

Source: Based on Samuelson (1954), Buchanan (1965), Ostrom (2010).

The classification of common-pool resources within the category of "common goods", however, is premised on two ideas: first, the resource is a fragile one, in the sense that it may collapse as a result of the resource being overexploited (if the multiple users do not agree on a set of rules that ensure that the resource will be used sustainably); second, it is difficult (if not impossible) to exclude some people from using the resource, which therefore is essentially subject to open access – indeed, it is this feature that results in the "tragedy" that Hardin referred to in his 1968 article cited above. However, both these premises may or may not be empirically verified in specific contexts. In fact, the common-pool resources studied by Elinor Ostrom herself illustrate that in many instances she observed, the resource was in fact exploited sustainably by the community of users, even as the products drawn from the resource were subject to rivalrous consumption. Once we distinguish between the resource itself and the units produced by the resource, it is indeed possible to define a "replenishment rate", and "as long as the average rate of withdrawal does not exceed the average rate of replenishment, a renewable resource is sustained over time" (Ostrom 1990: 30): for instance, whereas the fish appropriated by some individuals cannot be eaten by others, the fish stock itself, if managed sustainably, is a renewable resource, the exploitation of which is therefore not rivalrous *under the right institutional conditions*. Similarly, whereas Elinor Ostrom has sometimes located common-pool resources amongst the common goods in the classic typology described earlier, since excluding potential beneficiaries is difficult, the examples she studies lead her to identify as one important factor of success in the long-term viability of common management schemes the fact that CPRs have "clearly defined boundaries", a condition she describes as follows: "Individuals or households who have rights to withdraw resource units from the CPR must be clearly defined, as much the boundaries of the CPR itself" (Ostrom 1990: 91). Again, it is a matter of institutional architecture whether or not such exclusion (or such a "clear definition of the boundaries") will be effective and whether the transaction costs involved will be sufficiently reduced to ensure the scheme is viable.

Finally, what the classification above misses is that some resources in fact depend, for their long-term viability (or replenishment), on a number of users relying on the resource, thus contributing to its enhancement. Wikipedia is an example: without the continued collaboration of users, who improve the resource and constantly update it at the same time that they rely on it, its use-value would soon decrease. Plant genetic resources are another example: it is only by the patient process of saving and replanting seeds, performed by farmers generation after generation, that agro-biodiversity is enhanced. The cataloging of seeds in seed banks would not be a substitute for the use of such resources by farmers, which allows the genetic stock to be permanently renewed and improved (De Schutter 2011b); conversely, patent thickets or excessively strong plant-breeders' rights may make it difficult for new plant varieties to emerge, since innovations would not be able to build on existing (but patented, or otherwise restricted) genetic material. This is what Michael Heller called the "tragedy of the anti-commons", in which excessive barriers resulting from intellectual property rights delay innovation and thus are an obstacle to a competitive and efficient economy (Heller 1998, 2008). The peer-to-peer collaborative economy provides a wealth of other examples, as do the different varieties of "creative commons", which emerged in recent years in order to overcome the barriers to the dissemination of certain works resulting from copyright restrictions (see generally Ciorat 2015). In all these cases, we witness a positive correlation between the number of users and the use-value of the resource: far from there being a risk of overexploitation, the resource would be eroded if potential users were to be fenced off.

In fact, one could argue that all resources face the risk of under-exploitation at least in one sense: if a too-limited number of users rely on it, the rules regulating the use of the resource may be poorly enforced, since few people will have an incentive to contribute to such enforcement. Moreover, public goods are generally provided by the state and financed by the public purse, and they are thus dependent on people paying taxes. Therefore, it is to the extent that access is as broad as possible to all groups of the population that such taxation will be perceived as legitimate by the population, particularly by the wealthiest segments (who generally contribute relatively more, in systems of progressive taxation). If, for instance, only children from poor families had free access to schools, the wealthier households may be reluctant to contribute taxes to finance education. This is one major argument for the universality of social protection and for public services, even in polities in which income inequalities remain important. And it is one reason why public services in areas such as health, education or transport are threatened, not where *too many* people come to rely on them, but where (for example due to the coexistence with private service-providers that provide better quality services against fees) *too few* people use them – for it is then that they may be seen as not worth being financed by taxes.

In order to take into account these variations of the "tragedy of the anti-commons" (in a meaning broader than that considered by Heller), we may have to again revisit the classic typology and add a layer of complexity to include the situation where consumption is not only not rivalrous (in other terms, where the "subtractibility of use" is low: the fact that one actor enjoys access to the good does not diminish its enjoyment by others), but where, moreover, users contribute to maintain the resource or to co-produce and co-improve the good. In this situation, the larger the number of users, the better the resource will be maintained, or the more of the good will be produced. However, there is a difference between what, in this typology, we call "open-access" goods – in which any user may freely contribute without the rise in numbers of users raising significantly the coordination (or transaction) costs and "collaborative goods", which do require for their production a certain level of coordination between the users and the imposition and enforcement of rules that may lead to excluding users who do not comply. The logic of collaborative goods is that, while a larger number of users can benefit the community, allowing the resource to be better maintained or more of the good to be produced, the results may be suboptimal in the absence of adequate (rules-based) coordination between the users. In the following table, this hypothesis is equated to one in which certain beneficiaries may be excluded, because coordination requires the effective enforcement of rules that may lead to exclusion in cases of non-compliance:

| | | Subtractibility of use | | |
		High: overutilization is a risk to the resource	Low: there is no risk of overutilization	Negative: underutilization threatens the viability of the resource
Measures are taken to exclude potential beneficiaries or to make participation conditional upon the users contributing	No	Common goods: lakes, fisheries, forests, etc.	Public goods: national defense, public infrastructures (unless a toll is imposed), etc.	Open-access goods: users contribute to maintaining the good/resource, and all can easily contribute
	Yes	Private goods: food, clothing, housing, etc.	Club goods: infrastructures subjected to payment of a toll, private clubs, etc.	Collaborative goods: users contribute to maintaining the good/resource, but under certain conditions

Figure 12.2 A typology of goods, including goods that are co-produced by the users

Open-access goods and collaborative goods are thus goods to the production or maintenance of which the users contribute. As a result, the question of exclusion presents itself in a form that is almost the reverse than in the paradigmatic situation that Hardin had in mind when writing about the "tragedy of the commons". The problem here, as noted by Hanoch Dagan and Michael Heller (2001), is not *only* to avoid that users "overuse" the good (or exploit the resource beyond its carrying capacity); it is *also*, and perhaps *primarily*, to avoid that users are tempted not to contribute to the maintenance of the resource or to the production of the good by refusing to cooperate, though occasionally taking a free ride on the efforts of others. Consider for instance a collective vegetable garden that all families of the neighborhood are invited to contribute to and that grants them free access to the vegetables they grow collectively: opportunistic individuals might be tempted to take the vegetables without performing the work. Although the more neighbors who contribute to the vegetable garden, the better – in that the garden will be better maintained (it is in that sense that the garden may be classified as a "collaborative good"). This "commons" still requires that a certain balance be kept between the contributions of each participant (in work hours) and the benefits (in vegetables) he or she obtains. Of course, what counts as "contribution" and what counts as "benefit" is in part arbitrary (for people involved in collective vegetable gardens, a key motivating factor is the joy of working collaboratively and to build new social links), and there are situations where the two are truly indistinguishable. For instance, the larger the number of users of a car-sharing platform, the smoother the platform shall function, and using the platform *is* to contribute to its efficiency as a tool for all other users. A "tragedy" of a different kind may nevertheless emerge in more ambiguous or hybrid situations: it is in such cases that the questions of who has the authority to set the rules and how such rules shall be enforced take a decisive importance.

B. The deep democratic approach to the management of local affairs

What the previous discussion illustrates is that the classification of various goods or resources in the typologies outlined depends not on certain characteristics *intrinsic* to such goods or resources, but rather on an *institutional choice*, made within the particular society concerned, as to how such goods or resources should be governed. Elinor Ostrom spontaneously classifies a lake as a "common good", which is open to the public and where people may fish freely without fishing rights being reserved: in this scenario, the risks of overexploitation are indeed real, and it is to answer to this threat that she develops her alternative (see Ostrom 2010; and Figure 12.1 previously). That is not necessarily so, however. A lake located within a piece of land auctioned to a private company, which that company uses without any environmental restriction being imposed, will be treated simply as a "private good"; the same lake, managed by a community that designs its own rules to ensure that its fish stock will be exploited sustainably, but that develops means to ensure that no outside individual can fish in the lake, appears as a "club good". To borrow from the terminology of Carol Rose, quoted in this volume by Sheila R. Foster, such co-ownership appears like "commons on the inside", but operates very much like "private property on the outside" (Rose 1998). The lake would be a "public good", in which the use by some does not restrict use by others, and where regulations impose limits on fishing to avoid such overexploitation – again the result of an institutional choice, rather than a characteristic inherent to the resource itself.

Far from this being an infirmity, or a limitation, of the approach pioneered by Elinor Ostrom, this plasticity of the categories shows the potential for her model to have significance far beyond the category of resources we normally would see as common-pool resources – the fishing grounds, forests, grazing areas or irrigation systems she documents. Not only can Ostrom's approach apply, without much modification, to the urban commons (see Foster 2011), but in addition, it serves to broaden our institutional imagination, allowing us to design governance principles for both material and non-material resources and for institutions in the broadest sense of the expression. Indeed, the second avenue through which the commons are currently being revived is through the "deep democratic" current running through a number of contemporary social movements.

This current translates in the invention of various forms of direct democracy, beyond electoral politics and the delegation of powers to representatives appointed by political parties. Occupy Wall Street and equivalent Occupy movements in many parts of advanced industrial societies – from the *Indignados* in Madrid to the *Gezi Parc* in Istanbul – deny that they are adequately represented by the governing elites: even progressive parties, they assert, are complicit in a system that is perceived as working only for the better-off and as silencing minority voices. These groups are impatient. They have grown tired of waiting on solutions from either politicians or from the industry. Instead, they organize forms of solidarity and communality at a local level, inventing solutions that often take politicians by surprise. They set up community vegetable gardens or short food chains, local composting schemes, citizens-owned cooperatives to produce electricity from windmills or from solar panels (shared through local distribution grids) or platforms to share cars or tools. Occasionally, they violate the law, but as discussed in detail by Sonia Katyal and Eduardo Peñalver both in a book-form publication (Peñalver and Katyal 2010) and in Chapter 6 of this volume, they do so not so much as a means of protest than in order to bring about change directly, when such change cannot be expected to come from normal channels of democratic representation.

This is what David Bollier calls "commoning". It is fundamentally about people deciding collectively to co-govern a resource or an institution, designing rules that they find to be most suitable in the particular context in which they operate (Bollier and Helfrich 2015). Thus understood, the term encompasses a much broader set of social innovations by which relationships around resources and institutions are redefined by the social actors themselves, who occupy a space between the state and the market, escaping both bureaucratization and commodification – a space that these actors seek to democratize by inventing the rules by which it shall be governed (Dardot and Laval 2015; Hardt and Negri 2009). Such claims to self-government inevitably lead to questioning of representative democracy, in which a small group of elected politicians decide for the community without its members being involved in day-to-day decision-making. It is not by accident that, at the same time commoning practices develop in a number of areas, scholars and activists insist on the need for more direct forms of political participation to overcome the separation between the people and the ruling elites (Van Reybrouck 2013; Graeber 2013).

Is this second channel through which the commons are being revived competing with Elinor Ostrom's approach? Pierre Dardot and Christian Laval believe it is. They prefer to describe the phenomenon using a verb (*commoning*) rather than a noun (the *commons*) to emphasize the active participation on which it relies and to avoid reifying the commons. They see Ostrom's work as remaining stuck in a form of economicism and Ostrom herself as reformist, rather than as having a revolutionary potential: it would be premised on the idea that commoning can survive in a capitalist world, in which most institutions are still governed either by market relationships or by a state bureaucracy. This, they see as naïve. Instead, they see commoning as applicable across all society to a range of areas – from education to healthcare and from forest management to energy – which should be democratized in order to respond to the aspirations of this impatient public (Dardot and Laval 2015: 155–156; for an extended argument earlier, see Unger, 2000). If Ostrom were our Proudhon, they would see themselves as the Marx and Engels of these times.

C. Participation rights and social capital: from the management of common-pool resources to deep democracy

The apparent opposition between Ostrom's economicism and Dardot and Laval's radicalism should be nuanced, however. Indeed, two lessons drawn by Ostrom from her empirical work would appear to be relevant for governance in general, in all areas of life. First, she insists on the role of *self-government* in allowing particular communities, operating in particular contexts, to identify the rules that are best suited to their needs. For such self-government to succeed, she argues, these communities should be recognized as a "constitutional" authority. In other terms, they should not be limited to one level of rules (for instance, the operational rules alone, governing the use and exploitation of the resource, rather than collective-choice rules or even constitutional rules). Rather, the communities should be trusted to choose their own decision-making rules and to revise them: "self-organizing and self-governing individuals trying to cope with problems in field settings go back and forth across levels as a key strategy for solving problems" (Ostrom 1990: 54). Unless communities are recognized with such "constitutional authority", they will be stuck within a particular structure of the problems they face, with no ability to change the institutional setting in which they operate – and this may become an insuperable obstacle to the setting-up of effective cooperative schemes. Secondly, Ostrom insists on the idea that collaborative efforts result in the creation of *social capital* that, once it is reconstituted, can facilitate collective action in a wider set of circumstances to address a broader set of issues. "Success in starting small-scale initial institutions enables a group of individuals to build on the social capital thus created to solve larger problems with larger and more complex institutional arrangements. Current theories of collective action do not stress the process of accretion of institutional capital. Thus, one problem in using them as foundations for policy analysis is that they do not focus on the incremental self-transformations that frequently are involved in the process of supplying institutions. Learning is an incremental, self-transforming process" (Ostrom 1990: 190).

Both ideas remain highly relevant to the redefinition of the institution of property. Property is a social construct, and the bundle of prerogatives associated with it will vary as a result of societal choices (Commons 1893: 93; Hohfeld 1920). There were nine such prerogatives in the decomposition proposed by John R. Commons – including four "public partial rights" and five "private (and public) partial rights" – and there were four in the version of W. N. Hohfeld (the "right" in the narrow sense of the expression, which allows the right-holder to bring in the state to impose on others that they comply with certain obligations; the *privilege*, i.e. the freedom to do certain things; the *power* to change another individual's

juridical situation and the *immunity* from being imposed such a change by another's unilateral will). The commons approach shifts the focus from the various
prerogatives associated with the right to property (the sticks of the bundle, if you
wish) to the question of *who authors the rules that define such prerogatives* (how
the rules are set to govern the distribution of the sticks). Ostrom and other scholars
associated with this line of inquiry argue that such choices are best made at the
level of the community of users rather than by the imposition of uniform solutions
by the state or as the result of the blind forces of the market backed by private law.

Indeed, together with Edella Schlager, Elinor Ostrom discussed the "bundle of
rights" approach in order to provide a version that would be particularly suited
to situate the common property regimes she analyzed in 1990 in *Governing the
Commons* (Schlager and Ostrom 1992). The authors first distinguish between
"operational-level property rights", which are primarily the right of *access*
(defined as "the right to enter a defined physical property") and the right of *withdrawal* ("to obtain the 'products' of a resource") on one hand; and, on the other
hand, "collective-choice rights", which concern "the authority to define future
operational-level rights" (Schlager and Ostrom 1992: 250–251). Such collective-
choice rights include *management rights* ("the right to regulate internal use patterns and transform the resource by making improvements"), *exclusion rights* ("to
determine who will have access rights, and how that right may be transferred")
and *alienation rights* ("to sell or lease either or both of the above collective-choice
rights"). By listing these various prerogatives and associating them with various
positions (from the full "owner" to the "authorized user"), Shlager and Ostrom
can illustrate the variety of ways in which the relationship of any particular individual to the resource may be governed:

	Owner	Proprietor	Claimant	Authorized user
Access and withdrawal	X	X	X	X
Management	X	X	X	
Exclusion	X	X		
Alienation	X			

Figure 12.3 Bundles of rights associated with positions
Source: Reproduced from Schlager and Ostrom (1992).

Taking these distinctions as their departure point, the authors note that alienation rights are neither a sufficient nor a necessary condition for a sustainable
use of the resource. Indeed, alienation rights do not ensure that the owner shall
make a sustainable use of the resource since, if s/he applies a high discounting
rate to the potential of future gains, s/he may not care much about overexploit-
ing the resource. Nor are alienation rights a necessary condition to ensure such

sustainable use, since other ("weaker") prerogatives associated with property in the broad sense may suffice: "Owners and proprietors are reasonably assured of being rewarded for incurring the costs of investment (Posner 1975). Such investments are likely to take the form of devising withdrawal rights that coordinate the harvesting activities of groups of owners or proprietors so as to avoid or resolve common-pool resource dilemmas. In addition, owners and proprietors devise access rights that allow them to capture the benefits produced by the withdrawal rights (Dahlman 1980)" (Schlager and Ostrom 1992: 257). Therefore, contrary to the prejudice frequently encountered amongst economists (see in particular Demsetz 1967), full ownership rights are not a necessary condition for an efficient and sustainable use of resources.

Schlager and Ostrom put forward another distinction, however, and it is this second distinction that matters most for our purposes. That distinction is between "rights" and "rules": rights are certain authorizations (to do certain things, such as to have access to a good); rules are "the prescriptions that create authorizations" (Schlager and Ostrom 1992: 250). What may seem like a banal distinction does encourage us to identify, as a separate layer of prerogatives, what might be called "constitutional-level" prerogatives, which are rights to participate in the design of rules that will govern the distribution of both operational-level property rights and collective-choice rights. This complements one major implication of the findings of Elinor Ostrom: the self-government of communities, if it is to allow for a sustainable use of resources, should include the possibility not only of *choosing the rules that shall govern such use*, but also the possibility of *choosing how the rules shall be established*: it should include, in other terms, the constitutional-level prerogatives to choose the property regime that best suits the needs of the community and ensure that the rules are legitimate and well-tailored to the local context. It is in this sense that Ostrom's pioneering work on common-pool resources – far from being stuck in economicism or, even worse, in a "physicalist" perspective – contributes to and supports the deep-democratic approach to governance.

2. The contribution of international law to the revival of the "commons"

The preceding paragraphs discuss the question of which *autonomy* should be granted to local communities (*autonomy* being understood here in the etymological sense of one's ability to choose by which rules one shall be governed). That question is central, in particular, to the legitimate role of international law in contributing to the movement toward the "commons". Common-property regimes are increasingly referred to in recent international instruments, with a view to ensuring that such property regimes are protected from appropriation and encroachment. International law is therefore playing a major role in encouraging states to acknowledge that such forms of tenure are recognized as legitimate and adequately supported. However, another function of international law may be to ensure that, to the extent local communities are being granted a form of constitutional autonomy (the ability to choose how the collective-choice rules will be set in order to adopt and regularly revise the operational-level rules), such autonomy does not lead to the exclusion or marginalization of certain segments of the community.

A. Acknowledging the role of common-property regimes

Common-property regimes are spectacularly endorsed, for instance, in the *Voluntary Guidelines on the Responsible Governance of Tenure of Land, Fisheries and Forests in the Context of National Food Security*, adopted in 2012 by the Committee on World Food Security. These guidelines provide that states should "ensure that policy, legal and organizational frameworks for tenure governance recognize and respect, in accordance with national laws, legitimate tenure rights including legitimate customary tenure rights that are not currently protected by law" (guideline 5.3). They specifically note "that there are publicly-owned land, fisheries and forests that are collectively used and managed (in some national contexts referred to as commons)", and that "States should, where applicable, recognize and protect such publicly-owned land, fisheries and forests and their related systems of collective use and management, including in processes of allocation by the State" (guideline 8.3).

Though the terminology of *voluntary guidelines* may seem quite modest, such endorsement is significant, considering both the role of the CFS in global governance and the process through which the guidelines were adopted. Initially established in 1974, following the first World Food Conference as an intergovernmental committee within the United Nations Food and Agriculture Organization (FAO), the CFS was reformed in 2009 in order to become "the foremost inclusive international and intergovernmental platform for a broad range of committed stakeholders to work together in a coordinated manner and in support of country-led processes toward the elimination of hunger and ensuring food security and nutrition for all human beings" (Committee on World Food Security 2009: para. 4). It has since then been operating as a highly visible intergovernmental forum, with a strong legitimacy due to the fact that it involves in its deliberations, in addition to the governments as full members, civil society organizations, representatives of the private sector and of philanthropic organizations and the most important international agencies whose mandates relate to food security. In other words, the CFS expresses the consensus across the international community as to how global food security should be addressed, and the documents it has adopted – such as the 2012 Voluntary Guidelines on the Governance of Tenure (VGGT) – are the result of complex intergovernmental negotiations, with a view to achieving a consensus across all the member states of the FAO as well as other stakeholders.

Two years after the adoption by the CFS of the VGGT, another intergovernmental committee of the FAO, the Committee on Fisheries (COFI), adopted the *Voluntary Guidelines for Securing Sustainable Small-Scale Fisheries in the Context of Food Security and Poverty Eradication* (SSF guidelines). The guidelines were the outcome of a three-year participatory process conducted between 2010 and 2013 involving more than 4,000 representatives of governments, small-scale fishers, fish workers and their organizations, researchers, development partners and other relevant stakeholders from more than 120 countries in six regions, and more than 20 civil-society organization-led national consultative meetings. They provide that "States, in accordance with their legislation, should ensure that small-scale fishers, fish workers *and their communities* have secure, equitable, and socially and culturally appropriate tenure rights to fishery resources (marine and inland) and small-scale fishing areas and adjacent land, with a special attention paid to women with respect to tenure rights" (guideline 5.3 (emphasis added)). Like the VGGT, which were an important source of inspiration for the SSF guidelines, they encourage States to recognize forms of co-management of fisheries based on customary forms of tenure:

> Local norms and practices, as well as customary or otherwise preferential access to fishery resources and land by small-scale fishing communities including indigenous peoples and ethnic minorities, should be recognized, respected and protected in ways that are consistent with international human rights law.
>
> (guideline 5.4)

Indeed, for the same reasons why the generalization of individual property rights through titling schemes has been challenged as regards land tenure (as previously discussed in our introductory chapter to this volume), the attribution of fishing rights based on the allocation of quotas – in particular, with a view to avoiding overfishing – has been questioned in the organization of the fishing sector. For many years, the dominant view was that a clarification and strengthening of access rights, including by the use of transferable fishing quotas, would increase economic efficiency and avoid overfishing (see, for instance, World Bank 2004; or Cunningham et al. 2009). But another, opposite view has now emerged, according to which priority should go to poverty-reduction objectives and to improving access to fishing rights in the communities who need it most and who could be best placed to manage the common-pool resources concerned and monitor catches at the local level. This alternative approach to the allocation of fishing rights emerged from the concern that individual transferable quotas systems may lead to rent capture by certain actors in a privileged position, an outcome that is difficult to reconcile with poverty-reduction objectives, and that the Human Rights Committee found to be a potential source of discrimination in violation of Article 26 of the International Covenant on Civil and Political Rights[1] – a conclusion mirrored in the famous *Kenneth George* case presented to the South African courts.[2]

The shift to co-management of fisheries vesting collective rights with fishing communities is also based on the broadly positive assessment made of the establishment of fishing zones (whether lakes or coastal areas in seas) reserving fishing in these areas to local communities, allowing them to manage access rights (Sharma 2011). Indeed, one of the contributions that influenced the adoption of the 2014 SSF guidelines (see Ratner et al. 2014) was a report presented in 2012 by the

United Nations Special Rapporteur on the right to food, which (explicitly addressing the negotiations that were then being launched on this new instrument) noted that "top-down management strategies have been unsuccessful for the small-scale sector", and that "the active and meaningful participation by communities in the management of fisheries as well as the integration in decision-making of local or traditional knowledge on fish and marine habitats held by fishers is paramount" (Special Rapporteur on the right to food 2012, para. 58). The report cited a 2011 study that, comparing 130 co-management schemes (covering 44 developed and developing countries), demonstrated how local communities have often been able to develop legitimate institutions of self-governance and establish sustainable approaches to managing fishing intensity and ecosystems impacts, provided that strong community leaders emerge and robust social capital exists to monitor compliance with individual or community quotas (Gutiérrez et al. 2011). Other studies highlighted that co-management schemes could be successful, provided that certain conditions are present (Townsend 2008; Béné et al. 2009), including in particular an enabling institutional environment at the national level (Nielsen et al. 2004; Lewins et al. 2014) and a tradition of cooperation within the community (Jamu et al. 2011). Building on this literature, the report continued:

> Failures in co-management are partly explained by the fact that communities have been involved only in the implementation of policy, rather than in setting objectives of policy and ensuring that policy-making and evaluation are based on local knowledge on fish and marine ecosystems. The failure to integrate fishing communities in the design of policies affecting them, the top-down creation of community-based organizations to carry out functions for the State, approaches that are excessively donor-driven or that are captured by elites, have disappointed expectations. The solution to these difficulties is not to abandon co-management: it is to build it in a more participatory way, based on the needs of the fishing communities. This in turn will only be successful if the livelihoods of fishers are also better secured, taking into account that the environment in which they operate, and the markets on which they depend, are increasingly risky. Only by linking fisheries management to the broader improvement of the economic and social rights of fishers, in a multisectoral approach that acknowledges how fishing fits into the broader social and economic fabric, can progress be made towards solutions that are robust and sustainable.
>
> (Special Rapporteur on the right to food 2012,
> para. 59 (references omitted))

Finally and most recently, the revival of the commons in international human rights law can be seen in the process of adoption of a Declaration on the Rights of Peasants and Other People Working in Rural Areas by the UN General Assembly on December 17, 2018 (UNGA 2018).[3] The process of adoption of the Declaration was launched by Bolivia within the Human Rights Council and was strongly inspired by the *Via Campesina*, the transnational network of small-scale food producers (for background of this attempt, see Claeys 2015, 2018; Golay 2015 and the chapter by Claeys in this volume). Article 5(1) of the Declaration refers to the right of peasants and other people working in rural areas "to have access to and to use in a sustainable manner the natural resources present in their communities that are required to enjoy adequate living conditions", as well as the right "to participate in the management of these resources". Article 17(1) provides that peasants and other people living in rural areas have the right to land, *individually and/or collectively*, in accordance with Article 28 of the present Declaration, including the right to access the land; to sustainably use and manage the land and the water bodies, coastal seas, fisheries, pastures and forests therein; to achieve an adequate standard of living; to have a place to live in security, peace, and dignity; and to develop their cultures (emphasis added). In wording clearly inspired by the 2012 VGGT, Article 17(3) adds:

> States shall take appropriate measures to provide legal recognition for land tenure rights, including customary land tenure rights not currently protected by law, recognizing the existence of different models and systems. States shall protect legitimate tenure and ensure that peasants and other people working in rural areas are not arbitrarily or unlawfully evicted and that their rights are not otherwise extinguished or infringed. *States shall recognize and protect the natural commons and their related systems of collective use and management.*[4]

Thus, whereas international law originally emerged as a tool to justify colonial appropriation (Anghie 2005), recent trends in international human rights law exhibit a strong reaction against the push toward privatization and enclosures (see also Bakker 2007; De Schutter 2018). They also highlight the importance of rethinking doctrines such as Permanent Sovereignty over Natural Resources (PSNR) as right of communities, rather than states, as many TWAIL scholars have argued (Rajagopal 2003 chapter 8). However, these trends toward the recognition of communal forms of tenure leave open the question of the extent to which local communities (or the collectives of users of a particular resource) should be granted a constitutional role in choosing the rules by which collective-choice rules and operational-level rules shall be set, or whether the constitutional rules (i.e. defining how the collective-choice rules and operational-level rules shall be adopted) should be stipulated by a higher authority (whether at state or at international level). To which extent should local communities be trusted in setting the constitutional norms defining how collective-choice rules and operational-level rules shall be set? Should such constitutional autonomy be controlled at all?

B. Setting limits to the constitutional autonomy of local communities

It has been noted elsewhere that customary forms of tenure that support common property regimes have been found in many cases to exclude certain marginalized members of the community, including in particular women, and that this may call for certain restrictions to be imposed to the constitutional autonomy of local communities (see De Schutter 2018). Thus, in line with the requirements of human rights law,[5] the VGGT provide (in guideline 9.2) that:

> Indigenous peoples and other communities with customary tenure systems that exercise self-governance of land, fisheries and forests should promote and provide equitable, secure and sustainable rights to those resources, with special attention to the provision of equitable access for women. Effective participation of all members, men, women and youth, in decisions regarding their tenure systems should be promoted through their local or traditional institutions, including in the case of collective tenure systems. Where necessary, communities should be assisted to increase the capacity of their members to participate fully in decision-making and governance of their tenure systems.

A clear choice was made in the negotiation of the guidelines to prioritize full compliance with international human rights law, including as it regards the prohibition of discrimination against women in situations of conflict with customary forms of tenure: "where constitutional or legal reforms strengthen the rights of women and place them in conflict with custom, all parties should cooperate to accommodate such changes in the customary tenure systems" (guideline 9.6). This was also the choice made in the preparation of Articles 21 and 22 of the United Nations Declaration on the Rights of Indigenous Peoples, which calls for special attention to the needs of indigenous women and the adoption of special measures to protect them against all forms of violence and discrimination. In the VGGT that were adopted five years later, the constitutional prioritization of human rights over customary rules is affirmed more broadly, for the benefit of all "vulnerable and marginalized members" of the communities affected, whose "full and effective participation" states should ensure "when developing policies and laws related to tenure systems of indigenous peoples and other communities with customary tenure systems" (guideline 9.7).

Similarly, the Declaration on the Rights of Peasants and Other People Working in Rural Areas affirms the primacy of human rights, dedicating a specific provision to the rights of women peasants (Article 4), who are "often denied tenure and ownership of land" (Preamble, para. 9) and who in particular shall "have equal access to, use of and control over land and natural resources, independently of their civil and marital status and of particular tenure systems, and equal or priority treatment in land and agrarian reform and in land resettlement schemes" (Article 4(2)(h); see also, as regards women's right to land, Article 17(2)).

More generally, the recent recognition that international law should facilitate the recognition of common-property regimes based on customary forms of tenure – and, thus, the governance of the commons by local communities – raises the question of the constitutional framework that should be established in order to strengthen the ability of these communities to manage resources, in order to ensure that the outcomes are beneficial to societies as a whole. Some of the design principles for long-enduring common-pool resources institutions that E. Ostrom derived from her case studies on the management of common-pool resources (Ostrom 1990, pp. 88–102) can be said to be more or less independent from any recognition by the state. This is the case, for instance, of the (first) principle according to which clear boundaries should define both the community members and the perimeter of the resource itself. Similarly, the (second) principle of congruence (or adequate "fit") between the local conditions and the rules concerning the appropriation of the resource and the support given to its maintenance, does not require state intervention: the benevolent indifference of the public authorities generally shall suffice. Other principles relate to the substance of the primary (or operational-level) rules that govern the use of the resource. (These conditions, expressed as the fifth and sixth principles in Ostrom's typology, relate to the monitoring of the rules, to the adoption of a system of graduated sanctions, and to the accessibility of low-cost conflict-resolution mechanisms.) Yet, other principles do seem to be dependent on some form of endorsement by the state. The ability for the community of users to set the secondary (or collective-choice) rules, relating to how the primary (operational-level) rules are adopted (most individuals affected by the operational rules can participate in modifying the operational rules), expressed in the third principle, requires that some form of self-government be delegated by the state. Indeed, the seventh principle refers explicitly to the recognition by the official governmental authorities of rights to organize (rights of appropriators to devise their own institutions are not challenged by external governmental authorities).

Thus, some form of intervention of the governmental authorities appears to be not only inevitable but also, to a large extent, desirable. The framework enabling the emergence and endurance of common-pool resource management systems (with its institutional, regulatory and policy components) is not simply about allowing such systems to emerge or to exist. It is not just about not obstructing them. It can be conceived of as an active form of intervention, required both in order to ensure that the management by the local community of the common-pool resource will be perceived as legitimate and in order to ensure that the primary rules will maximize the chances of the system that is established will last. For instance, the system could benefit from a requirement that decision-making procedures within the community be fully inclusive; that the operational rules take into account certain requirements linked to sustainable use;[6] that monitoring of the rules by the community members and the system of sanctions complies with certain conditions related, for instance, to legal security and to proportionality, ensuring that the rules shall not be enforced in ways that shall be perceived as arbitrary, at the risk of creating divisions within the community (Nielsen et al. 2004); or even, that the community members be recognized certain basic rights related to the guarantee of an adequate standard of living, since more secure, less vulnerable, community members are better equipped to take part in participatory management systems and may feel greater freedom to experiment as a result of their improved material security (for an argument along these lines in the context of fisheries, see Allison et al. 2012). The establishment of this constitutional framework should not be seen by the community itself as a violation of the principle of self-governance of the common-pool resource; instead, it should be seen as an *enabling* framework – as facilitating self-governance, and as increasing the resilience of the system.

Internationally recognized human rights could provide a source of inspiration for the establishment of such a constitutional framework in support of the establishment and maintenance of common-property regimes. There is no necessary trade-off between the autonomy of the community that sets its own rules regarding the use of resources and the allocation of duties across the community members and the imposition of such a framework by the State authorities. Provided that the role of government is appropriately conceived – to enable and to support, rather than to obstruct and to micro-manage –, and the government is not captured by powerful interests, the two can in fact be mutually supportive. Self-governance by the community shall ensure that the rules that are set will be perceived as highly legitimate by the community members, since those members will have been involved in setting the rules,[7] and will be fully congruent with the local conditions and motivations. This allows the central governmental authorities to rely on such mechanisms for the effective management of the resource. Conversely however, the establishment by these authorities of an appropriate constitutional framework, in addition to ensuring that the common-property regime will be perceived as legitimate,[8] may ensure the appropriate functioning of the regime, in particular by ensuring that it will be fully participatory (not excluding any part of the community), that the operational rules comply with certain requirements of non-discrimination and proportionality and by protecting the resource from depletion.

Though the principle of a complementarity between the human rights-based constitutional framework on one hand and the self-governance by the community on the other hand may be easy enough to accept, a number of further questions are likely to be more controversial. A first question is whether the framework should prohibit the selling off, by the community, in accordance with its internal decision-making rules, of the resource that its members are co-managing and sharing. In the case of the *Ogieks*, citing Article 26(2) of the UN Declaration on the Rights of Indigenous Peoples (which speaks of the right of indigenous peoples "to own, use, develop and control the lands, territories and resources that they possess"), the African Court of Human and Peoples' Rights remarked that "the rights that can be recognised for indigenous peoples/communities on their ancestral lands are variable and do not necessarily entail the right of ownership in its classical meaning, including the right to dispose thereof (*abusus*). Without excluding the right to property in the traditional sense, this provision places greater emphasis on the rights of possession, occupation, use/utilization of land".[9] In other words, while recognizing the rights of the Ogieks to use and occupy the Mau Forest, the Court was agnostic (and perhaps skeptical) as to whether they also should be allowed to cede it, for instance against a monetary compensation or promises of relocation, in the absence of a strong public purpose that might justify eviction. Indeed, it may be argued that the recognition of the right of local communities to set the rules concerning the definition of appropriation/use rights and allocating responsibilities or duties to contribute should not extend to the right to liquidate the resource held in common, whether by tolerating an unsustainable use or whether by auctioning it to the highest bidder.

Another question concerns the role that the traditional authorities should be accorded. Involving traditional authorities (such as customary chiefs in indigenous communities) may strengthen the legitimacy of the common-property regime and thus favor its resilience. However, it has been found that the legitimacy of leaders elected by the members, and thus more directly accountable to them, could be as strong, and perhaps even stronger (Hara et al. 2002). Moreover, recognizing a leading role for traditional authorities may perpetuate older hierarchies and lead to elite capture (see, for instance, Sandford 1983; Baland and Platteau 1999; Bardhan 2002). Indeed, in situations where the traditional authorities are perceived to profit from their privileged positions and to act against the interests of the community, the trust on which the common management of resources relies may collapse entirely. It has been argued therefore that the traditional authorities "should support, but not control the co-management enforcement activities" (Wilson et al. 2010: 660), that a potential role for governmental authorities could be to "ensure transparency of punishments", and that enforcement of the rules by the community leaders does not lead to personal gain.

3. Rethinking private property law

Are these new aspirations of international law realistic? Can we credibly seek to move toward a recognition of multiple forms of property, including communal property, on which the management of the commons is based? A precondition for realizing these aspirations, we submit, is to critically analyze the private law regime that governs property and to understand the role of this legal regime – both essential and discreet – in the multiple crises that have beset the world since 2008. At the heart of this analysis is the overcommodified form of property, structured and legitimated by the legal regime of private property law, which is held up and sanctified as the only legitimate option for developing countries. Rather than give in to this, we suggest that a careful attention to the history of property relations in the West and the Rest yields entirely different lessons about the nature of property in land. We argue that a critique of displacement and eviction practices, food insecurity, grinding and stagnant poverty, inadequate and insecure housing and access to livelihoods based on land must rest on these lessons in order to inspire alternatives to current regimes of property rights.

The idea that property is overcommodified is simple. It means essentially that the property form has been abstracted and separated in terms of pure exchange value, to the total neglect of human values and welfare. It is the direct opposite of the vision of property expressed by Justice Weintraub in *State v. Shack*, assigning a social function to property: "Property rights serve human values. They are recognized to that end and limited by it".[10] Property in land is especially subjected to this limitation because unlike other fungible forms of property (such as a tool carved from a fallen branch) or intellectual property (such as a song), land did not originally belong to anyone and cannot be absolutely owned by anyone. Land grabs that seek to deny the poor any property rights over land while concentrating property in the hands of a narrow land-owning class of investors and government elites are fundamentally illegitimate. The idea behind this was expressed clearly by the philosopher J.S. Mill (quoted in Hollander (1985): 831):

> No man made the land. It is the original inheritance of the whole species. It is no hardship to anyone, to be excluded from what others have produced. But it is some hardship to be born and to find all nature's gifts previously engrossed, and no place left for the newcomer.

The status of property in land is even more precarious because the titles over land in most countries do not have a legitimate chain of ownership that can be defended credibly. Most countries witnessed the stealing and illegitimate (if not outright illegal) occupation of the lands of weaker neighbors, weaker communities and nations, and all of our titles have derived from those.

This is true, of course, in settler societies such as the United States of America, where the status of property in land is particularly precarious in terms of legitimacy because of the way land was stolen or coerced from Native Americans through methods that cannot be described as voluntary transactions in a free market or as a legitimate acquisition of sovereign territory. As Chief Justice Marshall noted in the historic case that doomed the fate of Native American title to land in the US by asserting the superiority of title by conquest over the actual property rights of Native Americans, "however extravagant the pretension of converting the discovery of an inhabited country into conquest may appear; if the principle has been asserted in the first instance, and afterwards sustained; if a country has been acquired and held under it; if the property of the great mass of the community originates in it, it becomes the law of the land and cannot be questioned".[11]

In other societies that are not settler societies, the status of property in land does not fare much better. As the philosopher J.S. Mill, again, puts it (quoted in Hollander (1985): 830):

> Landed property in all countries of modern Europe derives its origins from force; the land was taken by military violence from former possessors [and thence] been transmitted to its present . . . owners, the sellers, [who] could not impart to others better title than they themselves possessed.

The point we are making is simply that property in land has more grounds to be governed in a way that is not strictly according to commodity-form free market logic. Rather, it should take into consideration the precariousness of title, as well as the multiple human values that need to be reconciled by arranging uses of property in land. We see at least the following considerations about property in land as being important from the recent developments in private property law, practices of development actors including governments and investors and legal and political history, which may be used as a basis for developing alternative property regimes.[12]

A. *Legal titling*

For a little more than a decade, roughly between 1995 and 2010, titling was a triumphant and hegemonic way to bring the poor, especially the large mass of slum-dwellers, out of poverty. In 1993, the World Bank presented a report called *Housing: Enabling Markets to Work* where, while it warned against costly titling programs, it underscored the importance of "systems of property registration and titling and workable systems of foreclosure and eviction", as these were considered "necessary to ensure the collateral security of mortgage loans".[13] The emphasis in that report was more about ensuring security of tenure than about titling as one means to achieve this, but it did include a strong recommendation for the removal of any restrictions to the emergence of a market in property rights over land.[14] USAID, the United States international development agency, first supported programs for the privatization of land and titling in Russia in 1994, with the purpose of supporting the Russian authorities in creating real estate and land registries and clarifying ownership rights, first in a number of "hub" cities and later in larger areas, including the rural areas.[15] Then, in 1998, a major titling program was launched in Peru, with Hernando de Soto's Institute for Liberty and Democracy (ILD) in the leading role.

Titling henceforth became globally popular as a magic bullet for all development problems – from poverty alleviation to economic development, in no small measure thanks to Hernando De Soto. As discussed previously however, it has since emerged that the commodification of property rights can be a source of exclusion and *increased* insecurity of tenure – for instance because the formalization of property leads to an increase in taxes or because of the risk of over-indebtedness once loans are obtained by mortgaging the property. The problem in such instances is not, of course, that titling is wrong *in principle* (although it needs to be contextually assessed and implemented with an eye on its distributional and political consequences). It is, rather, that it has not benefited the poor either because they have remained unaware of their legal rights, or unable to rely on state institutions that guarantee them; or because, due to their low purchasing power, they were priced out of markets for land rights, especially in urban land markets.

Since the 1990s, the landless poor have been particularly affected by the commodification of land. The formalization of property rights and land registration aim to support the poor and are based, to a large extent, on the need to support smallholders and unlock their productivity potential (Deininger and Binswanger 1999; Platteau 2000). But they also give a premium to those who already occupy land, making entry into land markets more difficult. In that sense, they may be said to constitute a transfer of wealth from the landless to those who occupy land or those who command the money power to purchase land rights, and from the next generation to the present one: as titling increases the market value of land, land will become less affordable for the poorest part of the population or for the new entrants on the land markets, for whom *access* to land – not just the *consolidation* of unrecognized property rights – is vital. This consequence is, of course, particularly disturbing where inequality in the distribution of land is greatest, and where the population comprises a large number of landless rural workers or urban poor, often from lower castes or minority communities or those who lack formal social and legal protections, such as migrant laborers.

B. Land acquisition and eminent domain

The laws and procedures of most developing countries are outdated and lead to displacement and dispossession of the poorest and the most vulnerable. Often based on colonial era laws or practices, land acquisition procedures typically do not allow for the participation of the communities. Only rarely do they provide for an assessment of the economic, environmental or social/health impacts of the expropriation of land (or of the privatization of the commons), or do they explore alternatives to land acquisition. Eminent domain treats all land as an economic asset and mostly offers cash compensation for acquisitions that are mostly contested; land for land as compensation is rare and often poorly implemented. The process of calculating and awarding compensation during eminent domain is highly flawed in most countries, leading to enormous litigation. But most critically, the use of eminent domain has been expanded greatly and now covers land acquisition not just for public purpose or public benefit directly, but includes land takings for private enterprises in the name of vague promises of economic development for the public. We have seen this in the case of the West as in the *Kelo* case in the US;[16] we are also seeing it in the Rest, as in India in the *Narmada* case.[17] During the last two decades alone, more than 250 million people have been displaced due to large development projects using eminent domain in most cases. Large land deals are proliferating: according to some estimates, 1,150 deals have already been concluded since 1990, leading to a transfer of a total of 55 million hectares, facilitated by the use of eminent domain or claims of state ownership.[18] Big investors include not only private investors, including Western-based investment funds and agrifood companies, but also sovereign wealth funds and state-owned companies from countries such as Malaysia and India, or the Gulf states (Saudi Arabia and the United Arab Emirates in particular). Often, these land deals ignore the rights of marginalized populations like indigenous peoples.

C. Social basis of property and land law

Property is not a thing, and property law is not about relations between humans and things. In law, property is a bundle of rights and corresponding duties that structure social relations. It is a system of rules between humans about how to use and benefit from things. It is therefore completely social. This means that formal law, in statutes or rules or court decisions, is only one source of law. Property law reform that regulates property should therefore take into account different social relations with regard to the use of property in land, which are legitimated through different sources of norms, from formal/legal to informal/illegal. Most developing countries have a range of legal sources for property and land that are in constant interaction, in a state of legal pluralism. They include informal norms, illegal practices, social and cultural norms, customary and indigenous law and law of a variety of agencies of the state at different levels as well as certain rules of international law. In countries such as South Africa and India, courts have had to balance and mix different legal regimes that govern land, sometimes reconfiguring these regimes in order to avoid violating the constitutional guarantees of human rights. We see these admittedly few examples as models that can be used for property reform in land.

Titling is often described as "clarification" or "formalization" of property rights. The purpose is, ostensibly, to confirm existing use rights. But these use rights are often complex. It is not unusual that conflicting claims exist over any piece of land. And there are various types of land users, not all of whom are "dormant landowners" awaiting an opportunity to register the land they occupy. Moreover, prior to the formalization of property rights through titling, tenure generally is regulated by custom and past use status. Some of the claims for rights to property through these practices may even be illegal (Peñalver and Katyal 2010). The superimposition of titling on these preexisting, customary forms of tenure may result in more conflicts, rather than in more clarity, and in less security, rather than in improved security (as noted in Payne et al. 2007) – although the coexistence between different legal regimes may also be a source of creative solutions by the communities involved, as illustrated in Chapter 4 of this volume by An Ansoms and her coauthors in the context of the Democratic Republic of the Congo.

The importance of building on existing, customary forms of tenure was acknowledged by the United Nations Commission for the Legal Empowerment of the Poor, referred to previously. In its final report, presented in June 2008, the CLEP noted (CLEP 2008: 52):

> Customary tenure systems were once thought to provide insufficient security, but research shows that they can be flexible and responsive to changing economic circumstances. In many developing countries, particularly in Sub-Saharan Africa, customary tenure systems represent an appropriate and cost effective way for the rural poor to secure access to land. . . . Customary systems are thus able to provide some of the essential economic functions of a formal property rights system. . . . Whether through customary tenure, collective rights, or individual land titling, the poor need to be able to use their assets effectively.

D. *Tenure security and property rights*

There is often confusion between land tenure security and "hard" or "precise" property rights. The lack of hard and precise property rights in land are often said to be real reason for the lack of economic development in developing countries by development agencies such as the World Bank, who then push for the usual range reforms – titling, cadastral surveys, etc. This approach fundamentally misunderstands the law of property. One can have hard property rights and still most people in the country may have no security of tenure – as in apartheid South Africa. Security of tenure ranges on a continuum from free-hold property on one end to the situation of pavement dwellers. How law deals with each is not simply a question of having hard or precise property rights. In fact, there is evidence that hard property rights may adversely affect distributional consequences if policy choices for their implementation ignore how different social groups will take advantage of it (for the example of Kenya, see Ngugi 2004). That's what we have seen when property reform happens in countries that are dominated by narrow elites. There is substantial evidence, in fact, that property reform works only if there is more equal access to land and property by everyone, as already argued by F. Michelman in the 1980s (Michelman 1987): indeed, as seen earlier, private property reform under conditions of concentrated ownership may end up producing very negative development consequences.[19]

There is also evidence – based on the experience of countries known as the East Asian Tigers (Korea, Taiwan or Singapore) – that land reform is a fundamental prerequisite for economic and manufacturing takeoff that is broad-based and not concentrated in urban areas alone. This principle of distribution is central to private property reform, both as a precondition for development take off, as well as a principle for evaluating development as one goes forward. It has been argued that land reform serves economic development by "bringing idle lands of large estates into production; and increasing productivity levels through the transfer of land to family farms" (Palmer et al. 2009: 31). Empirical evidence suggests that countries that have made efforts toward a more equal land distribution, tend to achieve higher levels of growth: for instance, land reform in China in the late 1970s and early 1980s may have contributed to the largest and fastest rate of rural poverty reduction in modern times. A 2003 World Bank analysis of land policies in 73 countries between 1960 and 2000 shows that countries with more equitable initial land distribution achieved growth rates two to three times higher than those where land distribution was less equitable (Deininger 2003; see also Griffin et al. 2002: 315).

E. The conditions of reform

Making the institution of property more responsive to the various human values it should serve presents us with a number of challenges, however. First, to reform one institution or system, one may have to reform many others. One cannot reform the urban without reforming the rural. One can't have modern property law without a modern legal system as a whole. This includes an independent judiciary, a robust legal profession, a strong administrative law system and other well-functioning state institutions, including planning agencies and local government. Reformers may also need to reform laws in what appear to be unrelated areas. For example, titling reform in situations of deeply unequal gender relations can result in women being denied access to property and being more assetless and landless. Similarly, it may be impossible to have a fair and economically effective rental market operating without a fair housing law that prevents discrimination and ensures protection for tenants who have weaker security of tenure because of their race, color, national or place of origin or religion. In India for example, rental markets suffer from multiple horizontal inequalities of religion (for Muslims in cities) or place of origin (African nationals) and practices (meat eaters in upper caste-dominated neighborhoods). Free market approaches that ignore the human values to be achieved by rental markets will end up being unjust. When countries ignore this, they end up with modern laws that do not get implemented or that produce perverse results.

Perhaps the most difficult issue to grasp is that property systems implicate values. Some of these promote self-interest, autonomy of preferences, while others promote environmental stewardship or aggregate wealth. These values generate moral judgments about which of these values should guide the recognition of particular interests as property rights. For most countries, these values are contained in their expressed commitments in their constitutions or historical experiences. One can have a property system that reflects the worst values – as in apartheid South Africa – or a system that tries to reflect better values – as the current South African system does (although imperfectly realized in practice). The values we choose in which to embed property systems will determine how just and democratic societies are. In practice, this means that countries have the chance to develop a range of property systems, depending on the values they choose to respect. It is our belief that these values are universal, contained in the idea of human rights, which emanates from and is grounded in the actual struggles of social movements.

Notes

1 The Human Rights Committee found that the system established by the Iceland Fisheries Management Act No. 38/1990, in which the quotas originally held "can be sold or leased at market prices instead of reverting to the State for allocation to new quota holders in accordance with fair and equitable criteria," could result in discrimination in violation of article 26 of the International Covenant on Civil and Political Rights (Human Rights Committee, *Haraldsson and Sveinsson v. Iceland*, Communication No. 1306/2004, dec. of 24 Oct. 2007, CCPR/C/91/D/1306/2004).

2 See South Africa, High Court, *Kenneth George and Others v. Minister of Environmental Affairs & Tourism*, Order 2007, ordering a revision of the Marine Living Resources Act and requiring the development of a new framework take into account "international and national legal obligations and policy directives to accommodate the socio-economic rights of [small-scale] fishers and to ensure equitable access to marine resources for those fishers." This resulted in the adoption of a new Small-Scale Fisheries Policy in May 2012, which recognizes the importance of small-scale fisheries in contributing to food security and as serving as a critical safety net against poverty.

3 The resolution (73/165) was adopted with 121 votes in favor, eight against (Australia, Guatemala, Hungary, Israel, New Zealand, Sweden, United Kingdom, United States), and 54 abstentions.

4 Article 21(3) uses a similar formula with respect to access to water: "States shall respect, protect and ensure access to water, including in customary and community-based water management systems . . ."

5 The Convention on the Elimination of All Forms of Discrimination against Women has a specific provision on women in rural areas. Article 14(1) provides that "States Parties shall take into account the particular problems faced by rural women and the significant roles which rural women play in the economic survival of their families, including their work in the non-monetized sectors of the economy, and shall take all appropriate measures to ensure the application of the provisions of the present Convention to women in rural areas". Article 14(2) then sets out the implications, including a requirement that States Parties ensure to women in rural areas "to participate in all community activities" (f) and to "equal treatment in land and agrarian reform as well as in land resettlement schemes" (g). The CEDAW Committee also adopted a General Statement on Rural Women (Decision 50/VI, adopted on 19 October 2011 at the fiftieth session of the Committee (A/67/38, Annex II)).

6 For instance, the Voluntary Guidelines on the Responsible Governance of Tenure of Land, Fisheries and Forests, provides that "All tenure rights are limited by the rights of others and by the measures taken by States necessary for public purposes" insofar as such measure aim to promote, for instance, "general welfare including environmental protection" and are "consistent with States' human rights obligations" (guideline 4.4). They continue: "Tenure rights are also balanced by duties. All should respect the long-term protection and sustainable use of land, fisheries and forests". For an illustration, though the VGGT are not referred to, see African Court of Human and Peoples' Rights, *African Commission on Human and Peoples' Rights v. Kenya (in the case of the Ogiek Community of the Mau Forest)*, cited above, paras. 129–130 (noting that the Ogiek could not be expelled from the Mau Forest even in the name of the "preservation of the natural ecosystem", since there has been no evidence provided "to the effect that the Ogieks' continued presence in the area is the main cause for the depletion of natural environment in the area").

7 Conversely, the top-down imposition of operational rules would result in a "crowding-out" effect, undermining the legitimacy of the rules in the eyes of the community members (Cardenas, Stranlund and Willis (2000); Ostrom (2005)).

8 It is noteworthy that, in countries as different as Norway and Japan, fisheries co-management systems that have been the most enduring were provided a legal foundation (Jentoft and Kristofferson (1998); Ruddle (1989)).

9 African Court of Human and Peoples' Rights, *African Commission on Human and Peoples' Rights v. Kenya (in the case of the Ogiek Community of the Mau Forest)*, cited above, para. 127.

10 State v. Shack, 58 N.J. 297, 277 A.2d 369 (N.J. 1971).

11 *Johnson v. McIntosh*, 21 U.S. 543 (1823) at 591.

12 An inspiration to rethink property comes from recent scholarship, such as Alexander et al. (2009).

13 World Bank (1993), at 46 (recommending against ("costly titling programs") and 106. See also id., at 39: "Collateral security should be fostered by well-designed and enforced systems of titling and foreclosure".

14 See World Bank (1993), at 117: "Governments should establish land registration systems that cover the entire country, but which must be instituted gradually. Such systems need not be restricted to freehold titles, and may offer titles that can be upgraded to full freehold titles over time. Exchange of land and housing should be permitted without restriction, and ownership of land and housing should be available to all citizens. Governments should seek to dispose of occupied public lands by selling or granting secure land tenure to the occupying households". For an early discussion of the advantages of individualized property rights, see Feder and Feeny (1991).

15 See, for a summary description of these projects, http://usaidlandtenure.net/projects/ usaid-and-mcc-land-tenure-and- property-rights-completed-projects/view.

16 *Susette Kelo et al v. City of New London, Connecticut et al.*, 545 US 469 (2005).

17 *Narmada Bachao Andolan v. Union of India* (2000) 10 S.C.C. 664.

18 See www.landmatrix.org/en/. For an extensive discussion of these figures, see De Schutter (2011a).
19 In Hawaii in the 1960s, 72.5 percent of the land was owned by 22 land owners, and the Supreme Court approved the use by the Hawaii legislature to use eminent domain to break up this oligopoly, take the land the redistribute it to other private residents. See *Hawaii Housing Authority v. Midkiff*, 467 U.S. 229.

Works cited

Agarwal, A. (2001) Common Property Institutions and Sustainable Governance of Resources. *World Development*, 29 (10), 1649–1672.

Alexander, G. S., Penalver, E. M., Singer, J. W. and Underkuffler, L. S. (2009) A Statement of Progressive Property. *Cornell Law Review*, 94, 743.

Allison, E. H., Ratner, B. D., Åsgård, B., Willmann, R., Pomeroy, R. and Kurien, J. (2012) Rights-Based Fisheries Governance: From Fishing Rights to Human Rights. *Fish and Fisheries*, 13 (1), 14–29.

Anghie, A. (2005) *Imperialism, Sovereignty and the Making of International Law*. New York, Cambridge University Press.

Bakker, K. (2007) The 'Commons' Versus the 'Commodity': Alter-Globalization, Anti-Privatization and the Human Right to Water in the Global South. *Antipode*, 39 (3), 430–455.

Baland, J. M. and Platteau, J. P. (1999) The Ambiguous Impact of Inequality on Local Resource Management. *World Development*, 27 (5), 773–788.

Bardhan, P. (2002) Decentralization of Governance and Development. *Journal of Economic Perspectives*, 16 (4), 185–205.

Béné, C., Belal, E., Ousman Baba, M., Ovie, S., Raji, A., Malasha, I., Njaya, F., Na Andi, M., Russell, A. and Neiland, A. (2009) Power Struggle, Dispute and Alliance over Local Resources: Analyzing 'Democratic' Decentralization of Natural Resources through the Lenses of Africa Inland Fisheries. *World Development*, 37 (12), 1935–1950.

Bollier, D. and Helfrich, S. (2015) Overture. In: Bollier, D. and Helfrich, S. (eds.), *Patterns of Commoning*. Amherst, Commons Strategy Group and Off the Common Press, 18–31.

Buchanan, J. M. (1965) An Economic Theory of Clubs. *Economica*, 32 (125), 1–14.

Cardenas, J. C., Stranlund, J. and Willis, C. (2000) Local Environmental Control and Institutional Crowding-Out. *World Development*, 28 (10), 1719–1733.

Carruthers, I. and Stoner, R. (1981) *Economic Aspects and Policy Issues in Groundwater Development*. World Bank Staff Working Paper No. 496, Washington, DC.

Ciorat, B. (ed.). (2015) *Le retour des communs. La crise de l'idéologie propriétaire*. Paris, Les Liens qui Libèrent.

Claeys, P. (2015) Food Sovereignty and the Recognition of New Rights for Peasants at the UN: A Critical Overview of La Via Campesina's Rights Claims over the Last 20 Years. *Globalizations*, 12 (4), 452–465.

Claeys, P. (2018) The Rise of New Rights for Peasants: From Reliance on NGO Intermediaries to Direct Representation. *Transnational Legal Theory*, 1–14.

CLEP (High-Level Commission on the Legal Empowerment of the Poor). (2008) *Final Report*. New York, United Nations.

Committee on World Food Security. (2009) Reform of the Committee on World Food Security, U.N. Doc. CFS:2009/2Rev. 2.

Commons, J. R. (1893) *The Distribution of Wealth*. London, Macmillan and Co.

Cox, M., Arnold, G. and Villamayor Tomás, S. (2010) A Review of Design Principles for Community-Based Natural Resource Management. *Ecology and Society*, 15 (4), 38.

Cunningham, S., Neiland, A. E., Arbuckle, M. and Bostock, T. (2009) Wealth-Based Fisheries Management: Using Fisheries Wealth to Orchestrate Sound Fisheries Policy in Practice. *Marine Resource Economics*, 24 (3), 271–287.

Dagan, H. and Heller, M. A. (2001) The Liberal Commons. *Yale Law Journal*, 110, 549–623.

Dahlman, C. J. (1980) *The Open Field System and Beyond: A Property Rights Analysis of an Economic Institution*. Cambridge, Cambridge University Press.

Dardot, P. and Laval, C. (2015) *Commun. Essai sur la révolution au XXIème siècle*. Paris, La Découverte.

Deininger, K. (2003) *Land Policies for Growth and Poverty Reduction: A World Bank Policy Research Report*. Report No. 26384, Washington, DC and Oxford, World Bank and Oxford University Press.

Deininger, K. and Binswanger, H. (1999) The Evolution of the World Bank's Land Policy: Principles, Experience and Future Challenges. *The World Bank Research Observer*, 14 (2), 247–276.

Demsetz, H. (1967) Toward a Theory of Property Rights. *American Economic Review*, 57, 347–359.

De Schutter, O. (2011b) The Right of Everyone to Enjoy the Benefits of Scientific Progress and the Right to Food: From Conflict to Complementarity. *Human Rights Quarterly*, 33, 304–350.

De Schutter, O. (2018) From Eroding to Enabling the Commons: The Dual Movement in International Law. In: Cogolati, S. and Wouters, J. (eds.), *Commons and Global Governance*. London, Edward Elgar.

Feder, G. and Feeny, D. (1991) Land Tenure and Property Rights: Theory and Implications for Development Policy. *The World Bank Economic Review*, 5 (1), 135–153.

Foster, S. (2011) Collective Action and the Urban Commons. *Notre Dame Law Review*, 87, 57–133.

Golay, G. (2015) *Negotiation of a United Nations Declaration on the Rights of Peasants and Other People Working in Rural Areas*. Academy In-Brief No. 5, Geneva Academy of International Humanitarian Law and Human Rights.

Gordon, H. S. (1954) The Economic Theory of the Common-Property Resource: The Fishery. *Journal of Political Economy*, 62 (2), 124–142.

Graeber, D. (2013) *The Democracy Project: A History: A Crisis: A Movement*. London, Allen Lane.

Griffin, K., Khan, A. R. and Ickowitz, A. (2002) Poverty and the Distribution of Land. *Journal of Agrarian Change*, 2 (3), 279–330.

Gutiérrez, N. L., Hilborn, R. and Defeo, O. (2011) Leadership, Social Capital and Incentives Promote Successful Fisheries. *Nature*, 470 (7334), 386–389.

Hara, M., Donda, S. and Njaya, F. J. (2002) Lessons from Malawi's Experience with Fisheries Co-Management Initiative. In: Gehab, K. and Sarch, M.-T. (eds.), *Africa's Inland Fisheries: The Management Challenge*. Kampala, Fountain Publishers, 31–48.

Hardin, G. (1968) The Tragedy of the Commons. *Science*, 162 (3859), 1243–1248.

Hardt, M. and Negri, A. (2009) *Commonwealth*. Cambridge, Harvard University Press.

Heller, M. A. (1998) The Tragedy of the Anticommons: Property in the Transition from Marx to Markets. *Harvard Law Review*, 111 (3), 621–688.

Heller, M. A. (2008) *The Gridlock Economy: How Too Much Ownership Wrecks Markets, Stops Innovation, and Costs Lives*. New York, Basic Books.

Hohfeld, W. N. (1920) *Fundamental Legal Conceptions as Applied in Judicial Reasoning, and Other Legal Essays*, W. W. Cook (ed.). New Haven, Yale University Press.

Hollander, S. (1985) *The Economics of John Stuart Mill, Volume 2: Political Economy*. Oxford, Blackwell.

Jamu, D., Banda, M., Njaya, F. and Hecky, R. E. (2011) Challenges to Sustainable Management of the Lakes of Malawi. *Journal of Great Lakes Research*, 37 (1), 3–14.

Jentoft, S. and Kristofferson, T. (1998) Fishermen's Co-Management: The Case of the Lofoten Fishery. *Human Organization*, 48 (4), 355–365.

Lewins, R., Béné, C., Baba, M. O., Belal, E., Donda, S., Lamine, A. M., Makadassou, A., Mamane Tahir Na, A., Neiland, A. E., Njaya, F., Ovie, S. and Raji, A. (2014) African Inland Fisheries: Experiences with Co-Management and Policies of Decentralization. *Society and Natural Resources*, 27 (4), 405–420.

Michelman, F. (1987) Possession vs. Distribution in the Constitutional Idea of Property. *Iowa Law Review*, 72 (5), 1319.

Ngugi, J. M. (2004) Re-Examining the Role of Private Property in Market Democracies: Problematic Ideological Issues Raised by Land Registration. *Michigan Journal of International Law*, 25, 467.

Nielsen, J. R., Degnbol, P., Viswanathan, K. K., Ahmed, M., Hara, M. and Raja Abdullah, N. M. (2004) Fisheries Co-Management: An Institutional Innovation? Lessons from South East Asia and Southern Africa. *Marine Policy*, 28 (2), 151–160.

Olson, M. (1965) *The Logic of Collective Action: Public Goods and the Theory of Groups*. Cambridge, MA, Harvard University Press.

Ostrom, E. (1990) *Governing the Commons: The Evolution of Institutions for Collective Action*. New York, Cambridge University Press.

Ostrom, E. (2005) Policies That Crowd out Reciprocity and Collective Action. In: Gintis, H., Bowles, S., Boyd, R. and Fehr, E. (eds.), *Moral Sentiments and Material Interests: The Foundations of Cooperation in Economic Life*. Cambridge, MIT Press, 253–275.

Ostrom, E. (2010) Beyond Markets and States: Polycentric Governance of Complex Economic Systems. *American Economic Review*, 100, 1–33.

Ostrom, V. and Ostrom, E. (1977) Public Goods and Public Choices. In: Savas, E. S. (ed.), *Alternatives for Delivering Public Services: Toward Improved Performance*. Boulder, CO, Westview Press, 7–49.

Palmer, D., Fricska, S. and Wehrmann, B. (2009) *Towards Improved Land Governance*. FAO Land Tenure Working Paper 11.

Payne, G., Durand-Lasserve, A. and Rakodi, C. (2007) *Social and Economic Impacts of Land Titling Programmes in Urban and Peri-Urban Areas: A Review of the Literature*, paper presented at the World Bank Urban Research Symposium, Washington, DC, 14–16 May.

Peñalver, E. M. and Katyal, S. K. (2010) *Property Outlaws: How Squatters, Pirates and Protestors Improve the Law of Ownership*. New Haven, CT, Yale University Press.

Platteau, J.-P. (2000) Does Africa Need Land Reform? In: Toulmin, C. and Quan, J. (eds.), *Evolving Land Rights, Policy and Tenure in Africa*. London, DFID-IIED-NRI, 51–74.

Posner, R. (1975) Economic Analysis of Law. In: Ackerman, B. (ed.), *Economic Foundations of Property Law*. Boston, Little, Brown & Co.

Rajagopal, B. (2003a) *International Law from Below: Development, Social Movements and Third World Resistance*. Cambridge, Cambridge University Press.

Ratner, B. D., Åsgård, B. and Allison, E. H. (2014) Fishing for Justice: Human Rights, Development, and Fisheries Sector Reform. *Global Environmental Change*, 27, 120–130.

Rose, C. M. (1998) The Several Futures of Property: Of Cyberspace and Folk Tales, Emission Trades and Ecosystems. *Minnesota Law Review*, 83, 129–182.

Ruddle, K. (1989) Solving the Common-Property Dilemma: Village Fsheries Rights in Japanese Coastal Waters. In: Berkes, F. (ed.), *Common Property Resources: Ecology and Community-Based Sustainable Development*. London, Belhaven Press, 168–184.

Samuelson, P. A. (1954) The Pure Theory of Public Expenditure. *Review of Economics and Statistics*, 36 (4), 387–389.

Sandford, S. (1983) *Management of Pastoral Development in the Third World*. Chichester, John Wiley and Sons.

Schlager, E. and Ostrom, E. (1992) Property-Rights Regimes and Natural Resources: A Conceptual Analysis? *Land Economics*, 68 (3), 249–262.

Sharma, C. (2011) Securing Economic, Social and Cultural Rights of Small-Scale and Artisanal Fishworkers and Fishing Communities. *Journal of Maritime Studies*, 10 (2), 41–62.

Special Rapporteur on the Right to Food. (2012) The Fisheries Sector and the Right to Food. Interim Report of the Special Rapporteur on the right to food, Olivier De Schutter, to the 67th session of the General Assembly, UN doc. A/67/268.

Townsend, R., Shotton, R. and Uchida, H. (eds.). (2008) *Case Studies in Fisheries Self-Governance*. FAO Fisheries Technical Paper No. 504, Rome, Food and Agriculture Organization.

Unger, Roberto M. 2000. *Democracy Realized: The Progressive Alternative*. London, Verso.

United Nations General Assembly (UNGA). (2018) Declaration on the Rights of Peasants and Other People Working in Rural Areas, UN Doc. A/ RES/73/165.

Van Reybrouck, D. (2013) *Against Elections: The Case for Democracy*. London: The Bodley Head.

Wilson, D. C. K., Ahmed, M., Delaney, A., Donda, S., Kapasa, C. K., Malasha, I., Muyangali, K., Nyaja, F., Olesen, T., Poiosse, E. and Raakjær, J. (2010) Fisheries Co-Management Institutions in Southern Africa: A Hierarchical Analysis of Perceptions of Effectiveness. *International Journal of the Commons*, 4 (2), 643–662.

World Bank. (1993) *Housing: Enabling Markets to Work*. World Bank Working Paper No. 11820, by Stephen K. Mayo and Shlomo Angel), Washington, DC, World Bank.

World Bank. (2004) *Saving Fish and Fishers: Toward Sustainable and Equitable Governance of the Global Fishing Sector*. Washington, DC, World Bank.

Index

Note: Page numbers in *italics* and **bold** indicate Figures and Tables, respectively.

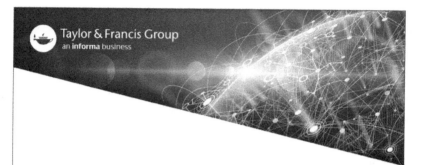